THE GRENADIER GUARDS
IN THE GREAT WAR OF
1914–1918

MACMILLAN AND CO., Limited
LONDON · BOMBAY · CALCUTTA · MADRAS
MELBOURNE

THE MACMILLAN COMPANY
NEW YORK · BOSTON · CHICAGO
DALLAS · SAN FRANCISCO

THE MACMILLAN CO. OF CANADA, Ltd.
TORONTO

Speaight Ltd. photographers   Emery Walker ph. sc.

Captain H.R.H. The Prince of Wales, K.G., M.C., &c.

THE
GRENADIER GUARDS
IN THE GREAT WAR OF
1914-1918

BY

LIEUT.-COLONEL
THE RIGHT HON. SIR FREDERICK PONSONBY
(LATE GRENADIER GUARDS)

WITH AN INTRODUCTION BY
LIEUT.-GENERAL THE EARL OF CAVAN

MAPS BY MR. EMERY WALKER

IN THREE VOLUMES
VOL. III

MACMILLAN AND CO., LIMITED
ST. MARTIN'S STREET, LONDON
1920

COPYRIGHT

Printed and bound by Antony Rowe Ltd, Eastbourne

CONTENTS

CHAPTER XXVIII

FEBRUARY, MARCH 1918 (4TH BATTALION) . . PAGE 1

CHAPTER XXIX

APRIL, MAY, JUNE 1918 (1ST, 2ND, AND 3RD BATTALIONS) 16

CHAPTER XXX

APRIL 1–14 (4TH BATTALION) 32

CHAPTER XXXI

APRIL 14 TO NOVEMBER 11 (4TH BATTALION) . . 53

CHAPTER XXXII

JULY AND AUGUST (1ST, 2ND, AND 3RD BATTALIONS) . 59

CHAPTER XXXIII

SEPTEMBER (1ST, 2ND, AND 3RD BATTALIONS) . . 104

CHAPTER XXXIV

OCTOBER (1ST, 2ND, AND 3RD BATTALIONS) . . 136

CHAPTER XXXV
November (1st, 2nd, and 3rd Battalions) . . 166

CHAPTER XXXVI
March into Germany (Guards Division) . . 191

CHAPTER XXXVII
The 7th (Guards) Entrenching Battalion . . 200

CHAPTER XXXVIII
The Reserve Battalion 206

CHAPTER XXXIX
The Band 212

CHAPTER XL
Regimental Funds and Associations . . . 215

APPENDICES
I. The Casualties in the Guards Division . . 229
II. The Title "Grenadiers" 230
III. Officers Killed in Action or Died of Wounds . 234
IV. Nominal Roll of W.O.'s, N.C.O.'s, and Men who have been Killed in Action, or who have Died of Wounds or Disease in the European War of 1914–1918 243

CONTENTS

	PAGE
V. OFFICERS WOUNDED	272
VI. REWARDS—OFFICERS	284
VII. REWARDS — WARRANT AND NON-COMMISSIONED OFFICERS AND MEN	296
VIII. "MENTIONED IN DESPATCHES"	318
IX. "CERTIFICATES FOR GALLANTRY"	328
X. PROMOTIONS TO COMMISSIONED RANK	331
INDEX TO NAMES OF OFFICERS	335

ILLUSTRATIONS

Captain H.R.H. The Prince of Wales, K.G., M.C., etc.	*Frontispiece*
	FACING PAGE
Brigadier-General C. R. Champion de Crespigny, D.S.O.	50
Brigadier-General B. N. Sergison-Brooke, D.S.O.	100
Brigadier-General Lord Henry Seymour, D.S.O.	150
Brigadier-General A. F. A. N. Thorne, D.S.O.	200

MAPS

Fourth Battalion at La Couronne—Position on April 13, 1918	42
Attack on Premy Chapel, September 27, 1918	114
Operations, October 11–14, 1918	142
Operations, October 20, 1918	164
Operations, November 1–11, 1918	178

CHAPTER XXVIII

FEBRUARY, MARCH 1918 (4TH BATTALION)

On February 12 the 4th Battalion left the Guards Division, and was played out by the drums of the 1st, 2nd, and 3rd Battalions Grenadier Guards, the pipers of the 2nd Battalion Scots Guards, and the band of the Irish Guards. Brigadier-General Lord Henry Seymour watched the Battalion march by, and congratulated Lieut.-Colonel Pilcher on its smart appearance.

Thus the newly formed 4th Guards Brigade joined the Thirty-First Division. On the 14th Major-General Sir Charles Fergusson, Commanding the Thirteenth Corps, inspected the Battalion, and expressed himself very pleased with its appearance on parade. On the 17th the Battalion relieved the Durham Light Infantry in the line near Arleux Loop, and was subjected to a slight shelling. This was the new Brigade's first tour in the trenches, and the 4th Battalion was the first of the three Battalions to go into the front line. The line taken over was an example of the new system of holding the front in depth. The Brigade frontage, 2000 yards in length, was held by one Battalion, and constituted the outpost line. Held very lightly by posts at long intervals, it was supported some 1000 yards in rear by a trench, known as the Arleux Loop, South and North, where the Battalion Headquarters were situated together with one company in reserve. Lieut.-Colonel Pilcher was aware that the arrival of a fresh Battalion in the line was likely to be observed by the enemy, and that therefore a raid was highly probable. If any confirmation of this theory was required it had already been supplied by a prisoner, who had been captured before the relief, and had stated that the enemy suspected the presence of the Guards Division, and intended shortly to make a raid to confirm the fact. Nothing, however, was observed either to indicate the exact time or the locality; in fact, everything seemed normal, and the officer commanding the 2nd Battalion Irish Guards went round the posts with Lieut.-Colonel Pilcher in the usual way in order to make the necessary arrangements for the relief the next morning.

From the evidence of the single surviving prisoner, who was captured, it was clear that the Germans had planned and rehearsed every detail of the coming raid with great thoroughness. Practice trenches, made from aeroplane photographs, had been dug in Beaumont, and the raiders were minutely trained in their duties. All the men who were to take part in the raid had been withdrawn from the line for three weeks, and had been well fed and cared for. They were the pick of the 469th German Infantry

Regiment, and had been selected on account of their physique and proved courage. Their equipment was of high quality, with every detail carefully thought out; it consisted of a short, light rifle of 1917 pattern with a leather sling, a trench dagger, an automatic pistol, wire-cutters, a watch, and a canvas bag for carrying stick-bombs.

CHAPTER XXVIII.

4th Batt.
Feb.
1918.

The raid, which had been planned by the Regimental Staff of the 469th Regiment, was carried out in two sections, each consisting of 1 officer and 28 other ranks, in all about 60. At 8 P.M. a concentrated bombardment was put down by the enemy from Oak Post on the left to Tommy Post on the right, and the bombardment was so intense that portions of our trenches were completely obliterated. An S.O.S. signal went up some way to the left of Oak Post, and our barrage came down with great promptitude opposite that part of the line; thus valuable time was lost in having it transferred to where the raid was actually taking place.

Shortly after the enemy's barrage was put down, the men in No. 8 Post saw a strong party of Germans advancing down Brandy Trench from Tee Trench, and a fierce fight commenced. Seeing they were greatly outnumbered, our men slowly closed in on No. 7 Post. After the bombardment began, Captain Benson at No. 2 Company Headquarters sent Second Lieutenant Wrixon to ascertain what was happening, and this officer, after passing through the enemy's barrage, came up just as No. 8 Post was joining No. 7. He at once took charge of both posts, and concentrated his men in Beer Trench, which he determined to hold to the last. He now had 2 N.C.O.'s and 12 men to oppose to the raiding party. The Germans on reaching Brandy Trench split up into two parties; one party continued to bomb up the trench while another, which comprised the majority, rushed across the open towards Beer Trench, with the obvious intention of cutting off these posts. Private Fletcher, No. 1 of the Lewis-gun team in No. 7 Post, saw them coming, and at once turned his gun on them. Several dropped, and the remainder fled, carrying their wounded with them. No sooner was this party disposed of than Lieutenant Wrixon saw a fresh group of men, advancing stealthily down the trench in front of him. Instead of waiting for them, he determined to attack them, and advancing down the trench he shot the first man he met dead with his revolver. His next opponent at once flung a bomb at him, which burst within a few feet, only slightly wounding him. Private Coles, who was just behind him, shot the man dead with his rifle at point-blank range. Then a bugle was blown, and the raiders disappeared. During this fight the Germans attempted an old ruse by calling out in perfect English: "Take off your gas respirators and return to your support line." Some of the men repeated these instructions under the impression they came from one of their officers, but Second Lieutenant Wrixon yelled at the men, and countermanded the spurious order.

At the commencement of the fight, when No. 8 Post was falling back on No. 7, Private Taylor, who had been sent back to No. 8 Post to fetch some bombs, which had been left behind, ran straight into the arms of a party of Germans, and was taken prisoner. He was ordered on pain of death to lead the Germans to No. 14 Post, and feigned to be willing to do so, when the raiders suddenly changed their minds, and told him to lead them back to their own lines. He at once acquiesced, but instead of doing so, led them to the strongest post in our line. When he knew he was within a few yards of Nos. 7 and 8 Posts, he shouted a warning to the garrison, and threw himself on the ground. His warning was heard by his comrades, who at once hurled bombs in the direction of his voice, and the Germans fled, abandoning their prisoner. Unfortunately, one of our bombs wounded Private Taylor, but he was finally rescued by Private Cunliffe, a stretcher-bearer who had already behaved with great gallantry, bringing in the wounded under heavy shell-fire.

Meanwhile a totally distinct fight took place at Nos. 13 and 14 Posts, generally known as Alton Post, where there was a machine-gun protected by a bombing-post, under Lieutenant W. B. Ball. It happened that a party of Royal Engineers, under an officer, was working at the machine-gun dug-out that night. The machine-gun itself was knocked out by the first few shells of the barrage, and a small party of Germans immediately afterwards emerged from the darkness, and rushed at the post. Corporal Horan, who was in charge of the bombing-post, disabled three of them with well-directed bombs, but one very tall German, followed by some more, broke through, and proceeded to throw bombs down the dug-out. It was all done in a moment, and the officer of the Royal Engineers, who was in the dug-out, having just escaped the first bomb, ran round to another exit, when he narrowly missed a second one, before he got out into the open. Meanwhile, Private Moore, a Grenadier attached to the Royal Engineers, closed with the leading German, and was stabbed to death. Corporal Horan then came up, and shot the tall German dead. Presumably the leaders of the party had all been accounted for, as the remainder turned and disappeared into the darkness.

It is difficult to estimate with any accuracy the enemy's casualties, since there is no doubt they were able to carry away most of their wounded and even their dead. It is only possible, therefore, to state the actual number of dead and wounded left in our lines. These were: 2 killed and 5 wounded, 4 of whom subsequently died. The casualties in the Grenadiers were: 2 killed, 2 died of wounds, and 5 wounded. It was a distinctly unfortunate raid for the Germans, who had taken infinite pains to make it a success; yet not only had they suffered heavy loss, but they had failed to obtain an identification of any kind either in the nature of a prisoner or a bit of equipment. With 2 officers and nearly 60 men, they imagined they would make short work of 12 men under one officer, but they had the misfortune to meet some tough fighters, who were anxious to come to close quarters with them.

Brigadier-General Lord Ardee two days later received the following message :

<small>CHAPTER XXVIII.</small>

<small>4th Batt. Feb. 1918.</small>

The Corps Commander requests that you will convey to the officers and men of the 4th Battalion Grenadier Guards his high appreciation of the gallant and successful resistance put up by the garrison of Arleux Post on the night of February 19-20. He wishes also to congratulate the Thirty-first Division on having completely repulsed for the fourth time in succession during the last two months determined and elaborately prepared attempts to penetrate their lines.

On the 21st the 4th Battalion was relieved by the 2nd Battalion Irish Guards, and retired to Ecurie Camp for four days' rest, after which it returned to the front trenches. On the 23rd the sad news of the death of Lieutenant Ludlow was received. He had been universally popular as Quartermaster of the Battalion, and had only just retired to take up an appointment at Chelsea Hospital, when he was killed by a bomb dropped by a German aeroplane during a raid on London.

On March 21 the 4th Battalion was in billets in the Cheiers—Guestreville—Bethencourt area, and the Brigade as part of the Thirty-first Division was in General Headquarters Reserve, when an order arrived, warning all Battalions to be ready to move the next morning. At 10 A.M. the 4th Battalion started off in buses, and with the rest of the Brigade moved *via* St. Pol and Doulens to Blairville. It was now to take part in ten strenuous days' fighting, digging, and marching, in open warfare of the kind associated with the retreat from Mons in 1914, and to forgo the comparative comforts of an established trench

CHAPTER XXVIII.

line. The following officers took part in these operations:

4th Batt.
Feb. 1918.

Lieut.-Colonel W. S. Pilcher, D.S.O.	Commanding Officer.
Capt. C. R. Gerard, D.S.O.	Adjutant.
Capt. M. Chapman, M.C.	Intelligence Officer.
Capt. I. H. Ingelby	Quartermaster.
Lieut. G. W. Selby-Lowndes	Transport Officer.
Lieut. G. R. Green	Attached to B.H.Q.
Capt. H. H. Sloane-Stanley, M.C.	No. 1 Company.
Lieut. C. E. Irby, M.C.	,, ,,
Lieut. E. H. Tuckwell, M.C.	,, ,,
2nd Lieut. A. J. Gilbey	,, ,,
2nd Lieut. R. B. Osborne	Replaced Lieut. Tuckwell on the 26th.
Lieut. G. C. Burt	Replaced 2nd Lieut. Gilbey on the 23rd.
Capt. C. E. Benson, D.S.O.	No. 2 Company.
Lieut. R. H. Rolfe	,, ,,
Lieut. R. L. Murray-Lawes	,, ,,
Lieut. the Hon. C. C. S. Rodney	Replaced Lieut. Murray-Lawes on the 26th.
Lieut. T. T. Pryce, M.C.	Replaced Captain Benson on the 25th.
Lieut. F. C. Lyon	No. 3 Company.
Lieut. M. D. Thomas	,, ,,
2nd Lieut. C. J. Dawson-Greene	,, ,,
2nd Lieut. J. Macdonald	(To Hospital on the 25th.)
Capt. G. C. Sloane-Stanley	Replaced Lieut. Lyon on the 26th.
Lieut. T. W. Minchin, D.S.O.	No. 4 Company.
Lieut. N. R. Abbey	,, ,,
Lieut. J. E. Greenwood	,, ,,
2nd Lieut. R. D. Richardson	,, ,,
Capt. N. Grellier, M.C., R.A.M.C.	Medical Officer.

Mar. 23.

During the early morning shells were heard passing over at a great height, and as the Battalion went through St. Pol it was clear that the enemy had begun a systematic bombardment of the back areas, and was paying particular attention to that town. Lieut.-Colonel Pilcher, who had gone on ahead with Lord Ardee, sent back word for the buses to proceed through Blairville to the cross-roads west of Boisleux-au-Mont. There he summoned the Company Commanders, and explained the situation to them. From where they were the men could see a large fire burning on the sky-line, and this proved to be the canteen at Boisleux-au-Mont, which was destroyed together with many thousand pounds' worth of food in order to prevent these stores falling into the hands of the Germans. Whether these drastic measures were necessary seems doubtful, since the enemy did not reach this place till four days later. Guided by Lieut.-Colonel Pilcher, the 4th Battalion moved through Hamelincourt to a ravine east of the Ervillers—Boyelles road, where it arrived on the morning of the 23rd. The line occupied by the 4th Guards Brigade ran through Judas Farm, to the east of Ervillers; St. Leger was in the hands of the Germans. The 4th Battalion and the 2nd Battalion Irish Guards held the front line, while the 3rd Battalion Coldstream Guards was in support. During the morning the news reached the Battalion that the enemy had broken through at Mory, and that the right flank of the Brigade was in danger; this was contradicted later. An order issued to the Battalion to feel its right, and take over ground occupied by the Fortieth Division was never carried out, as the troops on the right refused to move, stating that they had received no orders. Then commenced a most harassing

CHAPTER XXVIII.

4th Batt. March 1918.

Chapter XXVIII.
4th Batt.
March 1918.

shelling of our trenches by our own guns, which every effort on the part of the Commanding Officer failed to stop. Both British and German shells fell on our trenches and caused many casualties, including Second Lieutenant Gilbey, who was wounded. Nor was the shelling the only annoyance: the men in the front trench were constantly employed in repelling attacks, and fired off no less than 80,000 cartridges, inflicting continual losses on the advancing enemy. The fighting went on intermittently all day, and, although the enemy continually attacked the Brigade front, he was unable to make the slightest impression on the line. That night Lord Ardee issued definite orders for the whole Brigade to " side step " 1000 yards to the right, in order to close any gaps that might exist near Mory. When the order

Mar. 24. was carried out the next morning, the 2nd Battalion Irish Guards found no troops on its right, and was in a precarious position. During the whole day constant rumours of trouble on the right succeeded each other, and in the evening the news arrived that the Fortieth Division had suffered so severely that it had been relieved by the Forty-second Division. Still the line remained intact, and the German attacks only resulted in masses of their men being killed. The constant strain on our men was, however, beginning to tell, and all ranks were glad when darkness came down, and the attacks ceased. A curious order was issued warning the men against spies dressed as British officers, who were spreading false reports, with the object of hastening our retirement.

During the morning of the 25th the Companies were warned of a possible retirement under cover of darkness, and about noon it became certain that the line had given way on the right, for men from various units began coming back from the direction of Mory, followed by platoons led by officers ; and at 1 P.M. Captain Chapman, who went with the Commanding Officers of the Coldstream and Irish Guards to reconnoitre, reported Germans coming over the ridge on the right in large numbers. This information was at once passed on to Lord Ardee, who gave orders to evacuate the line and fall back north-west of Courcelles. The situation when the order for retirement arrived was extremely difficult, for not only had the right given way entirely, but the enemy was advancing in some force directly against the Battalion Headquarters of the Grenadiers and Coldstream, and there seemed nothing to prevent their penetrating to the rear of the two Battalions. Lieut.-Colonel Pilcher immediately withdrew Nos. 2 and 3 Companies under Captain Benson and Lieutenant Lyon, and placed them on the high ground behind Battalion Headquarters, whence they would be instantly available for a counter-attack in case of emergency. All the time the shelling continued, and the retirement had to be carried out with the enemy unpleasantly close. While the order was being executed Captain Benson was wounded, and was in danger of being left behind, but was gallantly rescued and carried back by Sergeant Marsh. Indeed the evacuation of all the wounded of the 4th Guards

CHAPTER XXVIII.
4th Batt.
March
1918.

Brigade was a notably fine piece of work. No wounded man was left to fall into the enemy's hands, although the medical officers of the Coldstream and Irish Guards and the sick-sergeant of the Grenadiers remained behind, after their Battalions had retired, and the enemy was within a few hundred yards of their aid-posts. Whether our artillery was imperfectly informed as to the movements of the infantry in front, or whether they gave the enemy credit for more rapidity than they possessed, is not clear, but an unfortunate incident occurred which completely prevented a counter-attack being made, when there was an opportunity of inflicting a severe blow on the advancing enemy. A Company of Coldstream had been formed up for a counter-attack, when, without any warning, our heavy artillery poured shells on their Battalion Headquarters, where they were assembling, causing a number of casualties. Although there was constant shelling, the enemy seemed unwilling to come to close quarters with the 4th Guards Brigade, and consequently when it became dark the position remained unchanged, save for a strong defensive flank drawn back on the right. That night the Companies were warned to assemble at Battalion Headquarters, but when once more our heavy artillery began to shell that particular spot, runners were despatched to alter the point of assembly. Captain O'Brien, Irish Guards, was wounded by a shell, and shortly afterwards Second Lieutenant Dawson-Greene was hit by another at the assembly point, and died of the wounds he received some days later. The Battalion formed

FEBRUARY AND MARCH 1918

up in the sunken road to the rear of Battalion Headquarters, and marched off to the Crucifix at Moyenneville, which it reached at 1 A.M. the next morning. Immediately it arrived, it dug a new line of trenches east of the village, and the men were supplied with hot food from the cookers which had been sent up. All the time the German artillery continued to shell Moyenneville without inflicting any casualties. At 4.30 A.M. the Battalion received orders to retire to Ayette, and to hand over its positions to the troops in front of it. Two hours later it moved back through Ayette to Douchy-les-Ayette, where the Battalion Headquarters were established. At noon an order arrived from Lord Ardee, assigning to the Battalion the special rôle of occupying and fortifying Quesnoy Farm, and two hours later it took up its new position. No. 3 Company, under Captain G. C. Sloane-Stanley, on the left; No. 4, under Lieutenant Minchin, in the centre; and No. 1, under Captain H. H. Sloane-Stanley, on the right, dug in east of the farm, while No. 2, under Lieutenant T. Pryce, remained in support behind the trench. The men were dead beat, having worked and fought unceasingly for the last three days, and it was a great relief to all ranks when the night passed quietly. An alarming message of undoubted German origin was received, stating that the enemy had broken through at Hebuterne with armoured motors, but this was subsequently refuted.

Early in the morning of the 27th it was reported that the 93rd Brigade was retiring on the left, and this information was at once passed on to the Brigade Headquarters; at first it was thought best to support this Brigade, and an order to that effect was issued. This was, however, cancelled later, and Lieut.-Colonel Pilcher was instructed to send one Company to each of the other two Battalions of the Brigade. Captain G. C. Sloane-Stanley and Lieutenant T. Pryce went off at once with Nos. 1 and 2 Companies, and did not come under the orders of the 4th Battalion again until the night of relief. In the meantime the enemy determined to take advantage of the retirement of the 93rd Brigade, and commenced to mass two battalions near the aerodrome outside Ayette. This tempting target was not lost on our artillery, but, in order that it might catch as large a number of the enemy as possible, it waited until the movement was nearly completed. Then with a deafening noise all available guns concentrated their fire on this spot, with the result that the most of the force was annihilated, and the survivors fled in disorder. It was as fine a bit of shooting as any one could wish to see, and the results astonished even the gunners themselves. Nos. 1 and 2 Companies, which had gone up to the front line, were able, in spite of the cold and wet, to dig and wire a formidable system of trenches. On the 28th Nos. 3 and 4 Companies moved to the left, and occupied a line that had been dug by the 3rd Battalion Coldstream Guards. The following three days passed quietly, and on the night of the 31st the Battalion was relieved by the 16th Battalion of the Lancashire Fusiliers, and marched back to Bienvillers. The total casualties incurred during the ten days' operations were : 4 officers wounded, and among the other ranks 9 killed, 1 died of wounds, 58 wounded, and 7 missing.

CHAPTER XXVIII.

4th Batt.
March 1918.

CHAPTER XXIX

APRIL, MAY, JUNE 1918

Diary of the War

Chapter XXIX.
1918.
THE Germans, finding that their advance was being brought to a standstill in the direction of Amiens, turned their attention farther north, and determined to threaten the Channel ports. On April 9 they began a concentrated attack with nine divisions on the British and Portuguese front between Armentières and La Bassée, and the fighting spread to Messines. Bailleul and Wulverghem, amongst other places, fell, and the Germans reached the Forest of Nieppe. Here they were checked, and at the end of April the German effort had spent itself, although Marshal Foch had been obliged to expend much of his reserve. The Germans had suffered enormous losses, and, though the German people rejoiced at the gain of territory, those who knew the true state of affairs were alarmed at the extravagant expenditure of men.

At the end of May Ludendorff determined to go straight for Paris, and with twenty-five divisions overwhelmed the French between Soissons and Rheims. This German onslaught continued

APRIL TO JUNE 1918

with varying success until it reached Château-Thierry. The stubborn resistance of the French made any farther advance impossible, and, although the battle still raged on a gigantic front, the Germans had to abandon their intention of striking at Paris.

In April Naval raids on Zeebrugge and Ostend were made, and two ships filled with concrete were successfully sunk at the entrance of the Bruges Canal, while an obsolete submarine and two other ships were blown up off the Mole at Ostend.

In Italy the Austrians began offensive operations on a large scale, and crossed the Piave River, but the Italians, by a series of counter-attacks, regained the lost ground, and by the end of June had driven back the Austrians with heavy loss across the river.

THE 1ST BATTALION

ROLL OF OFFICERS

Lieut.-Colonel Viscount Gort, D.S.O., M.V.O., M.C.	Commanding Officer.
Major C. H. Greville, D.S.O.	Second in Command.
Capt. R. D. Lawford, M.C.	Adjutant.
Lieut. R. F. W. Echlin	Transport Officer.
2nd Lieut. E. G. Hawkesworth	Intelligence Officer.
Capt. J. Teece, M.C.	Quartermaster.
Capt. P. Malcolm	King's Company.
Lieut. J. A. Lloyd	,, ,,
Lieut. L. G. Byng, M.C.	,, ,,
2nd Lieut. A. Ames	,, ,,
2nd Lieut. G. D. Neale	,, ,,
Capt. A. T. G. Rhodes	No. 2 Company.
Lieut. A. A. Moller, M.C.	,, ,,
Lieut. P. G. Simmons, M.C.	,, ,,

18   THE GRENADIER GUARDS

CHAPTER XXIX.
1st Batt. 1918.

2nd Lieut. S. J. Hargreaves	No. 2 Company.
2nd Lieut. O. W. D. Smith	,, ,,
Capt. O. F. Stein, D.S.O.	No. 3 Company.
Lieut. A. S. Chambers	,, ,,
2nd Lieut. W. A. Fleet	,, ,,
2nd Lieut. R. L. Webber	,, ,,
2nd Lieut. R. E. I. Holmes	,, ,,
Capt. R. Wolrige-Gordon, M.C.	No. 4 Company.
Lieut. J. F. Tindal-Atkinson	,, ,,
Lieut. the Hon. P. P. Cary	,, ,,
Lieut. H. B. Vernon	,, ,,
Lieut. R. C. Bruce	,, ,,
2nd Lieut. G. E. A. A. Fitz-G. Hamilton	,, ,,
Lieut. W. B. Evans, U.S.M.O.R.C.	Medical Officer.

April.   After the very strenuous days at the end of March, when the German attacks were successfully repelled, the 1st Battalion remained in the front line for two days, but whether the enemy considered it wiser to try some other parts of the line, or whether they were merely waiting for reinforcements, they showed very little signs of life. A heavy bombardment, directed against the Canadians on the left, which was vigorously responded to, seemed to indicate an attack in that direction, but by the time the 1st Battalion was relieved no move on the part of the enemy had taken place. After two days' rest at Blaireville the 1st Battalion returned to the trenches at Boisleux-au-Mont, where the line was singularly quiet. Early on the 5th a desultory bombardment commenced on our front line, but only with shells of light calibre. Later the railway station came under fire from the heavy guns, but by 9 A.M. all was quiet again, and no more shells were sent over by the enemy that day. Although infinite trouble had been taken to conceal Battalion Headquarters, a big flight of hostile aeroplanes flying low was able to locate it, and the enemy made some very accurate shooting. On the 8th the enemy began a gas bombardment, and obtained several direct hits on the entrance to the Battalion Headquarters dug-out and on two Lewis-gun posts. A new gas containing ether, which gave off little or no smell, was used by the enemy, and accounted for a large number of the Battalion Staff. After two more days' rest at Blaireville, the 1st Battalion returned to the trenches, where, although the shelling was light, the enemy's aircraft was very active, often flying low and firing into the trenches. Patrols were sent out along the whole frontage on the night of the 11th, and one under Second Lieutenant R. Holmes and Sergeant Brown failed to return. Little, however, was seen of the enemy, although a wiring party was encountered once, and another time the Germans could be heard demolishing a hut near the main Arras—Bapaume road. The next day the enemy occasionally fired with the Minenwerfer, but there was no shelling to speak of. In the evening Lieutenant R. Holmes and his patrol returned, having been cut off on the previous night by very strong parties of the enemy. Finding they were unable to regain our lines, they hid in shell-holes throughout the day, and took advantage of the darkness when night came to get back. On the 14th, when the usual patrols went out, Second Lieutenant W. Fleet took out a strong party to visit a German machine-gun post, which had come under the observation of a patrol on the previous night. Approaching it with caution, he found that it was unoccupied, but a German rifle, which he brought back, seemed to show that the enemy had been there lately. Four escaped British prisoners, who had been captured on the 21st, re-entered our lines near the sunken road; they belonged to the Sixth Division. The 1st Battalion went for ten days' rest to Barly until the 24th, when they marched to Bienvillers-au-Bois on their way to the trenches. Lieutenant Tindal-Atkinson and Second Lieutenant Paget-Cooke, who had just arrived to join the Battalion, were wounded by a shell that fell in No. 4 Company Mess. On the night of the 27th the 1st Battalion returned to the front line of trenches, but the Germans were singularly inactive except for occasional bursts of shell-fire. The patrols that were sent out failed to encounter any German parties, but one discovered that Calcutta Trench had been recently occupied by the enemy. Signs of its recent occupation were found in the shape of fresh bombs, rifles, etc., and a corporal's greatcoat proved that the occupants had belonged to the 453rd Regiment. Traces of German occupation could be seen all over the ground, but the most recent was the line of newly dug posts about 80 yards west of the Ablainzeville—Ayette road. The enemy evidently occupied an advanced picket line, as individual heads could be seen on the low ground, and the rapidity with which his light machine-guns and snipers opened fire from various points confirmed this surmise. On the 29th the enemy still remained inactive, and never engaged any targets which offered themselves. In the evening snipers were sent out from our lines to positions, where they could observe and engage any movement on the part of the enemy, who could be seen advancing in groups of two to occupy shell-slits. Parties were dribbled forward by the King's and No. 2 Companies, and told to occupy any empty enemy-slits, to check any advance of the enemy. These moves and counter-moves continued up to 9 P.M., when Lord Gort decided to withdraw all the advanced posts, and patrols continued to reconnoitre throughout the night.

The enemy's attitude during May was purely defensive, and except for two half-hearted raids he showed no inclination to come west of the line of the Ablainzeville—Ayette road. The Germans apparently were occupying an outpost line from Ablainzeville to Ayette, with a shell-hole line in rear and a line of resistance again behind that, and the situation depended very much on what was going on in other parts of the line: if the enemy succeeded in driving back the troops to the north and south, a retirement would become necessary, even without any movement of the hostile troops in front.

During the whole month the 1st Battalion remained either in the front trenches or in reserve. When in the trenches one and a half Companies held the front line, and one and a half Companies were in support, with one Company in reserve. On the days they became the Reserve Battalion,

CHAPTER XXIX.

1st Batt.
May
1918.

they were simply targets for the German artillery; every day there were casualties, and the number of men killed, wounded, and gassed amounted to a good many during the month. On some days the enemy activity was very slight, and on others the shelling would become intense. Patrols under officers were sent out every night, and the information gained varied. Occasionally bodies of Germans would be reported, moving about and talking, but when no attack developed such movements ceased to have any significance. The back areas were shelled with gas-shells daily, and so it happened that the casualties, when the Battalion was in reserve, were often greater than when it was in the front line. On the 17th the area occupied by the 1st Battalion was subjected to a severe bombing by aircraft; Second Lieutenant W. A. Fleet and Second Lieutenant G. E. A. A. Fitz-George Hamilton were killed, and Second Lieutenant S. J. Hargreaves and Second Lieutenant G. D. Neale were seriously wounded. The two latter never recovered from the wounds they received, and died the next day. The loss of these four keen young officers was deeply felt by the whole Battalion. At the same time Sergeant Robshaw and Lance-Sergeant Nicholson, the Lewis-gun instructors, were wounded and buried by the walls of a house, which were blown in by a bomb on the top of them. On the 20th the Cojeul Valley was bombarded with gas-shells, and Captain O. Stein, Second Lieutenant R. Holmes, and Second Lieutenant C. Brutton were gassed. A few days of rain and mist were welcomed by every one, since it made observation impossible, and therefore the enemy's artillery had to content itself with a small amount of inaccurate shelling. On the 24th Second Lieutenant O. W. D. Smith was seriously wounded by a shell. On the 28th a German propaganda balloon was shot down near Quesnoy Farm; it contained copies of the *Gazette des Ardennes*, a French newspaper, edited by the Germans. Although enemy transport activity could be often distinctly heard, the impending offensive never developed.

Much the same programme was followed at the beginning of June, and without any definite movement the enemy continued to bombard both the front trenches and the back area. On the 5th the Germans were located by a patrol, working on the road, and Stokes mortars were turned on to them, with the result that Véry lights went up in quick succession, no doubt an appeal for assistance. The guns on both sides were continually busy both day and night, and a great many shells of various sorts must have been fired. On the 8th the Battalion retired for a rest to Barly, where it remained until the end of the month.

The 2nd Battalion

Roll of Officers

Lieut.-Colonel G. E. C. Rasch, D.S.O.	Commanding Officer.
Major the Hon. W. R. Bailey, D.S.O.	Second in Command.
Capt. A. H. Penn	Adjutant.
Lieut. R. G. Briscoe, M.C.	Assistant Adjutant.

CHAPTER XXIX.
2nd Batt.
1918.

Hon. Capt. W. E. Acraman, M.C., D.C.M.	Quartermaster.
Lieut. G. G. M. Vereker, M.C.	Transport Officer.
Capt. F. A. M. Browning, D.S.O.	No. 1 Company.
Lieut. A. W. Acland, M.C.	,, ,,
Lieut. the Hon. H. F. P. Lubbock	,, ,,
2nd Lieut. J. S. Carter	,, ,,
2nd Lieut. G. F. Lawrence	,, ,,
2nd Lieut. R. C. M. Bevan	,, ,,
Capt. O. Martin Smith	No. 2 Company.
Lieut. R. H. R. Palmer	,, ,,
Lieut. W. H. S. Dent	,, ,,
2nd Lieut. C. A. Fitch	,, ,,
Lieut. A. C. Knollys	,, ,,
Lieut. S. T. S. Clarke, M.C.	No. 3 Company.
2nd Lieut. H. White	,, ,,
2nd Lieut. the Hon. S. A. S. Montagu	,, ,,
2nd Lieut. R. T. Sharpe	,, ,,
Capt. G. C. Fitz-H. Harcourt-Vernon, D.S.O.	No. 4 Company.
Lieut. R. A. W. Bicknell, M.C.	,, ,,
Lieut. F. H. J. Drummond, M.C.	,, ,,
Lieut. F. P. Loftus	,, ,,
2nd Lieut. P. V. Pelly	,, ,,
2nd Lieut. J. A. Paton	,, ,,
Capt. the Rev. and Hon. C. F. Lyttelton	Chaplain.
Lieut. L. J. Early	Medical Officer.

April. On the night of April 3 the Thirty-second Division captured Ayette, which considerably eased the situation on the right flank of the Guards Division. The 2nd Battalion went up into the line, and found the trenches very wet. On the 4th, during a heavy shelling, which was entirely directed against No. 1 Company on the right, Lieutenant the Hon. H. F. P. Lubbock was killed by a shell which pitched in the trench.

This was a great loss to the Battalion, for

he was an officer of sound judgment, who did not know what fear was. Corporal Teague, M.M., was killed at the same time, and 6 men were wounded. The 7th and 8th were spent in a camp behind Blaireville and Heudecourt, when Lieutenant F. H. J. Drummond and Second Lieutenant G. F. Lawrence joined. After two more days in the trenches the 2nd Battalion retired to Saulty, where they remained training till the 24th. On the 14th Second Lieutenant J. A. Paton and Second Lieutenant C. A. Fitch arrived from the Reinforcement Battalion, and on the 20th Second Lieutenant C. Gwyer joined.

On the 24th the 2nd Battalion proceeded in buses to Bienvillers-au-Bois, to relieve the 15th Battalion Highland Light Infantry, in reserve west of Douchy-les-Ayette. Two companies were billeted in the old German line just west of Monchy-au-Bois, and the remainder were in trenches between Douchy-les-Ayette and Monchy. The following day the Battalion moved up into the front line on the eastern outskirts of Ayette, and found everything very quiet. The explanation seemed to be that the Germans were thinning out their troops in this district, in order to increase their forces available for the thrust forward north on the night of the 29th. Second Lieutenant C. A. Fitch, who had gone out with a patrol to reconnoitre the German lines, was wounded in the head and right arm by a bomb thrown from a German post.

The same routine was carried out all during May: five days in the front line with inter-company relief, followed by two days in

CHAPTER XXIX.
2nd Batt.
May 1918.

reserve at Monchy-au-Bois. On the 4th an American Company Commander and three N.C.O.'s were attached to the 2nd Battalion under instruction. In order to ensure that the junior officers were proficient in technical subjects, special lectures were given by Officers from different branches of the service, and were attended by Officers and N.C.O.'s of the Battalion when it was in reserve. On the 11th Lieutenant J. C. Cornforth arrived, and on the 19th Lieutenant C. A. Gordon and Lieutenant H. A. Finch joined the Battalion. On the 22nd, during a heavy bombardment which was directed on the front line, Lieutenant A. W. Acland, M.C., was wounded, and almost every day there were casualties amongst other ranks. The exact spot the enemy would select for their next thrust was naturally not known, and a determined attack was expected daily, but except for intense shelling the enemy showed no signs of life. On the 27th the shelling increased, and the enemy aircraft became very active, with the result that there were 9 men killed and 8 wounded.

June.

The first week in June was spent by the 2nd Battalion in the front line, where the shells continued to fall with monotonous regularity. On the 3rd Lieutenant R. M. Oliver joined the Battalion. On the 6th, after a relief, rendered difficult by the enemy's barrage, which had been put down on the tracks leading to the trenches, the 2nd Battalion proceeded to Saulty, where they were billeted in the village and the Château grounds. There they remained till the end of the month, training, carrying out tactical schemes, and learning the latest developments in bombing. Colonel Rasch organised a platoon competition in the following: bomb-throwing, rifle-bombing, message-carrying by platoon runners, stretcher-bearer competitions, bayonet-fighting, Lewis-gunnery, musketry, tactical scheme and drill. The tactical scheme was judged by the two other Commanding Officers in the Brigade, and the drill by the three Regimental Sergeant-Majors. No. 7 Platoon, under Lieutenant Palmer, was the winner; No. 16 Platoon, under Sergeant Taylor, second; and No. 4 Platoon, under Second Lieutenant Bevan, third. At the Divisional Horse Show, which took place on the 22nd, the 2nd Battalion won Major-General Feilding's Cup, and Lieutenant G. Vereker, the Transport Officer, was congratulated on his horses having proved themselves the best in the Division. On the 23rd Lieutenant N. McK. Jesper, Lieutenant L. St. L. Hermon-Hodge, and Second Lieutenant F. J. Langley rejoined the Battalion, and in the absence of Colonel Rasch, who had gone temporarily to command the Brigade, Captain Harcourt-Vernon took over the command of the Battalion. On the 29th a Guard of Honour for H.R.H. the Duke of Connaught, under the command of Captain Browning, went in buses to the Third Army Headquarters at Hesdin, where their smart appearance created a great impression. Onlookers refused to believe that the men had just come out of the line, and maintained that they had been sent out from England for the purpose. The following day, the Army Commander, General Sir Julian Byng, in a message addressed to the

CHAPTER XXIX.

2nd Batt.
June
1918.

28   THE GRENADIER GUARDS

Chapter XXIX.
2nd Batt.
June 1918.

Division, expressed his satisfaction at their smart appearance, and added that their turn-out and bearing, their marching and handling of arms, were beyond all criticism.

THE 3RD BATTALION
ROLL OF OFFICERS

3rd Batt.

Lieut.-Colonel A. F. A. N. Thorne, D.S.O.	Commanding Officer.
Major R. H. V. Cavendish, M.V.O.	Second in Command.
Capt. the Hon. A. G. Agar-Robartes, M.C.	Adjutant.
Lieut. E. G. A. Fitzgerald, D.S.O.	Assistant Adjutant.
Lieut. F. J. Heasman	Transport Officer.
Capt. G. H. Wall	Quartermaster.
Capt. A. F. R. Wiggins	No. 1 Company.
Lieut. A. G. Elliott	,, ,,
2nd Lieut. C. L. F. Boughey	,, ,,
Capt. G. A. I. Dury, M.C.	No. 2 Company.
Lieut. A. H. S. Adair	,, ,,
2nd Lieut. W. A. Pembroke	,, ,,
Lieut. E. N. de Geijer	No. 3 Company.
Lieut. G. W. Godman	,, ,,
2nd Lieut. W. B. Ball	,, ,,
Capt. C. H. Bedford	No. 4 Company.
Lieut. H. St. J. Williams	,, ,,
2nd Lieut. E. J. Bunbury	,, ,,
Capt. Ffoulkes, R.A.M.C.	Medical Officer.
Capt. the Rev. S. Phillimore, M.C.	Chaplain.

April.

The 3rd Battalion spent the whole month of April either in the trenches, with three Companies in the front line, or in reserve. On the 7th Lieutenant E. G. A. Fitzgerald was wounded, and on the 8th the following officers joined the Battalion: Lieutenant F. A. Magnay, Second Lieutenant R. K. Henderson, Lieutenant C. Clifton Brown, and Second Lieutenant

H. W. Sanderson. The days spent in the front trenches were remarkably quiet, but as the ground on which these trenches were dug was overlooked by the enemy, very little work could be done except wiring, and this at night. On the 14th the Battalion, having "embussed" at Ransart, proceeded *via* Beaumetz-les-Loges to Lakerlière and Larbret, where it was billeted. On the 17th drafts reached the Battalion with the following officers : Second Lieutenant E. L. F. Clough-Taylor, Second Lieutenant R. Delacombe, Second Lieutenant W. B. L. Manley, Second Lieutenant H. J. Gibbon, and Second Lieutenant R. C. G. de Reuter. The days spent in billets were taken up with training, but as the men had to remain ready to move at one hour's notice in the morning and three hours' notice in the afternoon, it was impossible for Companies to go far. An attack from the enemy was expected on the 21st, and additional precautions were taken, but the Battalion was not called upon to go up into the front line. Major Lord Lascelles was appointed Second in Command *vice* Major Cavendish, and as Lieut.-Colonel Thorne had to take temporary command of the Brigade, he had at once to command the Battalion. Companies were now organised into three platoons with the headquarters of a fourth or depot platoon, to which all details were attached, when the Battalion went into action. On the 24th Lieut.-Colonel Thorne returned to the Battalion, and took it up into the front line the following day. On the 27th the front posts were subjected to an unusually heavy shelling, during which

CHAPTER XXIX.

3rd Batt. April 1918.

CHAPTER XXIX.
3rd Batt.
April 1918.

Second Lieutenant C. L. F. Boughey was wounded, and there were 6 killed and 5 wounded among other ranks. On the following day the Battalion retired into Brigade Reserve, where it remained till the end of the month.

May.

During the first week in May the Battalion remained in the line, with an inter-company relief, Major Lord Lascelles taking turns with Lieut.-Colonel Thorne. On the 3rd Second Lieutenant R. P. Papillon and Lieutenant the Hon. M. H. E. C. Towneley-Bertie joined. Officers' patrols were sent out every night and in the early morning, to lie out and listen for any hostile movement. After three days' rest the Battalion returned to the trenches, and came in for much shelling. Our artillery carried out nightly a harassing fire on the enemy's tracks, roads, and possible assembly areas, and this naturally brought down considerable retaliation. Lieutenant the Hon. M. H. E. C. Towneley-Bertie was wounded, and among other ranks there were 10 killed and 14 wounded. Another tour of duty in the front line from the 20th to the 24th caused 2 killed and 25 wounded among other ranks. On the 26th Captain G. F. R. Hirst, Lieutenant E. R. M. Fryer, M.C., and Second Lieutenant J. Chapman joined the Battalion. On the 28th the Battalion returned to the front trenches, and again came in for a harassing fire. Inter-company reliefs were carried out, and the work was concentrated on shelters and the deepening of lateral communication trenches.

June.

The Battalion remained in the front line until June 3, and was constantly bombarded with Blue Cross gas-shells. On the 2nd Lieutenant G. M. Cornish, M.C., joined. After four days spent in reserve the Battalion retired to La Baseque, where the men were billeted in the farms, or placed in tents and shelters in the wood. There they remained until the end of the month, training and practising tactical schemes.

CHAPTER XXX

APRIL 1–14, 1918

The 4th Battalion

Chapter XXX.
4th Batt.
April 1-14, 1918.

In April 1918 it fell to the lot of the 4th Guards Brigade to take part in some of the fiercest fighting of the war.

Ludendorff had opened a concentrated attack with nine divisions on the line north of La Bassée, and General von Quast, who commanded the German forces, had penetrated the portion of the line held by the Portuguese, and gained a considerable amount of ground. Reinforced by General von Arnim's infantry, he pushed on in the hope of gaining the Channel ports, or, at the least, of cutting the British communications. The German masses were pressing forward, and the general situation became more and more critical.

The attack commenced on April 9, and the Fifteenth Corps, under Lieut.-General Sir J. P. du Cane, which had been driven back, was holding the line between Merville and Vieux Berquin, south-east of Hazebrouck. Although the troops in Merville held fast, the enemy broke through at Robermetz, and, after capturing Neuf Berquin, moved down the road to Vierhoek.

APRIL 1918

Such was the state of affairs, when the 4th Guards Brigade was sent for to restore the line. After having "debussed" at Strazeele, it marched towards Vieux Berquin on the evening of April 11. Next day Brigadier-General the Hon. L. J. P. Butler received orders to attack Vierhoek, Pont Rondin, and Les Puresbecques, but before he could make much headway, was himself in turn vigorously engaged by the enemy. Reinforcements were being hurried up from several quarters, but everything depended on whether the line would hold. If the Australian Division, which was being sent up from the rear, could have time to detrain and take up good positions, the German rush would be checked. But should the enemy break through far enough to dislocate this arrangement, matters would become serious.

Realising the gravity of the crisis, General de Lisle, commanding the Fifteenth Corps, issued an order that no retirement must be made without an order in writing, signed by a responsible officer, who must be prepared to justify his action before a court-martial. Every inch of ground was to be disputed, and every company was told to stand firm until reinforcements could arrive.

The roll of officers of the 4th Battalion at the beginning of April was as follows:

Lieut.-Colonel W. S. Pilcher, D.S.O. . . . . Commanding Battalion.
Major C. F. A. Walker, M.C. . Second in Command.
Capt. C. R. Gerard, D.S.O. . Adjutant.
Capt. M. Chapman, M.C. . . Intelligence Officer.
Capt. I. H. Ingleby . . . Act.-Quartermaster.
Lieut. G. W. Selby-Lowndes . Transport Officer.

CHAPTER XXX.
4th Batt.
April
1918.

Capt. H. H. Sloane-Stanley, M.C.	No. 1 Company.
Lieut. C. E. Irby, M.C.	,, ,,
Lieut. E. H. Tuckwell, M.C.	,, ,,
Lieut. G. C. Burt	,, ,,
2nd Lieut. R. B. Osborne	,, ,,
Lieut. T. T. Pryce, M.C.	No. 2 Company.
Lieut. the Hon. C. C. S. Rodney	,, ,,
Lieut. R. H. Rolfe	,, ,,
Lieut. R. L. Murray-Lawes	,, ,,
Capt. G. C. Sloane-Stanley	No. 3 Company.
Lieut. F. C. Lyon	,, ,,
Lieut. the Hon. A. H. L. Hardinge, M.C.	,, ,,
Lieut. M. D. Thomas	,, ,,
Lieut. T. W. Minchin, D.S.O.	No. 4 Company.
Lieut. N. R. Abbey	,, ,,
Lieut. G. R. Green	,, ,,
Lieut. J. E. Greenwood	,, ,,
2nd Lieut. R. D. Richardson	,, ,,
Capt. N. Grellier, M.C., R.A.M.C.	Medical Officer.

The Battalion was in billets at Villers Brulin on April 10, when Lieut.-Colonel Pilcher received orders to move up in omnibuses to Strazeele Station *via* St. Pol. According to instructions it should have started " embussing " at 11.30 that night, but owing to some mistake the buses were twelve hours late, and all ranks spent the night and half the next day waiting by the roadside. It was impossible to cook any proper breakfasts, and too cold to sleep, so that when at last a start was made the men were already tired out. Then for twelve hours they jolted along in the buses, terribly cramped and without any opportunity for real rest. When it arrived at its destination next day, the Battalion marched to a field near Le Paradis, where Brigadier-General Butler held a conference. There were

APRIL 1918

to be two battalions in the front line and one in reserve; on the right was the 3rd Battalion Coldstream which was to take up a position from L'Epinette to Le Cornet Perdu. The 4th Battalion Grenadiers would be on the left, and the 2nd Battalion Irish Guards in reserve.

Chapter XXX.

4th Batt. April 1918.

Marching off at once, the whole force reached its position about dawn on the 12th. So promptly was the movement carried out that there was no time to issue rations, and the food had to follow on later in limbers. There was also a considerable shortage of tools, with the result that when daylight came the men were still very inadequately dug-in. In the 4th Battalion, No. 1 Company, under Captain H. Sloane-Stanley, was on the right, No. 4, under Lieutenant Green, in the centre, and No. 2, under Captain Pryce, on the left, with No. 3, under Lieutenant Nash, in support. As soon as it was light the enemy opened a heavy fire along the whole front with field-guns, while they swept with their lighter field-guns and machine-guns all places where they detected any movement. Battalion Headquarters seemed to come in for special attention, and, whenever any one went in or out, it was the signal for a shower of shells to fall round the spot.

April 12.

An order came to Brigadier-General Butler to secure the line from the College to Vieux Moulin with his brigade, and to prevent any movements along the Merville—Neuf Berquin road. He accordingly went up to Battalion Headquarters, and ordered an advance at 11 A.M. At the same time he sent up two companies of the Irish Guards to advance in échelon behind the right

36 THE GRENADIER GUARDS

CHAPTER XXX.
4th Batt. April 1918.

flank, in the hope of getting in touch with the Fiftieth Division. In the 4th Battalion Captain H. Sloane-Stanley was told to push forward two platoons to seize Vierhoek, and Captain Pryce to occupy Pont Rondin with a similar force.

The following were the officers who took part in the operations from April 12 to 14 :

Lieut.-Colonel W. S. Pilcher, D.S.O.	Commanding Battalion.
Capt. C. R. Gerard, D.S.O.	Adjutant.
Capt. M. Chapman, M.C.	Intelligence Officer.
Lieut. N. R. Abbey	Attached B.H.Q.
Capt. H. H. Sloane-Stanley, M.C.	No. 1 Company.
2nd Lieut. H. Stratford	,, ,,
2nd Lieut. R. B. Osborne	,, ,,
Capt. T. T. Pryce, M.C.	No. 2 Company.
Lieut. the Hon. C. C. S. Rodney	,, ,,
2nd Lieut. G. P. Philipps	,, ,,
Lieut. C. S. Nash, M.C.	No. 3 Company.
Lieut. M. D. Thomas	,, ,,
2nd Lieut. P. H. Cox	,, ,,
Lieut. G. R. Green	No. 4 Company.
2nd Lieut. J. E. Greenwood	,, ,,
2nd Lieut. G. W. Sich	,, ,,
Capt. N. Grellier, M.C., R.A.M.C.	Medical Officer.

The attack started at 11 A.M., but the Coldstream encountered such strenuous opposition that they were unable to advance more than 100 yards. Nor could No. 1 Company of the 4th Battalion Grenadiers make much headway towards Vierhoek, owing to the intense and accurate machine-gun and artillery fire, which swept the only road over the stream ; and it suffered severely in its attempts to carry out the orders. Second Lieutenant Osborne, however, had managed to push on about 200 yards with his platoon when he was wounded. But No. 2 Company made a most skilful advance towards Pont Rondin, led by Captain Pryce himself.

In the houses down the road, by which the Grenadiers had to come, the Germans were posted with light machine-guns, and before any progress could be made these houses had to be cleared. Slowly and systematically, No. 2 Company worked from house to house, and silenced the machine-guns. Thirty Germans were killed in this way—Captain Pryce alone accounted for seven—and were found afterwards in the houses or near by. Two machine-guns were taken, as well as a couple of prisoners.

During the whole operation, this company was under heavy fire, not only from machine-guns but also from a battery of field-guns, which was firing with open sights from a position some 300 yards down the road. It was a remarkably fine performance, and was watched with intense interest from Battalion Headquarters, which were some 200 yards in rear of the centre of the line, in a position from which the commanding officer could see most of the trenches occupied by his battalion. Lieutenant Nash, who had brought up one platoon to support No. 2 Company, was on his way back when his hand was carried away by a shell, and the command of No. 3 Company devolved on Lieutenant M. D. Thomas.

About 3 P.M. the situation of the 4th Guards Brigade became very critical. On the right the Coldstream reported that there was no sign of the Fiftieth Division, which should have been on

38 THE GRENADIER GUARDS

CHAPTER XXX.
4th Batt.
April 1918.

their right flank, and at the same time Captain Pryce sent back word that his left flank was in the air, and that Germans could be seen 1000 yards in rear of his company. He added that he was being engaged by trench mortars and field-guns, which were firing at him with open sights from the exposed flank.

Affairs on the right were improved by the arrival of a company of the Irish Guards, which, without orders, undertook a counter-attack in conjunction with a company of the Coldstream. But, having no troops to send up on the left flank, Brigadier-General Butler decided that that portion of the line must be withdrawn. Accordingly, Lieut.-Colonel Pilcher ordered Captain Pryce to fall back, but even then there was a large gap between his company and the troops on the left flank, of which the Germans took advantage. Having reached the position indicated, Captain Pryce held on to it in spite of several determined attacks by the enemy. Colonel Pilcher, accompanied by the Adjutant, Captain Gerard, visited the left of the line about 4.30 P.M. He found No. 2 Company rather scattered, as it had been compelled to form a defensive flank. Meanwhile, after an intense artillery preparation, the enemy attacked No. 1 and No. 4 Companies, and was driven back with severe losses.

All day the Battalion Headquarters were severely shelled by two German field-guns and also by trench mortars. The farm they occupied was set on fire, and both Captain M. Chapman, who had distinguished himself on many occasions as intelligence officer, and Lieutenant N. R. Abbey, who was attached to Battalion Headquarters, were killed by shells. A good many valuable men, who had served on Battalion Headquarters for a long time, were killed or wounded during the day. The farm was full of cows and horses, which had to be turned loose when the farm caught fire, and several casualties took place on this account. The Headquarters were afterwards moved to the garden of the farm. To some extent the fire was kept down by the skilful and gallant conduct of Lieutenant Lewis of the 152nd Brigade R.F.A., who exposed himself continually to get direct observation, while his guns undoubtedly inflicted heavy casualties on the advancing Germans.

At the close of the day, the front of the 4th Battalion remained intact, but the cost of holding this line against repeated assaults had necessarily been very heavy. No. 2 Company lost 80 men and 1 officer out of 120 who went into action, and No. 4 Company lost 70 per cent of its strength and all the officers. The total casualties in the Battalion were 250, including 8 officers. On the other hand, the enemy lost so heavily that the ground in front of the Battalion was strewn with their dead; in some places there were heaps of bodies piled up in front of the trenches. Some idea of the fierceness of the fighting may be gathered from the fact that during the day the 4th Battalion alone fired off no less than 70,000 rounds of ammunition.

In view of the situation on both flanks, Brigadier-General Butler gave orders on the

CHAPTER XXX.
4th Batt.
April
1918.

night of the 12th that the Brigade was to take up a new line. For this the 2nd Battalion Irish Guards was to have its right resting on Pont Tournant, with the 3rd Battalion Coldstream in the centre, and the 4th Battalion Grenadiers on the left, in touch with the 12th Battalion K.O.Y.L.I., which was to join up with the troops of the Twenty-ninth Division. In response to General Butler's request that the line held by his brigade might be contracted, the Fifth Division was ordered to take over the line as far as L'Epinette inclusive.

As soon as this relief was completed, the 2nd Battalion Irish Guards and one company of the Coldstream were withdrawn into Brigade Reserve, and the 210th Field Company R.E. went up, to help the 4th Battalion Grenadiers dig the new line. To replace some of the losses in the Battalion, Captain Minchin, Lieutenant Lyon, and Lieutenant Burt were sent up, and Lieutenant Murray-Lawes went to Battalion Headquarters. Colonel Pilcher's orders were to delay the enemy at all costs, so as to give the Australian Division time to detrain and come up to that part of the line.

The new Battalion frontage was 1800 yards long; the country was absolutely flat, with not a single hedge to mask the trenches, and the line was held by companies in isolated posts. So heavily had the Battalion suffered in the fighting on the 12th that it had only 9 officers and 180 other ranks left—that is to say, one man to every ten yards of front.

As the Battalion Headquarters had been

destroyed, Colonel Pilcher assembled the newly-arrived officers at the Irish Guards Headquarters, and explained to them that the new line was to be dug east of the Vieux Berquin—Neuf Berquin road, so that the village of La Couronne and the cross-roads south of it might be protected. When Captain Minchin reached the leading companies, Captain Pryce told him the men were so dead beat that he thought they were quite incapable of digging a new line, and the Adjutant of the K.O.Y.L.I. said his men were in much the same condition. When this was reported to Colonel Pilcher, he went up himself to explain how things stood. He could find no trace of the machine-guns from the Thirty-first Division, which should have been there. The Germans were so close that they could be heard talking quite distinctly. He found Captain Pryce, who was quite worn out from want of sleep, and made it clear that the orders must be carried out, as it was absolutely essential to alter the position of the trenches. The plans had been changed, and the line the Battalion was now to occupy lay between La Couronne and the burnt farm, that had been the Battalion Headquarters.

The men were awakened with difficulty, and led to the new position, where, exhausted as they were, they were set to dig themselves in. Having satisfied himself that the orders were understood, Colonel Pilcher went in search of Captain Minchin, but failed to find him in the dark. The field company of R.E., that was to have been sent up to help, did not appear, and as there were only 14 men left in No. 4 Company,

CHAPTER XXX.
4th Batt.
April 1918.

and 30 in No. 2, a continuous line of trenches was out of the question. Captain Minchin, therefore, ordered them to dig rifle-pits, capable of holding three or four men at intervals, and even so there were gaps of considerable length between companies. So utterly weary were the men that it was not at all easy to make them understand what had to be done, and naturally the darkness did not help to simplify matters. No. 1 Company, under Captain H. Sloane Stanley, had gone too far to the right, and instead of being up to the burnt farm was some 200 yards away. This made it necessary to post a strong sentry group, where it could guard the gap.

It was nearly dawn before the digging was finished; one man in each bay then took turns to watch while the other three slept. One source of constant anxiety to the officers was the ammunition, which had not been sent up. Just before dawn Lieutenant Lyon received a message that it had been dumped near La Couronne, but as it was then getting light he could not send men for it. Captain Pryce, however, succeeded in getting five boxes before daylight.

April 13.

Fog hung thickly round during the early morning of the 13th, and it was found that the Germans had taken advantage of it to work up machine-guns close to our line. Their first attack occurred at 6.30, and was directed against the 3rd Battalion Coldstream. With the aid of a tank, the enemy forced his way between the left and centre companies of the Coldstream, but was soon ejected. A company of the 2nd Battalion Irish Guards went up later to strengthen

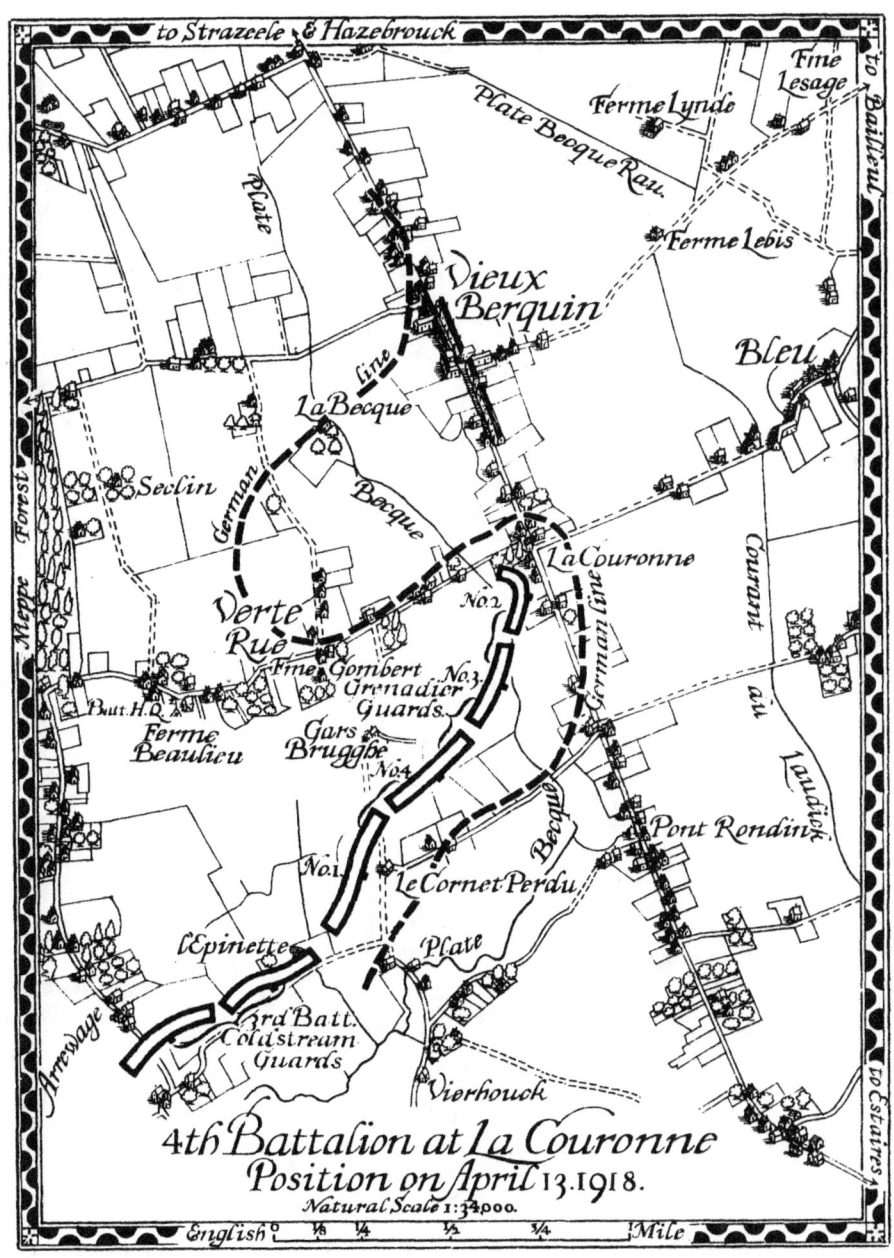

APRIL 1918   43

that part of the line. At 9.15 Colonel Pilcher found that strong German attacks were developing all down the line, and sent orders round to the companies that they must hold on to their line at all costs, and fight to the end. This message was duly acknowledged by all officers commanding companies.

As soon as the mist cleared away, the Germans opened fire with their machine-guns and swept the parapet with bullets. When the light improved, they brought up more machine-guns, and were able to enfilade the trenches. Under cover of this fire they crawled forward by ones and twos, and established sniping posts in some unfinished trenches not 150 yards off. The Brigade-Major came up to Battalion Headquarters, to confirm the report that the troops on the left had retired, and that the left was entirely in the air. He had also heard that the enemy had penetrated the centre of the Brigade. Colonel Pilcher and the Brigade-Major went down the road to within some 150 yards of La Couronne, where they met Private Bagshaw (afterwards killed), who was runner to No. 4 Company, and who reported that the centre was still intact. After going up close to the front line to verify this statement, the Brigade-Major returned to inform the Brigadier of what he had ascertained.

Captain Minchin meanwhile reported the precarious condition of affairs in front, and was told in reply that a company of Irish Guards and a platoon of Coldstream would be sent to his assistance, but these reinforcements never arrived. At one time the Germans seemed to be contemplating a determined attack; they stood up and advanced in extended order, in the hope of finding a gap and penetrating the line, but the steady fire poured on them by the 4th Battalion soon changed their minds, and sent them back to cover. About 12.30 P.M. the 12th Pioneer Battalion of the K.O.Y.L.I. at La Couronne was completely blown out of its trenches by the enemy's trench mortars. When the men of that battalion found that the troops on their left had been pushed back, and that the Germans were working round in rear of them, they had no choice but to retire. This placed the left flank of the 4th Battalion in the air.

Captain Pryce sent back an urgent message saying that the Germans were in Vieux Berquin and La Couronne, and that another column estimated at two battalions, was advancing from Bleu. Up to that point, he added, he had managed to beat off the enemy, and there was a large number of their dead in front of his trenches, but he was not strong enough to resist much longer the repeated assaults of so large a force. As soon as this message reached General Butler, he sent up the company of Irish Guards which had already been promised, but it never got to Captain Pryce, for by now the Germans had wedged themselves in some force between him and his hopes of relief. Advancing north of the road leading to La Couronne, the reinforcing company was met by large numbers of Germans coming from La Becque. It fought on till it was completely cut off, and only one sergeant and six men escaped.

An attempt was made to alter the position of a Lewis gun belonging to No. 2 Company, but the moment they moved the N.C.O. and the men with it were fired on, and the gun was disabled. Finding that all attempts to retrieve the gun were useless, Second Lieutenant Philipps, who was in charge of the party, decided to rejoin Captain Pryce, but was hit in the hip by a machine-gun bullet just as he reached the trench.

Their turning of the left flank allowed the Germans to creep round in rear of the Battalion, but they had not gone far before they were engaged by the Battalion Headquarters, as well as the 3rd Battalion Coldstream Headquarters, who offered a most determined resistance. This final effort kept them successfully at bay until the arrival of the Australian Division put a final and effective stop to any farther movements on their part.

There remains the epic story of Captain Pryce. One last message was received from him—that his company was surrounded and his men shooting to front and to rear, standing back to back in the trenches to meet the encircling enemy at all points.

Of what happened afterwards, an outline at any rate was gathered from a corporal of the company, who escaped from Vieux Berquin the following night. Reduced now to only thirty men, the gallant little band fought on all that day. Without a pause they fired at their advancing foes, steadily, calmly, with the same rapidity and deadly aim that caused the Germans in the Mons retreat to mistake our " contemptible "

CHAPTER XXX.
4th Batt.
April 1918.

riflemen for machine-guns. The enemy was puzzled. They could not for a moment believe that such a stout resistance could be put up by anything but a formidable force, and dared not make the attempt to come to close quarters.

By the evening the defenders were practically at the end of their tether. Only eighteen out of the thirty were left, and they had used up every scrap of ammunition. The Germans were in Verte Rue, and the beleaguered band could see the field-grey uniforms advancing towards Bois d'Aval. It was now 8.15. Suddenly Captain Pryce perceived a new move against him. A party of the enemy had made up their minds to test the strength of their obstinate opponents; they pressed forward, and got to within 80 yards of the stubbornly-held trenches. The position seemed hopeless, but not for a moment did he flinch. Though the last cartridge had been fired, the men still had their bayonets, and he ordered them to charge.

Straight at the advancing enemy he rushed at the head of his handful of men. The Germans were completely taken aback. They dared not fire, for fear of hitting their own men, who were now in rear of the Grenadiers' desperately defended position, and retired. Thereupon Captain Pryce decided to take his men back to the trench again.

But by now the enemy had seen. They had realised the almost incredible weakness of the hitherto unknown force, that had so long successfully kept them at bay. And, restored to confidence, they came on once more. Once more

APRIL 1918

Captain Pryce led the tattered remnant of his company—that now numbered only fourteen—to the charge, and when last seen they were still fighting fearlessly and doggedly against overwhelming odds.

In all the glorious record of the Grenadiers there has been no story more splendid than this. It was a Homeric combat—two battalions held up (and the advance of a whole enemy division thus delayed) by a few determined men. Of the losses they inflicted on their overwhelmingly superior foe, some idea was gathered by Lieutenant Burt, who when taken prisoner afterwards was shown by a German officer the heaps of enemy dead in front of the British trenches. If ever a niche were earned in the Temple of Fame it was by these brave men and their brave leader—who, having already won a bar to his Military Cross, was awarded the Victoria Cross for this crowning act of gallantry.

Meanwhile, No. 1 and No. 4 Companies, who had been enfiladed all day, had lost all their officers. Captain H. Sloane-Stanley had been killed and Captain Minchin wounded in three places, though he just managed to crawl back afterwards, being fired at all the way. In No. 3 Company Lieutenant Lyon was killed, and subsequently the whole company was surrounded and taken prisoners. The survivors of No. 1 and No. 4 Companies held on till night, although by then the Germans were in rear of them, and finally managed to get back to the Australians. The Headquarters of the Battalion took up a position in the evening just south of the Forêt

48 THE GRENADIER GUARDS

CHAPTER XXX.
4th Batt.
April 1918.

de Nieppe, in prolongation of the Australian line. Although the line had been saved, the whole Brigade had been cut to pieces. The Coldstream and Irish Guards had suffered the same fate as the Grenadiers, and few of them got back to the Australian line.

By April 14 the 4th Battalion had been three days and three nights fighting and digging without any rest, while of the nineteen officers who went into action only two were left. The casualties were:

Capt. H. H. Sloane-Stanley	Killed.
Capt. M. Chapman	,,
Capt. T. T. Pryce, V.C., M.C.	,,
Lieut. N. R. Abbey	,,
Lieut. F. C. Lyon	,,
Lieut. C. S. Nash	Wounded.
Lieut. G. R. Green	,,
2nd Lieut. J. E. Greenwood	,,
Lieut. G. C. Burt	Wounded and missing.
2nd Lieut. H. Stratford (died of wounds)	,, ,,
Lieut. the Hon. C. C. S. Rodney	,, ,,
2nd Lieut. G. P. Philipps	,, ,,
Lieut. M. D. Thomas	,, ,,
2nd Lieut. G. W. Sich	,, ,,
2nd Lieut. P. H. Cox	,, ,,

The total casualties amongst other ranks were 504, or 90 per cent of the strength of the Battalion

In the Brigade the casualties amounted to 39 officers and 1244 other ranks.

The following message was sent by Lieut.-General Sir H. de B. de Lisle, the Corps Commander, to General Sir H. S. Horne, commanding the First Army:

APRIL 1918

SECRET. XV. Corps No. 608/13/70.   CHAPTER
              Dated 23-4-1918.   XXX.
                 31D/211.A.   4th Batt.
                                      April
            SECOND ARMY   1918.

I forward the attached narrative of the action of the 4th Guards Brigade during the operations of the 11th to 14th April 1918, for the information of the Army Commander.

An account of the operations of the Corps as a whole is being prepared, but this record of the glorious stand against overwhelming odds made by the 4th Guards Brigade is of exceptional interest.

The history of the British Army can record nothing finer than the story of the action of the 4th Guards Brigade on the 12th and 13th April 1918.

The troops of the 29th and 31st Divisions by their stout defence covered the detrainment of the First Australian Division and saved Hazebrouck.

              (Signed) BEAUVOIR DE LISLE,
              Lieut.-General Commanding XV. Corps.
XV. Corps.
  23-4-18.

         Copy to 31st Division.

....
....

Forwarded for your information.

   (Signed)   W. H. ANNESLEY, Lieut.-Colonel,
  24-4-18.   A.A. and Q.M.G., 31st Division.

General Sir H. S. Horne, commanding the First Army, telegraphed as follows to the Commander of the Fifteenth Corps :

I wish to express my appreciation of the great bravery and endurance with which all ranks have fought and held out (during the last five days) against overwhelming numbers.

It has been necessary to call for great exertions and more must still be asked for, but I am quite confident that at this critical period, when the existence of the British Army is at stake, all ranks of the First Army will do their best.

(Signed)   H. S. HORNE, General,
Commanding First Army.

Sir Douglas Haig in his Despatch of October 21 describes the fighting as follows :

Next day (April 12) the enemy followed up his attacks with great vigour, and the troops of the Twenty-ninth and Thirty-first Divisions, now greatly reduced in strength by the severe fighting already experienced, and strung out over a front of nearly 10,000 yards east of the Forêt de Nieppe, were once more tried to the utmost. Behind them the First Australian Division, under the command of Major-General Sir H. B. Walker, K.C.B., D.S.O., was in process of detraining, and the troops were told that the line was to be held at all costs until the detrainment could be completed.

During the morning, which was very foggy, several determined attacks, in which a German armoured car came into action against the 4th Guards Brigade on the southern portion of our line, were repulsed with great loss to the enemy. After the failure of these assaults, he brought up field-guns to point-blank range, and in the northern sector, with their aid, gained *Vieux Berquin.* Everywhere except at *Vieux Berquin* the enemy's advance was held up all day by desperate fighting, in which our advanced posts displayed the greatest gallantry, maintaining their ground when entirely surrounded, men standing back to back in the trenches and shooting to front and rear.

In the afternoon the enemy made a further deter-

Brigadier-General C. R. Champion de Crespigny D.S.O.

mined effort, and by sheer weight of numbers forced his way through the gaps in our depleted line, the surviving garrisons of our posts fighting where they stood to the last with bullet and bayonet. The heroic resistance of these troops, however, had given the leading Brigade of the First Australian Division time to reach and organise their appointed line east of the *Forêt de Nieppe.* These now took up the fight, and the way to *Hazebrouck* was definitely closed.

The performance of all the troops engaged in this most gallant stand, and especially that of the 4th Guards Brigade, on whose front of some 4000 yards the heaviest attacks fell, is worthy of the highest praise. No more brilliant exploit has taken place since the opening of the enemy's offensive, though gallant actions have been without number.

The action of these troops, and indeed of all the Divisions engaged in the fighting in the Lys Valley, is the more noteworthy because, as already pointed out, practically the whole of them had been brought straight out of the Somme battlefield, where they had suffered severely and had been subjected to a great strain. All these Divisions, without adequate rest and filled with young reinforcements, which they had had no time to assimilate, were again hurriedly thrown into the fight, and in spite of the great disadvantages under which they laboured, succeeded in holding up the advance of greatly superior forces of fresh troops. Such an accomplishment reflects the greatest credit on the youth of Great Britain, as well as upon those responsible for the training of young soldiers sent out from home at this time.

Lieutenant C. Kerr of the 8th Battalion Australian Infantry afterwards reported that, when the Australian Division was establishing a line of defence for the troops in front to fall back upon, isolated parties from the front arrived.

Chapter XXX.

4th Batt. April 1918.

Sergeant E. Shaw of the 4th Battalion on reaching that line, collected all the men he could, and inquired where he should take up a position; but Lieutenant Kerr, who knew what hard fighting the Battalion had been through, offered to send these men back to his Battalion Headquarters. Sergeant Shaw, however, asked permission to stay in the line with his men until he received instructions to join his battalion. A position behind the hedge near Seclin Farm was allotted to these men, and there they stayed until the 15th, when they received orders to join their battalion.

Lieutenant Kerr added in his report:

The men of my company and battalion are full of admiration for the manner in which the Guards fought. We watched the fighting in the village and farms whilst consolidating new line. The moral effect on our troops of the stubborn resistance offered by these troops in denying ground to the enemy, the orderly withdrawal to our line, and the refusal of this sergeant to leave the line when offered the choice of comfortable quarters was excellent.

CHAPTER XXXI

APRIL TO NOVEMBER 1918

THE 4TH BATTALION

LIEUT.-COLONEL PILCHER brought the remnants of the 4th Battalion out of the line on the 15th, and after halting for a few hours at Grand Sec Bois, arrived at Borre. The billets into which the Battalion went, were between Hazebrouck and Borre, and the men were glad to get a rest after their hard fighting. Captain the Hon. F. E. Needham arrived, and took over command of No. 1 Company, and Second Lieutenant P. G. S. Gregson-Ellis, who joined at the same time, was posted to No. 2 Company. The Battalion was now so weak in numbers that Lieut.-Colonel Pilcher organised it into two companies of three platoons each. Being in reserve it was still in the area of operations, and on the 16th, while the Germans were shelling the back areas, one shell fell in one of the billets, killing three men, and wounding five more, including Company Sergeant-Major Pettit. On the 16th the Battalion marched to La Kreule, moving on the next day into billets at La Halte. Brigadier-General Butler found that these sadly depleted battalions were

CHAPTER XXXI.
4th Batt.
April 1918.

difficult to work with, since at any time his Brigade might be called upon to take over a portion of the line, and a battalion of six platoons would be expected to hold trenches, occupied by a battalion up to full strength. He therefore determined to make a composite battalion of the 4th Battalion Grenadiers and the 3rd Battalion Coldstream, and to place it under the command of Lieut.-Colonel Pilcher, with Major Gillilan as Second in Command. In all the history of the two regiments this had never been done before; not even at the first battle of Ypres, where battalions of each regiment had been decimated, had any amalgamation been attempted. This composite battalion now took over from the 5th Battalion of the 2nd Australian Regiment the billets in Le-Tir-Anglais, and was placed in support. During a severe shelling on the 20th Second Lieutenant R. D. Richardson was severely wounded, and died four days later. On the 22nd the composite battalion relieved the King's Own Yorkshire Light Infantry in the front line, and came in for a heavy bombardment of gas and high-explosive shells from the enemy's artillery, during which Lieutenant R. Rolfe was killed. After three days in the trenches the composite battalion moved back into support, and now that drafts of men had been sent up to both battalions, it was split up again into two. The officers of the 4th Battalion were:

Lieut.-Colonel W. S. Pilcher, D.S.O.	Commanding Officer.
Capt. C. R. Gerard . .	. Adjutant.
Lieut. R. L. Murray-Lawes .	. Intelligence Officer.
Capt. the Hon. F. E. Needham	. No. 1 Company.

Lieut. E. H. Tuckwell . . . No. 1 Company.
Lieut. C. E. Irby . . . . No. 2 Company.
2nd Lieut. P. G. S. Gregson-Ellis . ,, ,,

CHAPTER XXXI.

4th Batt. April 1918.

On the 27th the Battalion proceeded to Hondeghem, where Lieutenant A. A. Morris and Second Lieutenant the Hon. S. E. Marsham joined.

At the beginning of May the 4th Guards Brigade was transferred from the Second to the Third Army, and was placed directly under the orders of General Headquarters. On the 21st it marched *via* Wandicourt to Saulty, where it remained until the end of the month.

May.

The following officers arrived during May: Lieutenant M. P. B. Wrixon, M.C., Second Lieutenant H. V. Gillett, Lieutenant J. E. Greenwood, Lieutenant R. P. le Poer Trench.

The Battalion remained at Saulty until the 11th, when it moved to La Cauchie, where Captain J. H. C. Simpson and Lieutenant H. G. Wiggins joined. On the 30th, after church parade, Field-Marshal His Royal Highness the Duke of Connaught visited the Battalion.

June.

ROLL OF OFFICERS IN JULY

July.

Lieut.-Colonel W. S. Pilcher, D.S.O.   Commanding Officer.
Major C. F. A. Walker, M.C. . .   Second in Command.
Capt. C. R. Gerard, D.S.O. . .   Adjutant.
Capt. I. H. Ingleby . . .   Act.-Quartermaster.
Lieut. G. W. Selby-Lowndes .   Transport Officer.
Lieut. R. L. Murray-Lawes .   Intelligence Officer.
Capt. the Hon. F. E. Needham   No. 1 Double Compy.
Capt. J. H. C. Simpson . . .   ,,   ,,
Lieut. R. P. le Poer Trench, M.C. .   ,,   ,,
Lieut. H. G. Wiggins, M.C. .   ,,   ,,

56 THE GRENADIER GUARDS

CHAPTER XXXI.
4th Batt.
July 1918.

Lieut. M. P. B. Wrixon, M.C.	No. 1 Double Compy.
Lieut. J. E. Greenwood	,, ,,
2nd Lieut. the Hon. S. E. Marsham	,, ,,
Capt. the Hon. A. H. L. Hardinge, M.C.	No. 2 Double Compy.
Lieut. E. W. Nairn	,, ,,
Lieut. C. E. Irby, M.C.	,, ,,
2nd Lieut. A. F. Alington	,, ,,
2nd Lieut. P. G. S. Gregson-Ellis	,, ,,
2nd Lieut. H. V. Gillett	,, ,,
Capt. N. Grellier, M.C., R.A.M.C.	Medical Officer.
Capt. the Rev. E. Best	Chaplain.

At the beginning of July the Battalion went to Criel Plage. On the 20th the third anniversary of the formation of the Battalion was duly celebrated by a football match between the two half battalions, and a Sergeants' dinner and concert, which Brigadier-General Butler attended.

Aug. During August the Battalion remained at Criel Plage employed in training and fatigue work. Lieutenant C. C. Cubitt joined.

Sept. At the beginning of September Captain R. Wolrige-Gordon joined, and on the 25th the Battalion proceeded to Hiermont, where it was placed under the orders of the Cavalry Corps, as mobile infantry to be moved by motor transport. On the 27th it moved to Rorcourt, and two days later to Bray-sur-Somme, where it occupied a camp which had formerly been used for German prisoners. On the 30th Lieutenant B. Layton, Second Lieutenant A. G. Snelling, and Second Lieutenant W. R. Wearne arrived.

Oct. ROLL OF OFFICERS AT THE BEGINNING OF OCTOBER

Lieut.-Colonel W. S. Pilcher, D.S.O.	Commanding Officer.
Capt. C. R. Gerard, D.S.O.	Adjutant.
Capt. I. H. Ingleby	Act.-Quartermaster.

APRIL TO NOVEMBER 1918 57

Lieut. G. W. Selby-Lowndes	Transport Officer.	CHAPTER XXXI.
Lieut. R. L. Murray-Lawes	Intelligence Officer.	
Capt. R. Wolrige-Gordon, M.C.	No. 1 Double Compy.	4th Batt.
Lieut. B. C. Layton	,, ,,	Oct. 1918.
Lieut. M. P. B. Wrixon, M.C.	,, ,,	
Lieut. J. E. Greenwood	,, ,,	
2nd Lieut. P. G. S. Gregson-Ellis	,, ,,	
Capt. the Hon. A. H. L. Hardinge, M.C.	No. 2 Double Compy.	
Capt. E. W. Nairn	,, ,,	
Lieut. H. G. Wiggins, M.C.	,, ,,	
2nd Lieut. C. E. Irby, M.C.	,, ,,	
2nd Lieut. W. R. Wearne	,, ,,	
2nd Lieut. H. V. Gillett	,, ,,	
2nd Lieut. A. G. Snelling	,, ,,	
Capt. N. Grellier, M.C., R.A.M.C.	Medical Officer.	
Capt. the Rev. E. Best	Chaplain.	

On October 3 the Battalion moved to Frise, and on the 8th to Pœuilly. Its movements now depended on the Cavalry Corps, but as there was no scope for the latter, since the country was enclosed and full of barbed wire, its rôle was to march in the wake of the divisions, which were driving the Germans in front of them. In order to be at hand if wanted it was necessary to keep well up, and so the column was constantly under shell-fire. On leaving Pœuilly the Battalion marched to Bellenglise, moving on the following day to Montbrehain, where the British lines advancing and the Germans retiring could be plainly seen. On the 9th Major J. S. Hughes, M.C., arrived and took up his duties as Second in Command. The march was continued through Brancourt to Premont, where the main road was completely blocked, as the retreating Germans had blown down the church, through Montigny to Gouy, where the Battalion remained

CHAPTER XXXI.
4th Batt.
Oct. 1918.

Nov.

for three days. The men had an opportunity of seeing Lesbœufs and Morval, which had played so great a part in the battle of the Somme in 1916, and also the Grenadiers' Memorial erected there. On the 21st Second Lieutenant M. C. St. J. Hornby joined. On the 26th the 4th Guards Brigade left the Cavalry Corps and received orders to join the Guards Division. For the time being the Battalion was sent to its old billets in Criel, where Lieutenant R. D. Leigh-Pemberton, M.C., and Second Lieutenant O. Scott Russell joined, and there it remained until the Armistice was signed on November 11.

CHAPTER XXXII

JULY AND AUGUST 1918

Diary of the War

AFTER some successes on a small scale by the French at St. Pierre Aigle, and by the Americans at Château-Thierry, the Germans launched their third and last offensive on a fifty-mile front in the direction of Rheims, and penetrated the line to a depth of two to three miles. Thirty German divisions took part in this battle, and the fighting was very severe. On July 18 Marshal Foch began his brilliant counter-stroke on a twenty-seven-mile front from Fontenoy to Belleau, and drove the Germans back over the Marne, capturing a large number of prisoners. Although in full retreat, the Germans continued to offer a stubborn resistance, and counter-attacked all along the line.

In August Sir Douglas Haig struck with the Fourth Army under Sir Henry Rawlinson, and succeeded in inflicting a crushing defeat on the Germans and capturing 22,000 prisoners. Hardly had the enemy recovered from this blow, when the Third Army under Sir Julian Byng advanced on a nine-mile front, and recovered a large portion of the ground that had been lost in the spring.

In Italy the Austrians were completely defeated by the Italians, who took a large number of prisoners and guns, and the whole Piave Delta was cleared. These successes were quickly followed up until the Austrians were in full retreat.

In Albania the Allied Forces made considerable progress and compelled the Austrians to retire.

In Palestine the British positions covering the passages of the Jordan and the north of Jericho were attacked by the Turks.

OPERATIONS FROM AUGUST 21 TO 28

Divisional Account

After Rawlinson's success on the Somme Byng was ordered to advance, recover the Arras-Albert railway, and generally to hustle the Germans, who were now falling slowly back. This was to be the prelude to the main operation.

The attack on August 21 was planned and carried out at exceedingly short notice, and was completely successful. The subsequent daily attacks, executed in pursuance of the policy laid down by higher authority, gave the enemy no rest and no opportunity of organising a new line of resistance, but they rendered the task of co-ordination with the division on the flanks almost impossible. By the time the position of the advanced troops of the Guards Division at the end of the day's fighting had been ascertained (probably not before 4 A.M.), there was usually only just time to plan and issue orders for the next day's operations. It seldom happened that the situation and intention of the flank divisions could be ascertained before orders were issued, with the result that each division had to work independently.

The Guards Division was at that time in the Sixth Corps, which had been ordered to capture the Ablainzeville—Moyenneville spur on the morning of the 21st. The attack was carried out by the Second Division on the right, followed by the Third Division and 2nd Guards Brigade from the Guards Division on the left, with the 5th Infantry Brigade from the Second Division in reserve.

In the 2nd Guards Brigade (Sergison-Brooke) the attack was carried out by the 1st Battalion Coldstream Guards and 1st Battalion Scots Guards, with the 3rd Battalion Grenadier Guards in reserve. When the first objectives had been secured the 3rd Battalion Grenadier Guards was pushed through, and captured the line of the railway. The attack was supported by seven brigades of field artillery and heavy guns under Colonel Phipps. One company of the 4th Battalion Guards Machine Gun Regiment was attached, and sixteen tanks (Mark IV.) were to co-operate.

The 1st Guards Brigade (with Gort temporarily in command) was ordered to advance towards the railway, and be prepared to occupy Hamel Switch in the event of the leading brigade finding it unoccupied. There was very thick mist in the early morning, and the contact patrols were unable to work, but the enemy had expected this attack, and had withdrawn all his guns, leaving only a very small garrison in the forward area. Moyenneville was secured without difficulty, while the Second Division captured Courcelles. On reaching the railway the resistance stiffened; and when General Sergison-Brooke reported that all the tanks appeared to have been drawn away south-east, and that there were none operating on the front of the Brigade, Major-General Feilding warned him that no advance beyond the railway must be attempted without them. In the meantime the Third Division on the right had some stiff fighting on the railway, and the Fifty-ninth Division on the left made some progress towards Boisieux St. Marc. Gort's Brigade reached the quarries on the other side of the railway in the afternoon, and found there was heavy hostile shelling from the north of Courcelles. That night the patrols entered Hamelincourt Trench, and early the next morning the Germans counter-attacked, but failed to eject the companies which were occupying Hamel Works.

On the 22nd orders were issued for a farther advance the next day. Brigadier-General Sergison-Brooke, in command of the 2nd Guards Brigade, was instructed to advance. On his left the Third and Fifty-sixth Divisions would operate, and on his right the Second Division would capture Gomiecourt. The enemy was to be pressed continuously in order to conform to the attack by British and French troops elsewhere. On the 23rd the enemy shelled Boiry with gas and high-explosive shells, but did not offer any

JULY AND AUGUST 1918

serious resistance. Sergison-Brooke's 2nd Guards Brigade met with little opposition, and gained all their objectives along Hamelincourt Trench, capturing Hamel Mound. Orders were then sent to Brigadier-General Sergison-Brooke to advance on the line Judas Farm—St. Leger Mill, while Brigadier-General Follett was told to move up the 3rd Guards Brigade, and be prepared to relieve the 2nd Guards Brigade in the evening. Meanwhile the Second Division had captured Ervillers.

The great feature of the day's fighting was the advance of the 1st Battalion Grenadier Guards, which had been placed at the disposal of General Sergison-Brooke. After a long approach march, this Battalion, advancing with both flanks exposed, passed through Sergison-Brooke's Brigade, and seized the key-position south-west of St. Leger. The capture of this position enabled the divisions on both flanks to advance the following day with little loss.

That night when the 3rd Guards Brigade relieved the 2nd, the Guards Division had reached the line running through Mory Switch as far as Judas Trench, thence to Judas Farm, and on to Boyelles Reserve, where it was in touch with the Fifty-sixth Division.

The next morning—the 24th—the 3rd Guards Brigade continued the pursuit of the Germans, and was ordered to advance on St. Leger, which was not to be entered by the battalions engaged in the attack, as the battalion in reserve would be responsible for the " mopping up " of the town. This advance was successfully accom-

Chapter XXXII.

Aug. 1918

Aug. 23.

CHAPTER XXXII.

Aug. 1918.

plished, but after St. Leger had been secured, it was found impossible to make any further progress until Mory Copse was cleared. The Second Division was accordingly ordered to take and hold Mory Copse, while the 3rd Guards Brigade was to push forward at once, and conform to the general advance. As soon as Mory and Mory Copse had been secured, the Second Division advanced on Behagnies and Sapignies.

Aug. 25. The attack continued on the 25th, and the Guards Division advanced towards Ecouste and Longatte *via* Bank's Trench and Bank's Reserve, while the Fifty-sixth Division tried to gain the Hindenburg support line. The occupation of Behagnies and part of Sapignies was successfully accomplished by the Second Division on the right. Follett's 3rd Guards Brigade advanced supported by tanks, but these were quickly put out of action by the anti-tank rifles of the Germans. Considerable resistance was met with in Leger Wood, and there was heavy hostile machine-gun fire from Croisilles. The 1st Battalion Grenadier Guards made a wonderfully fine advance on the right of the Brigade, but was strongly counter-attacked and suffered heavy casualties. The Sixty-second Division was unable to capture Mory on account of the division on its right being held up; later in the evening it succeeded in reaching Camouflage Copse. That night De Crespigny's 1st Guards Brigade relieved the 3rd Guards Brigade.

The following day orders for a further attack were issued. The advance was to be continued by the Sixty-second, Fifty-sixth, and Guards

JULY AND AUGUST 1918

Divisions, the latter directed on high ground north and south of Ecouste and Longatte, while the Fifty-sixth Division was to envelop Croisilles, moving down the Hindenburg line. The advance was not to be pressed if strong resistance was encountered. The 1st Guards Brigade was to advance under barrage in a line from Croisilles Copse to the Crucifix, and the heavy artillery was to concentrate on Sensee Valley.

Early on the 27th the Sixty-second Division captured Bank's Trench, and De Crespigny's Brigade reached Burnhill Trench. Here the 2nd Battalion Grenadier Guards was held up by heavy machine-gun fire, while the 2nd Battalion Coldstream Guards was counter-attacked from both flanks, and driven back to the line of Leger Reserve—Bank's Trench. The Fifty-sixth Division was also in difficulties, and could make no headway against the machine-gun fire from Croisilles. The situation as regards the Guards Division was as follows: On the right the 2nd Battalion Grenadier Guards was in touch with the Sixty-second Division on the ridge south-west of L'Homme Mort, the line then reaching a sunken road leading to St. Leger. There were some men in Bank's Trench, but there were also isolated parties of the enemy still there, which made reorganisation impossible until dark. Major-General Feilding sent orders to Brigadier-General de Crespigny to reorganise the battalions in front, and to endeavour to secure the line from Bank's Trench to Leger Reserve. If it was found that the Germans had withdrawn, the 76th Brigade was to pass through the 1st Guards

66   THE GRENADIER GUARDS

CHAPTER XXXII.

Aug. 1918.

Brigade and follow them up. During the night Bank's Trench was cleared of Germans, and 150 prisoners were taken.

On the 28th De Crespigny's Brigade was holding a line along Mory Switch—Bank's Trench and St. Leger Reserve, and the enemy was reported to have withdrawn to Longatte support. At mid-day the Fifty-sixth Division captured Croisilles, and continued its advance towards Bullecourt. The whole of Bank's Trench up to the Mory—Ecoust road had now fallen into the hands of De Crespigny's Brigade, and patrols had been sent out some way in front. During the day the Germans withdrew towards Ecoust and Bullecourt, followed by our patrols. Orders were given for this brigade to be relieved by the 76th Infantry Brigade, and to retire to the area between the Arras — Bapaume road and the Arras—Albert railway.

The total number of prisoners taken by the Division from the 21st to the 29th was 30 officers, and 1479 other ranks.

The casualties were : Killed, 28 officers, 278 other ranks ; wounded, 58 officers, 1675 other ranks ; missing, 3 officers, 239 other ranks.

The 1st Battalion

July and August

Roll of Officers

1st Batt. Lieut.-Colonel Viscount Gort, D.S.O., M.V.O., M.C. . . . Commanding Officer.
Major the Hon. W. R. Bailey, D.S.O. Second in Command.
Capt. R. D. Lawford, M.C. . . Adjutant.

JULY AND AUGUST 1918

2nd Lieut. E. G. Hawkesworth	.	Intelligence Officer.
Lieut. R. F. W. Echlin . .	.	Transport Officer.
Capt. J. Teece, M.C. . .	.	Quartermaster.
Capt. P. Malcolm . . .	.	King's Company.
Lieut. J. A. Lloyd . . .	.	,, ,,
Lieut. L. G. Byng, M.C. . .	.	,, ,,
2nd Lieut. R. G. Buchanan .	.	,, ,,
2nd Lieut. C. O. Rocke . .	.	,, ,,
Capt. A. T. G. Rhodes . .	.	No. 2 Company.
Lieut. G. Hughes . . .	.	,, ,,
2nd Lieut. J. L. Campbell .	.	,, ,,
Capt. A. A. Moller, M.C. .	.	No. 3 Company.
2nd Lieut. A. Grant . .	.	,, ,,
2nd Lieut. A. A. J. Warner .	.	,, ,,
2nd Lieut. L. F. A. d'Erlanger	.	,, ,,
Capt. R. Wolrige-Gordon, M.C.	.	No. 4 Company.
Lieut. the Hon. P. P. Cary .	.	,, ,,
Lieut. H. B. Vernon . .	.	,, ,,
Lieut. B. H. Jones . .	.	,, ,,
2nd Lieut. R. L. Webber .	.	,, ,,
2nd Lieut. A. M. Brown .	.	,, ,,
Lieut. W. B. Evans, U.S.A.M.O.R.C.		Medical Officer.

CHAPTER XXXII.

1st Batt. 1918.

After six days spent at Barly, the 1st Battalion marched to Bavincourt, where it entrained for Blaireville. On arrival the men were provided with tea and cigarettes by the Thirty-second Division, and the Battalion took over trench shelters from the 2nd Battalion Manchester Regiment, whose Adjutant was Captain Kaye, formerly a sergeant in the King's Company, and whose Second in Command was Major Marshall, late Irish Guards. On the 10th the Battalion relieved the 2nd Battalion Scots Guards, which was the battalion in support, and some high-velocity shells fell in its area, wounding three men. On the 14th the Battalion moved up to the front line, which had become very

July.

CHAPTER XXXII.
1st Batt.
July 1918.

slippery owing to the heavy rainstorms, and the ground was so deep in mud in some places that the relief was not completed till 2 A.M. The enemy was quiet on the whole, but some movement was observed round Boyelles. The following day the Germans showed an inclination to push machine-guns forward on the south side of the railway in order to get close to our lines. Hostile aircraft was more active, but was kept well in hand, and in the evening two German aeroplanes were brought down near Hamelincourt. On the 19th the Battalion was relieved, and retired to the reserve line trenches. The period spent in reserve was uneventful, but on the 27th, when the Battalion had moved up in support, the Germans carried out a concentrated gas bombardment of the area Boisleux-au-Mont village and station, and eight men in No. 4 Company were gassed. On the 30th Second Lieutenant J. L. Campbell, Company Sergeant-Major Frost, and two men were wounded during some severe shelling. The former recovered, but Sergeant-Major Frost succumbed to the wounds he had received, and died that evening. On the 31st six platoons from the 320th Regiment of the American Army, in addition to the Second in Command and the Lewis-gun officer, were attached to the Battalion. The enemy's artillery that evening showed an increased activity, and put down a destructive barrage which lasted for three hours.

Aug.

From the 1st to the 6th of August the 1st Battalion was in the front line at Boisleux-au-Mont, where, except for intermittent shelling,

JULY AND AUGUST 1918

everything was unusually quiet. During one of the periods of shelling Lieutenant G. Hughes was severely wounded, and died in the evening. There were 2 men killed and 11 wounded, in addition to two of the American troops. On the 6th the Battalion returned to the reserve trenches at Blaireville, where it remained until the 15th. In the absence of Brigadier-General de Crespigny, Lord Gort assumed temporary command of the 1st Guards Brigade, and Major Bailey commanded the Battalion. On the 21st Sergison-Brooke's Brigade attacked in a thick mist on the right of the 3rd Guards Brigade, and the Germans put down a heavy barrage of shells and Minenwerfer on the trenches occupied by the 1st Battalion. The mist rendered smoke-bombs useless, and a patrol was sent out to get touch with the enemy, who was expected to retire. Lieutenant Hawkesworth with nine men entered Marc trench supported by a platoon from No. 3 Company, and captured two Germans; a strong party of the enemy which tried to recapture them, was beaten off with several men killed. On the 22nd the Battalion was relieved, and proceeded to Boiry St. Martin.

In accordance with General Follett's order, the 2nd Battalion Scots Guards and 1st Battalion Welsh Guards moved to the low ground east of Ayette, while the 1st Battalion Grenadier Guards was ordered to send an officer to Brigade Headquarters. Lieutenant Hawkesworth, who was selected for this duty, sent back word that the Battalion was to be ready to march at once. At 12.50 P.M. Major Bailey received orders to move

Chapter XXXII.

1st Batt. Aug. 1918.

Aug. 23.

Chapter XXXII.
1st Batt.
Aug. 1918.

up his Battalion to the east of Moyenneville, and to report to Sergison-Brooke's Brigade as soon as he arrived there. Accordingly the Battalion marched off, and reached its destination about 3.15 P.M. There was no time to issue written orders, and General Sergison-Brooke was able to explain only verbally to Major Bailey the objective of the Battalion. Having summoned his Company Commanders, Major Bailey informed them of the general situation. The 3rd Battalion Grenadier Guards and 1st Battalion Scots Guards were holding the general line of Hamerville trench and also Hamel trench, while the 1st Battalion Coldstream Guards was established on the high ground about Judas Farm. The situation on the right, however, was not clear, and no troops of the Second Division had been seen east of Ervillers. The 1st Battalion was therefore to move forward as soon as possible, gain touch with the Second Division about Ervillers, and in conjunction with it, capture Mory Switch.

LIST OF OFFICERS WHO TOOK PART IN THESE OPERATIONS

Major the Hon. W. R. Bailey, D.S.O.	Commanding Officer.
Lieut. J. A. Lloyd.	Acting Adjutant.
Lieut. E. G. Hawkesworth	Intelligence Officer.
Captain P. Malcolm	King's Company.
Captain the Hon. P. P. Cary	,, ,,
2nd Lieut. C. Cruttenden	,, ,,
2nd Lieut. C. O. Rocke	,, ,,
Lieut. H. B. Vernon	No. 2 Company.
Lieut. A. A. Morris	,, ,,
2nd Lieut. R. J. E. Conant	,, ,,

JULY AND AUGUST 1918

Captain A. S. Chambers.	. . .	No. 3 Company.
2nd Lieut. G. S. Lamont	. .	,, ,,
2nd Lieut. A. A. J. Warner	. .	,, ,,
Captain R. Wolrige-Gordon, M.C.	.	No. 4 Company.
Lieut. L. G. Byng, M.C..	. .	,, ,,
2nd Lieut. G. E. Barber	. .	,, ,,
2nd Lieut. R. L. Webber	. .	,, ,,
Capt. W. B. Evans, U.S.A.M.O.R.C.		Medical Officer.

CHAPTER XXXII.

1st Batt. Aug. 1918.

At 4.10 P.M. the Battalion advanced in approach march formation with the King's Company under Captain Cary on the right, and No. 2 Company under Lieutenant H. B. Vernon on the left, with No. 3 Company under Captain Chambers in support and No. 4 Company under Lieutenant Byng in reserve. The frontage occupied by the Battalion was 1000 yards, with strong patrols preceding the two leading companies at a distance of 300 yards. On reaching the line of the Ervillers—Hamelincourt road, the leading companies came under a light field-gun barrage and long-range machine-gun fire, which forced them to deploy, and the support company conformed as soon as it arrived at the same place. Captain Chambers then moved his company to a position écheloned in rear of the King's Company, so as to be in a position to protect the right flank. When the leading companies reached the neighbourhood of Jewel trench, the Germans offered a certain amount of resistance, which caused a momentary check, but the threat of an outflanking movement by No. 3 Company broke down their defence, and they fled, pursued by Lewis-gun and rifle fire, leaving fifty men who were taken prisoners.

No. 4 Company was moved to a position

72 THE GRENADIER GUARDS

CHAPTER XXXII.
1st Batt.
Aug. 1918.

on the high ground on the right to cover that flank, and was given orders to be prepared to move across the front of Ervillers, if a hostile counter-attack developed in that direction. The other three companies swept on to the next objective, which was carried without a further check. The three leading companies then proceeded forward to capture the final objective, and the defence of the enemy broke down, as soon as he saw that the victorious advance of the Battalion could not be stopped. By 5.45 P.M. the position was completely in the hands of the Battalion, many prisoners being taken, numbers of whom rushed forward with their hands up as soon as the leading companies appeared over the ridge. After the final objective had been secured, No. 4 Company returned to its proper position in reserve, its place on the right being taken by a sub-section of machine-guns. At dusk the Battalion was distributed as follows: No. 3 Company in Mory Switch trench as far as Hally Avenue (exclusive), No. 2 Company conformed from Hally Avenue (inclusive) to Judas trench while the King's Company formed a refused right flank in shell slits about Iscariot Work and No. 4 Company was in reserve in Jewel trench.

Considering the extent of ground that had been covered and the rapidity with which the objective had been secured, the casualties were not heavy: Lieutenant Rocke, who had been with the leading platoon of the King's Company was killed, and Captain Cary in the King's Company and Lieutenant Conant of No. 2 Com-

JULY AND AUGUST 1918

pany were wounded. The casualties amongst other ranks amounted to about forty.

At 4 A.M. Major Bailey received orders to continue the attack, and summoned a conference of Company Commanders. He explained to them that the Battalion was to advance at 7 A.M. on a front of 1000 yards and écheloned in depth. No. 4 Company was to lead the attack on a front of 500 yards, with the left flank on Hally Avenue; No. 3 Company écheloned at a distance of 250 yards on their right, No. 2 Company in support, covering the centre at a distance of 250 yards behind the left of No. 3 Company, and the King's Company in reserve.

The three leading companies were formed up by daylight in Mory Switch trench, but the King's Company remained in its position near Iscariot Work. The wire in front of Mory was too thick to cut before daylight, and the men were told to work their way through the gaps as best they could. As soon as the attack started, some thirty prisoners were taken; they were in positions outside the wire, and surrendered without firing a shot. A shrapnel barrage had been put down by our artillery, but it was placed too far in advance to be of any real assistance, and as the attack developed the Germans opened an intense machine-gun fire from Mory Copse and Hally Copse. It soon became evident that, until some advance was made on the right, there was no possibility of the attack succeeding, and even if it did succeed there seemed little prospect of the 1st Battalion retaining the position it had gained, unless the Second Division could keep

CHAPTER XXXII.
1st Batt.
Aug. 1918.

pace with them. Nothing could be done but to wait until the situation on the right developed, and the difficulty of the position was increased by the fact that all communication with the leading companies was cut off for the remainder of the day. During the morning Germans could be seen dribbling forward small parties to Mory Copse, and the sniping and machine-gun fire from this direction became more intense. At 10.45 the Second Division made an attempt to come up on the right, but was immediately checked and suffered considerably.

The casualties in the 1st Battalion were naturally heavy. Second Lieutenant G. E. Barber was killed, and Lieutenant L. G. Byng, M.C., was so severely wounded that he died that evening. Major Bailey, Captain Chambers, Lieutenant Vernon, Second Lieutenant Warner, and Second Lieutenant Webber were wounded, and amongst the other ranks there were 150 casualties.

Lord Gort, who had been temporarily commanding the 1st Guards Brigade, returned to the Battalion that evening, and Captain Wolrige-Gordon, M.C., came up to take over command of No. 4 Company, while Lieutenant Hawkesworth left Battalion Headquarters to command No. 3 Company. On learning that the Brigade was to continue the attack on the following day with the assistance of eight tanks, Lord Gort went round the line at dusk, and decided that, as the King's and No. 3 Companies had suffered fewest casualties, they should undertake the attack. He therefore gave orders for these two

JULY AND AUGUST 1918

companies to withdraw for the night, and get as much rest as they could in Mory Switch, while No. 2 and 4 Companies should supply the outposts; and he impressed on the officers commanding these companies, that in view of the attack the next day the men should be spared as much as possible, and that defensive measures for the night should be undertaken mainly by patrols.

After consultation with the officers commanding the 2nd Battalion Scots Guards, the 1st Battalion Welsh Guards, and the tanks, Lord Gort returned to his Battalion Headquarters, and summoned the Company Commanders—Second Lieutenant Cruttenden, King's Company; Lieutenant A. A. Morris, No. 2 Company; Lieutenant Hawkesworth, No. 3 Company; and Captain Wolrige-Gordon, No. 4 Company. The details of the attack were explained, and orders were issued. The total fighting strength of the Battalion was only 212 with 7 officers, including the Battalion Headquarters Staff.

In order to increase the number of officers, Captain Malcolm was sent up to join the King's Company. He received this order only at 10 P.M. the night before, and the distance he had to go made it most improbable that he could reach the Battalion before the attack started. But his determination to lead the King's Company into action helped him to overcome all difficulties. By dint of riding and walking all night over appalling country, without any guide, he managed to find the Battalion in time.

At 4.30 A.M. the attack started. A very thick

CHAPTER XXXII.

1st Batt.
Aug.
1918.

Aug. 25.

mist covered the ground, which made it difficult for the tanks to find their way. Lieutenant Hawkesworth started off with No. 3 Company supported by one tank, but when he reached the neighbourhood of Bank's Trench the tank broke down, and when the fog lifted he found he had only forty men quite unsupported. Unfortunately, at this moment he was badly wounded, and therefore ordered his men, who were without an officer, to fall back on to Mory Switch.

The King's and No. 4 Companies moved up Mory Switch supported by one tank, while another worked on the southern flank. The fog was still thick, and as the first tank advanced it was suddenly engaged at very close range by a stray machine-gun post. Armour-piercing bullets were used, and the engine and water jacket were penetrated. It was therefore necessary to find the other tank, which could be heard working in the fog, and after an unsuccessful attempt to get it going in the right direction, it eventually succeeded in moving forward at 8.30 A.M., supported by the King's Company and a platoon of No. 4 Company. But soon afterwards the fog lifted, and the tank was immediately put out of action. Germans in bodies of fifty and one hundred could be seen standing about in Bank's Trench, but as the King's Company and a platoon of No. 3 Company were close by, Lord Gort did not give the order to engage these hostile parties with machine-gun fire, until he could ascertain if they were prisoners surrendering or not. After a lapse of five minutes fire was opened on them, and they disappeared into their trenches. Meanwhile the enemy opened a very heavy and concentrated machine-gun fire on Mory Switch, and engaged the disabled tank with a field-gun. Lord Gort having been called back to Battalion Headquarters to speak to the Brigadier on the telephone with reference to the attack of the Sixty-second Division, which was timed to begin at 9 A.M., ordered Captain Wolrige-Gordon to hold on to Mory Switch and Camouflage Copse. But the enfilade machine-gun fire made this impossible, more especially as the right flank was quite unsupported, and the three companies had to withdraw from Mory Switch to the north-west of Mory.

At 4 P.M. after a severe bombardment the Germans developed a counter-attack, which was met by the Sixty-second Division, and driven back. Battalions of this division returned to the attack, and regained some ground, while the 1st Battalion reoccupied Mory Switch. Lord Gort told the captain of the leading company of the battalion from the Sixty-second Division that he was prepared to push on to the sunken road, if his company would co-operate, but the Company Commander replied that the right flank of his battalion was entirely unsupported, and that therefore any further advance was out of the question. The Sixty-second Division was subsequently withdrawn to the line from which they started, but the 1st Battalion was able to maintain its position and to clear Hally Copse of the enemy. That night it withdrew to Boiry St. Martin, and was relieved by the 2nd Battalion Grenadier Guards.

CHAPTER XXXII.
1st Batt.
Aug.
1918.

Captain Malcolm and Second Lieutenant Cruttenden were reported missing, and Lieutenant Hawkesworth was wounded. The total number of casualties during the three days' fighting was 13 officers and 258 other ranks, out of 18 officers and 489 other ranks who were engaged in the operations. 250 prisoners, 1 field-gun, and 20 machine-guns, in addition to several trench mortars, were captured by the Battalion.

In a letter which Brigadier-General G. B. S. Follett, commanding the 3rd Guards Brigade, wrote to Sir Henry Streatfeild, the Lieutenant-Colonel commanding the Regiment, he said :

As you have probably heard by now, we attacked on the 23rd, 24th, and 25th August—that is, this Brigade. The 1st Battalion Grenadiers gave the finest exhibition that has ever been made in this war. At 3 P.M. on the 23rd they were sent up to protect the right flank of the 2nd Brigade and take the heights south of St. Leger. There was just time to issue verbal orders and to collect the Company Commanders for a conference. Starting about 3.45 P.M. they had taken all objectives before 6 P.M.—that is, advancing 5000 yards from their starting point! Having been very highly trained by Gort during the past month or two, they proceeded to put their training into practice, with the result that it was a wonderful success. Commanded by Bailey (Gort was with the 1st Guards Brigade), they were magnificently manoeuvred by their company and platoon commanders, moving in great depth on a very wide extension. They captured 197 prisoners, 15 machine-guns and several trench mortars, and killed a lot. Their casualties were 2 officers and 50 O.R. I say again, the finest attack in open warfare that has ever been made. During the night 23-24 they even did a relief, and we were up against the junction of two fresh divisions in great strength, with the result that no great advance was made and many losses.

After remaining for twenty-four hours at Boiry St. Martin, the Battalion marched to Berles-au-Bois, where it occupied shelters in a bank. Lieutenant E. B. Shelley and twenty-five men joined, in addition to a large draft from the 4th Battalion under Captain Simpson, and the following days were spent in reorganising the companies.

The 2nd Battalion

Roll of Officers

Lieut.-Colonel G. E. C. Rasch, D.S.O.	Commanding Officer.
Capt. G. C. FitzH. Harcourt-Vernon, D.S.O.	Second in Command.
Capt. A. H. Penn, M.C.	Adjutant.
Lieut. R. G. Briscoe, M.C.	Assistant Adjutant.
2nd Lieut. S. C. K. George	Intelligence Officer.
Lieut. G. G. M. Vereker, M.C.	Transport Officer.
Capt. the Hon. W. E. Acraman, M.C., D.C.M.	Quartermaster.
2nd Lieut. J. S. Carter	Bombing Officer.
2nd Lieut. H. B. G. Morgan	Lewis-Gun Officer.
Capt. F. A. M. Browning, D.S.O.	No. 1 Company.
Lieut. S. T. S. Clarke, M.C.	,, ,,
Lieut. L. St. L. Hermon-Hodge	,, ,,
Lieut. G. F. Lawrence	,, ,,
2nd Lieut. R. C. M. Bevan	,, ,,
Capt. O. Martin Smith	No. 2 Company.
Lieut. R. H. R. Palmer	,, ,,
Lieut. W. H. S. Dent	,, ,,
Capt. J. C. Cornforth, M.C.	No. 3 Company.
Lieut. R. M. Oliver	,, ,,
2nd Lieut. H. White	,, ,,
2nd Lieut. F. J. Langley	,, ,,
2nd Lieut. the Hon. S. A. S. Montagu	,, ,,

80   THE GRENADIER GUARDS

CHAPTER XXXII.
2nd Batt. 1918.

Lieut. F. H. J. Drummond, M.C.	No. 4 Company.
Lieut. F. P. Loftus	,, ,,
Lieut. N. McK. Jesper	,, ,,
2nd Lieut. P. V. Pelly	,, ,,
2nd Lieut. J. A. Paton	,, ,,
Capt. the Rev. Hon. C. F. Lyttelton	Chaplain.
Capt. J. L. Early, U.S.A.M.O.R.C.	Medical Officer.

July. The 2nd Battalion, which had been training during the first few days in July at Saulty, proceeded by train on the 5th to Ransart, where tea was provided for the men by the Thirty-second Division. Guides from the Royal Scots led the Battalion to the position which it was to take up as reserve battalion of the brigade 500 yards east of Ransart. The Guards Division was occupying a sector of the line with its right joining the Second Division between Ayette and Moyenneville, and its left joining the Canadian Corps on the outskirts of Boisieux St. Marc. While in reserve, companies carried out training round the outskirts of Ransart, and scouting and patrolling by day were practised. In order to accustom the men to night-work they wore darkened glasses, which produced much the same effect as night. On the 11th the Battalion moved up into support, and relieved the 1st Battalion Irish Guards near the outskirts of Hendecourt. A place was found for a cricket-ground in a sheltered valley, and two matches were played with composition balls and bats made by the pioneers. From the 17th to the 23rd the Battalion went up into the front line, which had been formerly held by isolated posts, but which was now a continuous trench. The weather was fine and the casualties were not heavy, although there was usually a certain amount of shelling in the early morning. From the 24th to the 28th the Battalion returned to the reserve trenches at Ransart, when Lieutenant T. A. Combe, Lieutenant M. H. Ponsonby, Second Lieutenant A. P. J. M. P. de Lisle, and Second Lieutenant D. L. King joined the Battalion. During the days in reserve an increasing stream of American officers were attached to the 1st Guards Brigade for instruction, and the following amusing messages show the excellent relations that existed between the officers of the two armies :

From :—Guards Division Q.
To :—Transport Officer, 1st Guards Brigade.

Draw 6 bottles of Whisky from Divisional Soldiers Club and deliver to Brigade H.Q. for American Officers attached.

From G.O.C. 1st Guards Brigade.
To :—Guards Division Q.

On behalf of all officers of the American Army attached to the Brigade under my command, I wish to express my deepest thanks for the courteous present of whisky foreshadowed in your message. I am requested to add that these officers accept this gift as a proof of the solidarity of the union existing between the American and British nations, which will endure until the whisky runs out.

C. R. C. DE CRESPIGNY,
Brigadier-General.

While the Battalion was in support at Hendecourt, Captain A. H. Penn, M.C., resigned the

CHAPTER XXXII.
2nd Batt.
Aug. 1918.

adjutancy, much to the regret of all ranks, and was succeeded by Captain R. G. Briscoe, M.C. On August 4 the Battalion went up into the front line in front of Boiry St. Martin, and on August 5 six platoons of Americans who were to be initiated in the mysteries of trench warfare were attached for four days. The enemy was, however, not very active, and there was but little shelling. From the 10th to the 16th the Battalion remained in reserve at Ransart, where Lieutenant G. F. Lawrence took on the duties of Intelligence Officer from Second Lieutenant S. C. K. George, who was invalided home with dysentery. On the 18th the Battalion relieved the 320th American Regiment in the front line, where again the enemy was fairly quiet. Two advanced posts were established some 500 yards from the line, and the nights were spent in active patrolling to prevent the enemy occupying the dead ground in front of Moyenneville, which was to become the forming-up area for the attack on the 21st.

After three days spent in the reserve, the Battalion moved up into very inadequate trench accommodation in Boiry St. Martin. These trenches were now the reserve line, and out of range of enemy artillery owing to the advance on the 21st.

Aug. 25.

On the afternoon of the 25th the Battalion marched off to relieve a battalion in the 3rd Guards Brigade. A three hours' uncomfortable halt was made in a field at Hamelincourt, and as the ground had been well covered with gas, the companies had to move about to escape the drifting fumes. Respirators had to be worn, which rendered the eating of the evening meal no easy matter.

The relief in the front line of St. Leger was carried out without a hitch, although complicated by the fact that the Battalion was taking over a wide and sketchy front from the remnants of the 1st Battalion Grenadier Guards and the 1st Battalion Scots Guards. During the night Second Lieutenant H. A. Finch and eight men went out as a patrol to get in touch with the enemy and never returned. Second Lieutenant Finch was found killed 1000 yards in front of the line, when the Battalion advanced, which showed how thoroughly he had carried out his instructions.

August 26 was a very quiet day, with occasional shelling around Mory Trench. Judging by the extent to which he fired his machine-guns after dark, the enemy seemed very apprehensive. The following officers took part in the operations on August 26–28:

Lieut.-Colonel G. E. C. Rasch, D.S.O.	Commanding Officer.
Lieut. R. G. Briscoe, M.C.	Adjutant.
Lieut. G. F. Lawrence	Intelligence Officer.
Lieut. M. H. Ponsonby	No. 1 Company.
Lieut. N. McK. Jesper	,, ,,
Lieut. C. C. T. Giles	,, ,,
Capt. O. Martin Smith	No. 2 Company.
Lieut. C. Gwyer	,, ,,
2nd Lieut. A. P. J. M. P. de Lisle	,, ,,
Capt. J. C. Cornforth, M.C.	No. 3 Company.
Lieut. H. White	,, ,,
Lieut. R. M. Oliver	,, ,,
2nd Lieut. F. J. Langley	,, ,,
Lieut. H. B. G. Morgan	No. 4 Company.
2nd Lieut. J. A. Paton	,, ,,
1st Lieut. E. L. Major (U.S.A. Army)	Medical Officer.

84 THE GRENADIER GUARDS

CHAPTER XXXII.
2nd Batt.
Aug. 1918.
Aug. 26.

At midnight on the 26th a conference held at Battalion Headquarters was attended by all Company Commanders, at which Lieut.-Colonel Rasch explained the general situation and the objectives of the advance for the following day as far as they were known.

Definite orders were not received until 1.30 A.M. on the morning of the 27th. The instructions the Battalion received were to push forward at zero hour (7 A.M.), with the 2nd Battalion Coldstream Guards on its left, and the Sixty-second Division on its right, and to secure the enemy's trenches in and south of Ecoust and Longatte. Before dawn the Battalion was to be reorganised and disposed in battle formation. No. 3 Company under Captain J. C. Cornforth, M.C., extended along the whole Battalion frontage of 1500 yards, along the road in No Man's Land, running from Mory Copse to St. Leger. No. 2 Company under Captain O. M. Smith in left support lay concealed until zero in Hally Copse. No. 4 Company under Lieutenant Morgan was in right support in Mory Copse, and No. 1 Company under Lieutenant M. Ponsonby in reserve, with Battalion Headquarters in Mory Trench.

There were three points in these orders which caused a little uneasiness. In the first place, a very short space of time before dawn was allowed to re-dispose the Battalion, although fortunately strong patrols had been sent out earlier in the night to secure the Mory Copse—St. Leger road. In the second place, dawn being at 4.30 A.M. and zero at 7 A.M., No. 3 Company would be in an exposed position during daylight at some points within fifty yards of the enemy. It was a clear night, and even in the darkness this company got into difficulties, for while they were forming up, they were observed by the enemy, who spent the rest of the night sweeping the ground and putting up innumerable lights, probably thinking it was a patrol. Fortunately there were a number of large felled tree-trunks along the road, which enabled this Company to escape detection from ground observation, and from the low-flying aeroplanes, which continually patrolled No Man's Land at dawn. In the third place, although Bank's Trench was known to be held all along the whole front, the barrage table showed that on the left of the Battalion the barrage would open a considerable distance behind the trench, probably owing to the proximity of our front troops to the enemy position.

The reorganisation and forming up of the Battalion were successfully carried out before dawn. Unfortunately, while No. 1 Company was moving across the open to take up its position in reserve, a shell fell in the centre of No. 1 Platoon, mortally wounding Lieutenant M. Ponsonby, and causing casualties to the whole platoon, with the exception of three other ranks. Lieutenant Jesper took command of the remaining three platoons, and brought them to their allotted positions.

At zero hour (7 A.M.) the field-gun barrage came down on a line about 300 yards in front of No. 3 Company, creeping forward at the rate of 100 yards every two minutes. As soon as our troops moved off from their forming-up positions

CHAPTER XXXII.
2nd Batt.
Aug. 1918.

to close up to the barrage, the enemy covered his front with a deadly and accurate screen of bullets, fired from numerous carefully-sighted machine-guns, which were so well protected that our field-gun barrage had little or no effect upon them. In consequence we suffered heavy casualties from the very outset. On the left the troops of the leading company were mown down as soon as they got on to their feet, and were unable to advance. The right of the 2nd Battalion Coldstream Guards had also suffered severely, and was unable to push forward.

As No. 2 Company, under Captain O. Martin Smith, debouched from Hally Copse, it was caught by the machine-gun fire, and nearly cut to pieces before it could extend from artillery formation. Captain O. Martin Smith made a determined effort to reinforce the left of No. 3 Company, and push forward the advance, but long before his Company reached the front troops it had suffered over 50 per cent casualties. Captain O. Martin Smith and Lieutenant de Lisle were wounded, and Lieutenant Gwyer, who was pluckily pushing forward in spite of the storm of bullets, was killed. Captain O. Martin Smith ordered his Company to lie down in the open, while the N.C.O.'s collected the men who were nearest to them, and eventually got in close support of No. 3 Company. As, however, the enemy was entrenched on the top of the rise 200 yards in front, the slightest movement attracted a torrent of lead. This made it impossible to get communication in any direction or to collect the wounded, who had to remain in the open on the fire-swept ground until dark. Lieutenant R. M. Oliver, who had been in charge of the left platoon of No. 3 Company, had been killed earlier, so the left half of the Battalion was now without an officer.

CHAPTER XXXII.

2nd Batt. Aug. 1918.

In the centre, during the first 200 yards, the machine-gun fire, although equally intense, was slightly less accurate ; but on nearing the St. Leger—Homme Mort road Captain Cornforth found it swept by a practically impassable hail of machine-gun bullets, fired from three directions—the Homme Mort on the south, Bank's Trench on the east, and outskirts of St. Leger on the north. This last enemy position was off the Battalion frontage, and the troops opposite it had been held up. The only method of relieving this pressure on the left was to push on at all costs in our centre and right.

Lieut.-Colonel Rasch sent up No. 1 Company to reinforce the thinned ranks of No. 3, and to help in the capture of Homme Mort and the rushing of Bank's Trench. While going up this Company came under heavy fire, and Lieutenant Jesper and Lieutenant Giles were both wounded. Captain Cornforth therefore took over command of this Company in addition to his own.

With these reinforcements Lieutenant White and Second Lieutenant Langley led their platoons forward against the machine-gun nest at Homme Mort, but in advancing up the slope they were met with an increasing volume of accurate fire, and both the officers were mortally wounded before the position was reached. These platoons, however, with an inspired dash and determination

CHAPTER XXXII.

2nd Batt.
Aug.
1918.

took the position after a hard fight. Twenty prisoners were captured, in spite of the fact that, in the short rush up to the position, these platoons had been practically decimated.

At the same time Captain Cornforth decided to rush Bank's Trench, although the road was still swept by enfilade fire from the left, and by frontal fire from the trench itself. A party of men was sent over the road to cover the advance, but few succeeded in crossing it. Captain Cornforth thereupon collected a small number of men, led them across the road, and by short rushes succeeded with three other men in gaining Bank's Trench. Here fortunately they found a large supply of German hand-grenades, which they quickly detonated, and by this means succeeded in clearing the trench for 500 yards northwards, knocking out six German machine-guns and taking 40 men prisoners. Several other men soon succeeded in joining them, and this party, which eventually numbered one officer and 25 men, found that they were completely isolated. No other troops could be located on their flanks, and the ground was being swept by machine-gun fire from Bank's Copse in the front, from the high ground on the right, and from the outskirts of St. Leger on the left. It was impossible to advance farther, and the rest of the day was spent in resisting the efforts of the Germans to turn them out, and in endeavouring to gain communication on the flanks.

Lieutenant Morgan with No. 4 Company was more successful. At zero he advanced along Mory Switch and the southern end of Bank's

JULY AND AUGUST 1918

Trench, eventually establishing a position in Vraucourt Trench. The lie of the land and the cover afforded by the trenches enabled this Company to keep up with the barrage, and to avoid coming under the intense fire that the remainder of the Battalion had experienced. During the advance this Company captured a German Battalion Commander and 180 men —a remarkably fine performance. Lieutenant Morgan led his Company forward with such dash that they succeeded in penetrating the enemy's position to a depth of 2000 yards. However, it was soon clear that they were completely isolated, as they were being fired at from all directions. When it was dark Lieutenant Morgan decided that it would be unwise to remain in such an advanced position, since neither the Sixty-second Division on his right nor our own troops on his left showed any signs of coming into line with him, and he consequently withdrew his Company until he was in touch with troops on his flanks.

During the night the enemy retired from our front, and in the morning the remnants of the Battalion were reorganised, and continued the advance over the original frontage for about 1700 yards to a marked-out trench called Bank's Reserve. Here some machine-guns were encountered, but a good and continuous line was established with connection on both flanks.

This line was handed over to the 1st Battalion Gordon Highlanders on the night of the 28th-29th, and the Battalion marched back to the trenches east of Hamelincourt. The only officers left with the Battalion were Lieut.-Colonel Rasch,

Chapter XXXII.
2nd Batt. Aug. 1918.

Aug. 28.

90   THE GRENADIER GUARDS

Chapter XXXII.
2nd Batt.
Aug. 1918.

Captain Cornforth, Captain Briscoe, and Lieutenant Morgan. The total casualties were 12 officers and 278 other ranks. Amongst the officers the casualties were as follows :

Lieut. G. F. Lawrence	Killed.
Lieut. R. M. Oliver	,,
Lieut. C. Gwyer	,,
Lieut. H. White	,,
2nd Lieut. F. J. Langley	,,
2nd Lieut. H. A. Finch	,,
Lieut. M. H. Ponsonby	Died of wounds.
Capt. O. Martin Smith	Wounded.
Lieut. N. McK. Jesper	,,
Lieut. C. C. T. Giles	,,
2nd Lieut. J. A. Paton	,,
2nd Lieut. A. P. J. M. P. de Lisle	,,

In a message, which Major-General Feilding afterwards sent to Brigadier-General de Crespigny, he said: " All Battalions of the 1st Guards Brigade discharged their duty splendidly. The attack delivered by the 2nd Battalion Grenadier Guards and 2nd Battalion Coldstream Guards on August 27 not only inflicted heavy losses on the enemy and brought in large numbers of prisoners, but also compelled him next day to relax his hold on the high ground south of Croisilles."

The 3rd Battalion
Roll of Officers

3rd Batt.

Lieut.-Colonel A. F. A. N. Thorne, D.S.O.	Commanding Officer.
Major Viscount Lascelles, D.S.O.	Second in Command.
Capt. the Hon. A. G. Agar-Robartes, M.C.	Adjutant.
Lieut. E. G. A. Fitzgerald, D.S.O.	Assistant Adjutant.

JULY AND AUGUST 1918

Lieut. E. N. de Geijer	Intelligence Officer.	CHAPTER XXXII.
Capt. F. J. Heasman, M.C.	Transport Officer.	
Capt. G. H. Wall	Quartermaster.	3rd Batt.
Capt. A. F. R. Wiggins	No. 1 Company.	Aug. 1918.
Lieut. G. M. Cornish, M.C.	,, ,,	
Lieut. A. G. Elliott	,, ,,	
2nd Lieut. E. L. F. Clough-Taylor	,, ,,	
2nd Lieut. R. Delacombe	,, ,,	
Capt. G. A. I. Dury, M.C.	No. 2 Company.	
Lieut. C. C. Carstairs, M.C.	,, ,,	
Lieut. A. H. S. Adair	,, ,,	
2nd Lieut. W. B. L. Manley	,, ,,	
2nd Lieut. G. R. Gunther	,, ,,	
2nd Lieut. J. Chapman	,, ,,	
2nd Lieut. R. K. Henderson	,, ,,	
Capt. N. C. Tufnell	No. 3 Company.	
Lieut. E. R. M. Fryer, M.C.	,, ,,	
Lieut. C. C. Brown	,, ,,	
Lieut. G. W. Godman	,, ,,	
2nd Lieut. H. J. Gibbon	,, ,,	
2nd Lieut. A. D. Cooper	,, ,,	
Capt. G. F. R. Hirst	No. 4 Company.	
Lieut. C. H. Bedford	,, ,,	
Lieut. R. G. West	,, ,,	
2nd Lieut. E. J. Bunbury	,, ,,	
2nd Lieut. R. P. Papillon	,, ,,	
2nd Lieut. R. C. G. de Reuter	,, ,,	
Capt. R. Anderson, R.A.M.C.	Medical Officer.	
Capt. the Rev. S. Phillimore, M.C.	Chaplain.	

The first week in July was spent by the 3rd Battalion at Labazeque, and on the 7th it proceeded to Ransart, where it relieved the 10th Battalion Argyll and Sutherland Highlanders in the right sector of the front occupied by the Guards Division.

Two companies were placed in the front line with one company in support and one in reserve, and officers' patrols were sent out every night

July.

92 THE GRENADIER GUARDS

CHAPTER XXXII.
3rd Batt.
July.
1918.

from dusk to dawn, but there was no movement on the part of the enemy. On the 10th the Battalion moved back into support, and on the 15th into Divisional Reserve, where it remained for three days. From the 19th to the 24th the Battalion went up again into the front trenches, where the work consisted of improving the line by laying down duckboards and digging sumps and latrines. Fifteen officers, 30 sergeants, and 55 corporals from the American Army were attached to the Battalion, and were distributed between the four companies and Battalion Headquarters. Lieutenant S. G. Fairbairn, Second Lieutenant H. P. Gordon, and Second Lieutenant S. Calvocoressi arrived during this tour of duty in the trenches, and on the 25th the Battalion retired into support, where more officers and men of the American Army were attached for instruction. On the 30th the Battalion moved back into Divisional Reserve.

Aug.

After four days in reserve the Battalion went up into the front line near Adinfer, where it remained for a week carrying out inter-company relief. In this part of the line patrols were sent out every night, and a company from the 320th Regiment of the United States Army, which accompanied the Battalion, supplied a certain number of men for this purpose. On the 6th Second Lieutenant R. P. Papillon when out on patrol duty, encountered a German patrol in Observation Trench, and after severely wounding one of the enemy, succeeded in bringing back an identification mark. The Higher Command, however, required further information, and accordingly a special patrol was sent out on the night of the 10th. Captain Churchill, whose great experience in all kinds of incursions into the enemy's line rendered him eminently fitted for the task, was sent from the Brigade Headquarters, to take charge of the party, which consisted of Second Lieutenant de Reuter and seven men. A covering-party composed of thirteen men, under the command of Sergeant Birtles, accompanied the raiders. Hardly had the patrol started, when a shell fell among them, wounding one man, who had to be carried back to the trenches. Following the German outpost line, which consisted of small adjacent rifle-pits, but which showed no sign of frequent occupation, the patrol came on the German wire. This formidable obstacle consisted of barbed wire in concertina shape, staked to the ground, with strands running through it. After a careful search a gap was found, and through this the patrol went. After following the track for about forty yards a German sentry was seen. The patrol stood still, and the sentry walked away unconscious of its presence. Soon afterwards some more of the enemy were seen moving round to the left of the track. They were evidently suspicious, as they only whispered. Three of them came crawling slowly towards the patrol. In dead silence the patrol waited, but the Germans turned back, and apparently reported all clear, for thirty to forty more Germans appeared, and stood up close together. They came to within thirty yards of the patrol, when Lieutenant de Reuter gave the order " rapid fire." Several of them were seen to fall. It was now merely a question whether the Germans would attempt to capture the patrol or not, but they contented themselves with firing and throwing a few bombs, while Véry lights were sent up. Captain Churchill therefore retired unmolested through the wire, having only had one man wounded.

On the 10th Second Lieutenant de Geijer and twenty other ranks raided a German post under an artillery barrage. At 3.15 A.M. a Stokes mortar barrage supplemented the artillery bombardment, and the raiding party in two groups, under Second Lieutenant de Geijer and Sergeant Butler respectively, rushed the enemy's post. The Germans had, however, abandoned the post just before the raid took place, and the last two were seen to run from it, as the raiders started. Much valuable information was gained, as the Germans left everything behind, but, with the exception of Lieutenant de Geijer who was slightly wounded, there were no casualties.

On the 11th the Battalion was relieved by the 1st Battalion Coldstream, and went into support, moving on four days later to billets in Saulty, where it remained until the 20th.

On the 20th the Battalion "debussed" between Blaireville and Heudecourt, and took up its assembly positions east and south-east of Boiry.

The orders General Sergison-Brooke received were to attack Moyenneville in conjunction with the Second and Third Divisions on the right. In the operation orders which he issued the capture of the first two objectives was to be carried out by the 1st Battalion Scots Guards on the right,

JULY AND AUGUST 1918

and by the 1st Battalion Coldstream on the left. The 3rd Battalion Grenadiers was then to pass through, and secure the third objective. Eight tanks would co-operate in front of each Battalion.

The following officers of the 3rd Battalion took part in these operations:

Lieut.-Colonel A. F. A. N. Thorne, D.S.O.	Commanding Officer.
Lieut. E. N. de Geijer	Intelligence Officer.
Capt. E. R. M. Fryer, M.C.	No. 1 Company.
Lieut. C. C. Carstairs, M.C.	,, ,,
Lieut. R. Delacombe	,, ,,
2nd Lieut. E. L. F. Clough-Taylor	,, ,,
Lieut. A. H. S. Adair	No. 2 Company.
Lieut. S. G. Fairbairn	,, ,,
Lieut. J. Chapman	,, ,,
Capt. N. C. Tufnell	No. 3 Company.
Lieut. C. Clifton Brown	,, ,,
2nd Lieut. A. D. Cooper	,, ,,
Capt. G. F. R. Hirst	No. 4 Company.
Lieut. R. G. West	,, ,,
2nd Lieut. R. C. G. de Reuter	,, ,,
2nd Lieut. R. P. Papillon	,, ,,
Lieut. Graff, U.S.A.M.O.R.C.	Medical Officer.
Capt. the Rev. S. Phillimore, M.C.	Chaplain.

There was a thick mist in the morning, so thick that it was impossible to see more than a few yards ahead. On the one hand this favoured the attackers; on the other there was always the risk of the Battalion losing its way and never reaching the enemy's lines. In spite of everything, however, the leading Battalions eventually succeeded in securing the first two objectives.

The 3rd Battalion had breakfasted, water-bottles had been refilled, and the companies were beginning to get ready for the advance, when

Chapter XXXII.

3rd Batt. Aug. 1918.

Aug. 21.

96 THE GRENADIER GUARDS

Chapter XXXII.

3rd Batt. Aug. 1918.

this blanket of fog came down. At zero hour, 4.53 A.M., the barrage opened up and the attack began. Captain Smith, who commanded C Company 15th Battalion Tank Corps (Mark V. Star Tanks), arrived at Battalion Headquarters, and reported that his tanks had been delayed by gas in Coseul Valley, so that they would not be able to advance with the Battalion as arranged, but that they would endeavour to overtake it on the second objective. The Battalion started off with No. 3 Company under Captain Tufnell on the right, No. 4 under Captain Hirst on the left, No. 2 under Lieutenant Adair in support, and No. 1 under Captain Fryer in reserve. The fog was as thick as ever, and the smoke shells in the barrage increased its density. Keeping direction by compass was tedious and difficult, since it necessitated the removal of the steel helmet and box respirator, and even then it was far from accurate. To add to the difficulties, there were several pockets of German machine-gunners, which had been missed by the 1st Battalion Scots Guards in their advance, and which suddenly loomed out in the mist often in rear of the Battalion as it advanced. No. 12 Platoon captured two machine-gun posts in the first objective, and the markers under Lieutenant de Geijer, the Intelligence Officer, found German machine-gunners still holding out to the west of the second objective, in the area where the Battalion should have formed up. The 1st Battalion Scots Guards had captured the right and left of the second objective, but owing to the fog the centre was still in the hands of the Germans.

JULY AND AUGUST 1918

The 1st Battalion Scots Guards, on finding out what had happened, soon cleared out these Germans with the aid of No. 1 Company (the Reserve Company).

CHAPTER XXXII.
3rd Batt.
Aug. 1918.

By 6 A.M. the Battalion Headquarters had reached its destination, namely, the two trees between the first and second objectives, but was unable to get in touch with any of the companies. Tanks were moving about in the fog, and the Lewis guns were engaging the German machine-guns at close quarters, and were firing indiscriminately into the fog. To give an example of how confusing the situation was, the Battalion Headquarters was charged from the front by two platoons of the Scots Guards, who mistook it in the fog for a German machine-gun post.

By 7.30 No. 2 Company, under Lieutenant Adair, had gone through the junction of the 1st Battalion Scots Guards and 1st Battalion Coldstream, and was advancing on its objective, which was the valley between the railway and Moyenneville. A little later Captain Tufnell and Captain Hirst reported that Nos. 9 and 12 Platoons of No. 3 Company and all No. 4 Company were near Moyblain Trench, having completely lost their way. No. 11 Platoon had also lost its bearings, and after moving round in a semicircle, was discovered heading towards the rear instead of towards the front.

Meanwhile, Lieutenant Duff Cooper, with No. 10 Platoon, having entirely lost touch with the remainder of the company, had wandered too far to the south, and after pushing on in what

CHAPTER XXXII.
3rd Batt.
Aug. 1918.

he thought was the right direction for three hours, found himself in the outskirts of Courcelles. There he met a platoon of the 7th Battalion K.S.L.I., which had also lost its way, and, knowing that the Halte on the railway was the eventual objective, he determined to make for it. Together these two platoons started off, and as they were clearing the dug-outs on the road, they fell in with a tank which suddenly appeared out of the fog. With its assistance they attacked and captured the railway on each side of the Halte, where a German aid post was placed. There is no doubt that these two isolated platoons were the only units that succeeded in reaching the third objective for some hours, on the whole front of the two Northern Divisions.

When Lieut.-Colonel Thorne received a message from Lieutenant Duff Cooper, saying that the Halte had been taken, he sent up No. 1 Company under Captain Fryer to the assistance of this isolated platoon, and in order to save time directed No. 2 Company to advance on the objective originally assigned to No. 4. Lieutenant Forbes with two machine-guns was sent up to co-operate with No. 1 Company, and Lieutenant Hulme with two more to assist No. 2 Company. No barrage could be arranged for this attack, and it was impossible to obtain any assistance from the tanks, which were now returning to their rallying positions, since they were all suffering from engine trouble or the lack of petrol.

At 10 A.M. the fog began to lift, but Captain

Fryer had by this time brought up Nos. 1 and 2 Platoons to the assistance of No. 10 Platoon. Captain Fryer and Lieutenant Duff Cooper made a most valuable reconnaissance of the railway north of the Halte under heavy fire, and on returning decided at once to attack the German posts they had discovered. No. 10 Platoon started off, and supported by Nos. 1 and 2 Platoons succeeded in capturing the whole of the objectives allotted to No. 3 Company. This attack was carried out with great dash, but Lieutenant Delacombe and Second Lieutenant Clough-Taylor were wounded.

Nos. 7 and 8 Platoons of No. 2 Company had in the meantime commenced their advance on the railway cutting, but soon found that they were exposed to heavy enfilade fire from the railway north of the Halte. They made but little headway at first, but, when the attack of No. 10 Platoon lifted the enemy's fire off them, they pushed forward, and rushed the railway and hollow ground to the east of it, capturing 5 machine-guns and 60 prisoners, and gaining touch with the 1st Battalion Coldstream Guards on the left and No. 1 Company on the right.

No. 3 Company now moved up into support of No. 1, and four machine-guns were placed in Magazine Trench as barrage guns. No. 6 Platoon made a farther advance, and seized the hollow east of the railway and west of Hameau North, where 10 machine-guns and 60 prisoners were captured. Nos. 3 and 8 Platoons advanced to the east of the railway, and completed the capture of the whole objective allotted to the Battalion. Although twelve hours behind the

CHAPTER XXXII.
3rd Batt.
Aug. 1918.

scheduled time, Lieut.-Colonel Thorne was able to report that the task of the Battalion had been successfully carried out.

The leading of No. 10 Platoon and Nos. 1 and 2 Companies was particularly fine, and the response made by the men was beyond all praise. The fact that in spite of the fog each platoon managed to get to its own place was entirely due to the persistence with which Platoon Commanders advanced whenever opportunity offered, and to the determination on the part of the men to reach the enemy. After the fog lifted the attack was carried out steadily and relentlessly across ground swept by shell-fire and machine-guns, and succeeded in spite of the lack of an artillery barrage or tanks.

After dark, ammunition, water and rations were sent up by pack animals, and all the platoons rejoined their companies. Reconnoitring patrols under Lieutenant Clifton Brown and Lieutenant West were sent out to locate the new German line, and discovered that the enemy was holding the line of the sunken road about half a mile east of the railway. The Germans were apparently in some strength, and very much on the look-out.

Aug. 22.

The next morning a heavy hostile barrage came down on the whole position occupied by the Battalion, and the outposts could see the enemy advancing in three waves. The S.O.S. signal at once went up. Immediately our artillery put down a magnificent and accurate barrage, and the companies in front opened a concentrated fire with Lewis guns and rifles on the advancing

Brigadier-General B. N. Sergison-Brooke D.S.O.

enemy. The German counter-attack stood no chance at all, and completely crumbled away; only in one place did the Germans succeed in gaining a footing, and that was on the right, where they captured a trench. When the attack utterly failed, this party of Germans had to withdraw with heavy loss.

The following German orders that were subsequently taken from a prisoner give the details of this counter-attack. It will be seen that they advanced in some strength, and it is all the more remarkable that this carefully planned attack should have been repulsed by only two companies of the 3rd Battalion.

CAPTURED GERMAN DIVISIONAL ORDER

234 Div.   Div. H.Q.,
Abt. Ia. 2802.   21-8-18.

DIVISIONAL ORDER

1. According to information received from the Army we have repulsed $4\frac{1}{2}$ English Divisions to-day. The enemy has been beaten and he knows it.

The enemy has reached the Achiet le Grand Boisleux Railway. New artillery positions have been located, large enemy concentrations and movement observed.

2. XVIII. Corps will retake the old main line of resistance.

For this operation the 234 Div.—under the orders of the 40th Div.—will attack with the 2nd Guards Res. Div.—under the orders of the 6th Bav. Res. Div.—on its left.

3. The infantry will be divided into three attacking groups under the command of Col. Reichart (Comdr. 88 Inf. Bde.).

CHAPTER XXXII.

3rd Batt.
Aug. 1918.

Right attacking group.   Major v. Kluefer.
    181 I.R.
    3rd Bn. 452 I.R.
    3 Batteries, 32 F.A.R.
    Res. Pion. Coy. 55.

Centre attacking group.   Major v. Pape.
    104 I.R.
    451 I.R. less 2nd Bn.
    3 Batteries 32 F.A.R.
    3 Coy. Pion. Bn. 22.

Left attacking group.   Capt. Heine.
    1st and 3rd Bns. 453 I.R.
    2nd Bn. 452 I.R.
    359 Pion. Coy.
    360 Pion. Coy.

Objective :—   Moyenneville—Aerodrome ridge.

4. The 21st Res. Div. will detail one Bn. to support the attack on Moyenneville. 88 Inf. Bde. will establish liaison with this Bn. Zero hour on the whole front of attack will be 5.45 A.M. (German time).

5. 134 I.R. with three Batteries F.A.R. 32 as Divisional Reserve will be held in readiness N.E. of Mory.

6. Col. v. Bibra (Comdr. 234 Inf. Bde.) with the battalions formerly in support (1st Bn. 452 I.R., 3rd Bn. 451 I.R., 2nd Bn. 453 I.R.) will hold the artillery defensive position. These Battalions will remain as "safety garrison" and will hold the line at all costs in the event of a hostile counter-attack.

7. Duties of the Artillery :

    $X-15$ *to* X. Burst of fire on the enemy front line on the Railway embankment.

    X. Heavy bombardment on Moyenneville and Courcelles. Lift on to the line Eastern outskirts Moyenneville Eastern outskirts Courcelles, continue heavy bombardment on Moyenneville and Courcelles.

X plus 20. Lift to the line *Eastern* outskirts Moyenneville—*Western* outskirts of Courcelles.

X plus 40. Lift to the line W. of the Moyenneville—Ablainzeville Road.

X plus 60. Lift to the trench which extends from Moyenneville across Aerodrome ridge towards the S. (former main line of resistance).

X ,, 5.45 A.M.

Three Batteries F.A.R. 501 and Foot Art. Bn. 401 have occupied positions E. of Ervillers.

CHAPTER XXXII.

3rd Batt. Aug. 1918.

. . . .

11. Div. H. Q. . . . Queant.

v. STUMPFF,
G.O.C., 234 Div.

CHAPTER XXXIII

SEPTEMBER

Diary of the War

Chapter XXXIII.

Sept. 1918.

THE German retreat still continued, and the Allies gained ground all along the line. The salient at St. Mihiel was carried by the American Army, and the Hindenburg line was captured by the British. A combined attack of the British and Belgian troops under the command of King Albert succeeded beyond all expectation, and the British Fleet was able to join in and bombard the coast. An Austrian offer to enter into Peace negotiations was published, and at the same time the Germans made overtures to the Belgians, but the Allied conference at Versailles refused even to consider either of these proposals.

In Macedonia the Allied Forces inflicted a defeat on the Bulgarians, who retreated on a front of nearly 100 miles, and on September 25 the Bulgarian Government applied for an unconditional armistice.

In Palestine General Allenby commenced a series of attacks on the Turks between Rafat and the sea, and on the 30th Damascus was taken.

DIVISIONAL ACCOUNT

During September Marshal Foch followed up his successes all along the line, and the Germans were forced to abandon position after position. Ludendorff, however, always imagined that the Siegfried line was impregnable, and that if the German Army succeeded in getting back there intact, there was no reason why this position should not be held during the winter.

To the British Army was assigned the difficult task of piercing this impregnable line and rendering it untenable, but many doubts were expressed as to whether this was feasible. Sir Douglas Haig, however, was convinced that it could be done, and directed the First and Third Armies to open the attack in the direction of Cambrai, in the hopes that after they had advanced it would be possible for the Fourth Army to pierce the strongest part of the line farther south.

After the operations at the end of August the Guards Division had only five days' rest before it was again put into the line. On September 2 the Canadian Corps had broken the Drocourt—Queant Switch, whilst on the Sixth Corps front the Third Division had, after very heavy fighting, made ground in the neighbourhood of Noreuil and Lagnicourt. The Guards Division moved up from the Ransart area, and was ordered to continue the attack the following day. The position of the advanced troops of the Third Division was so uncertain that it was decided to form up for the attack, along the railway line just east of Noreuil, some distance in rear of the line which the Third Division claimed to have reached, the troops of this Division being then withdrawn. This necessitated the sacrifice of a certain amount of ground won by the Third Division at a heavy cost, but it ensured a straight jumping-off line, and enormously simplified the task of the artillery. (This procedure was repeated on October 9, and on each occasion was fully justified by results.)

After a long and tiring march from their rest areas, Sergison-Brooke's and Follett's Brigades formed up on the right and left respectively, with De Crespigny's Brigade in reserve south of St. Leger. The attack started under a very good barrage at 5.20 A.M. Reports soon showed that the enemy had withdrawn during the night, and the advance continued without opposition until the old British front line, just short of the Hindenburg line, was reached. By this time the troops were utterly exhausted, having covered since noon the previous day some twenty miles in full fighting kit and over hilly country.

During the course of the advance a number of prisoners and guns were captured, but the most noticeable feature on the ground which was recovered was the enormous number of the enemy's dead horses which littered and often blocked the roads : eloquent testimony of the work of our aeroplanes and long-range guns, but entailing heavy and unpleasant fatigue work for our tired troops.

On September 4 Follett's Brigade was ordered to push forward, and form an advance-guard for the rest of the Division, but it found that the

Germans were holding the Hindenburg line in some force. This prevented any ground being gained, and the line soon stabilised along the Army front.

The principal features of the operations that took place between September 5 and 26 were:

(*a*) Some fine trench fighting, by which the 1st Battalion Grenadier Guards, under the command of Lieut.-Colonel Lord Gort, reached the line of the Canal du Nord.

(*b*) The heavy and continuous fighting for the village of Mœuvres farther north, during which it changed hands several times before being finally captured and held by the Fifty-second Division.

(*c*) The heavy gas-shelling, with which the Germans searched all possible assembly positions every night in evident fear of an attack, and which, but for the improved gas discipline, would have caused heavy casualties.

During this period the troops had the satisfaction of seeing two huge German bombing 'planes brought down in flames, on successive nights by our night-flying scouts, working in conjunction with the reorganised searchlight system.

On September 11 Major-General Feilding left to take command of the London District on the retirement of Lieut.-General Sir Francis Lloyd, who had held that command with conspicuous success during the war. For four years Sir Francis Lloyd had occupied one of the most responsible and difficult positions in the Army, and had dealt, especially in the initial stages of the war, with innumerable problems requiring consummate skill, judgment, and tact.

There were several generals who were eligible to succeed Major-General Feilding in command of the Guards Division; all of them had fought consistently for four years, and had been proved and tempered in the furnace of war. The choice of the Commander-in-Chief fell upon Major-General T. G. Matheson, C.B., an officer of exceptional ability, who was reputed to be one of the best Divisional Commanders in the British Army.

On September 25 the orders for the forthcoming attacks were issued. The Guards Division was to attack and capture the ridge running east from Flesquières to Premy Chapel. On the right the Third Division would attack and capture the village of Flesquières, and on the left the Fifty-second Division would capture the Hindenburg line west of the Canal du Nord, after which the Sixty-third Division would pass through, and swinging right-handed would take the Hindenburg support line and the villages of Graincourt and Anneux. In the event of this operation being completely successful, further objectives were given, including Marcoing for the Third Division, Nine Wood and the outskirts of Noyelles for the Guards Division, Cantaing and Fontaine-Notre-Dame for the Fifty-seventh Division, which was to pass through the Sixty-third Division. The Sixty-second and Second Divisions were to be prepared to pass through the Third and Guards Divisions respectively, and capture Rumilly and the high ground east of the Canal de l'Escaut. In the Guards Division Sergison-Brooke's Brigade was to take the first objective (the Hindenburg support line) and form a defensive flank to the left during the next advance, until Graincourt had been secured by the Fifty-second and Sixty-third Divisions.

De Crespigny's Brigade would then pass through and capture the trench-system north-west, north, and north-east of Flesquières, moving on afterwards to the spur running from Flesquières to Cantaing with a view to capturing the batteries in that area and turning the Graincourt line. This advance was to synchronise with the attack by Follett's Brigade, but was not to be pressed against strong resistance.

Follett's Brigade was to pass through De Crespigny's Brigade, and to capture the third objective, including the high ground round Premy Chapel. Detailed orders for a farther advance were given in the event of no great resistance being encountered.

The attack would be supported by six brigades R.H.A., heavy artillery, and three machine-gun companies.

The assembly was rendered unusually difficult by reason of the exceptionally large number of troops that had to be accommodated, by the necessity of avoiding gas areas, and by the extreme darkness of the night. The 1st Battalion Scots Guards also suffered from a barrage, which the enemy put down on their assembly trench just before zero. The attack started at 5.20 A.M., and at once met with a check on the left, where the 1st Battalion Coldstream was held up by a machine-gun hidden under a fallen bridge. By the time this obstacle had been

CHAPTER XXXIII.

Sept. 1918.

overcome the barrage was lost, and this Battalion suffered heavy casualties before reaching its objective, particularly near Mammoth cross-roads, but the remainder of the Brigade reached the first objective with very slight loss.

The advance to the second objective was a very difficult operation. It was known that the Sixty-third Division could not reach Graincourt from the north for another two hours, and General de Crespigny had therefore to hold back his left, and push forward along Shingler Trench with his right. In the meantime Graincourt and the trenches south of it were kept under heavy artillery and machine-gun fire, in order to prevent, as far as possible, the Germans enfilading the troops advancing farther south. Flesquières was captured in conjunction with the Third Division, but the beetroot factory to the east of it held out, so that it was impossible for Follett's Brigade to get through in time to follow their barrage.

The Fifty-second and Sixty-third Divisions on the left had been held up, which prevented De Crespigny's Brigade from advancing, and the left flank of the Guards Division was therefore very much extended, and exposed to cross-fire from the left. General Follett, who had come up with General de Crespigny to see how the battle developed, before his Brigade came into action, was killed by this cross fire. His death was mourned by the whole Division, for there was no braver man in the Army, and indeed it was a serious loss to his Brigade just as it was going into action. Major-General Matheson sent orders that Lieut.-Colonel Lord Gort was to take command of the Brigade, but that pending his arrival General de Crespigny was to command both Brigades.

At this stage the battle might easily have died down, as the time-table was out of gear; the attack on the left had apparently failed, and the Germans in Graincourt village and Graincourt line were giving a great deal of trouble with their cross fire. Fortunately, however, a Commander of great enterprise and determination in Lord Gort was in the line, and before long the 1st Battalion Grenadiers, supported by the 1st Battalion Welsh Guards, had pushed out along the ridge east of Flesquières, and established itself only just short of Premy Chapel, while the 2nd Battalion Scots Guards, together with units of De Crespigny's Brigade, formed a defensive flank along Shingler and Silver Trenches.

Not long after, the Sixty-third Division, having organised a new attack, pushed down the Hindenburg support line, and the Germans began to pour out of Graincourt; as they streamed away, horse, foot, and gun, towards Cantaing, they were caught in flank by rifle, machine-gun, and artillery fire from the Guards Division, and suffered heavily. The 2nd Battalion Grenadiers at once pushed forward and captured Orival Wood, taking some guns, and driving the remaining batteries away.

The Second Division was ordered to pass through and pursue the retreating enemy, but dusk fell before it reached the front line, and all it could do was to take over the line occupied by the advanced troops of the Guards Division, which was withdrawn during the night to the area east and west of the Canal du Nord.

On September 27 the casualties in the Guards Division were 40 officers and 1200 other ranks. The total number of prisoners taken by the Division was 25 officers and 703 other ranks, in addition to 10 field-guns.

The 1st Battalion

On September 2 the Battalion proceeded to the area about Homme Mort, and halted for dinner near Moyenneville. In the afternoon the whole Brigade concentrated in Maida Vale, and Lord Gort rode forward with the Company Commanders towards Longatte, in view of an attack the following day. The orders for the attack were issued that night, and early the next morning the Battalion proceeded to Noreuil, where they went into old German dug-outs. The Germans had retired to the Hindenburg line, and a general advance on Bourlon and Mœuvres was ordered (on the whole Corps front). The 1st Battalion marched to a position west of Lagnicourt, where they remained for the night. A farther advance was made the next day, and on the 5th it reached Louverval Wood, where a week was spent training and practising open warfare.

On the 11th the Battalion moved up into the front line, but the relief was only effected by the infiltration of the companies through troops of the 50th Infantry Brigade. This Brigade, having made an attack that evening, had failed to secure its objective, and the relief was consequently not an easy one. Lord Gort and Captain Simpson spent the night reconnoitring the trenches in the outer zone of the Hindenburg line, in constant danger of being caught by the Germans, and the information they gained enabled the Battalion to establish itself by dawn the next morning in the objective, which the 5th Infantry Brigade had intended to secure the night before. At dawn a bombing attack was made up Brown Trench, and the line of Alban Avenue was secured. A barrage, supporting the attack on Havrincourt, was put down on the whole front, and soon brought retaliation from the enemy. Near the sunken trench in Alban Avenue a shell burst, killing Lieutenant E. B. Shelley, and wounding Second Lieutenant Payne severely and Captain Simpson slightly. In addition to the shelling, the enemy's machine-guns were very active, enfilading Alban Avenue. In the afternoon the 225th German Infantry Regiment carried out a bombing attack on Beatty and Babs posts, but was repulsed with several killed and wounded, leaving two machine-guns in our hands. Throughout the day the enemy maintained a heavy harassing fire, and in the evening again attempted a bombing attack on Beatty and Babs posts, but with the same result. The following day the shelling decreased considerably, and inter-company relief was carried out. First Lieutenant W. B. Evans, U.S.A.M.O.R.C., and Captain the Rev. J. O. Venables, in addition to 27 other ranks, were gassed on the 13th, and every day there were a number of men killed, wounded, and gassed.

CHAPTER XXXIII.

1st Batt.
Sept.
1918.

On the 15th the following letter from Brigadier-General W. S. Osborn, 5th Infantry Brigade, was received by Brigadier-General Follett:

The 5th Infantry Brigade much appreciates the support given them on their left by the 1st Batt. Grenadier Guards in Beatty Post and Alban Trench. The counter-attack repulsed by Grenadier Guardsmen would have fallen on their weakened Companies. A captured map showed the Hun main line running down Hunt Avenue with outposts in Slag Avenue, and the counter-attack was evidently made to gain this resistance line. Will you please thank Colonel Lord Gort from me on behalf of the 5th I.B.

The week preceding the attack on Premy Chapel was uneventful, and on the 25th Major-General Matheson explained the details of the operations. Captain Lawford was appointed to the Staff of the Fourth Army, and Captain Lovell, M.C., took over the duties of Adjutant.

The Attack on Premy Chapel

Sept. 26.

On the evening of the 26th the Battalion left its billets about a mile north-west of the village of Lagnicourt, and marched with its full battle equipment, accompanied by Lewis guns, limbers, field-kitchens, and water-carts, along the Lagnicourt—Doignies road, to its bivouacs about 1500 yards west of Louverval Wood. The strength of the Battalion was 15 officers and 395 other ranks actually going into action.

The officers who took part in the attack were:

Lieut.-Colonel Viscount Gort, D.S.O., M.V.O., M.C. . . . . Commanding Officer.
Capt. W. H. Lovell, M.C. . . Adjutant.

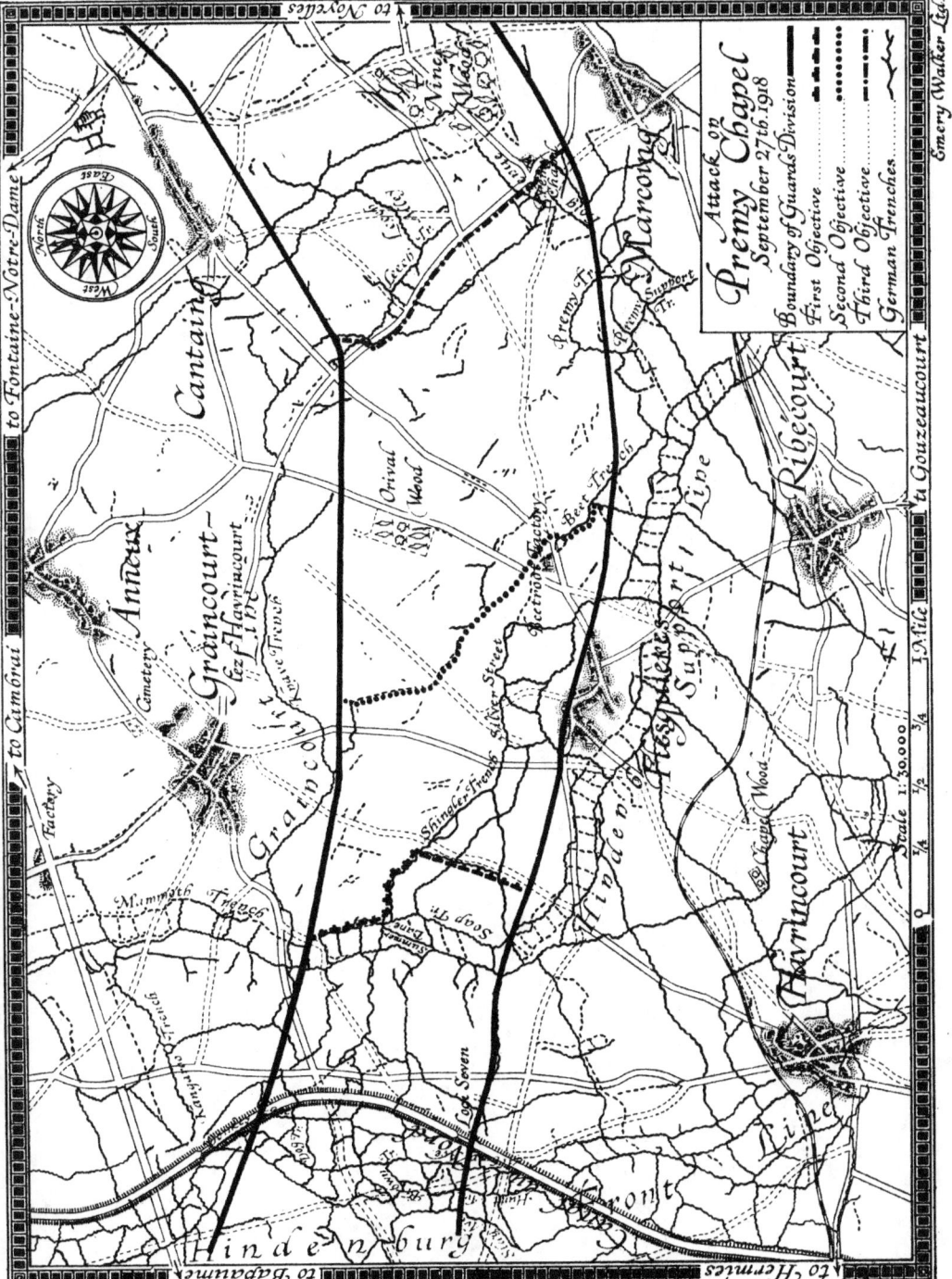

SEPTEMBER 1918

2nd Lieut. J. C. Blunt	. . .	Intelligence Officer.
Lieut. A. M. Brown	. . .	King's Company.
Lieut. C. G. Kennaway	. . .	,, ,,
Capt. J. S. Carter	. . .	No. 2 Company.
Lieut. A. A. Morris	. . .	,, ,,
Lieut. L. C. Jesper	. . .	,, ,,
Capt. J. H. C. Simpson	. . .	No. 3 Company.
2nd Lieut. L. F. A. d'Erlanger	. .	,, ,,
2nd Lieut. G. S. Lamont	. .	,, ,,
Lieut. B. H. Jones	. . .	No. 4 Company.
2nd Lieut. D. H. Clarke	. . .	,, ,,
2nd Lieut. A. Grant	. . .	,, ,,
Capt. W. Lindsay, R.A.M.C.	. .	Medical Officer.
Capt. the Rev. C. Venables	. .	Chaplain.

CHAPTER XXXIII.

1st Batt. Sept. 1918.

Lieut. R. W. F. Echlin was acting Brigade Transport Officer, and Lieut. R. G. Buchanan as Quartermaster.

Lord Gort issued the following operation orders :

The Battalion will attack Premy Chapel hill to-morrow the 27th, with the object of securing the line of the sunken road.

The attack will be made in conjunction with the 2/20th London Regiment, who will be advancing on Marcoing, and the 2nd Battalion Scots Guards, who will be attacking Leech Trench.

The strong patrols of the Battalion will debouch for the attack from the line of the sunken road at zero + 4 hours 20 minutes so as to cross the brown line (Beet Trench) at zero +4 hours and 30 minutes. Approach march orders have been issued separately.

The Battalion will attack with No.. 2 Company on right and No. 4 Company on left in front line, preceded at a distance of 300 yards by strong patrols.

Dividing line between the two leading Companies in the attack will be T of Beet Trench to A in Log Avenue, all inclusive to No. 4 Company.

No. 3 Company will be in support écheloned behind No. 4 Company at a distance of 500 yards in readiness to make a flank attack on Premy Hill from the north should it be found necessary.

The King's Company will be in Battalion Reserve and will follow No. 3 Company at a distance of 500 yards until the neighbourhood of Premy Trench is reached, when it will occupy suitable shell-holes and trenches.

Two Stokes mortars, each with 50 rounds, will move immediately in rear of and under the command of the O.C. No. 3 Company.

One section machine-guns will follow in rear of the King's Company and will be prepared to assist a flank attack on Premy from the north with covering fire and to assist the consolidation of Premy Hill by guns placed in the Graincourt line.

Corps heavy artillery will bombard Premy Hill until zero + 5 hours, when the guns will lift on to Nine Wood for half an hour and then cease firing.

The remainder of the orders contained detailed instructions for the action of the Battalion, if the attack on the right and left proved successful.

It was very dark when the Battalion started on its march, and the artillery on both sides was very quiet. The order of march was No. 2 Company under Captain Carter, No. 4 under Lieutenant Jones, No. 3 under Captain Simpson, and the King's Company under Lieutenant Brown, while Lord Gort, accompanied by Captain Lovell, the Adjutant, and some orderlies, walked at the head of the Battalion. On reaching the Bapaume — Cambrai road a halt was made to wait for zero hour, 5.20 A.M., at which time the Battalion was to advance towards Flesquières. At zero hour the advance began across country

to Demicourt. There was at first very little
shelling, but as the Battalion neared the
Canal du Nord the shells began to fall more
rapidly. There was no water in the Canal, and
by means of short ladders placed against the
banks the crossing was effected 100 yards north
of Lock Seven, with only a dozen casualties,
including Lieutenant Jesper, who was wounded
as he reached the near bank. Lord Gort
went back to Lock Seven to confer with the
officer commanding the tanks which were to
support the Battalion, and was unable to find
him; it was ascertained later that he had been
wounded. The Battalion had to be in position
east of Flesquières at 9.20 A.M., and Lord Gort
therefore continued the advance without further
delay. The ground over which it was necessary to pass was undulating, and was swept
by the enemy's fire, but the skilful manner
in which Lord Gort conducted this advance
accounted for the small number of casualties
the Battalion sustained. The situation did not
look very promising, for the Germans were still
holding Graincourt some 4000 yards to the left
rear. The 2nd Battalion was unable to advance
on Orival Wood, which should have been taken
before the 1st Battalion started, and the Third
Division, through which the 1st Battalion had to
advance, had failed to carry Beet Trench. On
nearing Flesquières, the enemy's machine-gun
fire from the direction of Graincourt became very
heavy, and Captain Carter was killed, being hit
in the head. On reaching Flesquières Lord Gort
took the leading companies round the northern

Chapter XXXIII.
1st Batt.
Sept. 1918.

edge of the village, threading a way through the houses, as the machine-gun fire was heavy from the left flank. Two enemy batteries were still in action in the neighbourhood of Beet Trench, and the Germans were also holding the Beetroot Factory and Beet Trench very strongly with infantry and machine-guns. No sign of any troops on the left could be seen, and tanks, which were to co-operate, had not yet arrived. Lord Gort himself took the leading platoons of the two leading companies into position for assault, and while doing so was slightly wounded over the left eye. While the patrol platoon of No. 2 Company was crawling forward to locate the exact position of the enemy, Second Lieutenant Clarke, with the patrol platoon of No. 4 Company, worked round the left flank of the enemy, captured Beetroot Factory, and took the garrison prisoners. It was a skilful and daring manœuvre, as the platoon was fired at from both flanks, and suffered heavily. One tank now arrived, and Lord Gort at once decided to push on towards Premy Chapel, in spite of the fact that no corresponding advance seemed to have been begun on either flank.

Second Lieutenant Clarke, who had returned with his prisoners, was now ordered to take a platoon from No. 3 Company in support, and again work round the left flank in order to attack Beet Trench from the rear. Lord Gort went across the open to a tank, that was working behind the sunken road, and showed the Commander where to cross, and in what direction to advance; but when it neared Beet Trench the tank was put out of action by direct artillery fire. It was now found that the 2nd Battalion Scots Guards, which should have been advancing on the left flank, was not in position, nor was the 2nd Battalion Grenadier Guards able to advance on Orival Wood. On the right the situation was better, for the Sixty-third Division was reported to be making good progress. The 1st Battalion Welsh Guards, which was in Brigade Reserve, undertook to come up and protect the left flank. All the time there were several hostile air balloons up directing the fire on the tank, and a German aeroplane had signalled the presence of troops in the sunken road, which immediately became a target for the enemy's artillery. One shell burst close to Lord Gort, wounding him severely in the arm, but although an artery had been cut and he lost a great deal of blood, he refused to go back to the dressing-station, and asked Captain Lindsay to bind his arm up temporarily.

His wound, however, proved more serious than he thought, and Captain Simpson took over command of the Battalion. Somewhat later Lord Gort insisted on starting off again to join the leading companies, but on reaching Beet Trench he collapsed from loss of blood.

Meanwhile the platoon of No. 3 Company under Second Lieutenant Clarke had succeeded in their turning movement, captured a German machine-gun post, and, in spite of being fired on by our tank, worked round to the east of Beet Trench. Two hundred Germans were driven into the sunken road, and forced to surrender,

Chapter XXXIII.
1st Batt. Sept. 1918.

while two batteries of field howitzers and six machine-guns were captured.

The two leading companies continued their advance and No. 3 Company moved forward in their support in échelon to their left flank, while the King's Company moved up to the sunken road in reserve. The enemy was now shelling the neighbourhood of Beet Trench, and sweeping the whole ground with machine-gun fire. No. 2 Company reached Labour Trench, leaving two platoons in support in Premy Trench, but in the face of point-blank artillery fire from Nine Wood was unable to advance any farther. Lieutenant A. A. Morris, who was the only officer left with the company, was killed while advancing with the leading platoons. Second Lieutenant A. Grant in No. 4 Company was killed about the same time, while Lieutenant B. Jones was wounded.

The enemy was holding Marcoing on the right flank and a spur by Leech Alley on the left, so that the whole attack had become wedge-shaped, and, while no advance was taking place on either flank, the 1st Battalion continued to drive this wedge into the enemy's lines. But however successful or daring a manœuvre like this may be, its ultimate success depends on the knowledge when to stop. In answer to a message sent by Captain Simpson, Brigadier-General de Crespigny said that any farther advance was not to be attempted in the face of such heavy fire, until the left flank had been secured by the advance of fresh troops through Graincourt. Captain Simpson decided to establish the main line of resistance in Beet Trench, with a line of outposts pushed well in front, to act as as creen for the advance of the Second Division, which was known to be advancing. Accordingly No. 2 Company was withdrawn to Premy Support Trench, No. 3 to the gun-pit and Beetroot Factory, and the King's and No. 4 Companies to Beet Trench, with outposts some 300 yards in front. This manœuvre was carried out under heavy fire, but was executed with such steadiness that the casualties were few. The men, however, seemed disappointed that they could not push farther on. The Adjutant, Captain Lovell, was hit by a machine-gun bullet whilst accompanying Captain Simpson, who had gone up to superintend the movement.

The Germans appear to have been thoroughly mystified by this attack throughout the whole operation, and to have imagined that the advance might eventually develop into a turning movement, threatening their line of retreat. When the Second Division came up at 2.30, they found the enemy retreating everywhere before them. As soon as the advance had been begun by this Division, the 1st Battalion was withdrawn to an area west of the Canal.

The extraordinary success achieved by the Battalion during this attack was entirely due to the courage, endurance, and determination of Lord Gort, who was awarded the V.C. for his conspicuous bravery. He was able by his example and the reckless exposure of his own life to infuse into all ranks an indomitable determination to reach the objective, no matter what the cost might be. He had himself brought the Battalion

122 THE GRENADIER GUARDS

Chapter XXXIII.
1st Batt. Sept. 1918.

to a very high state of efficiency, and there is little doubt that with a less highly trained battalion such an attack might have ended disastrously.

The casualties incurred during this attack were: Killed, Captain J. S. Carter, Lieutenant A. A. Morris, and Second Lieutenant A. Grant; wounded, Lieut.-Colonel Lord Gort, Captain W. H. Lovell, Lieutenant B. H. Jones, Lieutenant A. M. Brown, Second Lieutenant J. C. Blunt, Second Lieutenant L. C. Jesper; and amongst other ranks there were 35 killed and 24 wounded.

The last days in September were spent by the Battalion reorganising and re-fitting in bivouacs west of Canal du Nord, when the following officers arrived: Captain P. M. Spence, M.C., Lieutenant C. G. Kennaway, Lieutenant R. S. Challands, Lieutenant A. M. Brown, Second Lieutenant M. G. Farquharson, Second Lieutenant E. A. D. Bliss, Second Lieutenant N. P. Andrews, Second Lieutenant J. C. Blunt, and Second Lieutenant R. B. Osborne.

THE 2ND BATTALION

2nd Batt.

During the first week in September the Battalion near Adinfer was training and reorganising after the heavy losses incurred in the operations at the end of August. From the 7th to 11th the Battalion, under Major Harcourt-Vernon, went up into the front line, where it came in for much shelling, especially from gas-shells and, although the troops on each flank carried out offensive operations, it was not called upon to attack. After ten days spent out of the line during which Second Lieutenant K. B. Bibby and Second Lieutenant E. M. Neill joined, the Battalion moved up to Llama Post.

The following officers took part in the operations on September 27 :

Major G. C. FitzH. Harcourt-Vernon, D.S.O.	Commanding Officer.
Capt. R. G. Briscoe, M.C.	Adjutant.
2nd Lieut. the Hon. S. E. Marsham	Intelligence Officer.
Capt. L. St. L. Hermon-Hodge	No. 1 Company.
2nd Lieut. R. C. M. Bevan	,, ,,
2nd Lieut. E. M. Neill	,, ,,
Lieut. W. H. S. Dent	No. 2 Company.
2nd Lieut. D. L. King	,, ,,
2nd Lieut. K. B. Bibby	,, ,,
Lieut. R. H. R. Palmer	No. 3 Company.
Lieut. T. A. Combe	,, ,,
Lieut. R. T. Sharpe	,, ,,
Capt. F. H. J. Drummond, M.C.	No. 4 Company.
Lieut. C. C. Cubitt	,, ,,
2nd Lieut. P. V. Pelly	,, ,,
Lieut. E. L. Major (U.S. Army)	Medical Officer.

During the night rain fell, and the tracks were, in consequence, very slippery. This, added to the fact that some of the bridges which had been put across the trenches on the previous day had been broken, caused some delay, and prevented the pack animals, which were following the companies with hot food containers, from keeping up with the Battalion; they were consequently sent round by road, but failed to arrive before the companies left their assembly positions. The enemy's artillery was exceptionally quiet during the march, and only a few shells fell in Boursies, as the Battalion passed through. Walsh Trench and Walsh Support were reached at 4.30 A.M.

The general plan of attack was as follows: Sergison-Brooke's Brigade was to take the first objective, which was the Hindenburg support line between Graincourt and Flesquières. The 1st Battalion Irish Guards was then to pass through and take the second objective, which was the old British front line of December 1917 to March 1918, just north of Flesquières. The 2nd Battalion Grenadier Guards was to follow the Irish Guards, and pass through them in order to exploit any success gained towards Orival Wood and Graincourt, while Follett's Brigade on the right would push on towards Nine Wood.

The Battalion moved off at zero plus one hour from its assembly position, in the normal approach formation with No. 1 Company under Captain Hermon-Hodge, and No. 2 under Lieutenant Dent in the front line, and Nos. 3 and 4 Companies under Lieutenant Palmer and Captain Drummond in support. The ridge west of the Canal du Nord was being heavily shelled, but the Battalion passed over it with few casualties, and crossed the Canal itself easily enough with the aid of ladders on each bank. Any advance through the intricate labyrinth of trenches in the Hindenburg line was by no means a simple matter, especially under fire, and the instructions Major Harcourt-Vernon received were to bring up the Battalion to Soap Trench and Ship Trench in the Hindenburg support line, and then to advance to the forming-up area. The Battalion was unable to leave the Hindenburg support line until 8.20 A.M., partly on account of No. 4 Company having lost direction, and being engaged by machine-gun fire from the left, and partly on account of Summer Lane not having been completely cleared of the enemy. In order to deal with this machine-gun nest in Summer Lane, Major Harcourt-Vernon despatched one platoon under Second Lieutenant Pelly with orders to clear the Germans out. Second Lieutenant Pelly successfully carried out his orders, and not only chased the Germans away, but also took eight prisoners. The advance was then continued, but a heavy fire from the direction of Graincourt and Knave Trench caused many casualties, and Second Lieutenant Pelly was wounded. The mopping up had not been very thorough, and some casualties occurred from snipers' bullets from the rear.

The Third Division had taken Flesquières, but the Sixty-third Division had failed to occupy Graincourt, with the result that the Germans were able to enfilade the troops advancing to Flesquières. When the Battalion advanced to the Beetroot Factory, two batteries of field-guns fired at them with open sights, and machine-guns from Graincourt swept the ground over which they had to pass. On reaching the Beetroot Factory, the Company Commanders at once sent out patrols to make good the ground towards Orival Wood, and silence the batteries and machine-guns, which were causing the casualties, but the volume and accuracy of the enemy's fire prevented them from making much headway. Lieutenant Combe and Lieutenant Bevan were

CHAPTER XXXIII.
2nd Batt.
Sept. 1918.

wounded, whilst trying to push forward with patrols, and there seemed no prospect of advancing until Graincourt had been captured.

In the afternoon the situation underwent a change owing to Lord Gort's daring advance with the 1st Battalion Grenadier Guards. This had the effect of moving the whole German line. Graincourt was at last taken, and an advance on Orival Wood was begun. About 4.30 the Second Division began to arrive, and in conjunction with the King's Regiment advanced from Flesquières. This enabled the 2nd Battalion to push through Orival Wood, although it was unable to debouch from its north edge. Lieutenant Sharpe was wounded during this advance. The Battalion succeeded in capturing seven field-guns and three howitzers, in addition to some forty prisoners. Later in the evening the Fifty-seventh Division attempted to attack down the Graincourt—Marcoing Road, and met with little success.

The Battalion was withdrawn at 3 o'clock the next morning, and returned to a camp on the west of the Canal. The casualties were not heavy. The Battalion lost 9 men killed, 86 wounded, and 2 missing, in addition to the 4 officers already mentioned as having been wounded.

The 3rd Battalion

3rd Batt.

On the 24th the Battalion moved back to Ransart, and reorganised the companies which had suffered. Lieutenant J. A. Inglis-Jones joined on the 31st. Lieut.-Colonel Thorne left to take over command of the Ninth Corps School, and was succeeded by Major Viscount Lascelles.

On September 1 a warning order was received that the Brigade would take part in an attack, and the following morning the Battalion marched to Hamelincourt. Under the impression that it would stay there for the night, Lord Lascelles gave the men orders to collect material in the ruins of the village, bivouac, and cook their dinners; but bivouacking took rather longer than was expected, and just when dinners were cooked, orders were received for the Battalion to move at once to L'Homme Mort, near St. Leger. The result was that the men had a hurried meal. At a Brigade conference that was held, verbal orders for the attack were issued, and it was decided that, rather than risk finding pockets of Germans within the forming-up positions, it would be safer to ignore the advance made that morning, and form up on ground that had been in our possession for several days.

At 1 A.M. the leading company started for the assembly positions, and although the guide twice lost his way it arrived at the destination at 3 A.M. An hour later Lord Lascelles went round the positions and could find no trace of the other three companies. At 5.5 A.M., the hour at which the Battalion was to advance, they arrived, having been on the march for four hours, owing to inefficient guides.

The Germans had meanwhile decided not to wait for the attack and had already retired when the Battalion commenced to advance, so that there was no fighting. When No. 1 and No. 2

Chapter XXXIII.
3rd Batt.
Sept. 1918.

Companies, under Captain Fryer and Captain Dury, reached the final objective, it was merely a matter of rounding up a certain number of deserters. Lord Lascelles, on going up to the leading companies, found a stretch of undulating country in front with no sign of the enemy, and ordered an advance to the next ridge, at the same time directing No. 3 Company, under Lieutenant Cornish in support, and No. 4 Company, under Captain Hirst in reserve, to move forward as far as the position already occupied by the leading companies. This sweeping advance with no apparent opposition somewhat confused the leading companies, which were accustomed during the long period of trench warfare to short advances with definite objectives.

The fatigue of the men was beginning to tell, and this last advance was a distinct effort, but by two o'clock in the afternoon the leading companies had consolidated the position in Boursies. There were no casualties, although the enemy put up a few shells over the Battalion, as it topped the ridge 500 yards west of the village. During the afternoon the German artillery became very busy, and interfered a good deal with the patrols, but otherwise caused little or no damage. The men had been on the move since dawn the day before, and were consequently exhausted, but the Germans made no attempt to counter-attack, and it was therefore possible to get some rest.

At 5 o'clock the following morning the 3rd Guards Brigade passed through the Battalion, which was withdrawn to watch the exposed right flank. The visibility was good, and a few sentries were all that were required, while the remainder of the Battalion obtained some rest. On the 5th the Battalion relieved the Welsh Guards in the front line, and Lord Lascelles decided to move the Battalion Headquarters farther forward, and to hand over what had been the Welsh Guards Headquarters to the Medical Officer for an aid-post. Nos. 3 and 4 Companies were placed in the front line, with Nos. 1 and 2 in support. The right of the Battalion was not in touch with any troops, there being a gap of some 500 yards, and this was accounted for by the fact that the ground was covered with wire of the old Hindenburg line and of the old British line facing it. This wire was almost impenetrable laterally, and was at right angles to the line held by the Battalion. The enemy was in considerable strength in front, and held some 400 yards west of the Canal du Nord as an outpost line in the old maze of trenches, with a strong defensive position behind the Canal. The ground sloped down to the Canal, and the farther the Battalion advanced, the more they were overlooked from the opposite slope; but the necessity of gaining touch with the 1st Battalion King's Royal Rifles made an advance necessary. The line of resistance, about 600 yards behind the front line, which the Battalion received instructions to dig, was nearly finished, when the enemy put a concentrated gas bombardment on the valley, where the Company Headquarters of the two companies in support were placed. For an hour the Germans bombarded the valley with sneezing-gas shells, and all the officers and men

CHAPTER XXXIII.
3rd Batt.
Sept. 1918.

kept on their masks, but when the gas bombardment appeared to cease and was succeeded by one of H.E. shells, every one incautiously took off his mask. This new bombardment proved to be one of mustard gas. By the time this was realised every one was being sick, and all the officers and N.C.O.'s were casualties. Lord Lascelles came up from Battalion Headquarters to see what had happened, and met Captain Dury being led away blind. There were 61 men in No. 1 Company and 30 men in No. 2 who had been gassed, in addition to the following officers: Second Lieutenant S. Calvocoressi, Captain G. Dury, Second Lieutenant W. B. L. Manley, Lieutenant H. P. Gordon, and Second Lieutenant R. K. Henderson.

In the meantime Lieutenant Cornish, commanding No. 3 Company, had received orders from Lord Lascelles to close the gap on his right, and after reconnoitring the situation had established a liaison post with the King's Royal Rifles at Joan Post. When darkness came he managed to send out more men, and added two fresh posts south of Goat Trench; but the ground to be covered was over 500 yards, and the difficulty was that the line from the right of the Battalion to the left of the King's Royal Rifles ran diagonally over a crest, and not parallel to it. Lines of very thick and strong wire ran in irregular lines, and in various directions. What therefore seemed fairly simple by daylight was extremely difficult in the dark, since no patrol could keep direction on account of the wire. A compass was useless, owing to the wire, and there were no landmarks. Lord Lascelles, who was not at all happy about his right flank, ordered Lieutenant Cornish to double his liaison post, and to put up a Véry light perpendicular at dusk from his post on the left of the gap, so that a detachment from the liaison post could work towards it.

These measures, although far from satisfactory, were the best that could be done in the circumstances, and Lieutenant Cornish was afterwards highly commended for the energy and resource which he showed in dealing with an admittedly difficult situation.

On the 8th the Battalion was relieved by the 2nd Battalion Grenadiers, and retired to some trenches in Dunhelm Avenue. From the 8th to the 15th the whole of the 2nd Brigade went into reserve positions near Lagnicourt, where no incidents of any importance occurred. As a draft was shortly expected, the companies were not equalised in strength, but it was Nos. 1 and 2 Companies that had suffered most, and, as the other two companies would have to lead the attack at the end of the month, there was no objection to the half-assimilated draft being in reserve.

On the 20th the Battalion was warned that it would shortly have to take part in the attack on the Canal du Nord, and that it would relieve the 1st Battalion Scots Guards on the night of the 21st. A piece of ground was at once selected for practice purposes, and the enemy's trenches and salient features were taped out on it, while the Royal Engineers constructed a model of the area to be attacked. The expected draft arrived just in time to take part in the rehearsal, and was absorbed in Nos. 1 and 2 Companies. The following day after a Company Commanders' conference, the details of the attack were carefully explained by the Commanding Officer, Lord Lascelles, who had attended a conference at Brigade Headquarters. No. 3 Company and one platoon of No. 4 were to attack Slag Heap; the remainder of No. 4 Company would be in support; No. 2 Company would remain where it was in the front line, and No. 1 would be in Brigade Reserve. Thus all four companies were to be more or less in the front line, but No. 4 Company, under Lieutenant Bunbury, was the one most likely to come into touch with the enemy. During the relief No. 4 Company was raided, but the Welsh Guards had not yet left the line, and the enemy consequently received a very warm reception. The possibility of an attack on that part of the line had already occurred to Lieutenant Bunbury, as a similar raid had been attempted two days before, and the ground being a regular rabbit-warren of disused trenches made it extremely difficult to guard against a surprise; but he kept his company constantly on the alert, and was ready for the Germans when they came.

On the 25th a heavy barrage descended on the whole front line, and all wires became disconnected. The enemy raided the position of the line occupied by No. 4 Company, and managed to get into trenches at an unoccupied spot, but were ejected by a patrol. There were a few casualties from the barrage, but no men missing.

SEPTEMBER 1918

On the following day detailed orders for the attack were issued, and the Battalion proceeded to the assembly position.

LIST OF OFFICERS WHO TOOK PART IN THE OPERATIONS ON SEPTEMBER 27

Lieut.-Colonel the Viscount Lascelles, D.S.O.	Commanding Officer.
Capt. E. G. A. Fitzgerald, D.S.O.	Adjutant.
2nd Lieut. R. C. G. de Reuter	Intelligence Officer.
Capt. E. R. M. Fryer, M.C.	No. 1 Company.
Lieut. C. C. Carstairs, M.C.	,, ,,
Lieut. F. S. V. Donnison	,, ,,
Capt. A. H. S. Adair, M.C.	No. 2 Company.
Lieut. S. G. Fairbairn, M.C.	,, ,,
Lieut. C. B. Hollins	,, ,,
2nd Lieut. J. Chapman	,, ,,
Lieut. E. N. de Geijer, M.C.	No. 3 Company.
2nd Lieut. H. J. Gibbon, M.C.	,, ,,
2nd Lieut. A. D. Cooper, D.S.O.	,, ,,
Lieut. E. J. Bunbury, M.C.	No. 4 Company.
2nd Lieut. R. P. Papillon	,, ,,
2nd Lieut. G. R. Gunther, M.C.	,, ,,
2nd Lieut. H. I'B. Smith	,, ,,
Lieut. Graff, U.S.A.M.O.R.C.	Medical Officer.

The attack of the Battalion was at right angles to the main attack, which was somewhat confusing; but, as the Battalion was holding a salient, it was necessary to have the right half Battalion facing east, one company facing north, and one company (in échelon) facing east. There was still a pocket of Germans on the left between the Battalion and the Canal, but the ground was heavily wired and quite impassable. It was therefore necessary to attack northward, and as there were many lines of trenches and much wire, the attack had to be organised in small parties, working over the top of the ground but parallel with the trenches, so that the wire might be crossed by entering the trenches. Each party was in charge of an officer or a specially selected non-commissioned officer, and although there was undoubtedly a risk of losing many first-rate men, this decision was justified by the fact that, in spite of the maze of trenches, none of the parties failed to reach their objectives.

No. 3 Company, under Lieutenant de Geijer, reached Slag Heap, and got touch with the 1st Battalion Coldstream. An aid-post was established there, and parties began to move up Donkey and Dog Trench, when the Coldstream reported that they were suffering heavy casualties from their left flank. Instructions were at once sent by Lord Lascelles to keep down the machine-gun fire referred to, but the Battalion was itself subjected to a heavy fire from two machine-guns, which swept most of the ground crossed by carrying parties, and caused casualties among unsuspecting troops in rear. Two Stokes mortars were ordered up, but as soon as the Germans saw them coming into position they retired. Lance-Corporal Watson crossed the Canal with Private Parry in order to silence another machine-gun (probably the gun which was harassing the Coldstream), and succeeded in capturing not only the gun but an officer and seven men near Kangaroo Trench. Second Lieutenant Gibbon with three men took half a dozen prisoners, and sent them back down a trench. As the last German disappeared round the traverse, he treacherously drew a bomb from his pocket and threw it at Second Lieutenant Gibbon and his men, who had just enough time to run round another traverse. No. 3 Company took 83 prisoners, including the wounded, and 23 machine-guns, and their casualties were not heavy, for they only had 12 men wounded and 2 missing. In the evening verbal orders were received to move back to Doignies.

CHAPTER XXXIV

OCTOBER

Diary of the War

<small>CHAPTER XXXIV.
Oct. 1918.</small> IN France the German retirement continued, and the British Army made considerable progress, while the French were equally successful in hastening the retreat of the enemy near St. Quentin and later at Soissons. King Albert's attack threatened to cut off part of the German Army in Belgium, and in order to prevent this, the Germans were forced to retire precipitately, leaving behind them vast stores of war material. Ostend, Lille, and Douai were evacuated, and Sir Roger Keyes, who commanded what was known as the Dover Patrol, landed on the Belgian coast. The German intention appears to have been to retire from Belgium as speedily as possible, and in so doing to avoid any large number of men being surrounded.

In Italy the Austrians were in full retreat, and on the 27th sued for Peace.

In Palestine General Allenby, after a series of brilliant operations, succeeded in cutting off the main portion of the Turkish Army on the Tigris, with the result that Turkey asked for an Armistice.

The Guards Division

In October the Germans found the retirement more and more difficult. During September they had lost a quarter of a million prisoners and an immense number of guns, and their original intention of making a determined stand on one of their deeply fortified lines had long since been abandoned. The Allied Armies were pressing them back all along the line, and the continual retirement was beginning to affect the spirit of the Army. After the Siegfried line had been broken through, Sir Douglas Haig commenced operations on a seventeen-mile front from Cambrai to Sequehart with the Third and Fourth Armies, and the Sixth Corps, in which the Guards Division was, advanced to the south of Cambrai.

On October 6 Major-General Matheson received a warning order to be prepared to move to Havrincourt, but this move was postponed later for twenty-four hours. The Guards Division was in support of the Second and Third Divisions, and in the event of little opposition being encountered was to pass through and continue the advance on La Henières and Igniel-dit-les-Frisettes, but as the Germans offered a stubborn resistance the Guards Division did not go into the line until the next day.

All sorts of wild rumours were about, and as there seemed every danger of the enemy making use of them to gain time, Major-General Matheson issued the following order :

(1) Rumours are current that the German Government intends to propose a suspension of hostilities,

with a view to the discussion of Peace terms. It is possible that attempts at fraternisation may in consequence be made by German troops in the line.

(2) The German Army is hard pressed and the German High Command needs time to carry out its present withdrawal without heavy loss in men and material. German Peace talk is therefore circulated in order to relax our pressure, gain time for the withdrawal, and prepare for a long defensive campaign next year.

(3) All our troops will be warned against paying any attention to rumours of this kind. They are intended not to shorten the war but to save the German Army from the consequences of defeat this year and to preserve its strength for the defence of German soil next year. Any attempts made by the enemy to fraternise in the field will also be disregarded absolutely.

It is our intention to beat the enemy as fast as we can, not to allow him to recover his strength.

On the morning of October 9 De Crespigny's Brigade on the right, and Sergison-Brooke's Brigade on the left, passed through the Third and Second Divisions, and attacked under a barrage.

It was expected that the Caudry—Cambrai railway, running diagonally across the line of advance, with its steep embankments and deep cuttings, would form a serious obstacle, and special steps were taken to bring enfilade artillery and machine-gun fire to bear on it, till the infantry was within assaulting distance. It was soon found, however, that the enemy had withdrawn during the night, and it was not till late in the afternoon that the German advanced troops were again located, holding a line of trenches west of Boistrancourt and east of Igniel-dit-les-Frisettes. A night operation to capture Boistrancourt revealed the farther withdrawal of the enemy.

On the 10th De Crespigny's and Sergison-Brooke's Brigades followed up the enemy, and after some skirmishing with his rear-guards, took up an outpost line west of Quevy and St. Hilaire, with detached posts east of those villages.

On the morning of the 11th the 3rd Guards Brigade, which was now under the command of Brigadier-General Heywood, passed through the outposts, and was soon engaged with the German rear-guards, which were now fighting stubbornly.

The next few days were spent in clearing the enemy from the west bank of the River Selle, after which there was a pause to allow time for the reconstruction of the railways in rear. The most difficult problem of this period was the evacuation of the civil population from the villages on the banks of the Selle, which were occupied by both our own and the enemy's troops. The evacuation was carried out by night with scarcely a casualty.

On the 20th the Guards Division took part in a general attack, launched with the object of driving the enemy from his new positions, east of the River Selle. The attack, which started at 1 A.M., was carried out by De Crespigny's Brigade on the right, and Heywood's Brigade on the left. The Sixty-second Division was to clear Solesmes of the enemy on the right of the Guards Division, and the Nineteenth Division was to capture Haussy on the left. A great deal

Chapter XXXIV.
The Guards Division.
Oct. 1918.

of the success of this attack depended on whether the River Selle was held in any strength, but the Germans never attempted to dispute the passage, and both Brigades passed over with little loss. The first objective was secured without difficulty, but when the advance to the second objective commenced, a good deal of opposition was encountered, especially on the left, where the Nineteenth Division had been held up after capturing Haussy. The resistance was so stubborn that at one time artillery preparation was contemplated; but when the Sixty-second Division advanced towards Romeries, the Guards Division was able to secure the second objective, and even push out patrols as far as the River Harpies.

During the afternoon the Germans put down on the new positions an artillery concentration, which many officers present considered to have been the heaviest they had experienced since the battle of the Somme; our troops were, however, so well dug in that hardly any casualties were inflicted. On the night of the 22nd the Division was relieved by the Second Division, which continued the attack the following day.

The remainder of the month was spent in rest, which was, however, much interfered with by the constant change of quarters, necessitated by the withdrawal of the enemy.

THE 1ST BATTALION

1st Batt.

At the beginning of October Major the Hon. W. R. Bailey arrived, and took command of the Battalion. On the 7th orders were received to proceed to Havrincourt, where the Guards Division was to be in reserve during an attack by the Second and Third Divisions. The attack proved successful, and on the evening of the 8th the Battalion moved to Marcoing, where it was bivouacked in some old trenches. On the 9th the 1st and 2nd Guards Brigade attacked, and the 3rd Guards Brigade was in Divisional Reserve. The Battalion marched by platoons at 100 yards intervals to Seranvillers *via* Masnières and Crevecour. The next day it moved on to Cattenières, and Major Bailey, accompanied by the Company Commanders, rode on to Bévillers to reconnoitre.

LIST OF OFFICERS WHO TOOK PART IN THE OPERATIONS IN OCTOBER

Major the Hon. W. R. Bailey, D.S.O.	Commanding Officer.
Lieut. J. A. Lloyd	Acting Adjutant.
2nd Lieut. J. C. Blunt	Intelligence Officer.
Capt. P. M. Spence, M.C.	King's Company.
2nd Lieut. D. H. Clarke	,, ,,
Lieut. C. G. Kennaway	No. 2 Company.
2nd Lieut. R. B. Osborne	,, ,,
2nd Lieut. M. G. Farquharson	,, ,,
Capt. J. H. C. Simpson	No. 3 Company.
2nd Lieut. N. P. Andrews	,, ,,
Lieut. E. A. D. Bliss	No. 4 Company.
2nd Lieut. C. B. Hall	,, ,,
2nd Lieut. R. S. Challands	,, ,,
Capt. W. Lindsay, R.A.M.C.	Medical Officer.
Capt. the Rev. C. Venables	Chaplain.

On the 11th the Battalion moved off at 1 A.M., and reached the rendezvous just east of Bévillers at 4 A.M. It was a very dark night, drizzling with rain, and the marching was difficult owing to the mine craters, with which the enemy had

CHAPTER XXXIV.
1st Batt.
Oct. 1918.

endeavoured to destroy the road, transport wagons constantly falling in, and delaying the march. The Battalion had been allotted a front of about 2000 yards, which was covered by the King's Company under Captain Spence on the right, and No. 2 Company under Lieutenant Kennaway on the left, each with two platoons in the front line acting as fighting patrols, and two platoons in the second line with the Company Commanders. No. 3 Company under Captain Simpson was in support, and No. 4 under Lieutenant Bliss in Brigade Reserve. The country was quite open with no cover at all, and consisted of grass and stubble fields. The gently undulating ground was particularly favourable to the Germans, who were past-masters in the art of fighting rear-guard actions. At 5 A.M. the advance began. The first bound was to the railway east of the village of Quiévy, but no halt was made here, as it was found that the advanced troops of the 1st Guards Brigade had pushed farther on during the night. When the leading patrols reached the high ground immediately east of Quiévy, they were met by heavy machine-gun fire from the orchard north of Fontaine-au-terre Farm, and were enfiladed by numerous machine-guns along the St. Vaast—Solesmes road. The leading companies deployed here. The King's and No. 2 Companies, covered by their own fire, continued to advance by rushes, and captured the orchard, from which the Germans hastily retired. Captain Simpson halted No. 3 Company on the high ground west of the farm, while south of the farm touch was gained with the 2nd Bat-

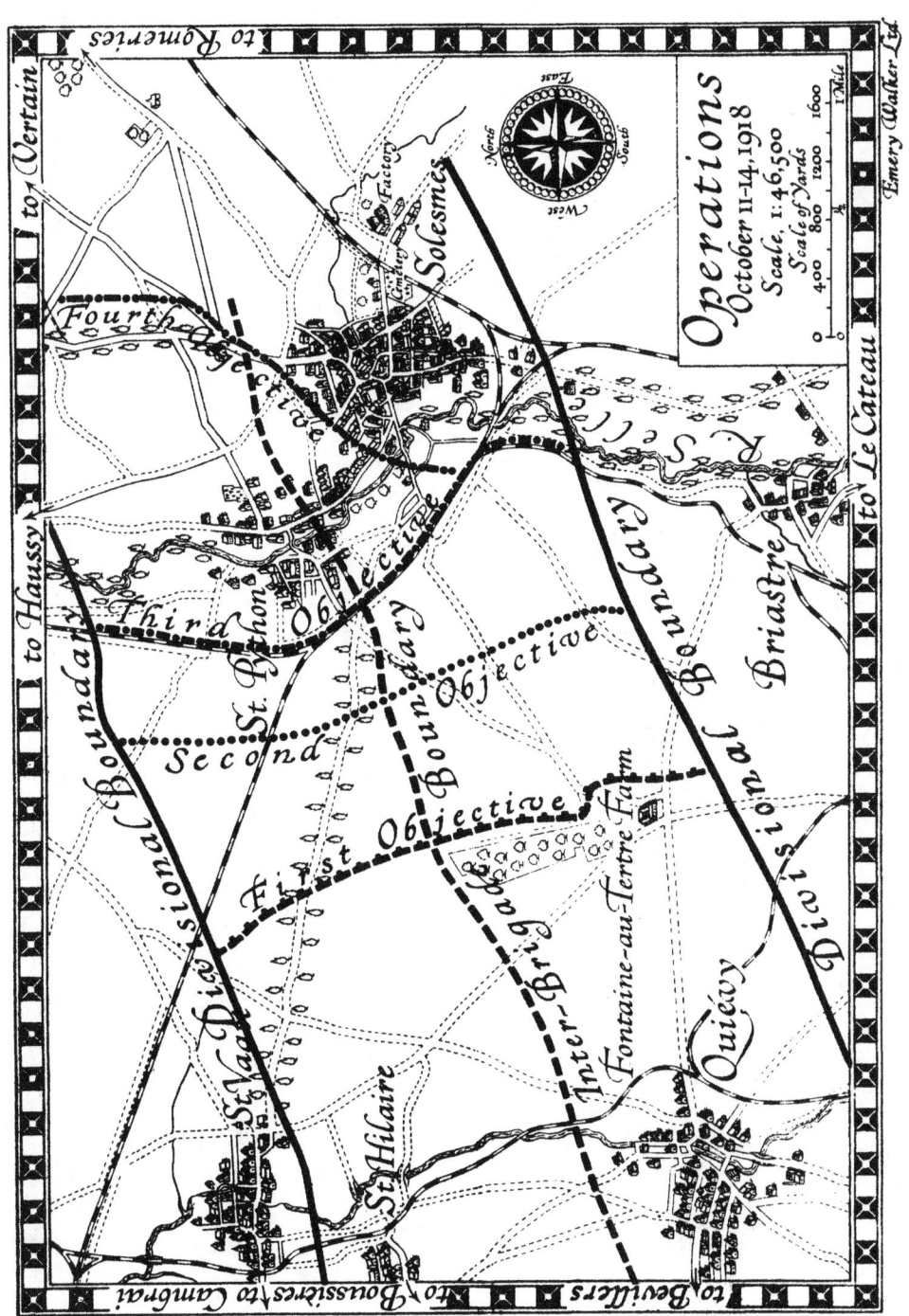

talion Auckland Regiment from the New Zealand Division. The machine-gun fire from the left flank, where the Scots Guards were checked, continued to be very severe, and completely held up No. 2 Company. Captain Spence decided to push forward with the King's Company to try and outflank the enemy's posts, and sent forward one platoon down the slope. Although this had the desired effect, and the German infantry retired, they left their machine-guns, which kept up a sweeping fire along the crest, and prevented the Scots Guards from advancing. It was thought that, if a demonstration was made straight towards them, it might perhaps force them to retire, but when No. 2 Company attempted this the German machine-guns never moved. Meanwhile the King's Company, with that dogged determination which has characterised all its movements during the war, drove away the Germans from the spur of the hill south of Solesmes, and working round in the area occupied by the New Zealand Division, pushed forward, and gained the spur itself. The ground over which the King's Company passed, consisted of a deep and broad valley quite devoid of cover, and the slightest movement could be observed from the opposite slope, where German field-guns and machine-guns were posted. The manner in which Captain Spence directed his company and surmounted all the difficulties, was specially mentioned by Lieut.-Colonel Bailey, and this advance undoubtedly made a considerable difference to the centre of the Guards Division. But the forward position, which the King's Company had gained, was by no means easy to retain, for the men were subjected to a heavy machine-gun fire from the north, whilst the enemy's 5·9 guns registered on them. These men remained unable to move a muscle until dark, when they dug themselves in. No. 3 Company was moved up to an orchard in close support, and, as there seemed no reasonable prospect of success during daylight without heavy loss, it was not pushed up into the attack. The German machine-guns were wonderfully well placed, commanding the flat plateaus on the top of the ridges, with no possibility of their being approached under cover, and our artillery was unable to help, as it was practically impossible to locate these machine-gun nests. The men were anxious to push on, and had to be restrained. All this time the shelling was heavy but promiscuous, and several men were hit by fragments. Captain Simpson, Second Lieutenant Clarke, and Second Lieutenant Osborne were wounded in this way, but the Battalion was really very fortunate in not having suffered more than it did. Although patrols were sent out during the night, they were unable to get very far on account of the enemy's machine-guns, which had evidently been pushed forward to hinder reconnaissance.

The next morning it was found that the Germans had retired, and that the machine-guns had all been withdrawn, the emplacements being full of empty cartridge cases. Except for some shelling the morning proved uneventful, and in the afternoon the 2nd Battalion Scots Guards and 1st Battalion Welsh Guards were ordered to attack on the left. Two platoons from No. 2 Company of the 1st Battalion were ordered to co-operate with them and guard their right flank. The advance was successfully carried out with little opposition, although the German artillery put down a heavy barrage on the west line. The company runners in this fight behaved with great gallantry, and throughout the day carried their lives in their hands, continually running great risks. Posts were ordered to be pushed down to the railway, and small reconnoitring patrols were sent out as soon as it was dark. Except at the commencement of the operations the Battalion saw few Germans, and the men realised they were fighting a very cleverly hidden enemy. Each machine-gun nest had to be located, and shot out in turn. During that night the King's Company was relieved by No. 4, and No. 3 by No. 2. Lieutenant Challands, who took over command of No. 3 Company, was knocked out temporarily by the bursting of a shell during the relief. The Battalion was the only one in the Division to reach its objective, and this was entirely due to the dash displayed by both officers and men in this entirely new form of open warfare.

The 2nd Battalion Scots Guards and 1st Battalion Welsh Guards advanced up to the same line, held by the 1st Battalion Grenadiers. The rest of the day was very trying for all troops in the forward area on account of the continual shelling, as the Germans had excellent observation, and were very accurate in their shooting. The line from Solesmes to St. Python was very strongly held, and the two posts on the right held by the

Battalion were in dangerous proximity to the enemy. One of these was rushed by a party of eighty Germans under cover of an intense Minenwerfer barrage, and only one man escaped. In the evening the Battalion was relieved by the 2nd Battalion Coldstream Guards, and marched by companies to Quiévy. The casualties during the three days' operations were 3 officers wounded, and of other ranks 11 were killed, 3 died of wounds, 45 wounded and 17 missing.

The next day Major Bailey received the following message from Brigadier-General C. P. Heywood, Commanding the 3rd Guards Brigade:

> I should like to put on record my appreciation of the good work done by you and your Battalion during the past three days. I was particularly impressed with the initiative and determined action of the King's Company in pushing forward on the afternoon of the 11th to the advanced position in D 12 central.

On the 15th Major-General T. G. Matheson, Commanding the Guards Division, addressed the following message to Brigadier-General Heywood:

> I wish to congratulate the Brigadier and all ranks of the 3rd Guards Brigade on the manner in which they carried out the task assigned to them from October 11th to 14th.
>
> The advance of the 1st Batt. Grenadier Guards towards Solesmes and of the 2nd Batt. Scots Guards to St. Python were carried out with very much gallantry and produced very valuable results in securing us command of the crossings of the River Selle. The hard fighting of the 1st Batt. Welsh Guards on the left flank contributed largely to the success of the other two Battalions.

OCTOBER 1918

I am much pleased with the performance of the Brigade and should like my appreciation to be conveyed to all ranks.

Two days, the 14th and 15th, were spent at Quiévy cleaning up and reorganising, but on the evening of the second day the enemy bombarded the billeting area with 8-inch shells, when two men were killed and nine were wounded. On the 17th the Battalion marched to Carmières, where Major Bailey attended a Brigade conference. On the 19th the Battalion marched by companies with intervals of 200 yards to St. Vaast, and sheltered in houses and cellars until 10.15 P.M., when they moved up to the assembly area, directed by guides from the 1st Battalion Coldstream Guards.

LIST OF OFFICERS WHO TOOK PART IN THE OPERATIONS OCTOBER 20–22

Major the Hon. W. R. Bailey, D.S.O.	Commanding Officer.
2nd Lieut. J. C. Blunt	Acting Adjutant.
Lieut. R. F. W. Echlin	Transport Officer.
Lieut. R. G. Buchanan	Act.-Quartermaster.
Capt. P. M. Spence, M.C.	King's Company.
Lieut. A. M. Brown	,, ,,
2nd Lieut. L. E. G. Wall	,, ,,
Lieut. C. G. Kennaway	No. 2 Company.
2nd Lieut. R. B. Osborne	,, ,,
2nd Lieut. M. G. Farquharson	,, ,,
Capt. J. H. C. Simpson	No. 3 Company.
2nd Lieut. G. S. Lamont	,, ,,
2nd Lieut. L. F. A. d'Erlanger	,, ,,
2nd Lieut. N. P. Andrews	,, ,,
Lieut. A. E. D. Bliss	No. 4 Company.
Lieut. R. S. Challands	,, ,,
2nd Lieut. C. B. Hall	,, ,,
Capt. W. Lindsay, R.A.M.C.	Medical Officer.
Capt. the Rev. C. Venables	Chaplain.

Chapter XXXIV.
1st Batt.
Oct. 1918.

The night was dark and it was pouring with rain, when the Battalion formed up along the line of railway between Haussy and St. Vaast. It is impossible adequately to describe the absolute wretchedness of forming up on a pitch-dark night in pouring rain. An operation seemed hopeless, and was only possible by giving careful instructions to every single man in the Battalion. Plenty of time was allowed to prepare for this fight, but the Battalion was only just ready when the time came to advance. No. 4 Company, under Lieutenant Bliss, was on the left; No. 3 Company, under Lieutenant Challands, in the centre; and No. 2 Company, under Lieutenant Kennaway, on the right. Touch was obtained with the 8th Battalion Gloucester Regiment in the Nineteenth Division on the left, and with the Irish Guards on the right. The Royal Engineeers had arranged to lay tapes from the railway to the eight temporary bridges, which they had put over the River Selle, but these tapes were not laid until shortly before zero hour, and one tape did not lead to a bridge, with the result that the platoon which followed it had to wade across the river.

Oct. 20.

From the very start everything went well, and the barrage moved with perfect precision. Chasing the Germans in the dark in this way was not without excitement, as no one knew whether they would remain and fight, or retire as soon as they were threatened. It was a great relief to Major Bailey to find that the enemy had no intention of disputing the crossing of the river, as this would have entailed the loss of a number of men at the start. As it was, the Battalion proceeded in artillery formation as far as the Haussy—Solesmes road, passing over five or six lines of rifle pits wonderfully well made in concrete. When the creeping barrage began to move forward, the Battalion moved with it, but there was little or no opposition, and the objective was gained according to scheduled time. The few prisoners that were captured said that the garrisons of their posts had fled as soon as the barrage began. Direction was admirably kept, and the men advanced close up to the barrage, in spite of the heavy plough on the side of the hill on which they had to advance. The 2nd Battalion Scots Guards and 1st Battalion Welsh Guards then came through, and continued the advance. In the evening the German artillery put down a very heavy barrage on the railway, shifting it later to the road, and then covering the objective and the reverse slope of the hill, but in spite of the shelling the casualties were not heavy.

The shelling continued all the next day, but the 3rd Guards Brigade was not required. In the evening the Battalion took over the whole Brigade front from the Scots Guards and Welsh Guards; the King's and No. 3 Companies were placed in the outpost line; and Nos. 2 and 4 Companies took over the main line of resistance on the high ground east of the Solesmes—Vendegies road.

The line of the Solesmes road was shelled all day, but the Battalion was very lucky, although No. 4 Company was rather seriously gassed.

Chapter XXXIV.
1st Batt. Oct. 1918.

Oct. 21.

Oct. 22.

Lieutenant E. A. D. Bliss and Second Lieutenant C. B. Hall and ten men were all gassed. In the evening the Highland Light Infantry relieved the Battalion, which marched back to billets in St. Vaast. These operations on the whole had been easy, as the Germans had put up very little resistance, but the rain and mud had made everything very miserable, and the men were soaked to the skin before the attack commenced.

In all the villages round about civilians emerged from cellars, having hidden there for five days in order to avoid being evacuated by the Germans. Among the German prisoners, who had been captured during the advance, were several regimental commanders of the true Prussian type, with florid faces and bristling moustaches. They presented a sorry spectacle in the cages, and seemed to feel their position acutely.

On the 23rd the following special order was issued:

> The Commanding Officer congratulates all ranks on the way in which the attack of the 20th was carried out. The difficulties of a night attack are always great, but in this case they were almost entirely eliminated by the obvious care with which the officers and N.C.O.'s had made their preparations and explained the scheme of attack to their men. No one lost direction, and the orders given out beforehand were carried out almost to the letter.
>
> The conditions have been very bad, but as always you have made the best of things and have kept up the Grenadier tradition of invariable cheerfulness under hardships. You are now out for a short time to reorganise and refit. In a day's time the Battalion will

Brigadier-General Lord Henry Seymour, D.S.O.

be as keen and smart as it was before, and I am confident that that spirit which has carried you through this attack so well will be as good and keen in any other operation which you may be called upon to perform in future.

I congratulate all ranks, and I sympathise with you for not having found more Germans to kill, which would have made up in some small degree for all the worry and anxiety of the preliminary preparations.

(Signed)   W. R. BAILEY, Lt.-Col.
Commanding 1st Batt. Gren. Gds.

While the Second Division continued the attack, the 3rd Guards Brigade remained in billets in St. Vaast. On the 25th Lieutenant H. Freeman-Greene and Lieutenant W. A. Pembroke joined the Battalion.

THE 2ND BATTALION

After the operations at the end of September the Battalion bivouacked close to the village of Demicourt for ten days' training. Meanwhile Lieut.-Colonel Rasch, having been appointed to command the 1st Provisional Battalion at Aldershot, left for England, and Major C. F. A. Walker, M.C., took over the 2nd Battalion.

The following officers took part in the fighting on October 9 :

Major C. F. A. Walker, M.C. . .	Commanding Officer.
Capt. R. G. Briscoe, M.C. . .	Adjutant.
Lieut. W. H. S. Dent . . .	Intelligence Officer.
Lieut. L. Holbech, M.C. . .	No. 1 Company.
Lieut. C. L. F. Boughey . .	,, ,,
2nd Lieut. E. M. Neill . . .	,, ,,
Capt. G. B. Wilson . . .	No. 2 Company.

2nd Lieut. D. L. King	. . .	No. 2 Company.
2nd Lieut. C. J. N. Adams	. .	,, ,,
Capt. J. C. Cornforth, M.C.	. .	No. 3 Company.
2nd Lieut. K. B. Bibby	. .	,, ,,
2nd Lieut. E. G. Harcourt-Vernon	.	,, ,,
Lieut. R. H. R. Palmer	. .	No. 4 Company.
Lieut. C. C. Cubitt	. . .	,, ,,
2nd Lieut. B. R. Osborne	. .	,, ,,
Lieut. E. L. Coffin	. . .	Medical Officer.

Chapter XXXIV. 2nd Batt. Oct. 1918.

During the night of the 7th the Battalion moved into some trenches near Marcoing, and next morning it crossed the St. Quentin Canal at Masnières. The canal was being shelled at the time, but the Battalion escaped without any casualties. Orders were now received for the Battalion to take part in an attack, the first objective being the La Targette—Forenville road, and the second the railway running north-east of Wambaix. In view of the possibility of the enemy being forced to retire, the instructions were that the leading companies were to push on in the general direction of Cattenières.

Oct. 9. Zero was 6 o'clock on the morning of October 9, and the assembly area for the 1st Guards Brigade was on the line of old German trenches, south-west of Seranvillers. Taking up its position on the left of the line, the Battalion had the 2nd Battalion Coldstream Guards on its right, with the 1st Battalion Irish Guards in reserve. In conjunction with this force, the 2nd Guards Brigade was to advance on the left and the New Zealand Division on the right, and the boundary between the two leading battalions was the main road through Seranvillers and Wambaix.

It had been arranged for the barrage to descend

on the first objective, and so the 2nd Battalion Grenadiers and 2nd Battalion Coldstream were able to start moving slowly forward ten minutes before zero hour. No. 3 Company of the Battalion, under Captain Cornforth, was on the right and No. 4 Company, under Lieutenant Palmer, on the left, while No. 2 Company, under Captain Wilson, was in support, and No. 1 Company, under Lieutenant Holbech, in reserve. The foremost companies advanced in waves, and the supports and reserves in artillery formation, preceded by strong patrols, Captain Wilson's company being responsible for clearing the village of Seranvillers. Two howitzers, a field-gun, several machine-guns, and a few prisoners were captured without any real opposition, and the Battalion pushed on very rapidly to within a short distance of Cattenières, where the patrols were sent ahead through the village.

But as soon as they emerged from Cattenières, and came on to the ridge to the north they were held up by heavy machine-gun fire from the wood surrounding the factory at Ignies-le-Petit. There was a considerable stretch of open ground in front of the wood, and progress became very difficult. Lieutenant Palmer, commanding No. 4 Company, ordered Second Lieutenant Osborne to try and advance with his platoon on the left in order to enfilade the enemy in the south-east corner of the wood. A certain amount of ground was gained by sectional rushes under extremely heavy machine-gun fire, but the complete lack of " dead " ground made real success impossible, and Major Walker decided to postpone any farther move until it could be made under cover of darkness.

A wonderfully gallant piece of work during this part of the fighting was done by No. 16796 Private Edgar Holmes, and won for him the Victoria Cross, which unfortunately he did not live to receive. He was acting as a stretcher-bearer, and calmly and fearlessly went on with his errands of mercy to the wounded under a withering machine-gun fire. He succeeded in getting two men in, and, quite regardless of the intense fire at close range, was attending to a third when he was himself hit in the stomach. He did not falter for a moment, and, paying no attention to his own wound, went forward once more to rescue yet another of the fallen. He had covered thirty yards in the direction of the enemy when he was hit again, this time fatally.

At 1 A.M. on October 10 Major Walker brought up the support and reserve companies, and directed them to attack the wood and factory at Ignies-le-Petit. They rushed the factory, encountering little resistance, and then took up a line and dug in on the farther edge of the wood, beyond the main road. The whole advance was a complete success, and the casualties of the Battalion were only one man killed and 12 wounded. Four hours after the attack began, the 1st Battalion Irish Guards passed through the Battalion, and went in pursuit of the retreating Germans.

For the week that followed the Battalion was in Brigade Reserve, and moved slowly forward through Fresnoy Farm, Bévillers, Quiévy,

OCTOBER 1918

Boussières to St. Hilaire, when it prepared for the forthcoming attack.

In the operations on the 20th the officers engaged were :

Chapter XXXIV.

2nd Batt. Oct. 1918.

Major C. F. A. Walker, M.C. . .	Commanding Officer.
Lieut. S. T. S. Clarke, M.C. . .	Adjutant.
2nd Lieut. A. F. Alington . .	Intelligence Officer.
Lieut. L. Holbech, M.C. . .	No. 1 Company.
Lieut. C. L. F. Boughey . .	,, ,,
2nd Lieut. E. M. Neill . . .	,, ,,
Capt. G. B. Wilson . . .	No. 2 Company.
2nd Lieut. D. L. King . . .	,, ,,
2nd Lieut. C. J. N. Adams . .	,, ,,
Capt. L. St. L. Hermon-Hodge .	No. 3 Company.
2nd Lieut. K. B. Bibby . .	,, ,,
2nd Lieut. E. G. Harcourt-Vernon .	,, ,,
Lieut. H. B. G. Morgan, M.C. .	No. 4 Company.
Lieut. C. C. Cubitt . . .	,, ,,
2nd Lieut. B. R. Osborne . .	,, ,,
Lieut. E. L. Coffin . . .	Medical Officer.

This attack was only part of a very extensive movement on the whole of the Third Army front. The Sixty-first Division was ordered to advance on the right of the Guards Division, and the Nineteenth Division, under Major-General Jefferies, on the left. Acting as the leading battalion on the right of the Guards Division, the 2nd Battalion Grenadier Guards had the Valenciennes—Solesmes road as its first objective, and, for its second, a line about a quarter of a mile west of the villages of Vertain and Romeries. The capture of Solesmes, which was known to be full of civilians, and strongly held by the enemy, was entrusted to the Sixty-first Division, while the Guards Division was to push right on to its final objective. This gave the Battalion the delicate and dangerous task of advancing the whole way with an exposed flank. Two other features added to the difficulty of the manœuvre. The long distance to the final objective had to be traversed under cover of darkness, and before it could reach the outskirts of Solesmes, known as St. Python, the Battalion had to cross the River Selle.

Leaving St. Hilaire at 9.30 P.M. on the 19th inst., the Battalion followed the 1st Battalion Irish Guards until it reached its assembly position, which was the railway running from Haussy to Solesmes. No. 1 Company under Lieutenant Holbech was on the right, No. 2 Company on the left under Captain Wilson, No. 3 under Captain Hermon-Hodge in support, and No. 4 under Lieutenant Morgan in reserve. A drizzling rain fell incessantly, and though the moon was full it was a very dark night.

At zero hour, 2 A.M., under a heavy and very effective barrage, the Battalion advanced to the river in artillery formation, guided by tapes. Very indifferent bridges had been erected by the Royal Engineers and the Pioneer Battalion of the Coldstream Guards, and it was no easy matter getting all the men across in single file on two extremely narrow planks. However, there were very few casualties, and the leading companies deployed into waves, and went forward, followed by the supports and reserves in artillery formation. Very soon after the start No. 1 Company got to St. Python, but as it was entering it came under heavy machine-gun fire from the houses.

OCTOBER 1918

Some useful bombing work was carried out at this juncture, especially by No. 1 platoon, led by Corporal Hunter. As the barrage was moving forward, Lieutenant Holbech decided to leave one platoon to complete the capture of St. Python, supported by No. 3 Company, while the rest of the leading companies went on to their first objective, which they reached almost to schedule time. About 50 prisoners and several machine-guns were captured in this stage of the attack.

There was an hour's halt at this point, in the course of which the remaining platoon of No. 1 Company joined up with the leading troops. It had been uphill work all the way, with a good deal of wire to get through, and it had been found necessary to constitute No. 3 Company a defensive flank. Just before another move was due, a party of the enemy was seen on the right rear of the Battalion, firing lights towards Solesmes. One platoon under Lieutenant Holbech wheeled about, and charged it from the rear, " getting home " with the bayonet and capturing several machine-guns.

The final objective was reached soon after 4 o'clock. But the Germans were inclined to hold on to their positions, and all the way the two leading companies met with resistance. This was partly owing to machine-gun fire from the right flank, as up to this time Solesmes had not yet been cleared by the Sixty-first Division. On the line of the final objective No. 1 Company took a field-gun with its garrison of one officer and 25 men—which brought the total captures

CHAPTER XXXIV.

2nd Batt.
Oct.
1918.

Chapter XXXIV.
2nd Batt.
Oct. 1918.

of the Battalion in the attack up to 200 prisoners, two field-guns, and a large number of machine-guns and trench mortars.

By daylight the leading companies had consolidated their line of outposts, and in order to protect the right rear of the Battalion, No. 3 Company dug in in échelon to the right flank, with No. 4 Company in rear of it. About 9 A.M. the Sixty-first Division continued its advance from Solesmes, and came up into line with the Battalion. Soon after dawn heavy enemy machine-gun fire had been brought to bear upon the leading companies, and continued for several hours, while the German artillery, which up to this time had taken little part in the operations, began to assert itself, and shells of every sort fell round the battalion. Lieutenant E. M. Neill, who had been conspicuous for his work and bravery during the advance, was wounded by shell fire, and the total casualties were one officer and 52 other ranks. On the evening of the 22nd the Battalion was relieved by the 24th Royal Fusiliers, and marched back to St. Vaast, where it " embussed " for Carnières. There it remained until the end of the month, when it moved on to St. Hilaire, proceeding the following day to Capelle.

The 3rd Battalion

3rd Batt

In the first week in October the Battalion remained at Doignies, where during a practice attack a barrage from a smoke rifle grenade was tried, and on the 8th moved to Premy Chapel. An attack was being made by the Sixty-second

OCTOBER 1918

Division, and the Battalion, which was not called upon, moved on later to Masnières. Cambrai could be seen in the distance burning fiercely throughout the night.

On the 9th the orders were not received until the Battalion was in its assembly position.

The following officers took part in these operations:

Lieut.-Colonel the Viscount Lascelles, D.S.O.	Commanding Officer.
Capt. E. G. A. Fitzgerald, D.S.O.	Adjutant.
Lieut. R. C. G. de Reuter	Intelligence Officer.
Capt. E. R. M. Fryer, M.C.	No. 1 Company.
Lieut. K. A. Campbell, D.S.O.	,, ,,
2nd Lieut. G. R. Gunther, M.C.	,, ,,
Capt. A. H. S. Adair, M.C.	No. 2 Company.
Lieut. S. G. Fairbairn, M.C.	,, ,,
Lieut. C. B. Hollins	,, ,,
Lieut. F. Anson, M.C.	No. 3 Company.
2nd Lieut. H. J. Gibbon, M.C.	,, ,,
Capt. E. J. Bunbury, M.C.	No. 4 Company.
2nd Lieut. A. E. F. F. Strangways-Rogers	,, ,,
2nd Lieut. H. I'B. Smith	,, ,,
2nd Lieut. R. P. Papillon	,, ,,
Capt. J. H. Graff, U.S.A.M.O.R.C.	Medical Officer.
Capt. the Rev. S. Phillimore, M.C.	Chaplain.

In the early part of the attack one of our guns appears to have been badly laid, with the result that it continued to shoot short, causing several casualties among the leading companies of the Battalion. This was particularly irritating, since only a short time before these companies had been mistaken for the enemy, and had been fired at by one of our own aeroplanes. The first objective was taken by 6.30, and no Germans were

160 THE GRENADIER GUARDS

Chapter XXXIV.

3rd Batt. Oct. 1918.

encountered, the only casualties being caused by our barrage.

The Battalion started off with No. 1 Company under Captain Fryer on the right, No. 2 under Captain Adair on the left, No. 3 under Lieutenant Anson in support, and No. 4 under Captain Bunbury in reserve. As there seemed every possibility of the Germans retiring rapidly, the scheme of attack was ambitious, with a large extent of ground to be covered. The first objective was a trench running from Niergnies to Seranvillers; the second objective the road running from Cambrai to La Targette; and after that there were four "bounds," ending up with the Cambrai—Beauvois road. There was no sign of the enemy, not even any hostile shelling at first, and no difficulty was experienced in securing the objectives. In the second bound, Wambaix Copse, which might possibly have been held by the enemy, was also taken without opposition. At 10.30 the capture of Estourmel was effected, and still the enemy had shown no sign of fighting. Lord Lascelles decided that the dinners should be eaten now, and as the 1st Guards Brigade had not come up there was plenty of time for the men to dine before resuming the advance. It was not until the Battalion reached the Cambrai—Beauvois road and Igniel-dit-les-Frisettes that the enemy's resistance stiffened, and it suffered casualties. Captain Adair with No. 2 Company occupied Igniel, but reported that casualties were occurring from machine-gun fire on his right, and from the enemy's heavy guns at long range. This village was in a clump of trees on the crest of a hill on the farther side of the Cambrai—Beauvois road, and was approached by a sunken road, on each side of which the ground rose in a gentle slope, and formed an ideal position for machine-guns. Captain Adair advanced up the sunken road, and as soon as his company appeared on the hill it was subjected to a harassing machine-gun fire. He at first ordered his men to dig themselves in, but later he decided to move up into Igniel-dit-les-Frisettes. When No. 2 Company moved into the trees and buildings, it was so heavily shelled that Lord Lascelles, who had come up to see how the situation was developing, told him his men would be safer out in the open. There seems little doubt that the German ammunition was already deteriorating, for when their shells burst the pieces did not scatter so well as before. But for this the casualties would certainly have been very heavy, and in all probability it would have been found necessary to retire from the hill altogether. At 4.30 P.M. Lord Lascelles received instructions to support a cavalry patrol of the Oxfordshire Hussars, which had been sent out through the 1st Battalion Coldstream on the left. He was surprised at this message, for he knew that no cavalry patrol could possibly go out in the face of this machine-gun fire, and when the officer commanding the patrol appeared at the Battalion Headquarters to say that it had been unable to go forward at all, he was able to disregard the order, and send in a report asking for confirmation of his action. In the evening orders were received to establish an outpost line

CHAPTER XXXIV.
3rd Batt.
Oct. 1918.

with two companies over the Cambrai—Beauvois road, with two companies in support near Estourmel. That night a warning order was received for a farther advance the next morning, and the Battalion Headquarters moved up to Grand Chanfemel.

Oct. 10.

The next morning the 1st Battalion Scots Guards passed through the outpost line, and continued the advance by bounds, while the Battalion moved forward in support. No. 3 Company on the right, under Lieutenant Anson, and No. 4, under Captain Bunbury, formed the support, with the other two companies in reserve. In the afternoon the Scots Guards were held up west of St. Hilaire, and were ordered to establish an outpost line for the night. Nos. 3 and 4 Companies were placed under the orders of the Officer Commanding the 1st Battalion Scots Guards, while two companies of the 1st Battalion Coldstream were sent up to take their place.

On the 11th the 1st Guards Brigade passed through the outpost line, and continued the advance, while the Battalion went into very comfortable billets in St. Hilaire, where the German baths were used. On the 13th the 2nd Guards Brigade passed through with the 3rd Battalion Grenadiers on the right, the 1st Battalion Coldstream on the left, and the 1st Battalion Scots Guards in reserve. These Battalions were ordered to be at immediate notice to move in case the 3rd Guards Brigade, which was crossing the Selle River, should require assistance, but the warning orders were later cancelled; and that night the Battalion relieved the 2nd Battalion

Scots Guards in the front line along the Selle River. Second Lieutenant Gunther with a patrol of eight men crossed the river, and surprised a German whom he gagged and brought back. He reported that the enemy seemed in a sleepy and disorganised state, and Lord Lascelles accordingly asked for permission to push a company across the river that night, but was told instead to establish a bridgehead on the following night north of St. Python.

The erection of a bridgehead so near to so many houses was a matter of some difficulty, since it was obvious that the crossing could not be held if the enemy occupied houses within 300 yards of it. Lord Lascelles therefore ordered Lieutenant H. I'B. Smith to occupy the nearest house to the bridgehead and Lieutenant F. Donnison to search the four or five houses near it and make sure they were empty. Second Lieutenant Smith had no difficulty in occupying the house, but found that the walls on the enemy's side were so full of large holes that the house was untenable. Lieutenant Donnison moved forward to reconnoitre but ran into the Germans in some force in the streets beyond, and was forced by machine-gun fire and bombs to fall back on Lieutenant Smith's party, leaving behind two men who were too badly wounded to move.

The alternatives open to Lord Lascelles were first, to hold the bridge with trenches dug practically on it, but this was dismissed as being strategically unsound; secondly, to dig trenches beyond the bridge, which was difficult, because the men would have to be on the top of the river bank, and overlooked by the houses 300 yards away ; thirdly, to occupy one house and strongly fortify it. This seemed at first to be the best solution of the difficulty, but when Second Lieutenant Smith and Second Lieutenant Donnison, who had behaved with great gallantry and coolness, reported that it was impossible to hold the nearest house, and that all the neighbouring houses would have to be cleared of the enemy, Lord Lascelles came to the conclusion that this would involve him in endless operations in the town. He therefore decided to have the bridgehead dug in on the banks of the river.

Captain Bunbury, who commanded No. 4 Company, from which the two platoons had been sent to secure the houses on the farther side of the river, was placed in a difficult position. He brought up the remainder of his company, and held a quarter of the village of St. Python, the houses on the other side of the stream being held entirely by the Germans. It was impossible to get to him in daylight, and by night all the streets were swept with machine-gun fire. He handled his men under circumstances of exceptional difficulty with some skill during the days he was there. Throughout these operations some five hundred civilians lived in the cellars and performed many acts of kindness to the men of the Battalion who visited them. It was impossible for them to move out of their retreat without being shot at. One little girl, eleven years old, quite unconscious of the danger she

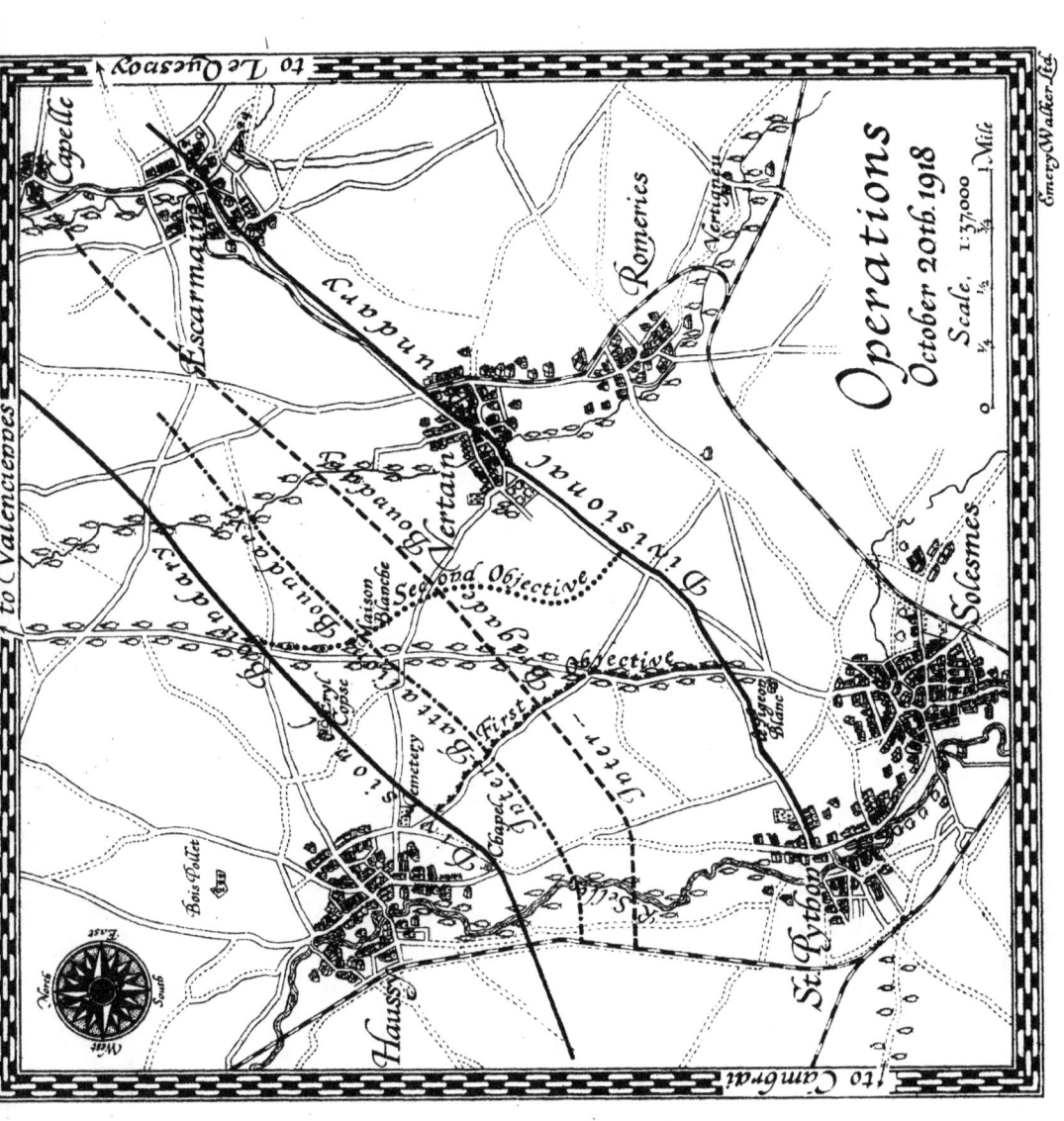

ran, walked out in the streets in broad daylight, and was brutally shot by a German; at great risk one of the men of the Battalion went out and carried her back, but she died.

This was the beginning of the period when the Germans seemed to spare all the buildings, and to concentrate their fire chiefly on the exits from villages.

On the 16th the enemy was reported to be massing men on the St. Python—Haussy road, and our artillery shelled the area indicated for two hours, but no counter-attack developed. The following day the Battalion was relieved, and went into billets at St. Vaast. On the 20th the 1st and 3rd Guards Brigades attacked, and captured the high ground east of Solesmes and St. Python, but the 2nd Guards Brigade was not wanted. On the 22nd the whole of the Guards Division was taken out of the line for a week's rest.

CHAPTER XXXV

NOVEMBER

Diary of the War

<small>Chapter XXXV.
Nov. 1918.</small> THE Versailles Conference opened. A mutiny among the German sailors at Kiel broke out, and had far-reaching effects. In France the Allied Armies continued to press forward, and the German retreat became more rapid. In reply to overtures made by the Germans, the Allies replied that if Germany wished for an armistice she must apply to General Foch, in the usual military form, for the conditions under which an armistice would be granted. On the 8th the German Envoys were received by General Foch, and were given the conditions drawn up by the Allies. A revolution broke out in Berlin, and the abdication of the Kaiser was announced. On the 11th the Armistice was signed.

At the beginning of November Austria surrendered unconditionally.

THE GUARDS DIVISION

<small>The Guards Division.</small> The advance in November, culminating in the capture of Maubeuge, was so rapid, the extent of ground covered in so short a time so great,

NOVEMBER 1918

and the number of prisoners and guns taken so large, that there was little doubt that an Armistice on any conditions was the only thing that could save the German army from absolute disaster.

The Guards Division moved up on the 2nd from Escarmain towards Villers Pol. The objectives or bounds were no longer measured in yards but in miles, and the ambitious programme produced by the Divisional Staff would have been considered beyond the bounds of possibility, even six months before.

It was known that the Germans must now stand and fight, if they were to gain time for the withdrawal of their armies elsewhere, and a final attack was ordered for November 4 in order to break through their resistance, and complete the victory of the Allied Armies. Preparations for the attack were somewhat disorganised by a partial withdrawal of the enemy during the afternoon of the 3rd.

General Sergison-Brooke and General de Crespigny felt their way forward, and Villers Pol was occupied during the night, but it was impossible to notify the artillery of the exact position of the leading companies by the time the attacks started on the 4th, and in order to allow a margin of safety the barrage had to start some way east of the village, with the result that some of our troops never caught it. Up to mid-day the Germans fought very stubbornly, but they were everywhere driven back, and by the evening Preux-au-Sart was in our hands, an advance of nearly four miles. So fierce had been the fighting that the losses on both sides

CHAPTER XXXV.

The Guards Division. Nov. 1918.

CHAPTER XXXV.

The Guards Division. Nov. 1918.

were exceptionally heavy, the Germans in particular leaving a large number of dead upon the ground.

During the two following days Heywood's Brigade drove back the enemy's rear-guards another five miles, and patrols of the 1st Battalion Welsh Guards entered Bavai, an important town, and the junction of no less than eleven roads. Bavai was not on the front allotted to the Guards Division, but during the whole of this advance the line on the left of the Division was very much thrown back, which caused great inconvenience, since it enabled the enemy to enfilade the troops from the north, for the Germans were now prodigal in the expenditure of shells, which they knew they could never carry away with them. The troops billeted in villages in rear suffered considerably, and as the left flank of the Division was thrown back the back areas were all within easy range from the north. In particular the village of Amfroipret was heavily punished, and General Heywood was severely wounded by a shell, which exploded in his headquarters just west of that village. Once more the 3rd Guards Brigade was without a commander. Brigadier-General Campbell, V.C., was sent for to take command, and in the meantime the Brigade was commanded by Lieutenant-Colonel Stirling, Scots Guards.

On the 7th Sergison-Brooke's Brigade, passing through the 3rd Guards Brigade, continued to drive the enemy back, but the following day the advance was checked owing to enfilade fire from the north. That afternoon a German orderly carrying an important message was captured. The message was at once sent by special despatch rider to Divisional Headquarters, and on being translated proved to be an urgent order to the rear-guard commander, telling him to hold on to his present position at all costs, and cover the withdrawal of the main body to a line east of Maubeuge. The resistance of the rear-guard, the message added, must be such as to gain time for the consolidation of this new line and thus save the rest of the army. General Matheson at once ordered General Sergison-Brooke to push forward his reserve Battalion (the 3rd Battalion Grenadiers) directly it was dark, with instructions to force its way through the enemy's rear-guard and straight on down the road to Maubeuge.

CHAPTER XXXV.

The Guards Division. Nov. 1918.

The 3rd Battalion Grenadiers moved forward at 10 P.M., and reached the citadel of Maubeuge at 2 A.M., but it was just too late to cut off the enemy's rear-guard. De Crespigny's Brigade was ordered to consolidate a line on the high ground east of the city; this was many miles east of any point reached by the remainder of the British Army. With the capture of Maubeuge the advance of the Guards Division ended, and at 11 A.M. on the 11th the Armistice was signed.

The final rapid advance had been made under circumstances of exceptional difficulty, since the systematic destruction of the railways by the Germans had necessitated the supply of ammunition and rations being brought up by road. The country was closely intersected by streams, and as all road bridges were destroyed, it was neces-

CHAPTER XXXV.

The Guards Division. Nov. 1918.

sary to erect temporary bridges with deviations through the fields leading to them, while the original bridges were being repaired. Constant rain and the continuous stream of transport soon turned these deviations into a quagmire, through which the horses, often up to their bellies in mud, had to pull their heavy load: only the persistent determination of the transport officers and men to get through at all hazards, and the fine condition of the horses made the task of supplying the troops possible.

Even then these efforts would have been of no avail, but for the work of the Royal Engineers in repairing the innumerable bridges to carry lorry traffic: day and night, without rest and with scarcely time for food, they worked, and never failed to do what was asked of them.

But the finest part of the advance, without which victory could not have been enforced in 1918, was the dash and courage of the infantry in face of the insidious knowledge that peace was within sight. Every officer and man who went into those attacks in November knew that it might be the last engagement of the war, and that if he avoided unnecessary risk he would probably get through safely; if he took it, he might be throwing away his life on the last day of the war. That knowledge had not the smallest effect upon the conduct of the troops, and the attack on November 4 was carried out with a dash and reckless courage that had never been surpassed in the war.

The result cannot be over-estimated: instead of a half-hearted Armistice with the Germans still under the impression they were, as far as the army was concerned, virtually the victors, the last attacks had shown them that it was merely a matter of estimating how far their defeat had been completed, and had made them understand that their safest course lay in bringing about an Armistice as speedily as possible, to save the reputation of their army.

CHAPTER XXXV.
The Guards Division.
Nov. 1918.

THE 1ST BATTALION

After ten days' rest spent in billets at St. Vaast the Battalion went in pursuit of the retreating Germans, and marched to Escarmain, which was being shelled by the enemy. On the 4th the 1st and 2nd Guards Brigades attacked, while the 3rd Guards Brigade was in Divisional Reserve. The Battalion moved by companies at 200-yards intervals to Mortre Farm, where it bivouacked in the orchard, moving on again in the afternoon to Villers Pol. Here orders were received that the Battalion was to go through the 3rd Battalion Grenadier Guards and to continue the advance.

1st Batt.

LIST OF OFFICERS WHO TOOK PART IN THE OPERATIONS FROM NOVEMBER 4 TO 7

Lieut.-Colonel the Hon. W. R. Bailey, D.S.O.	Commanding Officer.
Major C. H. Greville, D.S.O.	Second in Command.
Lieut. J. A. Lloyd	Acting Adjutant.
2nd Lieut. J. C. Blunt	Intelligence Officer.
Capt. J. Teece, M.C.	Quartermaster.
Capt. P. M. Spence, M.C.	King's Company.
Lieut. R. G. Buchanan	,, ,,

172 THE GRENADIER GUARDS

CHAPTER XXXV.
1st Batt.
Nov. 1918.

2nd Lieut. A. D. Anderson	King's Company.
Lieut. C. G. Kennaway	No. 2 Company.
2nd Lieut. M. G. Farquharson	,, ,,
2nd Lieut. G. S. Lamont, D.S.O.	,, ,,
Lieut. R. S. Challands	No. 3 Company.
Lieut. W. A. Pembroke	,, ,,
2nd Lieut. N. P. Andrews	,, ,,
Lieut. H. Freeman-Greene	No. 4 Company.
2nd Lieut. L. F. A. d'Erlanger	,, ,,
2nd Lieut. C. A. Fitch	,, ,,
Capt. W. Lindsay, R.A.M.C.	Medical Officer.
Capt. the Rev. C. Venables	Chaplain.

Nov. 5. At 2.15 A.M. the Battalion moved out from Villers Pol with intervals of thirty yards between platoons, and marched to La Buvette cross-roads, where a halt was made, and the Lewis guns were taken off the limbers. Directed by two guides from the 1st Battalion Scots Guards, the Battalion made its way across country to a bridge, where a long halt was made to find the Headquarters of the 3rd Battalion Grenadiers—no easy matter in the dark. The Battalion eventually managed to get into position close behind the front line posts. No. 2 Company, under Lieutenant Kennaway, was on the right and in touch with the 2/20th London Regiment from the Sixty-second Division; No. 3 Company, under Lieutenant Challands, on the left in touch with the 2nd Battalion Scots Guards; No. 4 Company, under Lieutenant Freeman-Greene, was in support; and the King's Company, under Captain Spence, was in reserve.

At 6 A.M. the advance began. Rain fell and continued intermittently during the three days' operations. The advance was much hampered, especially in the initial stages, by a creeping barrage put down by the Sixty-second Division, without any warning having been given to the Battalion. The going was very heavy, and the very enclosed country, intersected by thick hedges and wire fences, made it difficult for the companies to keep their directions. Little opposition was encountered, until the leading platoons reached Amfroipret, when one German officer and five men were taken prisoners in the village. Immediately east of the village and in the wooded country south of the railway, the Battalion began to encounter the enemy's rear-guard, but after driving it in some way the advance came to a standstill about the line of the road from Bout la Haut to Cambron Farm. The extraordinary difficulty of locating a hidden enemy in such an enclosed country made the advance hazardous, and the Germans appeared to be holding very strongly with machine-guns a line some five hundred yards east of this road. Lieutenant Kennaway, with No. 2 Company, attempted to secure the cross-roads in front of him, and failed to make any headway against the enemy's machine-guns. During this gallant attempt Lieutenant Lamont, who was with the leading platoon, was killed, in addition to many men.

The situation was not without anxiety, for on neither flank could any British troops be seen. It looked as if the Battalion had been going on too fast for the rest of the line, and Lieutenant-Colonel Bailey decided to wait until the situation on the right developed. No. 2 Company accordingly dug in where it was, and the King's Company was moved to Cambron Farm to fill up the gap there was between the right of the line and the Sixty-second Division. The situation on the left required some adjustment, for the 2nd Battalion Scots Guards had been apparently held up, and No. 3 Company had to be responsible for that flank of the Battalion. About mid-day a company of the Scots Guards came up through the village, and occupied Bermeries without opposition, making the left flank once more secure. This enabled No. 4 Company to push forward through the orchards and drive out an enemy's post, but again the enemy's machine-guns prevented any farther advance. The difficulties in this action were that, when once a company or platoon had been sent off anywhere, it could not be found again owing to the enclosed nature of the country. No communication between the various parties was possible, and the operations therefore developed into small isolated parties fighting independently of each other. The Germans began to shell the village with heavy shell during the afternoon, and the front line posts were fired on at close range by field artillery. During the evening No. 3 Company took over the outpost line from No. 4 Company, which was withdrawn to cellars in the eastern end of the village.

Lieut.-Colonel Bailey received orders for a farther advance next day, and the King's and No. 2 Companies were to secure the cross-roads, if possible during the night. It was, however, so dark, and the enemy was in so great strength, that the operation was not attempted that night. Brigadier-General Heywood, commanding the 3rd Guards Brigade, was wounded in the evening, and the command devolved upon Lieut.-Colonel Stirling, commanding the 2nd Scots Guards.

It poured with rain all night. The Battalion formed up south of the railway on the line of the forward posts, with the King's Company, under Captain Spence, on the right; No. 4 Company, under Lieutenant Freeman-Greene, on the left; No. 3 Company, under Lieutenant Challands, in support (their position north of the railway being taken over by the Welsh Guards), and No. 2 Company, under Lieutenant Kennaway, in reserve. The King's Company and No. 2 Company were ordered to make good the line of the Bavai—Queve-au-loup road, where Nos. 2 and 3 Companies would advance through them, and secure the last two objectives. The King's and No. 4 Companies were comparatively fresh, as they had had some hours' rest in barns and cellars during the night, but Nos. 2 and 3 Companies were soaked through by the rain, and tired out after a hard day constantly on the move and a night spent in digging in on the outpost line. At 6 A.M. the advance began, and was again most difficult, on account of the enclosed country. The Battalion met no opposition until it reached some high ground, when the leading platoons came under a very heavy machine-gun fire from the far side of the valley, and a harassing fire from field-guns. No. 4 Company was temporarily checked, but the King's Company, under cover of the houses and hedges along the Mecquignies

CHAPTER XXXV.

1st Batt.
Nov.
1918.

road, seized the crossing over the river, and worked up till it got in touch with a company from the Sixty-second Division on the right. This advance through houses was well carried out, and the Lewis gunners performed wonders in getting their guns into houses. One party of German machine-gunners was shot down in the church tower. No. 3 Company was halted on the road, and No. 2 Company in reserve moved up to the cross-roads at Bavisiaux. The grounds of Mecquignies Château were strongly held by machine-guns, but after a sharp fight the King's Company drove out the enemy and seized the Château. In this fighting Second Lieutenant A. D. Anderson was killed, while gallantly leading his men to the attack. Lieutenant Freeman-Greene, seeing the King's Company advance up the farther slope, at once began to push on with No. 4 Company, and in spite of a hail of machine-gun bullets reached the line of the river with little loss, and gained touch with the left of the King's Company. After this the fighting became very promiscuous, and platoons became scattered among the orchards and fields of the Château. Touch was established with the Welsh Guards, who had been temporarily checked in Buvigny, and who were now moving on, and the enemy seemed to be retiring all along the line. Lieut.-Colonel Bailey was ordered to push on and try and seize the line on the Bavai road before night, and he accordingly moved up No. 2 Company to the Château grounds. The King's and No. 4 Companies had in the meantime made good the high ground north of the Château, driving out some advanced posts of the enemy. No. 3 Company was ordered to move through Mecquignies village and to seize the orchards north-east of the village. This it succeeded in doing, meeting with little opposition. The King's and No. 4 Companies at once prolonged the line to the left, and pushed out patrols to the east. This line was consolidated, and as the night was very dark no farther advance was considered advisable.

CHAPTER XXXV.
1st Batt.
Nov.
1918.

The 466th German Regiment which opposed the advance fought extremely well, and was cleverly handled by its commander, who thoroughly understood how to fight a rear-guard action. The wet weather and the mud made these operations peculiarly trying to men who had had little training in close country fighting, but the discipline in the Battalion was so good that each platoon, however isolated, could be relied on to act intelligently. The scenes in the various villages were most touching, for the civilians who emerged from cellars and underground dug-outs all acclaimed the men as their deliverers, and were highly excited in their joy.

Early on the 7th the 1st Battalion Scots Guards advanced through the Battalion, which was withdrawn to Amfroipret. Lieut.-Colonel Bailey issued the following message to the Company Commanders:

Nov. 7.

Please let all ranks know that I consider the advance on the 5th and 6th to have been carried out excellently in spite of very heavy going and the difficulties of keeping direction. On the 5th Nos. 2 and 3 Companies, though they had little fighting, had a thoroughly miserable and uncomfortable time, which as usual was borne with the greatest cheerfulness. The King's Company and No. 4 Company were better off, as they got a few hours' rest under cover.

On the 6th, in spite of very heavy machine-gun fire from front and flank and most difficult country, the King's Company and No. 4 pushed ahead and drove in the rear troops of the enemy, thus making good the passage of the river Du Moulin de Bavai. The greatest credit is due not only to the fine fighting powers of the men but also to the good leading and forethought of the leaders.

The two days' fighting were unsatisfactory as far as the killing of Germans was concerned, and the conditions miserable from the start to finish, but the Battalion, as always, went quicker and farther than any other Battalion in the Brigade, and the distance you went undoubtedly helped the 24th Division by threatening the communications of the enemy, holding the ground north-west of Bavai, and causing them to retire. You have well kept up the traditions of the Regiment and maintained the Grenadier spirit—the most magnificent in the world. I congratulate officers, non-commissioned officers, and men, and I know that you will never fail.

W. R. BAILEY, Lieut.-Colonel,
Commanding 1st Battalion Grenadier Guards.

On the 9th the Battalion marched to La Longueville, and the 1st Guards Brigade entered Maubeuge. On the following day it reached Douzies, where the news arrived that the Armistice had been signed. On the morning of the 11th the Battalion paraded, and the Commanding Officer read out the official telegram declaring the Armistice to be in force.

The 2nd Battalion

In the fighting on November 4 the following officers took part :

Lieut.-Colonel C. F. A. Walker, M.C.	Commanding Officer.
Capt. R. G. Briscoe, M.C.	Adjutant.
Lieut. L. Holbech, M.C.	Intelligence Officer.
Capt. L. St. L. Hermon-Hodge	No. 1 Company.
2nd Lieut. D. L. King	,, ,,
Lieut. W. H. S. Dent	No. 2 Company.
2nd Lieut. C. J. N. Adams	,, ,,
Lieut. R. H. R. Palmer	No. 3 Company.
2nd Lieut. K. B. Bibby	,, ,,
2nd Lieut. E. G. Harcourt-Vernon	,, ,,
Lieut. C. C. Cubitt	No. 4 Company.
2nd Lieut. B. R. Osborne	,, ,,
Lieut. E. L. Coffin	Medical Officer.

The Battalion marched from Capelle through La Croisette and Villers Pol to its assembly area, which was a line 100 yards east of the Jenlain—Le Quesnoy road. Villers Pol was being heavily shelled at the time, and a good number of casualties resulted. Lieut.-Colonel Walker was ordered to advance in support of the 2nd Battalion Coldstream Guards, until the capture of the first objective, the Fresnay—Wargnies-le-Petit road, had been completed, then to pass through and secure the second objective, a line some 3000 yards farther east. Zero hour was fixed for 7.20 A.M. The rain ceased early, but a very heavy mist hung low over the ground and made it impossible for troops to see more than 200 yards ahead. No. 4 Company, under Lieutenant Cubitt, was on the left of the line; No. 3 Company, under Lieutenant Palmer, on the right; No. 2 Company, under Lieutenant Dent, in support;

Chapter XXXV.
2nd Batt. Nov. 1918.

and No. 1 Company, under Captain Hermon-Hodge, in reserve.

The 2nd Guards Brigade under Brigadier-General Sergison-Brooke went forward on the right of the Battalion. Owing to mist the Coldstream lost their direction, and proceeded at a right incline. Seeing troops ahead moving along close to the barrage, the foremost companies of the Battalion imagined that they were Coldstream Guards making for the first objective. It was only discovered later that these were really the Germans in retirement. As No. 4 Company passed over the high ground near the wood south-west of Wargnies-le-Petit, the mist suddenly lifted, and they came under heavy machine-gun fire from the north. Lieutenant Cubitt was wounded, and the company had a considerable number of casualties. Second Lieutenant Osborne, who now took command, led two platoons a bit farther by short rushes, but was eventually stopped by a sweeping machine-gun fire, which made farther progress impossible. German field-guns were also firing at a short range, and the Battalion lost a good many men. Lieutenant Osborne therefore took it upon himself to make a personal reconnaissance of the enemy's positions, and see whether there was not a better line of advance. With almost reckless gallantry he went out, and carefully examined the German line, but the result of his scrutiny was never known, as he was shot through the heart by a machine-gun bullet on the way back. As No. 4 Company was now without an officer, Sergeant E. Carter took command.

NOVEMBER 1918 181

Meanwhile No. 3 Company under Lieutenant Palmer had made its way through the southern part of the wood near Wargnies-le-Petit. On leaving the wood along the eastern edge, they came under machine-gun and rifle fire from the enemy, who was barely 200 yards away. Lieutenant Palmer advanced by short rushes, and not only took the position, but captured or killed the whole garrison. It was found impossible to proceed, and the company dug in a line of outposts. During this attack the field-guns of the Guards Divisional Artillery were brought up at a gallop to within a very short distance behind the leading troops—a daring and difficult achievement that is worthy of record. As soon as these guns opened fire on the village of Wargnies-le-Petit, the companies on the left were able to continue their progress. Touch was then gained with the 3rd Grenadier Guards on the right, and with the Forty-second Division on the left. Nothing more could be done that afternoon, and the Battalion consolidated its position. Early on the morning of the 5th the 1st Battalion Irish Guards passed through, and pursued the retreating Germans, who had fallen back during the night. The Battalion moved up into billets in Wargnies-le-Petit, and reorganised. Owing to casualties among officers and men, Nos. 3 and 4 Companies were amalgamated into a composite company under Lieutenant Palmer.

Two days later the Battalion moved on to Bavai. On the 9th it was in Brigade Reserve, and supported the 2nd Guards Brigade in the advance on Maubeuge. No. 1 Company was

Chapter XXXV.

2nd Batt. Nov. 1918.

Nov. 5.

Nov. 7.

CHAPTER XXXV.
2nd Batt.
Nov. 1918.

in support of the 2nd Battalion Coldstream Guards, and No. 2 Company in support of the 1st Battalion Irish Guards, taking the main Bavai—Maubeuge road as the centre of the Brigade frontage. The composite company followed in support, ready to form a defensive flank in either direction. There was no opposition, and at 5.30 the Battalion entered Douzies, and occupied the high ground east of Maubeuge. The 2nd Battalion Coldstream Guards consolidated the outpost line, with No. 1 Company forming a Brigade defensive flank. The remainder of the Battalion was billeted at Port Allont. On entering Maubeuge the troops had a great reception from the civilians in the town.

On the 11th the cryptic news arrived :

Hostilities will cease at 11 A.M. to-day.

The Armistice had been proclaimed.

THE 3RD BATTALION

3rd Batt.

On November 2 the Battalion left St. Python, where it had been billeted, and moved up to Capelle.

The following officers in the 3rd Battalion took part in the operations from November 4 to 9 :

Lieut.-Colonel the Viscount Lascelles, D.S.O.	Commanding Officer.
Lieut. G. M. Cornish, M.C.	Adjutant.
2nd Lieut. R. C. G. de Reuter	Intelligence Officer.
Lieut. K. A. Campbell, D.S.O.	No. 1 Company.
Lieut. C. C. Carstairs	,, ,,
2nd Lieut. G. R. Gunther	,, ,,
Capt. A. H. S. Adair, M.C.	No. 2 Company.

NOVEMBER 1918 183

Lieut. S. G. Fairbairn, M.C. .	. No. 2 Company.	CHAPTER XXXV.
2nd Lieut. A. E. F. F. Strangways-Rogers	. ,, ,,	3rd Batt.
Capt. E. N. de Geijer, M.C. .	. No. 3 Company.	Nov. 1918.
Lieut. F. Anson, M.C. . .	. ,, ,,	
2nd Lieut. H. J. Gibbon, M.C.	. ,, ,,	
Lieut. E. J. Bunbury, M.C. .	. No. 4 Company.	
Lieut. G. W. Godman . .	. ,, ,,	
Capt. J. Lawson, R.A.M.C. .	. Medical Officer.	
Capt. the Rev. S. Phillimore .	. Chaplain.	

The Battalion moved off early to bivouac at Capelle. After slipping and stumbling along a greasy chalk track, the companies reached their positions, and were told to dig in. This order was easier to give than to execute, for the men had only their light entrenching tools, which were ill suited for excavating a flinty chalk ground. A few shells came over to enliven the proceedings, but otherwise the day passed quietly. On the following day orders were received for an attack by the Guards Division, and battle stores were drawn.

On the 4th the Battalion started to take up its assembly positions in rear of La Flaque Wood, and was much hampered on the approach march by the crowded state of the roads and the congestion of traffic. On reaching Villers Pol, it was forced to halt, as the bridge across the Rhonelle had been destroyed, and the stream had to be crossed by a single plank. During the crossing a few high-explosive and gas shells were sent over, and the men had to put on their masks. Owing to the dense fog the Company Commanders experienced some difficulty in finding the way to the assembly positions, but fortunately they had been provided with the

Nov. 4.

Chapter XXXV.
3rd Batt.
Nov. 1918.

large-scale aeroplane reconnaissance maps, and were able to go unerringly by the shortest route. The attack was led by the 1st Battalion Coldstream, which had the 1st Guards Brigade (2nd Battalion Coldstream) on their left. The Battalion was to pass through the 1st Battalion Coldstream Guards, whilst the 2nd Battalion Grenadier Guards was to pass similarly through the 2nd Battalion Coldstream Guards, and to continue the attack across a gully and on to the villages and woods beyond. On the way No. 2 Company had some casualties from shell-fire.

Though somewhat late on account of the fog, the Battalion started off with No. 1 Company (under Lieutenant Campbell) on the right, and No. 2 Company (under Captain Adair) on the left, and advanced through Flaque Wood. Passing through the leading Battalions they found the 2nd Battalion Coldstream had occupied the frontage of the 2nd Guards Brigade, and throughout the day (as indeed throughout the whole advance) units were apt to incline to the right, owing to the fact that the enemy retirement was north-east, and the enemy units gave way more readily opposite our right flank.

Lord Lascelles had issued orders that he would move Battalion Headquarters to a sunken road, on the edge of the gully, two hours after the leading companies were timed to pass that spot. The approach of this road was shelled by a field-gun at short range, but fortunately the arable ground, on which the shells fell, was so soft that one of them bursting in the middle of Battalion Headquarters caused no casualties.

On arriving at the road, the leading companies did not advance beyond it, but at this moment the enemy were seen removing their gun, and a patrol from each company was hurried forward, down the gully, whilst Lewis guns were set to fire over their heads at the retiring gun.

On the far side of the gully an abandoned 5·9 was taken over by No. 1 Company, and on reaching the crest of the hill an enemy trench was found defended by machine-guns. Whilst reconnoitring to organise his attack, Captain Adair was wounded in the leg.

In the meanwhile the Sixty-second Division (on the right) had got well forward, and the right of No. 1 Company was able to push on whilst the left of No. 1 Company and the whole of No. 2 Company were held up. Second Lieutenant A. E. F. F. Strangways-Rogers, reconnoitring along the hedgerows on the right of No. 2 Company, was fatally wounded.

Lieutenant Campbell then organised an attack with his right platoon, under a barrage of smoke bombs, which, though they were badly handled and burst innocuously in the air, so astonished the enemy that he abandoned the key to his position, and withdrew down his trench to a position in rear.

Farther on were some thick-set hedges, admirably adapted for a rear-guard action, and on reaching them Lieutenant Carstairs found there was only one gap sufficiently large to let one man through at a time. He led the way, followed by his platoon, and immediately came under fire from the left flank. While trying to locate the enemy, he was severely wounded, and as there were no stretcher-bearers available he had to lie where he was. Lieutenant Campbell on hearing this came up, and seeing that the men were lying bunched up together, ordered Lieutenant Gunther to straighten out the line, while he went to get a platoon to reinforce his right flank. The Germans were unpleasantly close, but their exact position had not yet been located. Lieutenant Gunther, having carried out his orders, went out to where Lieutenant Carstairs was lying on the ground, and was shot through the head.

Meanwhile the left of No. 2 Company was not in touch with the 2nd Battalion Grenadier Guards, and the enemy was trying to creep round that flank into the gully. Fortunately Lieut.-Colonel R. Bingham with a section of the Guards Machine Gun Regiment was there, and had managed by skilful sniping to hold them back. Lord Lascelles decided to bring up No. 3 Company under Captain de Geijer to protect that flank, and ordered the two leading companies to take advantage of the delay to eat their rations.

During this delay the enemy opposite No. 2 Company, finding their southern flank had been driven in, retired off the hill, and evacuated the greater part of the village of Preux, which lay below. As soon as his flank was secure, Captain Adair sent a platoon, under Lieutenant Fairbairn, forward, and this platoon occupied the northern end of the village without resistance. In No. 4 Company Lieutenant Godman was wounded.

The enemy still held a trench in front of the

southern end of the village, but an attack launched by Lieutenant Campbell drove them out of a position, which was really untenable when the houses in their rear were held by us. They abandoned their machine-guns and their equipment.

There remained only a few detached houses at the southern end of the village, with a trench in front of them, to complete the capture of the line east of Preux, from which the following day's attack was to start. This position was approached down an open slope, and the attacking party was driven back, Lieutenant Campbell (the only officer left in No. 1 Company), Sergeant Bennett, Sergeant Stevenson, and Sergeant Valerio being wounded.

Lieutenant Campbell remained with his company, and organised a fresh attack to take place at dusk, but left the execution of it to Company Sergeant-Major Marks, who carried it out with great skill and resource. He captured the trench but not the houses, and consolidated his position.

Lord Lascelles ordered the attack on the houses to be postponed until 10 P.M., when it would be dark. This was accomplished without difficulty, and the jumping-off line for the next day's attack was completed. During the night Lieutenant F. Anson was sent to take command of No. 1 Company.

The casualties among stretcher-bearers had been particularly heavy, but Captain S. Phillimore did the work of four men in attending to the wounded and relieving the medical officer of some of his work, which owing to the shortage of stretcher-bearers was scattered all over the field.

Captain Adair and Lieutenant Campbell were afterwards specially mentioned by the Commanding Officer in his report of the operations, not only on account of the skill and courage they displayed in handling their companies, but also for their tenacity and courage in carrying on their duties for some hours after they were wounded.

On the 5th the 3rd Guards Brigade passed through, and continued the advance, while the Battalion remained behind at Preux, and was employed on salvage work.

On the 7th the Battalion was placed, at the last moment, on the left of the attack, but, owing to the state of the roads, it did not reach the line from which it was to start for the attack, until twenty minutes after the other Battalions had started. The enemy had, however, retired, and the objectives were occupied without opposition. Since the area allotted to the Battalion was in the Twenty-fourth Divisional Area, the Battalion was relieved by the 9th Battalion East Surrey Regiment, and went into support to the 2nd Guards Brigade at Audignies.

On the 8th the 2nd Guards Brigade was again ordered to continue the attack. The Battalion, being in support, moved off at 6 A.M., but was forced to halt west of Longueville, where the bridge had been demolished. After a bridge had been constructed by the Battalion the limbers were pushed across at once, and the companies crossed without difficulty. Billets in Malgarni were taken, until the news arrived that no farther move forward was likely that day, when the Battalion moved up north into Longueville. From despatches captured from the Germans it was known that a general retirement had been ordered that night, and the Brigadier asked Lord Lascelles whether his Battalion was fresh enough to attempt the capture of Maubeuge that night. He answered that it was, and the Battalion was ordered to advance along the main Maubeuge road. It was a very dark night; and a straight high road, often above the level of the surrounding fields, where the enemy might still be lurking, was not the best route to take, but as rapidity was the main point, Lord Lascelles moved the Battalion in advance-guard formation straight down the road, instructing the companies to occupy the ditches on either side of the road if attacked.

Although hampered by mine craters, the Battalion reached Maubeuge at 4 A.M., and occupied the town and citadel. It met no opposition, but three German officers and 35 men were taken prisoners. So rapid was our advance that Lieutenant Bunbury sent a platoon to capture a German field-gun still in action. This platoon got within 150 yards of the gun before it was taken away at a gallop. The only civilian Lord Lascelles was able to find above ground in Maubeuge was a priest, who told him that the enemy had all retired a few hours before the Grenadiers arrived, which confirmed the information extracted from the German despatches. The inhabitants came out in the morning, and welcomed the Battalion with the greatest enthusiasm.

On the 11th the cessation of hostilities was announced, and the Battalion attended a thanksgiving service.

CHAPTER XXXVI

THE MARCH OF THE GUARDS DIVISION INTO GERMANY, AND THE RETURN HOME

AFTER an impressive thanksgiving service at Maubeuge, the march into Germany began, and the Guards Division moved by stages to Cologne. The weather broke, and on several days the men were soaked before they reached their billets in the evening. At first the advent of the British troops was hailed with enthusiasm by the inhabitants of the towns and villages, and the people on whom the men were billeted vied with each other to make things as comfortable as possible for their visitors. Flowers were thrown at the men, speeches were made, and cheering crowds of peasants greeted the Battalions as they arrived, but as the march continued, and they reached the Flemish part of Belgium this good feeling changed to one of apathy, bordering at times on incivility. The people of this district had been untouched by the war, and regarded the mass of troops who swarmed into their houses as an intolerable affliction.

When the British troops arrived at the frontier of Germany, they supposed that the march would

CHAPTER XXXVI.

The Guards Division. 1918.

be continued through a hostile population, but so far was this from the truth, that the people of Germany cringed before the British soldier, and seemed only surprised at the considerate manner in which they were being treated. Whether the Germans expected to be as brutally treated as the Belgians had been by their own soldiers, or whether they were under the impression that their conduct would in some way affect the peace terms it is difficult to say; but the fact remains that the British troops received nothing but kindness at the hands of the inhabitants. In some of the towns that were passed through, the inhabitants did not appear to grasp the fact that they belonged to a conquered nation, and that the best they could do was to remove their hats respectfully, as the Commanding Officers rode past at the head of their Battalions, but the escorts had much pleasure in teaching them manners, by knocking off their hats and caps as they passed.

The routes taken by the four Battalions were as follows:

THE 1ST BATTALION

1st Batt.
Nov. 18. Left Maubeuge.
          To Villers Sire Nicole.
,, 19. ,, Binche.
,, 20. ,, Marchienne-au-Pont.
,, 24. ,, Châtelet.
,, 25. ,, Fosse.
,, 28. ,, Naninne.
,, 29. ,, Sur Huy.
Dec. 5. ,, Modave.
,, 6. ,, Ocquier.
,, 10. ,, Grimonster.
,, 11. ,, Lierneux.
,, 12. ,, Rodt.

THE GUARDS DIVISION   193

Dec.	13.	To	Büllingen.	CHAPTER XXXVI.
,,	14.	,,	Oberhausen.	
,,	15.	,,	Sötenich.	1st Batt.
,,	16.	,,	Schwerfen.	1918.
,,	17.	,,	Lechenich.	
,,	18.	,,	Efferen.	
,,	20.	,,	Cologne.	

THE 2ND BATTALION

Nov.	18.	Left Maubeuge.		2nd Batt.
		To Estinne-au-Mont.		
,,	19.	,,	Anderlues.	
,,	20.	,,	Montignies-sur-Sambre.	
,,	24.	,,	Bambois.	
,,	28.	,,	Assesse.	
Dec.	5.	,,	Verlée.	
,,	6.	,,	Aisne.	
,,	7.	,,	Arbrefontaine.	
,,	11.	,,	Born.	
,,	12.	,,	Mürringen.	
,,	13.	,,	Oberhausen.	
,,	15.	,,	Sinzenich.	
,,	16.	,,	Lechenich.	
,,	17.	,,	Efferen.	
,,	18.	,,	Widdersdorf.	
,,	20.	,,	Ehrenfeld (Cologne).	

THE 3RD BATTALION

Nov.	18.	Left Maubeuge.		3rd Batt.
		To Rouvcroy.		
,,	19.	,,	Mont St. Geneviève.	
,,	20.	,,	Charleroi.	
,,	24.	,,	Presles.	
,,	25.	,,	Lesves.	
,,	28.	,,	Maillen.	
Dec.	5.	,,	Havelange.	
,,	6.	,,	Barvaux.	
,,	7.	,,	Werbomont.	
,,	10.	,,	Wanne.	

194 THE GRENADIER GUARDS

Chapter XXXVI.

3rd Batt. 1918.

Dec. 12. To Deidenburg.
,, 13. ,, Nidrum.
,, 14. ,, Weywertz.
,, 15. ,, Ehrenfeld (by train).

The 4th Battalion

4th Batt.

Nov. 17. Joined Guards Division.
,, 19. To Binche.
,, 20. ,, Marchienne au Pont.
,, 24. ,, Châtelet.
,, 25. ,, Sart St. Laurent.
,, 28. ,, Dave.
,, 29. ,, Brionsart.
Dec. 5. ,, Pont de Bonne (Modave).
,, 6. ,, Houmart.
,, 10. ,, Ferrières.
,, 11. ,, Lierneux.
,, 12. ,, Blanche Fontaine.
,, 13. ,, Büllingen.
,, 14. ,, Blumenthal.
,, 15. ,, Scheven.
,, 16. ,, Kommern.
,, 17. ,, Friesheim.
,, 18. ,, Efferen.
,, 20. ,, Kriel (Cologne).

The Guards Division.

Cologne, it was feared, might be difficult to manage, for, although the country people had submissively borne the mass of British troops inflicted upon them, it seemed probable that the inhabitants of a large town like Cologne would resent the occupation. The disorderly elements might take advantage of the arrival of troops, belonging to their most hated enemy, to make a hostile demonstration, and even to shoot. But here again a surprise awaited our men, for the greater portion of the inhabitants hailed the Battalions, as the only means of escape from anarchy. The British military authorities found that the population readily submitted to the most stringent measures, that were considered necessary for the maintenance of order.

CHAPTER XXXVI.

The Guards Division. 1919.

The life at Cologne was on the whole pleasant, but after a short time monotonous. After the novelty of playing the part of conquerors in a German town had worn off, the men naturally wished to go home. The only event that is worth chronicling was the arrival of the colours of each Battalion in January. Colour parties consisting of picked officers and N.C.O.'s were despatched to London to bring them out: in the 1st Battalion Lieutenant J. A. Lloyd and Second Lieutenant M. G. Farquharson, M.C.; in the 2nd Battalion Lieutenant W. H. S. Dent, M.C., and Lieutenant L. Holbech, D.S.O., M.C.; and in the 3rd Battalion Lieutenant K. A. Campbell, D.S.O., and Second Lieutenant E. L. F. Clough-Taylor.

The 4th Battalion, having been specially raised during the war, had no colours, and was presented with a Union Colour by Major H.R.H. The Prince of Wales. The ceremony took place on the 14th of January, and in presenting the colour His Royal Highness said:

Colonel Pilcher, Officers, Warrant Officers, Non-Commissioned Officers, and Men of the 4th Battalion Grenadier Guards—The King, the Colonel-in-Chief of the Regiment, has commanded me to entrust to your safe-keeping this colour which His Majesty has presented to you in recognition of your gallantry. Less than three months after your formation you were fighting at Loos. At once you showed how completely

196　THE GRENADIER GUARDS

CHAPTER XXXVI.
The Guards Division.
1919.

you had absorbed the great traditions of the First or Grenadier Regiment of Foot Guards. You added fresh laurels to your record in the great attacks of the Guards Division in the battle of the Somme in September 1916. In the advance on Passchendaele in 1917, and later in the year at Cambrai, you still further enhanced your fighting reputation. Your historic stand in front of Hazebrouck in April last year earned your Battalion its second V.C., and was largely responsible for checking the enemy's advance. It is a special pleasure to me to hand you this colour in the hour of victory, having like yourselves the honour of serving in this our great regiment. May it be a perpetual reminder to you of the honour you have won for yourselves and for the whole regiment in this war.

Colonel Pilcher replied as follows :

Your Royal Highness—On behalf of the Officers, Warrant Officers, Non-Commissioned Officers, and Men of the 4th Battalion Grenadier Guards, I beg to thank you for the generous words you have addressed to the Battalion under my command in presenting this colour, the gift of His Majesty, the Colonel-in-Chief of the Regiment.

This gracious mark of His Majesty's recognition of the services of the Battalion during the war is most deeply appreciated by all ranks who are in Your Royal Highness's presence amongst us here to-day on enemy soil—a memorable symbol of the completeness of the victory of our arms.

In thanking Your Royal Highness for coming here to-day, may I request you to beg His Majesty the King, the Colonel-in-Chief of the Regiment, to accept the grateful and loyal thanks of the 4th Battalion Grenadier Guards.

In February orders for the Guards Division to return home were received, and one by one the

Battalions went to Dunkirk, where they embarked for England. The 2nd Battalion was the first to reach London, and its reception by the crowd, assembled to welcome the men home, was most enthusiastic.

On March 22 all the Battalions had a great ovation when they marched past the King at Buckingham Palace, and afterwards went on to the Mansion House. Though it was a bitterly cold day, thousands of people thronged the streets, and filled the windows and house-tops to cheer the men as they passed. Demobilised officers and men in plain clothes followed their battalions, and all the wounded who were able to march joined the procession, while lorries were provided for those who had lost a leg or who were too badly wounded to march. Even the blind joined in, and marched with men to guide them. The Household Cavalry came first, and were followed by the Battalions of the Guards Division, headed by Lieut.-General the Earl of Cavan and his Staff. Amongst them rode the Prince of Wales, who was greeted with the greatest enthusiasm as he passed. Major-General Feilding and his Staff also rode past, in addition to many Brigadier-Generals, who had commanded one of the Guards Brigades, while officers, who had been in command of the Battalion at any period during the war, rode alongside the officer actually in command.

Representatives of the Artillery with guns, the Engineers with pontoons, the Army Medical Corps, and Army Service Corps, who had been attached to the Guards Division in France, all took part in the procession. In the City the crowds were, if possible, denser and more enthusiastic than in the West End, and the scene at the Guildhall was a sight that no one will forget. After marching through the City the procession returned to the West End, and some battalions went to barracks, while others, not quartered in London, proceeded to the railway station.

After the march every man was handed the following message from the King, bearing a facsimile of His Majesty's signature:

BUCKINGHAM PALACE.

Officers, Non-Commissioned Officers, and Men of the Guards Division—It is with pride and satisfaction that I take the Salute of the Guards Division on this memorable occasion of their triumphal march through London, and on the same spot where Queen Victoria in July 1856 welcomed back three battalions of Guards from the Crimea.

The Guards Division, first formed in 1915, practically served in every sector in the Western Front, and my visits to the British Armies in the field gave me opportunities of seeing the battle grounds on which it has made so great and enduring a name.

The Division, which commenced its brilliant career at Loos, took a prominent part in 1916 in the hard fighting on the Somme, when on two occasions three Battalions of the same regiment were in the line together.

At the third battle of Ypres the Division responded to the call of its Commander by capturing all allotted objectives in three separate attacks.

The fighting round Cambrai, and the historical counter-attack which broke up a dangerous German thrust at Gouzeaucourt, will ever be remembered.

During the critical days of 1918 an heroic resistance

was offered to the vigorous assaults of an enemy numerically stronger and elated by success, while during our subsequent rapid advance the efforts of the Division were crowned by the capture of Maubeuge, the flag of which is carried on parade to-day, a grateful tribute from its citizens.

<small>CHAPTER XXXVI.

The Guards Division. 1919.</small>

Nor do I forget the other Arms which enabled the three Brigades of Guards for the first time in the history of the British Army to fight as a Division. The Guards Division Royal Artillery, composed of the 74th and 75th Brigades of Field Artillery; the Guards Division Royal Engineers, formed of the 55th, 75th, and 76th Field Companies; the 3rd, 4th, and 9th Field Ambulances, constituting the Guards Division Field Ambulance, and the Guards Division Train and Supply Column.

All these, inspired by the best traditions of their respective regiments and corps, fostered the invincible spirit and dogged determination of a Division which knew no defeat.

Now, after three and a half years of close co-operation in the field, through the ever-changing fortunes of war, the units of the Guards Division are about to separate.

As your Colonel-in-Chief I wish to thank you one and all for faithful and devoted services, and to bid you God-speed. May you ever retain the same mutual feelings of true comradeship which animated and ennobled the life of the Guards Division.

(Signed)   GEORGE R.I.

March 22, 1919.

CHAPTER XXXVII

THE 7TH (GUARDS) ENTRENCHING BATTALION

Chapter XXXVII.
Entrenching Battalion.
1915-18.

THE enormous amount of spade work, required for the long and intricate network of trenches, rendered some measures necessary for supplementing the work, usually done by the fighting forces; and thus entrenching battalions were formed, composed of drafts for the front, awaiting absorption in their respective units; but the system of detaching men from Battalions of Guards and sending them to fill any vacancies that might occur in one of the entrenching battalions was not at all satisfactory. In the first place, to allow men on arrival in France at once to go to an entrenching battalion, where the discipline was more lax, and the habits and customs different from those which obtained in the regiments of Guards was a measure hardly calculated to improve them as fighting men. And in the second place, it was contrary to the regulations for men of the Guards to be commanded by any but their own officers.

The idea of forming a Guards Entrenching Battalion seems to have come from certain

Brigadier-General A.F.A.N. Thorne, D.S.O.

THE ENTRENCHING BATTALION 201

officers at the base. Shortly before the arrival of the new battalions of the Guards in France, rumours were afloat that an entrenching battalion for the Guards Division was about to be formed. Captain Viscount Lascelles wrote a letter to the effect that a platoon from the reinforcements of every battalion of Guards was to be diverted to an entrenching battalion. The platoon from the 2nd Battalion Grenadiers had already been told off, and was to be commanded by an officer of the Connaught Rangers, while the Battalion itself was to be placed under a cavalry captain. Captain Viscount Lascelles deplored the fact that there was no one of sufficient seniority at the base, to combat these proposals, and thought the whole matter should be referred to the Lieutenant-Colonel rather than let it lapse, on the judgment of half a dozen ensigns at the base.

Nothing, however, appears to have been done until November, when a Guards Entrenching Battalion was formed, and Major E. C. Ellice, Grenadier Guards, was sent out to take command. He arrived at Chipilly on the Somme, about five miles from Bray, on December 1, 1915, and took over the Battalion from Major Clutterbuck, who had been temporarily in command. The Battalion consisted of 230 Grenadiers, 300 Coldstream, 250 Scots Guards, and 200 Irish Guards, with 40 tunnellers from the Royal Engineers.

Major Ellice, having made the acquaintance of his new Battalion, appointed Lieutenant Ian Bullough, Coldstream Guards, to be Adjutant, while Captain Jones, who had hitherto occupied that post, became Quartermaster. The Battalion

Chapter XXXVII.

Entrenching Battalion. 1915–18.

CHAPTER XXXVII.

Entrenching Battalion. 1915–18.

was divided up into four companies: No. 1 Company Grenadiers under Captain M. Lloyd, No. 2 Coldstream under Lieutenant Viand, No. 3 Scots Guards under Lieutenant Maitland, and No. 4 Irish Guards under Lieutenant Hanbury. The billets in which the men lived were not only uncomfortable but also extremely inconvenient, being sometimes over a mile apart, and so cramped were the men for room that pigsties even were made use of to house them: it was therefore with pleasure that Major Ellice received instructions to move the men to Wood Camp, which was no paradise, but still preferable to the pigsties, and much nearer the trenches. An old stone quarry, worked by a gang of twelve quarrymen under a Lieutenant in the Royal Engineers, provided the material for draining the camp and improving the roads. Water carts were obtained to provide sufficient water for cooking parties, and fatigue parties were sent every evening to draw water for other purposes from the Somme.

The great advantage of an entrenching battalion was quickly seen by the rest of the Army, since the battalions that came out of the front line were relieved of working during their rest. It had formerly been the custom for resting battalions to dig reserve lines, but now this duty was taken over by the entrenching battalion. All reserve trenches were made by it; emplacements for field-guns, howitzers, and machine-guns constructed, brushwood cut for revetting, roads repaired, carrying parties for all materials necessary for trench warfare supplied.

The staff of the Battalion was kept as per-

THE ENTRENCHING BATTALION 203

manent as possible, but the Battalion itself was used as a stepping-stone from the base battalion to the Battalions in the front line. The training the officers received was invaluable, as it accustomed them to shell-fire. One or two shells invariably fell near the working-parties; sometimes as many as thirty to forty shells would explode in the neighbourhood. This showed the officers that the effect was local, unless the shell happened to strike a hard surface. It gave them confidence, and they gradually became used to unaimed shell-fire.

At the end of December 1915 Captain Bullough was ordered to join his Battalion, and Captain M. K. A. Lloyd, Grenadier Guards, succeeded him as Adjutant.

In January 1916 the Entrenching Battalion was employed on the second-line trenches, and in constructing gun emplacements for the artillery. This latter duty involved technical knowledge on the part of the officers, who had to work from plans supplied to them by the gunners. About this time it was found that the Amiens—Somme Canal afforded better means of transport for rations and road-making material than the lorries, which had hitherto been used for that purpose; and it was necessary to make a light railway across some marshy ground between Bray road and the Canal. The Entrenching Battalion was employed in making 3000 fascines for this purpose, and the men became so expert at their work that there was keen competition between the various companies as to which should turn out the most fascines.

CHAPTER XXXVII.

Entrenching Battalion. 1915–18.

1916.

Chapter XXXVII.
Entrenching Battalion 1916–17.

In April 1916 preparations for the offensive operations on the Somme were begun, and the Entrenching Battalion played a great part during this battle, which lasted six months. The Guards Division was not employed in the initial stages of the battle, and it was therefore not until July that the Entrenching Battalion moved up to the vicinity of Fricourt, to take over the forward roads in the battle area. The constant shelling, combined with the heavy traffic, made it peculiarly difficult to keep the roads in sufficiently good repair for constant use, but in spite of all difficulties the roads were kept open all the time, and this was entirely due to the ability and energy of the officers and the efficiency and discipline of the men. Throughout the year the duties of the Entrenching Battalion were many and various, and at times the work was very heavy, but it was always cheerfully undertaken, because the men prided themselves on being part of the Guards Division, and knew that more than the average amount of work done by the other entrenching battalions was expected from them.

1917.

In January 1917 the Battalion was employed in strengthening the defences of Ginchy and Combles, and in the successful operations against the Germans early that year it participated in the various works, on which all arms were engaged. In April it was encamped for some months in the neighbourhood of Havrincourt Wood, and was employed in preparations for the offensive in the direction of Cambrai, which, however, did not take place till November. In June the Battalion made a farther move to Roisel, where for some months

THE ENTRENCHING BATTALION 205

it was busily employed in digging a line of trenches some nine miles long, from Epeley to within three miles of St. Quentin. The strength of the Battalion had now risen to over 2000 men. The work on these trenches was very interesting, as it was in sight of the Hindenburg line, and although works of some importance were undertaken, Major Ellice and his Entrenching Battalion were given complete charge of this area.

Although the Guards Entrenching Battalion had constantly worked in the forward areas, the other entrenching battalions had been employed mostly in rear on work which could as easily have been done by labour battalions or Chinese, and they had consequently diminished in strength. In September 1917 the attention of the military authorities was directed to these entrenching battalions, with the result that it was decided to disband them. General Feilding asked that the Guards Entrenching Battalion might be maintained, but this was not considered possible. In October the final disbandment took place.

Chapter XXXVII.

Entrenching Battalion. 1917.

CHAPTER XXXVIII

THE RESERVE BATTALION

Chapter XXXVIII.
Reserve Battalion. 1914–18.

THE Reserve Battalion, originally known as the 4th Battalion, sprang into existence at the School of Mines at the London University at Kensington as soon as war was declared in 1914. Within five days one thousand seven hundred reservists had arrived from all parts of England and Wales, and retired officers appeared on the scene, whether they belonged to the Reserve or not. This mass of men had to be converted into a disciplined Battalion, non-commissioned officers appointed, and the whole machinery of a battalion created. Yet so smoothly did the mobilisation work that within a few days every man was fully equipped, and companies were drilling in the Park, with N.C.O.'s shouting out their drill as if they had never been away.

Lieut.-Colonel G. D. White was appointed Commanding Officer, Major G. W. Duberly Second-in-Command, Captain E. N. E. M. Vaughan, Adjutant, and Lieutenant J. C. Rolinson, Quartermaster.

The whole conditions of service were now different. Instead of the usual apathy on the part of the men to learn anything new, they now eagerly seized every occasion to acquire knowledge. The Army was no longer a profession, where a man could reduce to a science the practice of doing the least possible amount of work without getting into trouble. It was now a matter of life and death. The latest developments of modern warfare had to be learnt quickly, and the men, who were already seasoned soldiers, set to work with a will to learn from officers and N.C.O.'s at first as ignorant as themselves, the new drill and the latest method of attack and defence. By the time the Reserve Battalion moved to Chelsea Barracks, about three weeks later, it had already become a serviceable body of men. A large number of N.C.O.'s and old soldiers, mostly " D " section reserve, were selected and sent as instructors to train the new battalions of " Kitchener's Army." Nearly all proved excellent instructors, and many privates rose almost at once to be sergeants and even warrant officers. In the early days of the war the National Guard and Volunteers did not exist, and consequently the duty of finding guards to protect the reservoirs, electric power stations, and other vulnerable points, devolved on the regular troops in London. The number of small guards all over London was so great that it took the field officer, whose duty it was to visit them, over five hours in a motor to go his rounds. About October 1914 the majority of these guards were taken over by the Special Home Service Units.

Soon the heavy casualties incurred by the battalions in France made the sending of large drafts necessary, and the Reserve Battalion began

CHAPTER XXXVIII.

Reserve Battalion. 1914–18.

to change completely, with new officers and new men constantly arriving from Caterham. The number of men in the Battalion became so great that there were two thousand five hundred men in barracks, and the problem of accommodation was a very difficult one. Early in 1915, Aylwin huts were erected at Burton's Court, which somewhat relieved the pressure. On the formation of the Welsh Guards in February 1915, five officers and six hundred and thirty-four other ranks were transferred to this new regiment, and in July of the same year, when it was decided to form another battalion of the Grenadier Guards from the Reserve Battalion, the latter automatically became the 5th Battalion.

The officers at that time were as follows:

In Command—
    Lieut.-Colonel G. D. White

Major—
    Du Plat Taylor, G. P.

Captains—
    Stewart, E. O.
    Ellice, E. C.
    Macdonald, G. G.
    Taylor, E. R.
    Halford, C. H.
    Webster, Sir A. F. W. E., Bart.
    Lethbridge, Sir W. P. C., Bart.
    Coventry, St, J. H.
    Glyn, A. St. L.
    Loftus, D. F.
    Vaughan, E. N. E. M.
    Lygon, Hon. R., M.V.O.

    Cary, Hon. L. P.
    Needham, Hon. F. E.

Lieutenants—
    Stewart, W. A. L.
    Harcourt-Vernon, G. C. FitzH.
    Cecil, A. W. J.
    Ward, E. S.
    Stanhope, Hon. R. P.
    Pearson-Gregory, P. J. S.
    Kenyon-Slaney, R. O. R.
    Sitwell, F. O. S.
    Williams, M.
    Graham, H. A. R.
    Duckworth-King, Sir G H. J., Bart.
    St. Aubyn, F. C.
    Mildmay, A. S. L. St. J.
    Westmacott, G. R.
    Cary, Hon. P. P.
    Parker-Jervis, T.

THE RESERVE BATTALION

Lieutenants (continued)—
  Rumbold, H. C. L.
  Eyre, J. B.
  Asquith, R.
  Walker, P. M.

Second Lieutenants—
  Llewelyn, H.
  Loftus, F. P.
  Crosland, C.
  Yorke, Hon. A. E. F.
  Charteris, Hon. I. A.
  Sloane-Stanley, G. C.
  Sloane-Stanley, H. H.
  Miller, E. E.
  Combe, T. A.
  Parker, R. W.
  Chapman, M.

North, J. B.
Farquhar, R.
Joicey-Cecil, J. F. J.
Bonham-Carter, F. G.
Manners, the Hon. F. H.
Alexander, H.
Gordon-Lennox, V. C. H.
Irvine, A. F.
Nairn, E. W.
Kendall, R. Y. T.
Worsley, J. F.
Hopley, F. J. V. B.
Benyon, J. W. A.

Adjutant—
  Hon. L. P. Cary.

Quartermaster—
  Rolinson, J.

CHAPTER XXXVIII.
Reserve Battalion.
1914–18.

In February 1916 Lieut.-Colonel G. D. White left to take up a Staff appointment in France, and was succeeded by Lieut.-Colonel G. C. Hamilton, D.S.O. From January 1916 until the end of the war, the Battalion was organised on a nine-company basis in the following manner: the first four companies were composed of recruits who were being trained to feed the Battalions at the front. No. 5 Company consisted of men employed on various duties, and the remaining four companies, six to nine, comprised sick and wounded men from France.

On May 29, 1916, Lieut.-General Sir Francis Lloyd, commanding the London Districts, inspected the Battalion, and expressed himself much pleased with its appearance on parade. General Sir George Higginson also paid a visit to the Battalion that year, and both officers and men much appreciated this attention from a veteran

Grenadier, who had fought in the Crimean War. In September a duty, somewhat out of the ordinary routine, was assigned to the Reserve Battalion. During an air raid over London, one of the German Zeppelins was brought down in flames in Essex, and the Battalion was ordered to provide a guard over what was left of it during the two following days. In December Lieut.-Colonel Hamilton was given command of the 4th Battalion in France, and was succeeded by Lieut.-Colonel Lord Francis Montagu-Douglas-Scott, D.S.O.

Nothing of interest occurred until 1918, when, owing to the large numbers of men who joined in consequence of the protected trades being brought under the Military Enlistment Act, a Provisional Battalion was formed at Tadworth. This Battalion, under the command of Lieut.-Colonel Maitland, D.S.O., proceeded to Aldershot four companies strong, leaving behind two companies under Captain Lord Forbes. A month later Lieut.-Colonel Maitland was succeeded by Lieut.-Colonel G. E. C. Rasch. Throughout the war the Reserve Battalion found the public duties in London, and on several occasions provided guards of honour, notably at the funeral of Field-Marshal Earl Roberts at St. Paul's Cathedral on November 19, 1914.

Field training was carried out by one company at a time at Basildon Park, lent by Captain J. A. Morrison, during the autumn of 1914, and at Bovingdon Green Camp, Marlow, during the summer of 1915, and after that at Tadworth Camp. In addition, there were specialist courses: bombing at Southfields and Godstone, Musketry

THE RESERVE BATTALION 211

at Rainham and Hythe, Machine Gun courses and Gas Instruction at Chelsea.

The arduous and somewhat thankless task of continually training men as quickly as possible, to feed the battalions in France, was successfully carried on during the four years of the war, and letters from the four Commanding Officers bear ample testimony to the efficiency of the Battalion organisation. The greater part of the work fell on the Commanding Officer, Adjutant, and the senior Captains, whose untiring efforts will ever be gratefully remembered by the regiment. Day in and day out, during four long years, these officers strived to maintain with each draft the high standard of the regiment, and this result could not have been effected without the invaluable assistance of the warrant officers and sergeants.

CHAPTER XXXVIII.

Reserve Battalion. 1914–18.

CHAPTER XXXIX

THE BAND

<small>Chapter XXXIX.
The Band.
1914–18.</small>
In the first year of the war it does not appear to have occurred to any one that the Battalions at the front would wish to have a band, but when the Guards Division was formed in 1915 the lack of music was much felt, and it was decided that the regimental bands of the five Guards Regiments should be sent out in turn. The Grenadier Guards Band was naturally sent out for the first tour of duty at the front, and was therefore fortunate enough to earn the distinction of being the only band that received the 1914–1915 Star. It embarked on October 22, with Captain A. Williams in command, and proceeded to France. While in mid-Channel, the ship on which it crossed over collided with a four-masted Norwegian vessel, and sank her. A thorough search was made in the darkness for any survivors, and eventually nine of the Norwegian crew were picked up. The British ship itself was badly damaged, and for some hours there was great uncertainty whether it would ever reach port, but it eventually arrived at Havre some six hours overdue.

THE BAND

On arrival the band at once proceeded to Harfleur, which it reached in time to play the National Anthem, when the King, on one of his periodical visits, inspected the Guards depot. Later it moved up to Sailly-la-Bourse, and was warmly welcomed by all ranks of the Guards Division. Captain Williams at once set to work to organise concerts, and to make arrangements to play at each Battalion Headquarters. Two and even three performances were given daily, and visits were paid to the troops in rest billets and in the clearing stations. The people of Paris, anxious to take advantage of the presence of this famous band in France, invited Captain Williams to give a concert at the Hippodrome in aid of the French Red Cross. This proved to be a remarkably successful performance, and a sum of no less than £650 was raised. In January 1916 the band was relieved by the Coldstream band, and returned to London.

A second tour of duty in France was undertaken in 1917, when the Guards Division was on the Somme, and three months were spent at Mericourt l'Abbé.

A third visit to the front took place in August 1918, just at the time when the German last effort had spent itself, and the Allied Armies were making a general advance. On the night of August 21, when the Guards Division was commencing its advance, the Germans bombed the whole area in which it was throughout the entire night. Among the many casualties were three Grenadier bandsmen, and although none of their wounds proved fatal, the solo clarinettist, a very fine musician, lost his arm, and thereby his livelihood.

In July 1918 the band attended the French Fêtes in Paris, and remained there for the celebration of the Belgian Independence. This function took place in the grounds at Versailles, and was attended by the principal bands of Great Britain, France, America, and Belgium. On another occasion in August 1918 the band played in the Tuileries Gardens in Paris in aid of the American Red Cross Society.

CHAPTER XL

REGIMENTAL FUNDS AND ASSOCIATIONS

"Grenadiers look after themselves" has become an accepted axiom not only in war but also in peace time. A short time before the commencement of the war the Old Comrades Association was instituted under the auspices of Colonel Scott Kerr, who commanded the Regiment at that time, and its object was to ensure that no Grenadier after he had left the Regiment was ever in want. This Association proved a great success, and although two years' service was a necessary qualification for membership, the officers, non-commissioned officers, and men who joined soon rose to a considerable number.

Another tradition in the Regiment was that those who remained behind should look after those who went to fight. In the South African war especially the custom of sending out comforts to the Battalions in the field was brought to a pitch of perfection, and during the two years that campaign lasted the 2nd and 3rd Battalions were well provided for. When the war broke out in 1914, the first care of the regimental authorities was to see that the men in the Expeditionary Force wanted for nothing, and also that

CHAPTER XL.

Regimental Funds and Associations.

their families were adequately provided for. Colonel Gordon-Gilmour, who was temporarily in command of the Regiment in August 1914, came to the conclusion that the mass of routine work was as much as the Regimental Orderly Room could cope with, and that if a Comforts Fund was to be a success, it would be necessary to invoke the aid of an old officer. He therefore asked Major-General Sir Reginald Thynne (an old Commanding Officer of the 3rd Battalion) to undertake the arduous task. At that time all existing organisations were being strained to their utmost to cope with the vast numbers of men who were flocking to the army.

As soon as Sir Reginald Thynne grasped the immensity of the task he had undertaken, he sent round an appeal to all officers past and present, and raised a substantial sum for the initial expenses. Two funds were started: the Comforts Fund and the Families Relief Fund. The former was entirely for men at the front, and was managed by Sir Reginald Thynne himself. The latter was under the direction of Sir Reginald Thynne as Treasurer and Colonel C. Rowley as Secretary until November 1915, when Lieut.-Colonel Viscount Colville became Treasurer and Mrs. Stucley, Secretary. In September 1914 a small Committee, consisting of the wives of officers and presided over by Lady Florence Streatfeild, was formed, and the whole organisation was put on a thoroughly business-like footing, but the number of men who joined the Regiment increased with such rapidity that it was found necessary to enlarge the Committee.

FUNDS AND ASSOCIATIONS 217

The following ladies eventually formed the Committee :

Lady Ardee, the Hon. Mrs. Wilfred Smith, Mrs. Fisher-Rowe, the Hon. Mrs. Corry (who resigned later on account of illness), the Hon. Mrs. Dalrymple-White, the Hon. Mrs. Earle (who resigned later and went to Switzerland to join her husband), Mrs. Montgomerie, the Hon. Mrs. G. Legh, Mrs. Ricardo, Viscountess St. Cyres, Lady Helen Seymour, Mrs. Barrington-Kennett, Mrs. St. Leger Glyn, and Mrs. Stucley.

When the Committee first started it was decided to look after families only on the married roll, leaving the others to be dealt with by the Soldiers' and Sailors' Families Association, to which the Regiment sent a subscription of £100; but it was found that families were so well provided for by Separation Allowances, that it was only in special cases that assistance was needed. The Committee, therefore, undertook to assist special cases, whether they were married people on the strength or not. The ladies of the Committee kept in constant touch with each family either by correspondence or by personal visit, and by degrees they were able to ensure that every case was looked after.

When the cold weather arrived, the needs of the men at the front became of paramount importance, and the wives of officers, non-commissioned officers, and men set to work to make warm mittens and hand-made socks, the wool being provided to a great extent by the Comforts Fund.

Owing to certain officers contributing large

CHAPTER XL.

Regimental Funds and Associations.

CHAPTER XL.

Regimental Funds and Associations.

sums to the Comforts Fund, which had already been generously supported by the officers, Sir Reginald Thynne was able to send, in addition to what are called comforts, newspapers, tobacco, and cigarettes every fortnight, as well as footballs, boxing-gloves, and other things that the men love. Colonel Streatfeild also decided to supplement the appliances supplied by the War Office, and sanctioned the supply by the fund of such articles as trench periscopes, telephones, and bicycles for orderlies. Later, gramophones were provided, and when Christmas came Sir Reginald Thynne was able to send a plum-pudding to each man at the front. This necessitated 2000 plum-puddings being sent in 1914, and 4000 in 1915 and 1916, in addition to a certain number to the Grenadiers on the Brigade and Divisional Staffs. During the last two years of the war, the supply of plum-puddings for all the Expeditionary Forces was undertaken by the Director-General of Voluntary Organisations.

PRISONERS OF WAR FUND

Early in the war the problem of how to deal with the Prisoners of War had to be faced, and Sir Reginald Thynne, having organised the Comforts Fund, now turned his attention to this at the request of Colonel Streatfeild. The Grenadiers were fortunate in having far fewer prisoners than other regiments, but the fact that there were men of the Regiment at the mercy of a country, which had proved itself capable of the most dastardly cruelty, was enough to warrant

FUNDS AND ASSOCIATIONS 219

energetic steps being taken at once to ensure that the men in Germany should not starve.

Major-General Sir Reginald Thynne set to work to devise some organisation by which parcels of food would reach the prisoners regularly, and a Prisoners of War Fund, to which many old officers of the Regiment contributed, was started, and in the initial stages was partly financed by the Comforts Fund.

In the first place it was decided to send all men in Germany a good parcel of food and some tobacco every fortnight, but this was not enough, and a system was started by which many prisoners of war of the Regiment were "adopted" by a lady belonging to the Regiment, a wife, a mother, or a sister of an officer. The adopter was asked to undertake the despatch of a parcel once a fortnight, so that with the parcels from the Fund each prisoner received weekly a sufficient supply of food. This worked admirably, but the labour involved was necessarily heavy, since the men were constantly moved from one place to another.

By an arrangement with the American Embassy in Berlin a complete refit of outer and under clothing was sent to each prisoner by Colonel Streatfeild, but these were not provided by the Prisoners of War Fund.

This method of supplying food to the prisoners in Germany was not altogether satisfactory. In the first place, men in good regiments were much better looked after than those who belonged to regiments where there was no organisation for the care of prisoners; and in the second place,

Chapter XL.

Regimental Funds and Associations.

it was open to abuse. Some men, for instance, wrote to various people in England and obtained by this means more parcels than they could possibly want. One prisoner managed by diligent writing to obtain as many as fifty parcels. The difficulty of getting food into Germany increased as the war went on, and it was soon found that the whole problem had become too big for voluntary effort. Accordingly in October 1916 a Central Prisoners of War Committee was formed under the auspices of the Government, and the supply of regular food was officially taken in hand with the aid of the American Embassy in Berlin. This did not entail the abolition of the various regimental funds, but it ensured every prisoner being provided with an adequate amount of food. After this the packets of food were sent with a Red Cross label, provided by the authorities, and no parcel could be sent, unless it had been packed by the Central Committee, or under their authority, as they were responsible that the parcels contained nothing that contravened the regulations. No prisoner was allowed to receive parcels from more than one authorised organisation.

The following memorandum was issued for the guidance of the prisoners' relations and friends:

SYSTEM OF SENDING PARCELS TO GRENADIER PRISONERS OF WAR IN GERMANY

1. No parcels either of food, tobacco, tea, or clothing can now be sent by private individuals to these prisoners, nor should monetary assistance be given to any agency

FUNDS AND ASSOCIATIONS 221

except our own. Books can be sent to them only through authorised publishers, such as Mudie's, W. H. Smith, and Bumpus. Gramophones, boxing-gloves, and a few other such articles can sometimes be sent by special request through the Central Prisoners of War Committee, 4 Thurloe Place, S.W.7.

Chapter XL.

Regimental Funds and Associations.

We cannot accept parcels from individuals to be forwarded to prisoners, but only subscriptions to our funds.

2. Details of parcels are as follows :

(1) Assorted food parcels (weight under 11 lbs. gross) are sent three times per fortnight to each prisoner at the cost of £6 : 15s. per man per quarter, or £2 : 5s. per parcel per quarter. Each parcel contains 1 cake of soap, and frequently other necessaries applied for by the men.

(2) 1 lb. of tea (in a separate parcel) is sent out per month to each man, costing 1s. 8d. per month, duty free.

(3) 250 cigarettes or ½ lb. of tobacco, as preferred, is sent to each man (in a separate parcel) costing 3s. 8d. per month, duty free.

(4) A separate supply of bread or biscuits, according to season, is sent to the Camps by the Central Prisoners of War Committee, and each man should receive 4 lbs. per week. In future we shall have to pay for this, and it will cost us 8s. per man per month (based on 7s. 6d. per four weeks).

(5) A complete outfit of clothing is sent out to each man twice yearly.

3. We classify our subscribers as follows :

(a) *Adopters*, who subscribe for parcels to specified and named men, paying £2 : 5s. per quarter for each fortnightly parcel. In some cases an adopter pays £4 : 10s. for two, or £6 : 15s. for three fortnightly parcels all sent to the same man; in other cases an adopter takes over two men or three men, or more, and pays

Chapter XL.
Regimental Funds and Associations.

for one or more fortnightly parcels each. The names of the senders cannot, owing to shortage of labour, be written on parcels, and the subscriber writes to the prisoner to let him know what is being done for him.

(*b*) *Friends or relations*, who subscribe monthly, or occasionally, for the tea, tobacco, or bread, at the prices above quoted, or pay 7s. occasionally when they wish to provide for one of the regular parcels.

(*c*) *Givers of donations*, of various amounts to be used as we think best.

N.B.—It is possible for relations of prisoners by applying to the Regimental Orderly Room to get allotments made to them out of the prisoner's pay, in order to enable them to subscribe to us. This can only be done when a prisoner writes to say he wishes it, and defines the amount of the allotment.

These instructions were altered several times, and new rules and conditions were added. Soon after the official system came into force, there was an unfortunate hitch about the bread. The Central Prisoners of War Committee, which had undertaken the supply, found that the arrangements they had made for its manufacture and despatch from Copenhagen were anything but satisfactory; complaints from the prisoners showed that the system was not working well. Steps were at once taken by the Central Prisoners of War Committee to rectify the fault, and afterwards the supply was carried out satisfactorily from Copenhagen and Berne.

One prisoner, who wished to inform his friends of the true state of affairs, and who feared his remarks would not pass the Censor, wrote on a postcard, " 1 Corinthians iv. 11." The German Censor's biblical knowledge was fortunately weak,

FUNDS AND ASSOCIATIONS 223

and he allowed the card to go. The text referred to was:

Even unto this present hour we both hunger, and thirst, and are naked, and are buffeted, and have no certain dwelling-place.

Early in 1917 the relatives of the men in Germany began to hear more frequently from them, and to learn how badly some of them were being treated. Thus a considerable correspondence grew up with these anxious people, as well as with the prisoners themselves, and General Thynne had to ask the Lieutenant-Colonel to give him some help. Lieutenant Bernard Samuelson, who was at that time incapacitated for active service by wounds, therefore joined in the work; in July of that year, General Thynne requiring a short holiday, Lieutenant A. O. Whitehead (also wounded) helped; and when General Thynne returned, and Lieutenant Samuelson, who had rendered most able assistance, had rejoined for active duty, Lieutenant Whitehead continued to work with General Thynne. Being a business man with more than common capacity and experience, Mr. Whitehead's assistance and powers of organisation were invaluable, for the clerical work and correspondence had become considerable, and he devoted himself to the work with the greatest zeal and interest.

In the autumn of 1917 it became very difficult to procure the necessary supplies of provisions; in fact, some essential articles were absolutely unobtainable. It was, therefore, decided to ask

Chapter XL.

Regimental Funds and Associations.

CHAPTER XL.

Regimental Funds and Associations.

the Central Prisoners of War Committee to pack and despatch the parcels, which they were able to do, as they had very large contracts for supplies; and this they continued to do with most satisfactory results until the cessation of hostilities, November 11, 1918.

During 1918 the number of prisoners greatly increased, principally because the 4th Battalion had been surrounded by the enemy, when under orders to hold the position at all costs near Merville, and, whilst losing heavily in casualties, had had over 250 men captured. The other Battalions lost some men captured during the fighting in August and September, thus bringing the total up to 475, including 27 men interned in Holland, and 6 in Switzerland, besides several badly wounded men repatriated, 3 who died in captivity, and 2 who escaped.

HOSPITAL VISITING COMMITTEE

President—Colonel Sir HENRY STREATFEILD, K.C.V.O., C.B., C.M.G.

Secretary—Mrs. H. ST. L. STUCLEY.

Assisted by the ladies of the Regiment.

The members of this Committee visited the sick and wounded men of the Regiment in hospitals in the London district every week, taking them cigarettes, books, and other comforts. The good work done by this Committee cannot be too highly valued. The patients appreciated the kindly sympathy of the Regiment conveyed by the ladies, and looked forward to the weekly visit.

826 men were visited in the London hospitals, and the work of the Committee was extended to provincial hospitals when visitors were available.

FUNDS AND ASSOCIATIONS

SERGEANTS PAST AND PRESENT CLUB

President—Mr. J. HINGLEY.

Hon. Treasurer—Mr. A. HASKELL.

Hon. Secretary—Supt. Clerk W. FAWCETT, M.B.E.

CHAPTER XL.

Regimental Funds and Associations.

The Club has been inactive during the war, but was revived on the return of the Battalions from France. Many old members maintained their connection with the Club, and the total number of members is now 230.

OLD COMRADES ASSOCIATION

President—Lieut.-Col. Lord F. G. MONTAGU-DOUGLAS-SCOTT, D.S.O.

Hon. Treasurer and Secretary—Lieut.-Col. W. GARTON, O.B.E., 87 Merton Hall Road, Wimbledon, S.W.19.

This Association numbered 4000 members. All Old Comrades who required help were assisted from Regimental Funds, in the manner most suitable to the needs of the applicants. The annual meeting of the Association was held at Chelsea Barracks on March 29, 1919.

H.R.H. the Prince of Wales was present, and a large number of members attended.

A Dinner was given at the close of the meeting by the Officer Commanding 5th (Reserve) Battalion.

RELIEF AND CHARITABLE WORK CARRIED OUT AT REGIMENTAL HEADQUARTERS

Discharged Men

A letter was sent to all discharged men, offering assistance and giving information regarding the Guards Employment Society.

Discharged men were encouraged to communicate with Regimental Headquarters in all their troubles, and help was always given in one form or another.

Chapter XL.

Regimental Funds and Associations.

Many letters and applications were received, and all were sympathetically replied to and assisted where necessary.

Memorial Fund

This Fund was founded in 1915 by sums of money given by relatives to perpetuate the memory of Officers who have been killed in action or died of wounds.

Various sums have been given to this Fund by relatives of deceased Officers, and, in addition, the late Major-General Hon. W. S. D. Home and Captain T. F. J. N. Thorne each bequeathed £1000 to the Fund. A total of £18,000 was invested in addition to the sum of £2100 placed at the disposal of the Lieut.-Colonel, the interest of which was paid to this Fund.

All money received was invested, and only the interest is used in relieving distress amongst the widows, wives, and children, and assisting discharged N.C.O.'s and men.

Roehampton Hospital Beds Endowment

An appeal was made in 1916 to Officers, past and present, to enable Grenadier Guards Beds to be endowed in Queen Mary's Convalescent Auxiliary Hospital, Roehampton, where limbless men receive special treatment, are fitted with artificial limbs, and taught how to use them.

A sum sufficient to endow eight beds for two years was obtained, and sufficient donations have been received since to enable the Lieut.-Colonel to renew the endowment of two beds for four years.

Star and Garter Hospital

In June 1918, a room at the Star and Garter Hospital at Richmond was endowed by G. H. Windeler, Esq., the father of the late Second Lieutenant H. W. Windeler, the necessary funds having been subscribed by the Boston friends of that officer and of the late Second

Lieutenant Hartley, Coldstream Guards, and Mr. Farnsworth, French Foreign Legion. The room was named after these officers. Nomination to the occupation of the room was in the hands of the Officers Commanding Grenadier Guards and Coldstream Guards, the right to nominate to run alternately, commencing with the Grenadier Guards.

CHAPTER XL.

Regimental Funds and Associations.

Holiday Homes

By the generosity of an Officer of the Regiment and his wife, a number of the wives and children of warrant and non-commissioned officers and men were sent to the seaside for a holiday every year. These holidays began first in 1918, and have been greatly appreciated.

APPENDIX I

THE CASUALTIES IN THE GUARDS DIVISION

	Officers.		Other Ranks.	
	Killed.	Wounded.	Killed.	Wounded.
Grenadier Guards	203	242	4,508	6,939
Coldstream Guards	168	328	3,510	9,061
Scots Guards	107	149	2,072	4,002
Irish Guards	115	199	2,234	5,540
Welsh Guards	34	55	822	1,700
Guards M.G. Regiment	21	47	187	2,090
Total	648	1,020	13,333	29,332

APPENDIX II

THE TITLE "GRENADIERS"

During 1915 the whole Regiment was much perturbed by the official use of the word "grenadier" as applied to men in all regiments who were being trained to throw bombs. This expression began to creep into official documents in April, and about this time a memorandum was published by General Headquarters on the training and employment of "grenadiers." In June the Army Council addressed a circular letter to officers commanding battalions, by which authority was given for the training of a detachment in each battalion, consisting of one officer, two sergeants, and 56 other ranks, as "grenadiers." Badges for "regimental and battalion grenadiers" were described in some additional paragraphs to the Dress Regulations, which were issued in Army Orders in October.

Eventually Colonel H. Streatfeild decided to take up the matter officially, and on November 29 sent the following letter to Major-General Lord Cavan, commanding the Guards Division:

"I respectfully beg to bring to your notice, and to strongly protest against, what I consider is an usurpation of the rights and privileges of the Regiment under my command, by the establishment of 'GRENADIERS' to all battalions of the Army by Army Order of the 11th October 1915, and would venture to suggest that the name of 'GRENADIERS' given to Regimental Bomb Throwers be altered to 'BOMBERS.'

THE TITLE "GRENADIERS" 231

"In the *London Gazette* of 29th July 1815 the First Regiment of Foot Guards had bestowed upon it the title of 'First or Grenadier Regiment of Foot Guards' in commemoration of their having defeated the Grenadiers of the French Imperial Guard at the Battle of Waterloo.

"This distinction the Regiment has proudly borne for the past 100 years, and it is a source of regret to all ranks that at this period, when there are four battalions of the Regiment upon Active Service, this title, which was granted exclusively to the Grenadier Guards as a reward for services in the Field, should in any way be invalidated."

On receipt of Colonel Streatfeild's protest, Lord Cavan wrote to General Headquarters:

"I beg with great deference to raise a question of privilege. The word and title Grenadier is now seen in all official documents to denote a man who throws a bomb. This title was given to the First Guards for service rendered at Waterloo, and they are naturally jealous of the honour.

"In conversation the word bomber is general, but if this is not sufficiently dignified for official documents I most respectfully suggest that 'bomb thrower' be the recognised title."

To this the Adjutant-General at General Headquarters in France sent the following reply:

"The term bomb is officially confined to projectiles fired from trench mortars or dropped from aeroplanes. Projectiles thrown by hand are 'grenades.'

"The G.O.C. Guards Division is in error in supposing that the Grenadier Guards are the only Regiment in which the word grenadier forms part of the title of the Regiment.

"It would appear that the term Grenadiers is merely an unofficial abbreviation of Grenadier Guards, and

Appendix II.

does not appear in any official documents in relation to that Regiment.

"The Grenade fired proper is the badge of many Regiments, and it would seem that a claim to the sole use of the title 'Grenadier' has as little foundation as one to be the only wearers of the Grenade badge.

"It would seem that Modern Warfare has necessitated a partial return to the Grenadier Companies of former days which it is believed existed without any prejudice to the rights of the Grenadier Guards."

Lord Cavan, however, could not let the matter rest there, and again wrote to the Adjutant-General on December 22, meeting the arguments put forward by him. He said:

"I beg respectfully to reply to the remarks of the A.G.

"In Para. 2. He says the G.O.C. Guards Division is in error in supposing that the Grenadier Guards are the only Regiment in which the word 'grenadier' forms part of the title of the Regiment. The G.O.C. Guards Division never made this supposition, and is perfectly aware that the Indian Army contains the 101st Grenadier and the 102nd King Edward's Own Grenadiers, and there are also some Colonial Grenadiers, but he is not aware that any British Regiment has the word grenadier as part of its title except the First Guards.

"Reference Para. 4. No claim to be the only wearers of a Grenade Badge was made, but the title Grenadiers was officially given in the *London Gazette* of July 1815 to the First Guards in commemoration of their having defeated the Grenadiers of the Imperial Guard at Waterloo.

"The title of Grenadier Company is of course of ancient origin and was almost universal. If resuscitated it would be welcome and would solve the problem; if a report stated that 'the Grenadier Company of the —— Battalion then attacked' no objection would be

THE TITLE "GRENADIERS" 233

raised, but if the report was worded 'the Grenadiers then advanced,' I consider it not only an infringement of privileges but misleading to future historians.

"Had the weapon been the carbine or carabine or the Fusil the same confusion would have arisen with the Carabineers or Fusiliers.

"It is in no carping spirit that this letter is written, but I most respectfully beg to emphasise my point that the title 'Grenadiers' was a battle honour given to the First Guards and as such should be respected."

Finding it impossible to get any redress in France, Colonel Streatfeild in January 1916 appealed to the King, as Colonel-in-Chief of the Regiment, and His Majesty promised to look into the question. Nothing was done till March, and then at last, in deference to the King's expressed wish, the Army Council decided that in future the word "Bomber" should be used instead of "Grenadier." The decision was embodied in the following Order:

WAR OFFICE,
28th March 1916.

673. BOMBERS.

The term "Grenadier" will no longer be applied to men trained or employed in the use of hand grenades. Such men will in future be designated "Bombers."

121/7862 (A.G. 1).

By Command of the Army Council,

(Signed)   R. H. BRADE.

APPENDIX III

OFFICERS KILLED IN ACTION OR DIED OF WOUNDS

Batt.	BRIGADIER-GENERAL	Date.
	Nugent, G. C., M.V.O.	31/5/15

LIEUTENANT-COLONELS

Batt.		Date.
	Clive, P. A. (wounded 6/8/15 and 3/11/16) (attached Lancs. Fus.)	5/4/18
1	Fisher-Rowe, L. R.	13/3/15
1	Hope, G. E., M.C. (Actg. Lieut.-Col., attached Lancs. Fusiliers) (wounded 4/11/14)	10/10/17
2	Smith, W. R. A., C.M.G.	18/5/15
	Trotter, E. H., D.S.O. (attached Liverpool Regiment)	8/7/15

MAJORS

Batt.		Date.
2	Barrington-Kennett, B. H.	18/5/15
1	Colby, L. R. V.	25/10/14
	Crichton, H. F. (Irish Guards)	1/9/14
1	Duberly, G. W.	13/3/15
2	Gordon-Lennox, Lord B. C.	13/11/14
3	Molyneux-Montgomerie, G. F.	22/10/15
1	Nicol, W. E., D.S.O. (wounded 29/5/15)	1/10/15

KILLED OR DIED OF WOUNDS

Batt.		Date.
4	Ponsonby, Hon. C. M. B., M.V.O. (wounded 29/10/14)	27/9/15
	Quilter, J. A. C. (M.E.F., Comdg. Hood Batt. Naval Brigade)	7/5/15
1	Stucley, H. St. L.	29/10/14
1	Weld-Forester, Hon. A. O. W. C., M.V.O. (wounded 29/10/14)	1/11/14

CAPTAINS

1	Baker, C. D. (wounded 25/1/16)	29/7/17
2	Beaumont-Nesbitt, W. H., M.C. (wounded 25/9/16)	27/11/17
	Blackett, W. S. B. (attached Leicester Yeo.) (wounded 18/11/14)	25/11/14
4	Burke, J. B. M., M.C. (wounded 6/8/17)	1/12/17
2	Carter, J. S.	27/9/18
2	Cecil, Hon. W. A.	16/9/14
4	Chapman, M., M.C. (wounded 6/7/16 and 25/11/17)	12/4/18
2	Cholmeley, Sir M., R. A., Bart.	24/12/14
2	Cunninghame, A. K. S. (slightly wounded 9/7/16)	25/9/16
1	Douglas-Pennant, Hon. G. S.	11/3/15
2	Derriman, G. L. (wounded 20/7/15)	9/8/15
1	Drury-Lowe, W. D., D.S.O.	25/9/16
4	Filmer, Sir R. M., Bart. (wounded 24/1/16)	26/1/16
1/4	Goschen, C. G. (wounded 23/7/15 and 11/9/16)	25/9/16
2	Gosselin, A. B. R. R., D.S.O. (wounded 14/9/14)	7/2/15
1	Graham, A. C.	10-12/9/16

APPENDIX III.

APPENDIX III.

Batt.		Date.
3	Gunnis, G. G., M.C. (wounded 14-17/9/16)	13/10/16
4	Houstoun-Boswall, Sir G. R., Bart. (missing 27/9/15), assumed to have died	27/9/15
2	Lloyd, M. K. A. (wounded about 24/10/14)	15/9/16
2	MacDougall, I. (missing 1/9/14)	1/9/14
3	Mackenzie, A. K. (wounded 14/9/14)	16/9/16
1	Malcolm, P. (wounded 27/9/15 and 16/4/17)	25/8/18
	Maxwell, A. E. (wounded 8/10/14) (attached Naval Brigade)	9/10/14
3	Murray, W. R. C. (wounded 27/9/15)	25/2/17
3	Parker, R. W. (wounded 26/7/17 and 27/3/18)	28/3/18
4	Paton, G. H. T., V.C.	1/12/17
2	Payne-Gallwey, Sir W. T., Bart., M.V.O., assumed to have died on or since	14/9/14
4	Penn, E. F.	18/10/15
4	Pixley, J. N. F.	12/10/17
1	Rennie, G.	29/10/14
1	Sartorius, E. F. F. (wounded 11/3/15)	5/4/15
1	Shelley, E. B. (wounded 10-12/9/16)	12/9/18
4	Sloane-Stanley, H. H., M.C.	13/4/18
3	Stanhope, Hon. R. P. (missing 14-17/9/16)	16/9/16
2	Stephen, D. C. L.	8/9/14
4	Stewart, W. A. L. (wounded 14/9/14)	25/9/16
2	Symes-Thompson, C.	18/11/14

KILLED OR DIED OF WOUNDS

Batt.		Date.	
4	Thorne, T. F. J. N.	27/9/15	APPENDIX
1	Wellesley, Lord R.	27/10/14	III.

LIEUTENANTS

Batt.		Date.
4	Abbey, N. R.	12/4/18
3	Anson, A.	11/10/15
1	Antrobus, E.	24/10/14
3	Asquith, R.	15/9/16
1	Bibby, J. P.	12/10/17
1	Brabourne, W. W., Lord	11/3/15
4	Boyton, H. J.	14/12/16
1	Byng, L. G., M.C.	24/8/18
1	Chamberlain, N. G.	1/12/17
4	Chitty, J. M. (on or since)	1/12/17
2	Congleton, H. B. F., Lord	10/11/14
1	Corry, A. V. L., M.C. (wounded 10/8/15)	10-12/9/16
M.G.C.	Cottle, W. E. W.	31/7/17
3	Crabbe, C. T. E.	27/9/15
1	Darby, M. A. A.	11/3/15
1	Dashwood, W. J. (wounded 21/9/16)	2/8/17
2	Des Vœux, F. W.	14/9/14
1	Douglas-Pennant, Hon. A. G. S.	29/10/14
3	Dunlop, B. J.	31/7/17
4	Ellice, A. R. (wounded 25/9/16)	29/9/16
1	Ethelston, H. W.	13/3/15
4	Farquhar, R.	17/9/17
M.G.C.	Fraser, J. C. (missing, believed drowned)	9/9/18
3	Gardner, C. G. (missing 14-17/9/16)	14-17/9/16
1	Gascoigne, I. C. (wounded 6/4/18)	12/4/18
2	Gwyer, C.	27/8/18

Batt.		Date
2	Harter, H. H.	9/10/17
2	Harvard, K. O'G.	1/8/17
M.G.C.	Higginson, T. C.	15/9/16
1	Hughes, G.	5/8/18
1	Johnson, H. J. G.	7/8/17
4	Joicey-Cecil, J. F. J.	25/9/16
	Keating, H. S. (attached Irish Guards)	20/1/15
2	Knatchbull-Hugessen, M.A., M.C.	25/9/16
2	Lawrence, G. F.	27/8/18
2	Lawson-Johnston, A. Mc.W., M.C.	22/2/17
1	Leeke, C. (wounded 7/4/16)	12/4/16
2	Lubbock, Hon. H. F. P.	4/4/18
4	Lyon, F. C., on or since	13/4/18
4	MacLear, B. G. H., M.C.	26/7/16
2	Manners, Hon. J. N.	1/9/14
2	Marshall, F. G.	22/3/15
	Maurice, F. T.	29/10/18
2	Miller, F. W. J. M.	23/10/14
1	Morris, A. A.	27/9/18
2	Napier, R. G. C. (wounded 31/7/17)	2/8/17
2	Oliver, R. M. (wounded 26/8/18)	27/8/18
3	Orris, W. G. (wounded 9/2/17 and 28/3/18)	29/3/18
2	Parnell, Hon. W. A. D., M.C.	25/9/16
3	Pauling, G. F., M.C. (wounded 30/7/17)	25/3/18
4	Payne-Gallwey, M. H. F.	25/9/16
2	Ponsonby, M. H. (wounded 29/1/18)	27/8/18
4	Pryce, T. T., V.C., M.C. (Actg. Capt.)	13/4/18
	Radcliffe, D. J. J. (attached Corps School)	31/10/17

KILLED OR DIED OF WOUNDS

Batt.		Date.
4	Rolfe, R. H. (wounded 24/7/17 and 25/3/18)	22/4/18
3	Stainton, W. A. (missing 14-17/9/16)	15/9/16
2	Stocks, M. G.	10/11/14
4	Stratford, H. D. (wounded 9/10/17)	13/4/18
4	Tennant, Hon. E. W.	22/9/16
3	Tetley, J. C. D.	9/10/17
M.G.C.	Thomas, O. C. (wounded 14/9/17)	1/12/17
4	Tompson, R. F. C.	11/9/16
2	Tudway, H. R. C. (wounded 11-13/11/14)	18/11/14
2	Tufnell, C. W.	6/11/14
1	Van Neck, P.	26/10/14
M.G.C.	Vernon, H. D.	15/9/16
2	Welby, R. W. G.	16/9/14
2	Williams, E. G.	12/8/15
3	Worsley, J. F. (wounded 31/7/17), on or since	27/11/17
3	Wynne, E. H. J.	16/9/16

SECOND LIEUTENANTS

	Adams, C. J. N.	14/11/18
1	Alexander, H.	17/10/15
1	Anderson, A. D.	6/11/18
2	Arbuthnot, G. A.	25/9/16
2	Arbuthnott, J. (wounded 15/9/16)	16/9/16
	Ayles, F. P.	1/6/18
2	Bailey, Hon. G. S.	10/8/15
1	Barber, G. E.	24/8/18
M.G.C.	Bentley, F. D.	30/11/17
2	Blackwood, Lord I. B. G. T.	3/7/17
1	Burnand, C. F.	11/3/15

APPENDIX III.

APPENDIX III.

Batt.		Date.
2	Burton, J. S.	16/5/16
	Bury, H. S. E. (attached Scots Guards)	28/1/15
1	Carson, R. H.	4/9/17
2	Cecil, G. E.	1/9/14
1	Chapple, J. W.	31/7/17
1	Charteris, Hon. I. A.	17/10/15
1	Cholmeley, H. V.	7/4/16
2	Corkran, R. S. (wounded 7/6/15)	11/6/15
4	Constable, D. O.	25/9/16
2	Creed, C. O. (wounded 18/5/15)	2/6/15
1	Crisp, F. E. F.	5/1/15
4	Dawson-Greene, C. J.	25/3/18
4	Denman, R. C.	1/12/17
1	Dudley-Smith, C. J.	16/6/15
3	Durbin, P.	25/3/17
2	Finch, H. A.	27/8/18
1	Fleet, W. A. (wounded 5/9/17)	18/5/18
	Fletcher, G. H. (attached Scots Guards)	25/1/15
4	Flower, A. C.	25/9/16
1	Foster, A. C.	11/3/15
4	Gault, R. A.	16/9/16
1	Gelderd-Somervell, R. F. C. (wounded 11/3/15)	11/3/15
1	Grant, A.	27/9/18
3	Greenhill, F. W. R.	10/10/17
3	Gunther, G. R., M.C.	4/11/18
1	Hall-Watt, R.	13/10/17
1	Hamilton, G. E. A. A. FitzG.	18/5/18
2	Harbord, P. A., M.C.	1/12/17
1	Hargreaves, S. J.	19/5/18
1	Harvard, L. de J. (wounded 25/9/16)	30/3/18
2	Harvey, D. (wounded 15/9/16)	27/3/18

KILLED OR DIED OF WOUNDS

Batt.		Date.
2	Hasler, A. (wounded 15/9/16)	18/9/16
1	Hoare, E.	9/5/16
2	Hopley, G. W. V.	12/5/15
4	Hubbard, B. J., M.C.	1/12/17
3	Jackson, G D., on or since	14/9/16
1	King, E. G. L. (wounded 10-12/9/16)	22/7/17
1	Lamont, G. S., D.S.O.	4/11/18
	Lang, A. H. (attached 1st Batt. Scots Guards)	28/1/15
2	Langley, F. J. (wounded 6/3/18 and 30/3/18)	22/8/18
2	Lee Steere, J. H. G.	17/11/14
1	Mays, C. C.	30/3/18
1	Neale, G. D.	18/5/18
2	Nevill, J. H. G.	24/12/14
2	Osborne, B. R.	4/11/18
4	Pearce, N. A.	25/11/17
2	Pearson, S. H.	1/12/17
1	Phillipps, R. W.	26/10/15
2	Pickersgill-Cunliffe, J. R.	14/9/14
3	Ranney, R. van T.	28/3/18
4	Richardson, R. D. (wounded 21/4/18)	26/4/18
1	Rocke, C. O.	23/8/18
3	Roper, W. H. S.	11/10/17
1	Sim, L. G. E.	14-16/9/16
1	Somerset, N. A. H.	23/10/14
	Stewart, H. W. (wounded 11/10/17 and 27/3/18)	27/8/18
3	Strangways-Rogers, A. E. F. F. (wounded 4/11/18)	4/11/18
3	Thrupp, M. (wounded 3/8/16 and 14-17/9/16)	31/7/17
4	Tompson, A. H.	27/9/15

APPENDIX III.

APPENDIX III.

Batt.		Date.
2	Vereker, R. H. M.	25/8/14
1	Wakeman, E. O. R.	15-18/5/15
1	Walter, S.	23/10/14
1	Warner, A. A. J.	24/8/18
3	Webster, G. V. G. A.	4/8/17
2	White, H.	27/8/18
3	Williams, R.	9/10/15
4	Windeler, H. W.	28/11/17
3	Worsley, E. G.	17/9/16

APPENDIX IV

NOMINAL ROLL OF W.O.'s, N.C.O.'s, AND MEN WHO HAVE BEEN KILLED IN ACTION, OR WHO HAVE DIED OF WOUNDS OR DISEASE IN THE EUROPEAN WAR OF 1914–1918:—

SERGEANT-MAJORS

11487 Hughes, W., M.C. 20875 Thomas, A.

QUARTERMASTER-SERGEANT

11652 O'Connor, W. G.

COMPANY SERGEANT-MAJORS

8517 Bradbury, G.	8013 Garrard, E. J.	11219 Littleton, S.
6384 Chamberlain, W. C.	10372 Hearn, C., M.M.	9950 Percival, R.
12424 Clarke, H.	11771 Huddlestone, F.	11963 Streten, W. H.
12138 Dunn, G., M.M.		11718 Tyson, L. C.
8421 Frost, E., D.C.M.	13347 Kendrick, F. A.	11290 Waterworth, W. H.

COMPANY QUARTERMASTER-SERGEANTS

11550 Barrett, C.	11059 Moore, F.	13716 Thomas, W. J., M.M.
14620 Langley, W. J., D.C.M.	12978 Parrott, H.	
11818 Malcolm, G.	10217 Richardson, G. L.	10463 Thompson, E. J.

COLOUR-SERGEANTS

7987 Mansfield, A. 4126 Napier, W. H.

SERGEANTS

14107 Akers, G. F.	13094 Batchelor, W. J.	14102 Brahon, E.
19015 Alderson, W.	16634 Belcher, W. W., D.C.M.	11366 Brain, T. H.
12631 Anness, T. A.		15955 Bray, J. H.
15754 Ashman, E. W.	10609 Bevan, F.	18654 Brewer, A.
15444 Ayres, C. E.	10627 Bosworth, J., M.M.	14049 Brewster, A.
14930 Bartlett, F. W.		11772 Briggs, J. H.

244 THE GRENADIER GUARDS

APPENDIX IV.

- 15494 Buckle, E., M.M.
- 10592 Butler, F. G.
- 11330 Buttle, R. W.
- 15362 Bygrave, E. T.
- 14058 Campion, A. F.
- 12203 Carson, E.
- 13053 Cartwright, J. T.
- 13195 Chantrell, A. R.
- 14539 Clinton, W.
- 20460 Collyer, C. M.
- 13580 Comley, E.
- 19583 Cooper, W. T., D.C.M., M.M.
- 15959 Cornwell, A. W.
- 7727 Croft, H.
- 14562 Cross, A.
- 14512 Currie, A.
- 16707 Curtis, E. E.
- 15376 Cushen, W. H.
- 12436 Cutler, M.
- 11996 Davis, F. E.
- 13714 Dench, A. C.
- 6036 Digby, J. H.
- 16109 Dix, E. H.
- 13549 East, B.
- 13055 Entwistle, C.
- 11752 Evans, L. L.
- 17673 Ewell, R. C., M.M.
- 9388 Fry, E.
- 14284 Gordon, H. W.
- 9552 Gosling, R.
- 13447 Gotts, W. A.
- 12489 Gray, A. E.
- 11440 Green, A.
- 19461 Greenhill, D.
- 8563 Grubb, T.
- 13678 Grundy, H.
- 15331 Hackett, H.
- 16379 Hales, P. J.
- 15393 Hall, L.
- 14859 Harding, O. G.
- 9419 Harmer, R. H.
- 12295 Harper, E. J. H.
- 13491 Harrison, G. H.
- 13841 Harrison, J. C., D.C.M.
- 17118 Harrop, W.
- 11580 Harte, M.
- 13727 Hatton, C. G., M.M.
- 15655 Hawkes, W.
- 15025 Hawkins, R.
- 16096 Hayes, J. W.
- 6680 Helyer, E. W.
- 14729 Hollett, S.
- 12687 Hopkins, F.
- 16443 Hughes, J.
- 19688 Hurley, H. L.
- 15087 Jarman, G., D.C.M.
- 12552 Jerram, A.
- 15128 Jones, A. F., D.C.M.
- 11916 Jones, H., D.C.M.
- 16255 Jones, S. L.
- 14910 Kent, F. G.
- 10840 Lack, W. B.
- 12056 Lafferty, W.
- 11856 Lawrence, A. J.
- 13832 Lee, W. R.
- 13886 Lewis, S. T., M.M.
- 11153 Locke, H. J.
- 10371 Lyon, J., D.C.M., M.M.
- 11448 Macey, C. F.
- 7987 Mansfield, A.
- 11517 Marshall, I.
- 7799 Martin, G. E.
- 11278 Mattock, D.
- 15219 May, A. H.
- 8278 Maynard, W. J.
- 14772 Mills, A. J., D.C.M.
- 10394 Munns, F. J.
- 10176 Myson, E.
- 11854 Oldham, A.
- 8785 Packer, C. E.
- 14265 Packwood, A. W. H.
- 12836 Parker, F. C. M.M.
- 12733 Philpin, C.
- 10825 Pitt, W.
- 20856 Prior, C. A.
- 8355 Quinn, T.
- 15122 Rhodes, J. H., V.C., D.C.M., and clasp.
- 14429 Ritchie, W.
- 15166 Roberts, H. R.
- 13115 Russell, W. J.
- 17790 Rymer, R. G.
- 10765 Sanday, S.
- 11816 Shakespeare, E.
- 12002 Sharpe, A.
- 11124 Sheehan, D.
- 13373 Singleton, W.
- 11761 Skerry, T.
- 13260 Slim, H.
- 13654 Smith, H.
- 14785 Smith, J.
- 12108 Smith, J. J.
- 11836 Smith, W. J.
- 15156 Snailham, C. H.
- 13211 Spowage, A., D.C.M.
- 20003 Stafford, R. C.
- 16440 Stone, A.
- 15179 Stone, A. G.
- 18391 Teebay, J.
- 14801 Thomas, J., D.C.M., M.M.
- 15052 Thomas, J.
- 11848 Thomas, W. J.
- 11083 Thompson, F.
- 14057 Todd, J.
- 11946 Turner, H.
- 11919 Tyler, A.
- 14261 Upperton, W.
- 13214 Vaughan, W. M. J.
- 16043 Vowles, H. J.
- 14465 Walters, A.
- 14892 Walton, B., M.M.
- 12778 Watts, W. A.
- 14210 Webb, C. D.
- 15491 Wentworth, W. H., M.M.
- 11367 White, G.
- 10928 Wiggins, A. W.
- 9426 Williams, H., M.M.
- 15392 Wood, E.
- 15400 Wonnacott, T. J., D.C.M.

LANCE-SERGEANTS

- 21630 Anning, G. T.
- 10507 Asplin, F.
- 15856 Bailey, A. C.
- 18707 Bailey, E.
- 19144 Bailey, J.
- 17602 Barnes, J. B.
- 19475 Barton, R.
- 15792 Bell, E.
- 13338 Bennett, A. E.
- 10715 Bentley, A. W.
- 10910 Bingham, J. W.
- 15872 Blakemoor, G. C.
- 14565 Brenchley, G. T.

NOMINAL ROLL

Appendix IV.

11665 Brown, A.	11489 Hunt, H. G.	17071 Robotham, W.
23152 Brown, C., M.M.	15799 Jackson, J.	16243 Roper, W., M.M.
12371 Butler, W.	21382 Jeffcoat, W.	12280 Ruck, H. J.
12472 Cæsar, A. J.	12821 Kendall, W.	18347 Rumfitt, H.
14340 Carnall, H. E.	19633 Kibble, E.	17577 Ryder, S. G.
22783 Challis, J. A., M.M.	20906 King, T.	16616 Sayer, H. J.
21432 Clark, S. E.	14447 Lamb, F.	12960 Shea, H.
23653 Cogdell, W.	12043 Leech, E., M.M.	10964 Shipton, M.
14511 Cole, E.	15632 Lees, F.	20146 Shrimpton, H. E.
19467 Cook, A. H., M.M.	18919 Leeves, W.	18259 Smith, W.
20826 Cook, W. F.	17149 Lloyd, F.	14788 Stenner, E.
22054 Coulton, E.	19634 Locke, F., M.M.	23846 Stephenson, G., M.M.
19867 Cripps, G. E.	14898 Lockwood, C. A.	12353 Stockdale, F. J., M.M.
15919 Croucher, A. T.	13220 Lowdell, A. G.	11912 Stokes, C.
23813 Crundwell, F.	12957 McCulloch, G.	16779 Stolle, H. J.
24711 Dale, R. C.	13062 McDowell, J.	12062 Street, B.
20399 Davies, H. R.	14417 McKanna-Maulkin, A.	20961 Stride, F. C.
11714 Dowsell, E. W.	18825 Manley, F. H.	13079 Strutt, H. C.
12593 Eden, E. G.	16915 Mann, C. W.	12136 Studd, J.
23456 Eyers, A. G.	13577 Mann, F.	10785 Tamblin, P. J.
14975 Farr, F. C. J.	20356 Marsh, H., M.M.	13805 Tarlton, F. J.
15446 Ford, R.	14830 Marshall, F. J.	20939 Trotter, A.
15275 Fox, F.	17654 Mason, F. W.	14288 Turner, W. D.
15666 Galer, F. J.	12430 Matthews, W. C.	12796 Varley, J.
12646 Garnett, J. E.	16446 Miller, A. R.	18930 Wakely, W.
17175 Gladding, C. T. R.	11314 Milnes, J. W.	19488 Walsh, P., M.M.
14724 Golding, S.	16843 Mitchell, F. C.	13789 Ward, H., M.M.
14911 Gregory, B.	17045 Mortimer, E. J.	11158 Watkins, R. J., M.M.
19830 Goodwin, F.	30294 Mountain, R. J.	15814 Watt, G.
15922 Green, T.	13820 Mulvey, J.	11238 Webster, H. M.
18085 Hains, J. E. M.	13283 Nash, F.	19537 Webster, S.
16828 Harding, W.	19574 Needham, E. C.	15607 Weller, S.
20217 Hardy, H.	15604 Newsome, W.	19059 Whitaker, T., D.C.M.
17506 Harris, R.	14274 Nix, A.	16339 Whitehouse, T. A.
17407 Hartfield, F. G.	11091 Nuttall, H., M.M.	19372 Wigginton, F.
15169 Hatton, G. L.	17608 Palmer, W. C.	12206 Wilkinson, T.
10996 Hawker, A. A.	23840 Parr, J. W.	10172 Williams, E.
16429 Haynes, E.	14421 Patten, J.	18100 Wilson, A., M.M.
16070 Hayward, C. M.	19563 Payne, T. H.	10015 Wiltshire, H.
15629 Hearn, R. C.	15138 Perrins, E.	10612 Winfield, J. H.
23197 Herriman, V.	19057 Phipps, R. E.	14266 Wood, A. A.
13350 Hickling, G.	14079 Pickerill, T.	19041 Wood, J. A., M.M.
12285 Hiles, W. C.	13982 Pickering, J. W.	18339 Ward, A. W.
16864 Hill, J. C. W.	11803 Pretty, W.	
18396 Hinks, F. E.	19332 Rains, H. G.	
15657 Holley, F. W.	26798 Reynolds, S. E. C.	
13246 Hook, W.		
14221 Horgan, A. H.		
11706 Hunt, A. E.		

CORPORALS

21635 Allen, S.	13325 Boocock, J.	19946 Crutchley, J. A.
19112 Bennett, D. W. (Signalling Corpl.)	11203 Burke, V., M.M.	20869 Dale, P. J.
	25119 Cartwright, H.	10819 Davey, J.
	15833 Collard, P. C.	

246   THE GRENADIER GUARDS

APPENDIX IV.

23763	Dickens, T. G., D.C.M.
14382	Dickinson, J.
14739	Dunphy, C. N.
24092	Fasey, J. W.
15466	Franklin, H. G.
12370	Gregory, F. D.
11698	Gundry, A. J.
16445	Hammond, H. N.
16983	Harris, J.
15630	Horn, O. J.
13458	Horwood, H. A.
8464	Ingleby, H.
19226	Jackson, H.
15558	James, J.
17006	Jones, A. H.

13914	Jones, F.
20346	Keep, P. W., M.M.
21175	Kemp, C. W.
13555	Kenney, H.
8592	Kilmartin, E.
13107	Lloyd, W. H.
34446	McGrath, J.
15365	Matthews, W. H.
11208	Moore, W.
16786	Orpwood, W.
12827	Palfrey, E. G., M.M.
11828	Palmer, I.
14861	Parkes, E.

17080	Pavitt, H.
15719	Porter, C. A.
15560	Potten, C. H.
11454	Rees, J.
16116	Ryall, H. E., M.M.
15808	Sharpe, G.
15147	Shaw, S.
11056	Shipp, J.
15720	Smith, E.
10497	Stone, W.
14471	Thomas, W., D.C.M.
16778	Trevett, G.
11880	Tuttle, A. H.
12301	Wallis, A.
16496	Weavin, W. H.

LANCE-CORPORALS

17647	Abbott, A. C.
26948	Abbott, J.
15602	Abbott, W. J.
26799	Abernethy, H.
18248	Adam, J.
21254	Aggett, E. W.
23510	Alford, A. O.
28647	Allen, F.
29675	Allen, G.
21123	Alway, F.
19094	Archer, S.
10729	Armstrong, A.
23094	Armstrong, C.
17286	Arland, J. W.
24132	Arthur, W. J.
20561	Ashman, J. C.
12395	Askew, G.
10067	Aspin, A.
12517	Atherton, F.
17069	Atkins, W. R.
16358	Ayers, T. F.
22086	Back, G. H.
29600	Baker, H.
18154	Balsdon, H. G.
22849	Barker, E.
28351	Barker, E. J.
10847	Barker, J.
16781	Barnes, F. H.
20924	Barnes, M.
28757	Barrett, W. R.
14780	Beard, G. H.
18564	Bebb, D. W.
21347	Beer, T. J.
27727	Bell, J.
15688	Belson, A. G.
17133	Benstead, F. M.
23207	Bentley, F.
24764	Berry, E.

16848	Bessant, C. E.
14112	Betty, S.
24103	Bicknell, P. G.
27290	Binns, J.
25581	Birch, C. H.
19874	Birch, W. H.
22524	Bird, H. H.
19224	Blackburn, D.
14344	Blakeman, E.
26544	Bond, E.
25203	Bond, J. W.
21243	Boston, J.
27438	Boulter, C. H.
13553	Boulton, A.
19314	Boulton, F.
22088	Bowden, H.
18961	Boyce, J.
27381	Bradley, T. H.
23879	Bradshaw, E. C.
23239	Brailsford, W. J.
15469	Braine, L. F. H.
13396	Bramwell, J.
15036	Brandon, G.
14784	Brennan, T.
21791	Bridge, A.
24962	Briggs, W. J.
19937	Brighton, C. H.
15474	Brignell, J. H.
15583	Brisley, L. C.
20817	Broadfoot, J. F., M.M.
16633	Brotherwood, C.
26327	Brown, C.
20824	Bruce, J.
13312	Burch, G. A.
17448	Burgess, E. F.
15387	Burr, S. A.

12520	Bushell, W. T.
27598	Buxton, H. S.
24803	Cadman, J.
28277	Campbell, J.
21505	Campion, L.
13937	Campion, R. P.
19496	Cansfield, H. D.
29555	Carey, G. V.
15007	Carter, J. T.
17923	Cartwright, J.
23168	Caygill, T.
28241	Catanach, A.
18539	Champ, R.
12895	Church, C.
29717	Clare, E. F.
10362	Clark, A.
22932	Clark, B.
19426	Clark, E. W.
22464	Clarke, W.
23819	Colclough, W.
17077	Coles, J. T.
15269	Collard, L. E.
24243	Colwell, A.
20867	Cooke, E.
18595	Coombes, A. E.
15037	Comley, S.
19066	Cooper, T.
30441	Cooper, W. E.
23144	Corbett, G.
13142	Corben, L. W.
15506	Corby, C.
14504	Cox, F.
17450	Cox, G.
21991	Cox, G. H.
15339	Cox, W. G.
17082	Cozens, A. W.
22155	Cresswell, A. E.
12656	Critchlow, T. P.

NOMINAL ROLL 247

23347	Cross, V.	11327	Francis, T. W.	14352	Holton, T.
16418	Curtis, J. L.	15994	Franklin, F.	14808	Hopkins, C.
26827	Daines, B.	20111	Gard, G.	17528	Hopkins, L.
23313	Daniels, L. G.	16233	Gaskin, C.	17290	Hosking, A.
22438	Dann, T. A.	28030	Gibson, T. H.	21136	Hudson, W.
28721	Dardani, P.	22413	Gladstone, T.	20896	Huggett, A.
23025	Darrell, H.	10129	Glover, J. E.	27223	Hyde, W. J.
13362	Davenport, S. D.	12628	Goodley, H.	9813	Hyman, C.
		16906	Gould, J. W.	18519	Ingram, G.
24032	Davidson, T. W.	14089	Gould, T.	16947	Jacobs, G. E.
		15470	Gransden, C. E.	23020	James, W.
25773	Davidson, W. E.	16344	Green, C. H.	7848	Jarvis, F.
		16083	Green, J.	22130	Jarvis, H.
16199	Davies, C.	16568	Greene, W.	10304	Johnson, F.
16927	Davis, L.	17768	Griffiths, T.	26651	Jones, C. T. R.
26302	Davison, G.	13092	Groce, F. H.	14793	Jones, G.
23029	Dawson, W. J.	17130	Grocott, J.	12539	Jones, S.
21880	Deade, R. G.	21106	Grout, J. T.	29943	Joyce, A. T.
20416	Deal, J. T.	23809	Gunn, J.	12654	Kane, T. A.
17187	Dean, F. J., M.M.	21559	Hales, G.	22418	Keeble, G.
		18445	Hales, L. W.	29886	Keen, S. G.
19120	Dickinson, H.	20995	Hall, A. G.	13633	Kendall, F. A.
18997	Dillon, F. L.	17157	Hall, H. D.	17988	Ketchell, T. C.
24838	Dixon, E. B.	20054	Ham, J.	11793	Kettlety, H. E.
12950	Dobson, J. S.	20328	Hamilton, F. S.	18015	Kings, A. R.
27617	Donnison, A.	17359	Hancock, W. C.	23480	Kissane, M.
13675	Donovan, F. W.	20707	Handley, J.	17596	Kitchen, J. E.
30407	Dore, S. W.	16361	Hardstaff, J.	20552	Kitchener, H.
16075	Doughty, S. W.	19862	Hargreaves, A.	21149	Knight, R.
19619	Douthwaite, G. R.	23664	Harris, H. E.	18421	Lane, F. G.
		17086	Harvey, W. H.	22439	Lane, W. H.
16952	Dufty, W. J., D.C.M.	24909	Harwood, G.	14754	Langford, F.
		21964	Hassell, F.	22900	Langham, J. L.
21651	Dungate, W. J.	13700	Hawkins, F.	14174	Laughlin, H. J.
20181	Dunn, W.	17445	Hawkins, W. J.		
23697	Dunscomb, F. T.	15979	Hawkswood, R. H.	17360	Leach, T.
				25822	Leach, T. A.
24525	Dutton, J. T.	16965	Haycock, E.	11138	Lee, J.
18600	Earnshaw, T.	22739	Hayes, F. R.	19208	Leggott, R. H.
22328	Eastham, R.	13006	Hazlewood, R.	15661	Lester, W.
23908	Edwards, H. J.	15106	Heath, T. H.	8305	Levett, W. J.
23243	Elkin, W.	12806	Hemsley, W.	29136	Lilley, J.
25839	Ellis, W. T.	22617	Henshaw, T. W.	11349	Litchfield, H.
15521	Eustace, G.			22472	Littler, C. W.
16251	Evans, I.	23415	Henson, E.	24756	Llewellin, L.
26764	Fairhurst, H.	23015	Hewett, J. F.	23210	Lloyd, W.
23159	Farlam, T. H.	21525	Higgins, H., M.M.	12501	Locke, H.
30334	Fielden, E. H.			24996	Long, W. F., M.M.
27158	Fields, A. H.	19617	Hill, C. A.		
21554	Fisher, F. G.	17565	Hillman, R.	20273	Longfield, T.
16817	Fisher, W.	25024	Hirons, W.	23372	Longhurst, H. E.
20126	Fletcher, H.	31746	Hobbs, A. E.		
20249	Flynn, M.	17138	Hobbs, C. B.	20673	Lord, F. C.
18138	Fooks, J.	13228	Hodges, A.	25783	Lord, J.
11575	Ford, E.	14438	Hodgson, M.	16291	Love, J.
13885	Foreman, B. W.	23885	Hoffman, F. J.	16839	Lowe, L. G.
19115	Foster, J.	17060	Hollingbery, S.	20472	Lumley, J. F.
16377	Foster, J. H.	23897	Holloway, W.	23672	Lusted, H. V.
20811	Fox, W. T.	26381	Holt, H. S.	23396	Lyes, J. H. P.

APPENDIX IV.

248 THE GRENADIER GUARDS

APPENDIX IV.

13922 Lyes, J. W., D.C.M.
20646 McGuinness, J.
20061 McHale, W.
24458 McKenna, H. J.
18333 McLellan, A.
29290 Mag, M.
25844 Major, E. F.
21334 Maley, T.
12463 Mankelow, G. A.
16899 Marbe, A. R.
22728 March, J. H.
27035 Marl, G. T.
16930 Marrows, R. D.
14378 Marsh, H.
15704 Martin, C. W.
29191 Maskell, S.
22618 Mason, J. E.
24973 Maycock, F.
22850 Mead, J.
16923 Mellor, E.
11109 Mepstead, A.
22159 Meredith, E. H., M.M.
18456 Merrick, T.
19359 Merrilees, E. G.
25619 Merry, J.
17893 Miles, E. G.
26493 Mills, L.
11883 Miner, C. G.
18491 Montague, W.
20556 Moore, B.
14052 Moore, H.
26620 Moore, J.
24986 Moore, M. M.
24707 Morley, J. L.
17028 Morris, W. C.
22527 Morris, W. G.
15941 Mosley, V.
13800 Mottershead, A.
25819 Moulding, A. J., M.M.
21384 Munn, A., M.M.
20976 Munro, J.
18364 Murfin, A.
14297 Murrell, W. J.
30429 Myall, H. L.
27739 Mycock, J. H.
30285 Newbury, H.
21386 Newman, C. V.
14388 Newman, T. H.
14624 Nicholls, W.
27804 Nicholson, C.
16001 Nisbet, A. C.
24218 Noon, A.
17439 Norman, L. C.
25821 North, E.
10526 Noutch, J. W.

26417 Nunn, A. S.
13734 Odell, W.
16108 Oliver, G. G.
17011 Ollerenshaw, J. R.
25328 Olliffe, H.
15965 Onion, F.
16355 Orchard, F. J.
14867 Orris, T. C.
26270 Orth, H.
29345 Outen, G. A.
21648 Page, J. L.
14498 Painter, H.
23205 Palk, S.
17610 Palmer, A. G.
18153 Palmer, J.
11584 Palmer, V.
17619 Parker, E.
22150 Parker, H.
19025 Parker, J.
15532 Parkinson, E.
19841 Parr, W. F.
20174 Parrott, F. H.
18487 Parsons, P. A.
29522 Pearce, L. R.
24047 Pearson, J. C.
17181 Peartree, C.
21003 Pell, R. H.
27980 Pennell, G.
20957 Perrin, G.
17012 Perry, J. A.
17757 Peters, H. F.
22352 Phillips, W.
28147 Phillipson, A. M.
13589 Pilkington, H.
24736 Pillage, A.
28300 Place, T.
13932 Posh, W. N.
19595 Pratley, F.
21947 Price, R.
24876 Prickett, W. G.
17520 Prickman, H. G.
23825 Prince, J. W.
24109 Pullen. W.
29323 Pybus, H.
17370 Quinn, T.
17472 Radford, G. C.
15402 Radford, S. J.
12768 Randall, F. C.
11979 Randall, L. T. R.
18034 Read, C. S.
22004 Reece, R. C.
14577 Reed, A. G.
12508 Reid, S.
21528 Renard, A. B.
9517 Reynolds, F. J.

19333 Reynolds, J. H. G.
19643 Reynolds, J., M.M.
21235 Rhodes, S.
12246 Richardson, G.
15006 Richardson, H. G.
17925 Roberts, F. T.
16312 Roberts, J.
28377 Robinson, J. W.
11602 Robinson, W. H.
23129 Robson, C.
26863 Rogers, H., M.M.
20012 Roome, A.
24474 Rossiter, F.
24266 Rowbotham, S. J., M.M.
16780 Rudman, W. H. W.
19473 Ryder, J., M.M.
11917 Sander, L. J.
14033 Sapsford, A. W.
25533 Saunders, H.
23509 Scholes, J.
23013 Shaw, G. H.
14921 Shipley, G. E.
20745 Shorthose, A. R.
23222 Simmonds, G. W.
19037 Singer, F. C.
15346 Slater, W.
25055 Smith, A. B.
30401 Smith, A. H.
15516 Smith, E. J.
16453 Smith, E. R.
17076 Smith, F., M.M.
19494 Smith, F. W.
19388 Smith, H. P.
14427 Smith, J. W., D.C.M.
23494 Smith, T.
23738 Snow, C. T.
18998 Southwood, T.
22602 Spencer, J.
19003 Spencer, T. R.
13657 Spencer, W.
22633 Squirrell, S. A.
20050 Stanley, H.
18612 Stannard, G. W.
16158 Stead, J. E.
20972 Stebbing, L. C.
17748 Stevens, F.

NOMINAL ROLL

18817 Stevenson, H., M.M.	13468 Todd, T.	20178 Westmoreland, M., M.M.
20091 Stevenson, T.	17881 Toms, N.	21016 Weston, H.
22636 Stevenson, T.	24825 Travis, A. B.	23791 Westwood, J. T.
18218 Stewart, J.	11272 Tuck, H.	15728 Wheeler, F. E.
24187 Stockley, R.	24708 Tucker, W. H.	20024 White, F. A.
21169 Stockton, J.	17516 Turner, A.	21013 White, J.
27284 Stothard, H.	16637 Turner, C. F. T.	22031 White, J.
21228 Strange, W. R.	22188 Turner, C. W.	23112 White, J.
15762 Street, F.	21408 Turner, E.	21609 Wilfred, S.
24791 Street, H., M.M.	32326 Turner, W. H.	28735 Wilkinson, E.
27084 Strickland, J. T.	22248 Tusler, G.	12695 Willetts, L.
12136 Studd, J.	13409 Tyne, J.	19038 Willett, J. H.
21367 Styles, W.	18150 Vesey, G. E.	26492 Williams, A. B.
26393 Swallow, H.	14348 Vickerman, C.	8671 Williams, D. J.
32280 Swindlehurst, H. H.	28061 Vincent, J.	17229 Williams, W.
24472 Tate, C.	16542 Wakefield, T.	18956 Williamson, P.
19340 Taylor, A.	19442 Walker, C. W.	19616 Wilson, H. W.
25186 Taylor, H.	22480 Walker, E.	22110 Wilton, A. J.
18187 Taylor, R. J.	12704 Wall, A., M.M.	21103 Wincer, G. H.
15861 Taylor, T.	21172 Wallis, F. W.	25022 Wiseman, A. J.
15058 Teagle, T., M.M.	16059 Walton, L.	17714 Witcher, A. H.
20689 Teasdale, A.	13559 Ward, R. G., M.M.	29408 Wood, A. S.
20104 Tebbutt, E. W.	16600 Ward, W. E.	21843 Worswick, D. N.
18957 Tegg, A.	11546 Washington, W. J.	14444 Wright, W. H.
21093 Tennant, A.	23274 Waters, A. C.	9468 Wright, W. J.
18914 Thorpe, A. E.	24661 Webb, W.	21460 Wright, F.
16928 Tippett, H. E.	22782 Welch, T. V.	18189 Wylie, J.
	16378 Weller, T. J.	24807 Wynne, R. T.
	22966 West, A. J.	16746 York, J. E.

APPENDIX IV.

DRUMMERS

12607 Abbott, W. T.	12302 Jowett, H. A.	14314 Tomlinson, H. W.
14327 Clark, H.	13953 Langrish, A. C.	20649 Wadeson, W.
13660 Copping, A. A.	16217 Marsden, S. J.	15439 Ward, A. E.
12175 Haines, O. P. H.	14367 Roe, E. W.	
16064 Hook, L. G.	14451 Steed, C. S.	

GUARDSMEN

16125 Abbott, E. W.	20338 Alder, A. E.	21425 Allerston, J. T.
20947 Abbott, J.	22486 Alder, A. F.	18521 Allin, W. F.
24805 Abbotts, J.	24371 Alderson, R., M.M.	29093 Allison, T. R.
29017 Abery, E. S. F.		11452 Allman, F.
17894 Abram, F. C.	15232 Aldridge, H.	18878 Allport, E. H.
26566 Abram, L.	14804 Alexander, A. R.	18480 Allsopp, J.
9628 Ace, T.		25665 Almond, W.
14095 Acres, J. J.	23652 Alexander, G.	30483 Amos, W. S. E.
17312 Adams, E. G.	16332 Allen, A. W.	33690 Amos, W.
15610 Adams, G.	17700 Allen, E. R.	27601 Amsbury, D. P. J.
9774 Adams, W. H.	21888 Allen, E. T.	
10170 Adby, W.	17159 Allen, F.	25414 Anderson, W. A.
14758 Adey, C. A.	18543 Allen, J.	
28672 Admans, A. H.	14650 Allen, W. G.	29300 Andrews, A.
23368 Adnitt, R. F.	18298 Allen, W. G.	14422 Andrews, A. J.
15976 Alesbury, F.	30117 Allen, W. H.	20289 Andrews, E.

250 THE GRENADIER GUARDS

Appendix IV.

23184 Andrews, H. S.	13825 Bagshaw, J. H.	20923 Barker, S.
18727 Andrews, J. C.	31322 Bailey, A.	24833 Barker, J. A.
25322 Angus, W. A.	20816 Bailey, C.	25676 Barlow, B.
16614 Aulton, C. H.	18222 Bailey, E.	30486 Barlow, R. A.
16165 Antill, H.	23581 Bailey, E.	12115 Barnes, J.
13737 Anthony, W.	13426 Bailey, E. E.	15972 Barnett, H. L.
19215 Appleby, E. F.	22660 Bailey, F.	17562 Barnett, G.
14215 Apps, W.	30360 Bailey, F. A.	21337 Barr, C.
30582 Archer, H. G.	23070 Bailey, H. G.	27050 Barraclough, B.
18254 Armison, G. J.	25267 Bailey, J. C.	13624 Barrell, C. A.
11516 Arms, C. E.	26390 Bailey, R. J.	26483 Barrett, A.
18962 Armson, G. E.	29015 Bailey,	22009 Barrett, G.
24044 Armstrong, E.	W. E. H.	16068 Barrett, J. F.
31543 Armstrong, J. S.	30434 Bailey, W. D.	13284 Barson, C.
26696 Armstrong, W.	20514 Bailey, W. J.	30436 Barter, P. H.
16622 Arnall, H.	13339 Bain, R.	28356 Bartle, F.
20431 Arnold, C.	18299 Baines, W.	11843 Bartlett, A.
19766 Arnold, H. S.	14748 Baker, A.	25291 Bartlett, G.
16467 Arnold, J.	30485 Baker, A.	16973 Barton, J. T.
29217 Arnold, R. G.	28907 Baker, A. C. C.	19650 Barton, J.
27639 Arrowsmith, I.	15114 Baker, B. H.	23102 Barton, J. T.
24679 Arrowsmith, J., M.M.	28423 Baker, E.	28255 Barton, R.
	26711 Baker, H. G.	12799 Bartram, E.
20531 Ashman, A. J.	16380 Baker, P. G.	22394 Bassett, A.
17108 Ashton, J. J	20333 Baker, R. W.	15929 Batchelor,
22398 Ashton, J. W.	17773 Baker, T.	A. H.
22259 Ashworth, A.	22500 Baker, T.	24409 Batchelor, J. H.
28758 Ashworth, E.	20716 Baker, T. W.	24410 Batchelor,
27355 Ashworth, G. W.	15092 Baker, W. J.	W. T.
	25271 Baldock, F.	29252 Batchelor, C.
20263 Ashworth, I.	23432 Baldry, D.	25095 Bate, J.
28024 Askey, W.	24514 Baldwin, C. W.	15141 Bateman, G.
9465 Aspin, W.	28522 Baldwin, S.	14281 Bates, W. J.
13846 Astle, A. E.	20666 Ball, A. C. J.	18359 Bates, F. G.
15196 Astle, W.	24276 Ball, G.	17578 Bates, T. P.
21518 Atherton, J. T.	16875 Ball, P. H.	25723 Batstone, J. T.
21661 Atherton, J.	27935 Ball, T.	14160 Batt, A. R.
21579 Atkinson, A.	11119 Bale, T. H.	25493 Batt, L. W.
19391 Atkinson, A. E.	27002 Ball, W.	21865 Battersby,
31615 Atkinson, A. H.	31120 Ball, W.	W. A.
27603 Atkinson, G. G.	15080 Ballard, J. G.	13463 Battle, P. U.
	10869 Bamber, E.	29854 Bave, E. A.
16770 Atkinson, H.	28810 Bamfield, G.	25745 Bavin, A. R.
28627 Atkinson, J.	17403 Bamford, A.	25611 Baxendale, H.
25978 Attridge, G. S.	25858 Bamford, H.	17555 Baxter, B.
27951 Austin, E.	27889 Bamford, J. H.	21566 Baxter, J. A.
21259 Austin, G. G.	28877 Banks, A.	13940 Bayliss, T.
12890 Austin, H. S.	22052 Banks, J.	26502 Bazett, H. C.
32281 Austin, J.	23164 Banner, J. H.	17300 Beaden, J.
13895 Austin, R.	24632 Banning, A. J.	17346 Beale, C. W.
31130 Avery, F. W.	25484 Banton, A.	28936 Beames, E. R.
17850 Aylott, H. C.	15518 Barber, E., V.C.	19420 Bean, L. W.
11679 Ayres, R.	24684 Barker, A.	14527 Beard, G. W.
27349 Ayres, G. E.	28546 Barber, A.	25286 Beard, H.
31262 Ault, J. T. F.	21775 Barber, A. E.	20753 Beasley, G. W.
14608 Bacon, A.	27882 Barber, B.	9783 Beauchamp, J.
19873 Bacon, T.	21581 Barber, G. A.	22697 Beck, A. W.
20733 Bagnall, H.	23605 Barber, J. H.	23851 Beck, T. R.
16750 Bagnell, N.	18292 Bargh, W.	14939 Beddis, J. H.

NOMINAL ROLL 251

		APPENDIX IV.
17795 Beddoes, G.	25255 Birch, W.	25875 Boraman, P. H. C.
27430 Bednall, A.	12164 Birchley, F.	29716 Borle, J. C.
13048 Beebee, J. H.	27411 Bird, F.	29022 Bott, A. H.
16084 Beech, A. H.	19768 Bird, W.	14928 Bottrill, J.
28620 Beedle, W. J.	25999 Birkett, W. G.	19899 Boucher, J. C.
21129 Beeks, C.	29763 Birrell, T.	18544 Boult, A. E.
24094 Beeston, T.	22349 Birtles, H.	24808 Boultbee, A.
17195 Belfield, T. H.	9694 Birtwistle, A.	16631 Boulton, F.
22558 Bell, F. M.	28739 Bishop, F. W.	13415 Boulton, G.
27936 Bell, H. D.	23338 Bishop, R. J.	20515 Boumford, C.
28466 Bell, R.	15838 Bishop, W. H.	18440 Bourke, W.
24897 Bellwood, G. W.	27672 Bishop, W. H.	27093 Bourne, E.
24773 Benford, A. A.	24076 Biswell, S. G.	25368 Bourton, A. E.
21374 Bennett, A.	29817 Bizzell, F. A.	30554 Bovey, W. P. C.
24628 Bennett, A.	17062 Blackburn, S.	29344 Bower, H.
10707 Bennett, A. G.	11499 Blackman, H. G.	21540 Bower, L.
15471 Bennett, A. T.		23106 Bowers, J.
27010 Bennett, C.	17931 Blades, J. P.	15205 Bowers, J. T.
17109 Bennett, F.	21299 Blair, W. J.	22920 Bowes, H.
21056 Bennett, G. D.	22407 Blake, F. C.	21211 Bowes, J.
29985 Bennett, J.	16598 Blake, H. H.	26605 Bowler, J. H.
30157 Bennett, S.	24957 Bland, H.	16022 Bowles, H. F.
23627 Bennett, T.	25697 Bland, V. V.	22950 Bowmer, J.
29085 Bennett, T.	15999 Blanton, J. H.	21133 Bowsher, H.
20361 Bennett, T.	27933 Blatchley, A. W.	20730 Bowtell, W.
15445 Bennett, T. E.		23842 Boyes, T.
11810 Bennett, W.	20993 Blay, S.	19530 Bracegirdle, A.
20498 Bennett, W. F.	27658 Blease, W. R.	20698 Bracewell, J.
14474 Bennett, W. H.	15676 Blenkinsop, C.	17984 Brackley, T.
26820 Bennison, T. P.	23162 Bligh, A. C.	19738 Bradburn, P.
18592 Benson, W.	14391 Bligh, P.	18813 Bradbury, H.
27422 Bentley, J. H.	22938 Bloomfield, T. R.	23105 Bradbury, J.
20123 Bent, J.		17447 Bradbury, P.
19060 Berkin, S. T.	28229 Blurton, L.	29708 Bradbury, S. E.
22801 Berry, T.	24045 Bly, G.	21418 Braddock, C.
29012 Berry, W.	27747 Blythe, C. E.	23264 Bradford, T.
19898 Besant, H. G.	14696 Board, A. F.	28238 Bradley, F. H.
16295 Besant, W. J.	16913 Boarder, F. J.	16403 Bradley, G. H.
11428 Bestley, H.	18841 Boardman, J.T.	17300 Bradon, J.
20266 Beswick, H.	21355 Boden, E.	8852 Bradshaw, T.
19582 Bethel, A.	17373 Boden, W. R.	29027 Brain, C. A.
23536 Bettles, J. H.	25244 Boffin, W.	20138 Brain, W. J.
13297 Bevan, M.	29340 Bogie, R. L.	27540 Braithwaite, H.
25480 Bew, E. E.	21025 Bolstridge, B.	23095 Bramidge, R.
13065 Biggerstaffe, J.	26857 Bolt, W. H.	18695 Brand, L.
16019 Biggin, A. W. T.	21583 Bolton, F.	19007 Brandon, J.
	28395 Bolton, H.	26291 Brant, D.
26448 Biggs, H. G.	27328 Bolton, J.	12944 Brassington, J.
17268 Biggs, J.	10946 Bond, A.	17725 Brayshaw, C. T.
19079 Biggs, J. W.	16282 Bond, P.	29384 Breach, H.
14806 Bilbie, C.	15385 Bonfield, R. W.	19635 Breakspeare, H.
17856 Billingham, J.	18748 Bonfield, S.	
13178 Billingsley, T.	25790 Boniface, R.	21281 Breakwell, E.
21539 Bilsbury, H.	18593 Boon, A.	19975 Breakwell, H.
24906 Binding, C.	18036 Boorer, H. G.	19014 Brearley, H.
20075 Birch, F.	22367 Boote, J.	8310 Brennan, J.
17343 Birch, J.	22670 Booth, J.	24812 Brett, J. A.
25011 Birch, J.	23044 Booth, W.	13747 Brett, J. W.
24912 Birch, T. M.	28921 Booth, W.	

252 THE GRENADIER GUARDS

Appendix IV.

14542 Brewer, J.	28248 Brown, G.	25062 Burr, H. D.
27339 Brewis, R. W.	28849 Brown, G.	15348 Burr, S. F.
13021 Brewster, A.	18281 Brown, G. S.	20198 Burrell, F. H.
25744 Brewster, A.	11907 Brown, H.	24578 Burrell, J.
15646 Brice, J. J.	19315 Brown, H.	21866 Burrows, E.
20311 Briddon, J.	21531 Brown, H.	24153 Burrows, J. B.
18621 Bridgen, J. G.	13540 Brown, J.	15621 Burrows, W. J.
25937 Bridges, F.	18665 Brown, J.	20699 Burslem, H.
26082 Bridges, H.	26085 Brown, J.	13138 Burton, A.
22759 Bridgland, E.	17115 Brown, J.	17796 Burton, A. E.
13124 Brierley, A.	15540 Brown, J. A. H.	17105 Burton, B.
29076 Briggs, G. R.	24526 Brown, P.	17095 Burton, E.
32003 Briggs, T.	20542 Brown, R.	28650 Burton, R. F.
20645 Bright, P. M.	13863 Brown, R.	28422 Burton, W.
7789 Bright, S.	16529 Brown, T. G.	21891 Bush, H.
14343 Brighton, W.	25863 Brown, W.	23814 Bush, J.
10716 Brimson, T.	28919 Brown, W. G.	11356 Bush, P. E.
18847 Brindley, G. W.	11339 Brown, W. R.	13150 Bush, W. H.
17179 Brinkman, A. T.	28995 Browne, G. J.	18349 Bushby, J.
27939 Britton, S.	26581 Browne, J. M.	29688 Bushell, A. T.
24806 Broadhurst, G.	31711 Brunger, F. J.	22770 Bussey, E. A.
29550 Brock, A. T.	20681 Brunskill, J.	13199 Butcher, A. E.
22332 Brocklehurst, T. A.	31063 Brunton, T. S.	19265 Butcher, C. E.
16476 Bromage, W.	29573 Bryan, F. R.	25889 Butchers, J. T.
23852 Bromwich, J. E.	24457 Bryan, J.	28889 Butler, F.
28101 Brookbanks, J.	18447 Bryant, C. B.	29155 Butler, F. E.
26442 Brooke, Henry	16186 Bryant, H. J.	16963 Butler, F. G.
16859 Brooker, J.	24530 Bryce, N.	12149 Butler, G. H.
18694 Brooker, F. W.	26979 Buck, C.	25010 Butler, J.
18655 Brookes, J. E.	27243 Buckham, F.	17972 Butler, R.
29475 Brookes, T. S.	20216 Buckland, H. C.	25564 Butlin, F. S.
24943 Brooks, A.	17261 Buckle, F.	28808 Butt, A.
19072 Brooks, A. J.	25816 Buckman, S.	16414 Butt, H. J.
18934 Brooks, H.	17734 Buggs, A.	24360 Butterfield, W. S.
16805 Brooks, H. J.	17063 Bull, H., D.C.M.	31140 Butterton, H.
15860 Brooks, J.	22149 Bull, T. H.	17968 Butterwich, E.
17220 Brooks, J.	12378 Bullen, H. E. T.	14584 Button, H. J.
19679 Brooks, J.	20108 Bullock, G.	21152 Button, L.
23265 Brooks, W. A.	19047 Bullock, G.	22923 Buxton, T.
26886 Broster, A. E.	20283 Bullock, H.	11743 Bye, F. T.
25601 Broughton, S. E.	24517 Bullock, S.	23853 Bye, L. J.
11369 Brown, A.	23294 Bullock, W. J.	23368 Bywater, G.
11811 Brown, A.	12407 Bunce, F.	23598 Cady, G.
25126 Brown, A.	23014 Bunce, F.	29381 Caffyn, E. H.
30337 Brown, A.	18968 Bunker, J. T.	27347 Cain, J. W.
25606 Brown, A. B.	30341 Bunker, P.	17092 Calderbank, W.
22610 Brown, A. J.	16289 Bunnett, H. A.	22400 Calland, A.
27096 Brown, A. W.	24557 Bunyan, J.	28635 Callen, E. H.
29545 Brown, B. R.	22432 Burden, J.	29612 Callister, J. L.
12011 Brown, C. D.	30488 Burden, R. J.	26391 Calloway, W.
21429 Brown, C. W. T.	28687 Burdett, T. R.	11288 Calvert, G. W.
23276 Brown, D.	11767 Burge, A. J.	27413 Calvert, W.
19460 Brown, E.	17033 Burge, I.	14106 Cameron, R.
17400 Brown, F. E.	18972 Burgin, J.	13200 Campfield, A. M.
10049 Brown, G.	23048 Burke, A.	25471 Campbell, G.
	31062 Burke, J. S.	11694 Campbell, P.
	16036 Burleton, R.	14558 Campion, J. A.
	31497 Burney, G.	
	30587 Burney, T.	

NOMINAL ROLL 253

24009	Candy, R. J.	24960	Chapman, W.A.	29949	Clutterbuck, F. G.	APPENDIX IV.
16701	Cannavan, T.	17965	Chappell, J.			
14292	Cannell, S. J.	15897	Chard, F.	14909	Coates, W. G.	
24946	Canner, W.	28797	Charlton, M.	27512	Coates, W.	
15461	Cannon, J.	22687	Charlton, T.	30045	Cochill, P.	
18444	Cannon, W. J.	16386	Charnock, J.	13545	Cockayne, W.	
26859	Capel, A.	29387	Chatters, R. J.	21145	Cockbill, R.	
24616	Capewell, S.	19135	Cheeseman, A.	12787	Cockle, B. W.	
18710	Caple, W. J.	19476	Cheetham, J.	26415	Coe, R.	
24761	Capper, R.	22753	Chesnaye, W. C.	20015	Coker, J. A.	
23604	Careless, F.	16305	Chester, F. G.	24087	Coker, J. H.	
28785	Carlton, G. A.	22754	Chetter, H.	19383	Coker, W.	
23400	Carman, E.	24337	Chetwyn, E.	17177	Colbeck, H.	
31273	Carmichael, J.	11072	Cheverton, W.J.	16350	Cole, J. W.	
16338	Carpenter, R.	12610	Chevins, G.	3404	Cole, W.	
26558	Carr, J.	29399	Chilton, H. W.	16329	Cole, W. S.	
27040	Carr, W. N.	26824	Chilver, E. J.	22878	Cole, W. T.	
29147	Carr, W.	31487	Chinnick, C. F.	28521	Coleman, H.	
21585	Carrier, T.	18360	Cholerton, G.	14800	Coles, G.	
14564	Carrington, S.	21237	Clack, H.	26650	Colley, D. G.	
30357	Carr, F.	21431	Clanchy, H.	24893	Collier, E. J.	
10565	Carroll, J.	22621	Clapham, P.	15787	Collier, G.	
11140	Carson, C.	24967	Clapson, F. T.	28874	Collier, I.	
21193	Carter, A., M.M.	9838	Clare, J.	28063	Collins, A. W.	
29210	Carter, B.	15228	Clark, C. T.	17110	Collins, B.	
14618	Carter, C. R.	18114	Clark, J.	31029	Collins, D. G.	
15121	Carter, J. C.	25208	Clark, J.	27190	Collins, E. H.	
26771	Carter, J. L.	25939	Clark, J. W. F.	13461	Collins, G.	
25188	Carter, O. F.	28164	Clark, P.	28041	Collins, R.	
18343	Carter, T. J.	26784	Clark, R.	9598	Collins, T.	
10806	Carter, V. A. B.	23635	Clark, R. W.	23504	Colven, W.	
13510	Carter, W.	17275	Clark, T. S. W.	24561	Comfort, A. H.	
26339	Carter, W.	24431	Clark, W.	29645	Commander, A. E.	
25120	Cartwright, W.	25342	Clark, W.			
28569	Casson, O.	24902	Clarke, A.	28370	Condon, F. F.	
14301	Catchpole, H.	20267	Clarke, E. S.	18624	Connell, J.	
14522	Caunt, G. P.	20885	Clarke, G.	12337	Connell, R.	
28048	Causer, W. A.	14844	Clarke, H. F.	21831	Consterdine, J.	
18675	Cave, A.	8231	Clarke, N.	12793	Coogan, M.	
17898	Caveney, J.	17623	Clarke, T. J.	31820	Cook, C.	
24589	Chadbourne, A.	16681	Clarke, W. H.	27252	Cook, C. G.	
13850	Chadwick, P. E.	17542	Clarkson, J., M.M.	11918	Cook, E.	
26897	Chadwick, R.			20227	Cook, E. G.	
26802	Chadwick, T.	27148	Clarkson, T.	26674	Cook, F.	
25019	Chainey, W. G.	25906	Clasper, J.	22682	Cook, J. W.	
21036	Challoner, E. C.	21587	Claxton, R. W.	13425	Cook, P. G.	
26137	Chambers, C. E.	26340	Clay, T.	26800	Cook, W.	
21586	Chambers, M.	21700	Clayton, G. A.	16644	Cooke, G. M.	
25918	Chambers, R.W.	26465	Clegg, S. W.	14181	Cooke, P. T.	
12829	Chandler, J.	14488	Clements, B. R.	22771	Cooke, W.	
24712	Chant, C. W. F.	14363	Clements, W.	22409	Cookson, J.	
28962	Chant, J. R.	8151	Clewes, W.	25847	Cooley, B.	
18545	Chantler, H.	24375	Clifford, G. J.	11456	Cooling, H.	
13388	Chapman, A. H.	24580	Clinkard, H. A.	16275	Coombe, O.	
28974	Chapman, A. T.	16370	Clissold, W. C.	29049	Coombs, W.	
15468	Chapman, E. J.	28293	Cloak, G. H.	26438	Coop, G. W.	
26587	Chapman, F.	16398	Clowes, J.	27518	Cooper, A. G.	
20700	Chapman, H. S.	16393	Clowes, R.	13571	Cooper, E.	
16431	Chapman, W. A.	27047	Clune, L. V. F.	21244	Cooper, F. W. A.	

254 THE GRENADIER GUARDS

APPENDIX IV.

21350 Cooper, H.	14017 Creed, A.	16397 Daniels, D.
26885 Cooper, O. T.	21365 Cripps, A. E.	16495 Dann, E. E.
21722 Cooper, T.	16250 Cripps, E.	29842 Dann, F. T.
16689 Coote, R. G.	22401 Croan, P.	24305 Darg, D. B.
24295 Cope, A.	11614 Crockford, A. G.	12901 Darlington, G., M.M.
24509 Copnall, F.	12129 Croft, E.	
30345 Coppard, C.	22775 Croft, P.	15859 Dash, P.
18424 Coppard, W.	28033 Crook, E.	25531 Davey, J.
18025 Copperthwaite, W. A.	28800 Crooker, D. V.	25303 Davey, M.
	24026 Cross, F.	28149 Davidson, C. E.
10845 Corbett, E.	25522 Cross, G.	24377 Davie, C. F.
21444 Corbett, W.	28220 Cross, G. W. C.	21936 Davies, A.
29126 Cordwell, C. F.	15397 Cross, J.	26775 Davies, B. D.
21356 Cork, C.	28754 Cross, J.	26772 Davies, C.
24939 Corlett, A. A.	24664 Cross, L.	16410 Davies, D.
24940 Corlett, R. R.	25358 Cross, W. R.	20327 Davies, F.
20834 Cormack, L.	27982 Crouch, H.	26439 Davies, O. T.
16311 Cornelius, J. W.	19455 Crouch, W. G.	28386 Davies, P. H.
21844 Cornish, S. E.	16017 Croucher, W.	24979 Davies, R. T.
25605 Cornish, W.	21726 Crow, A. E.	22084 Davies, T.
27584 Cornthwaite, R.	28046 Crowder, S. F.	26665 Davies, T.
20679 Cornwell, T.	21663 Crowley, E. W.	16208 Davis, C.
18854 Corps, A. E.	24328 Crumpton, E.	24117 Davis, E.
20200 Corrigan, G.	24148 Crundwell, G.	15513 Davis, E. J.
19628 Corrigan, J. T.	19539 Cubitt, G.	19384 Davis, G. P.
18250 Cossey, J. W.	21215 Cull, A.	23286 Davis, J.
19146 Cotgreave, J.	20453 Cullen, J.	29052 Davis, J. H.
26268 Cottam, W.	14122 Cullum, J. S.	18156 Davis, J. S.
21859 Cottrell, J.	27289 Cummins, J.	19848 Davis, M. G.
26430 Couldrey, F.	15399 Cummins, R. J.	21096 Davison, R. V.
23310 Couling, S.	25107 Cunliffe, S.	15201 Dawe, A. H.
23124 Coulthard, A.	17114 Cunliffe, T.	17207 Dawes, H. L.
21210 Couchman, A. E.	24370 Cunliffe, W. B.	25359 Dawes, T.
	13033 Cunningham, A.	28787 Dawson, A.
27775 Counsell, C.	19593 Cunningham, H.	22451 Dawson, G. E.
18293 Coupe, F. W.	8915 Cupit, J. P.	15822 Day, A. V.
26089 Coupland, E. C.	18625 Curbishley, H.	18910 Day, E. G.
12563 Court, G.	20926 Curtis, B.	22496 Day, H.
26247 Cousins, T. A.	12803 Curtis, E.	24542 Day, H. W.
13467 Coventry, J. E.	22465 Curtis, J. S.	22369 Day, J. H.
20938 Cowens, J. T.	14651 Curtis, W.	25285 Day, M.
21061 Cowley, T.	25439 Curtis, W. A.	27237 Day, P. R.
19921 Cox, A. F.	11185 Curzon, W.	23557 Day, R.
30489 Cox, E.	21892 Cutler, J.	22561 Day, W.
23575 Cox, E. S.	25132 Cutting, H. W.	16185 Day, W.
9535 Cox, J.	14048 Cutts, M.	29267 Day, W.
17550 Cox, J.	21269 Dabell, A.	20461 Daykin, M.
20175 Cox, J. D.	18906 Dadley, R. J.	12091 Deakin, H.
29826 Cox, S. J.	26230 Dagger, D.	32283 Deamer, C. A.
12060 Cox, W.	23717 Dale, H.	11442 Dean, F.
18093 Coxall, R. W.	22807 Daley, J.	15198 Death, H.
22604 Coxhead, W. A.	14969 Dalton, A.	14657 Deeley, S. T.
13098 Coxon, T.	15939 Dalziel, W. G. M.	30320 Deem, B. T.
20343 Coy, C.		23786 Delaney, J. T.
31099 Cradock, W.	24166 Danby, T.	14373 Dell, W.
27385 Craig, B.	21893 Dangerfield, S. T.	28879 Denison, H.
20627 Crane, C. A.		28320 Denison, J. W.
25301 Crawford, H.	27021 Daniel, E. J.	24844 Dennis, F. J.
11160 Crawford, J. R.	26000 Daniell, F. G.	31641 Dennis, W. M.

NOMINAL ROLL

16035 Denny, F.	25425 Drayton, P. H.	26636 Eggleton, H., M.M.
27641 Dent, G. N.	28295 Dresser, E. E.	16432 Elder, A. G.
28945 Denton, J. D.	31237 Drew, F.	18066 Eldridge, H. B.
29513 Derbyshire, H.	25811 Drew, G.	22873 Elford, F. W.
28216 Derbyshire, W. J.	28459 Drewitt, R.	17597 Elkin, A.
14545 Devine, J. T.	22645 Drewry, S. T.	35214 Elkin, H.
13035 Devonshire, D.	11183 Drinkwater, P.	24189 Elliott, A.
20141 Dibble, R. J.	16590 Duckhouse, L.	22823 Elliott, F. R.
17707 Dickaty, C.	23483 Duckmanton, T.	9316 Elliott, R.
13717 Dickens, H. C.	26416 Duckworth, E. R.	18327 Ellis, A. R.
24995 Digby, F. R.	17551 Duddy, J. L.	27713 Ellis, E.
25713 Dignan, W.	17966 Dudley, D.	25672 Ellison, A.
18816 Dill, H.	20915 Duffitt, W.	22492 Ellson, A.
19640 Dillon, T.	28604 Duke, R.	17078 Ellwood, E. P.
25905 Dilloway, G. J.	7794 Duncan, A.	17781 Ellwood, W. E.
14486 Dinham, S. G. V.	13378 Duncan, P.	25518 Elsey, A. G.
25598 Dipple, G. E.	28474 Dunne, J. M.	10501 Elson, J. H.
31573 Dix, H. V.	11215 Dunning, H. J.	24701 Elvidge, A. H.
26980 Dixon, C. J. S.	16464 Durant, L.	31950 Ely, W. C.
29112 Dixon, G. M.	23680 Dutton, T.	26472 Emmott, L.
11710 Dixon, J.	15877 Dyde, A.	24714 England, R.
22076 Dixon, R.	28720 Dyer, A. E.	24831 Engley, J.
21792 Dixon, T.	15472 Dyer, H.	23946 Enstone, H. J.
18126 Dixon, W.	25892 Dyer, J. R.	18094 Entwistle, A.
23723 Dixon, W.	17383 Dyke, H.	30085 Erdbeer, G. H.
22090 Dixon, W. J.	18065 Eagle, E. A.	21895 Errington, C. W.
18489 Dobbs, H.	19163 Eaglestone, W. A.	23418 Errington, R. S.
24444 Dobbs, H. A.	23643 Ealden, F.	16472 Essery, F. W.
21673 Dobby, H. T.	29008 Easey, B.	19584 Espley, A.
24641 Dobson, A.	17295 Easley, S.	22832 Evans, A. F.
12715 Dodd, J.	16728 East, R. F.	20250 Evans, A. G.
16883 Dodd, J.	16425 Easton, J.	17912 Evans, A. L.
31333 Dodd, S. J.	27716 Eaton, E. W. C.	15047 Evans, D.
28406 Dodding, E. G. S.	16270 Eaton, J. H.	25838 Evans, E. E.
23656 Dodman, E.	14886 Eaton, W.	21664 Evans, H. D.
16057 Dodsley, W. G.	16673 Ecclestone, R.	8154 Evans, I.
18754 Doherty, J.	15732 Eden, G.	23187 Evans, J.
24281 Dolphin, G.	20583 Edgar, H.	28408 Evans, J.
15239 Dominey, S. W.	26149 Edgell, S.	26684 Evans, J. H.
16743 Donlan, W.	23967 Edmonds, F. W.	30561 Evans, J. P.
20651 Dooley, T.	18450 Edwards, A. W.	23344 Evans, S.
24015 Dorey, A. P.	22337 Edwards, A. W.	7851 Evans, T.
25722 Dorricott, J.	17375 Edwards, B.	20481 Evans, T. J.
29940 Douglas, H. J.	11644 Edwards, G.	15735 Evans, V.
16626 Dowd, J.	27896 Edwards, G.	25496 Evans, W.
16306 Dowdon, E. L.	25225 Edwards, G. W.	27097 Evans, W.
22138 Dowling, H. J.	16769 Edwards, H. J.	28707 Evans, W.
11210 Downing, G. H.	10972 Edwards, J.	12488 Eve, F.
22497 Dowse, W. H.	23381 Edwards, J.	16366 Everitt, G. F.
26567 Doyle, P.	11840 Edwards, J. G.	24289 Evers, T.
18969 Drackett, C.	4859 Edwards, S. G. L.	24280 Every, A.
16375 Drain, G.	20618 Egan, J.	19623 Evison, J.
18064 Drake, A.	16399 Eggenton, W.	30185 Exton, W. T.
19757 Drake, M.		22454 Eyden, W.
26631 Drakett, W.		24820 Eyre, J.
• 13430 Draycott, W.		18144 Eyre, S.
16183 Draycott, W. H.		25735 Fancourt, F.

APPENDIX IV.

256 THE GRENADIER GUARDS

APPENDIX IV.

29961 Farleigh, E.	26681 Fletcher, S. E.	15927 Frazer, W. T.
28398 Farmer, R. L.	30446 Fletcher, W.	20202 Freeman, E.
18425 Farmer, W. M.	28845 Flook, F. W.	16373 Freeman, G. E.
23527 Farnsworth, J. H.	17254 Flower, J.	11740 Freeman, W.
	20417 Flynn, J.	28913 Freeman, W. E.
14717 Farrell, J.	10552 Flynn, T.	25583 Freer, F. H.
20948 Farthing, T.	23999 Fogg, H. N.	14912 French, P.
22226 Faulkner, J. W.	11680 Foley, J.	14035 French, T. F.
28309 Faulks, J.	16847 Foote, O. J. H.	11277 French, W.
20868 Fawcett, M.	16625 Footman, T. B.	16904 Freshwater, W. G.
20842 Fawcett, R. G.	18451 Ford, A.	
24073 Fayle, D. H.	13676 Ford, C. S.	15885 Fretter, H. M.
24975 Fear, A.	15740 Ford, D.	29641 Friend, A.
14081 Fearn, W.	19174 Ford, F. H.	26192 Frisby, F. T.
12754 Fears, A. C.	31164 Ford, I.	29392 Frost, G.
14918 Feary, E. B.	12286 Ford, J.	28901 Frost, J.
13371 Featherstone, T. C.	28828 Ford, P.	15455 Frost, W. S.
	20078 Ford, W. H.	27944 Fry, A. C.
21497 Fell, C.	10068 Foreman, E.	11624 Fry, W. A.
28065 Fellender, T.	23067 Foreman, W. G.	21739 Fullard, J.
28223 Felsted, A.	27849 Forgan, A.	28341 Fuller, A.
26031 Felton, F.	18371 Forknell, H.	26560 Fuller, C. H.
28334 Fenn, A.	20182 Forrester, W.	11012 Fuller, J. W.
25683 Fenn, R. W.	11009 Forshaw, T.	20093 Fullman, S. G.
31695 Fenson, G.	17934 Forster, F. H.	22444 Fulonger, V.
18873 Fenton, E. V., M.M.	13884 Forster, J. B.	28258 Furness, J.
	16037 Forster, J. S.	15902 Furniss, D. L.
27033 Ferguson, H.	27134 Fortune, J.	28361 Fyfield, C. M.
12532 Few, R.	14479 Fosher, A.	24386 Gaffney, J.
27946 Fewtrell, W.	22607 Foster, C. J.	21002 Gage, L. V.
21982 Fiddies, C.	28882 Foster, F.	28387 Gale, B. A., M.M.
26405 Field, J. C.	22260 Foster, G. J.	
24107 Field, W.	16438 Foster, H.	13859 Gale, G. S.
24829 Field, W. J.	21794 Foster, S.	14227 Gale, W.
25469 Fieldhouse, G.	17873 Fountain, E.	21860 Gallagher, M.
20887 Fields, J.	20362 Fowler, G.	22537 Gallear, W.
22091 Fieldsend, F.	22208 Fowler, J.	17218 Gamble, C.
20345 Figgis, J. B., M.M.	18757 Fowler, R. G.	21322 Gambrill, F. A.
	13324 Fox, E.	23407 Gamlin, F.
9187 Final, G.	15598 Fox, G.	29199 Gamman, S.
33242 Fineran, W.	29603 Fox, H.	25529 Gane, W.
25386 Finnamore, E.	26369 Fox, J.	13968 Gardiner, H.
30027 Finneran, C.	29561 Fox, J. S.	17243 Gardiner, H.
22062 Finney, F.	28747 Fox, M.	15044 Gardiner, S.
26658 Firth, H.	24498 Fox, W. J.	21154 Gardner, H. F.
21635 Fisher, E.	22103 Foxon, H. J. C.	24144 Garlick, S.
17604 Fisher, J. H.	29047 Frampton, S. H.	22647 Garment, W. S.
14937 Fisher, R.	30227 Frampton, W. F.	29454 Garner, J.
13797 Fitch, H. E.		26157 Garner, R. A.
11156 Fitzgerald, J.	25167 France, H.	29914 Garnett, E.
10557 Fitzgerald, T.	29718 France, W.	31635 Garratt, T.
21452 Fixter, W. R.	11096 Francis, A.	25014 Garrett, A.
24365 Flavell, W. C.	28929 Francis, F. C.	21168 Garrett, E.
25390 Fleming, W. M.	13581 Francis, J.	20088 Garton, H.
20155 Fletcher, A.	21220 Francis, R. C.	23873 Garvey, W.
13303 Fletcher, F. J.	21537 Frankton, W. F.	22487 Gascoigne, A.
28557 Fletcher, G. E.	17332 Fraser, R.	14678 Gates, A.
13375 Fletcher, O.	24483 Fraser, W.	20072 Gawthorn, J. E.
18512 Fletcher, R.	26914 Fray, W. S.	23399 Gaywood, J. N.

NOMINAL ROLL

12494 Gee, W.	28618 Goodwin, J.	20355 Griffin, M.
25588 Geeves, A.	29274 Goodwin, J. P.	21613 Griffin, T.
27564 Gelder, W. D.	15487 Goodwin, P. W.	16328 Griffith-Williams, A. F.
27968 Gentle, H.	15312 Goodwin, R.	
14816 George, C. W.	20668 Goodwin, W. J.	29916 Griffiths, A. L.
26352 George, J.	28049 Goom, N.	20115 Griffiths, D.
25669 Gibbons, A.	25825 Gordon, A.	10442 Griffiths, E. R.
26961 Gibbons, L.	23552 Gorton, P.	30016 Griffiths, J.
18660 Gibbons, T.	18936 Gosling, T. G.	25421 Griffiths, P.
25196 Gibbs, B.	26322 Gott, J. H.	27588 Griffiths, R. A.
14214 Gibbs, J.	14098 Gough, C. H.	30597 Griffiths, W. H.
15033 Gibbs, W. T.	11085 Gough, F.	28700 Grime, J.
26474 Gibson, C. H. B.	11928 Gough, G.	27735 Grime, W.
20549 Gibson, J.	13034 Gough, F. E.	20919 Grimsdale, H.
20819 Gibson, S.	24245 Goulding, C.	25449 Grimshaw, S.
25435 Gibson, W. H.	23583 Goulding, W.	24460 Grindley, E.
15244 Giffen, W. C.	30596 Gower, V. A.	28158 Gritten, H. A.
26372 Gilbert, E. H.	29889 Grace, A. H.	24264 Grocott, G. H.
30399 Gilbert, C. T.	26111 Gramshaw, E.	13788 Grooms, E.
23502 Gilding, A.	19397 Grant, J. T.	18547 Grove, W. T.
27316 Giles, W.	15155 Gray, F.	11477 Grundy, J., D.C.M.
27008 Gilham, R. J.	24976 Gray, E. W.	
28432 Gill, R. H.	23036 Gray, H. C.	28327 Grundy, J.
15918 Gillett, F.	24595 Graydon, W.	26663 Grundy, R. T.
21271 Gillott, W.	20378 Greaves, W. A. G.	30352 Grundy, W.
15278 Gilmore, J.		18656 Gunn, A.
26500 Gilroy, J.	11082 Greaves, W. H.	25006 Gunn, A. E. L.
15616 Gilson, A. G.	29997 Green, A.	20229 Guthrie, M.
23465 Gilson, J.	22858 Green, A. E.	30241 Guttridge, C. F.
20565 Gittus, H.	21063 Green, F. G.	22592 Guy, G. R.
17875 Gleed, G.	10606 Green, G. H.	24889 Guy, H. C.
22355 Glover, H.	20371 Green, J.	11099 Guymer, H.
14423 Glynn, J.	16205 Green, J. D.	19419 Gwinnett, H.
30565 Goddard, A. H. J.	12758 Green, R.	28826 Hack, L.
	27377 Green, S. M.	21486 Hackett, E.
14932 Godden, D.	30404 Green, T. P.	28252 Haddock, A.
12368 Godfrey, J. A.	27194 Green, W.	20402 Haddow, A. J.
24850 Godfrey, F.	29835 Green, W. A.	17102 Hadley, T.
21545 Godman, W.	27425 Greene, W.	16993 Hague, H.
22158 Godsafe, A. E.	25005 Greenland, G.	23384 Hague, J.
19018 Goff, G. H. W.	27955 Greenough, J.T.	26396 Haigh, W.
27376 Goldfinch, E. T.	16123 Greenstreet, J. R.	28082 Hale, L.
30338 Golson, J.		16919 Hales, G. H.
19585 Gomer, C. E.	21314 Greenway, E.	21848 Hales, W. J.
22748 Goodacre, S. E.	23351 Greenwood, A.	13708 Halfpenny, C.
17473 Goodall, A. S.	20419 Greenwood, W. A.	24023 Hall, A.
10236 Goodall, S.		18513 Hall, A. F.
16080 Goodchild, W.	28381 Gregory, J.	26819 Hall, A. W.
31019 Goodchild, L. J. T.	12972 Gregory, J. W.	24935 Hall, B.
	23938 Gregory, H.	13705 Hall, E.
26265 Goodedge, T.	25731 Gregory, W. H.	18649 Hall, E.
15490 Gooderham, G.	26579 Gregson, E.	21112 Hall, E.
25459 Gooderham, W.	26043 Gribble, H. C. E.	16836 Hall, E. A.
24621 Goodes, R. B.		28872 Hall, E. F.
30205 Goodeve, E. A.	17176 Grice, G.	16392 Hall, F. J.
22152 Goodier, H. B.	30773 Griffen, W. W.	21142 Hall, G.
18486 Gooding, A. M.	28783 Griffin, C. R.	21570 Hall, H. D.
22599 Goodwin, A. V.	28081 Griffin, E. G.	22648 Hall, J. H.
14929 Goodwin, F. T.	14313 Griffin, H. J.	29258 Hall, R.

APPENDIX IV.

258 THE GRENADIER GUARDS

Appendix IV.

27745 Hall, R.	16771 Hardy, R.	20566 Harvey, W.
16179 Hall, W.	12864 Hargreaves, F.	15568 Hasell, W. J.
24397 Hall, W.	22908 Hargreaves, J. R.	29171 Hatcher, A. E.
23470 Hallam, A.		16611 Hattemore, W. C.
18116 Hallam, J. H.	21728 Harker, J.	
22818 Hallam, W. T.	18791 Harkness, F.	16161 Hawkes, H.
28773 Hallett, H. S.	26589 Harlow, C. A.	16334 Hawkes, T. A. J.
21845 Halls, F.	21419 Harney, H.	
21756 Hamblin, R.	22918 Harper, A. F.	16449 Hawkins, A. G.
23088 Hambridge, S. J.	25165 Harper, C. T.	24735 Hawkins, H.
	28840 Harper, E.	19715 Hawkins, R.
13666 Hamer, R. C.	21943 Harper, S.	28993 Hawkridge, L.
26695 Hamer, E.	30041 Harper, W. F.	25177 Haxton, W.
25654 Hames, W. H. J.	17500 Harrick, J. J.	25552 Hay, C. E.
	15978 Harrington, T. A.	18208 Hayden, W.
21217 Hamilton, T.		25716 Hayes, J. H.
26354 Hammond, C. H. G.	7956 Harris, A.	19483 Hayes, R.
	22860 Harris, A. E.	32284 Hayhurst, J.
29968 Hammond, F. M.	23856 Harris, A. J.	27859 Haynes, A. G.
	17675 Harris, C. N.	29334 Haythornthwaite, R. W.
12732 Hammond, W.	16023 Harris, F.	
24998 Hammond, W.	22649 Harris, F.	20876 Hayward, F.
17929 Hampson, J.	23438 Harris, F. G.	26776 Haywood, T.
12602 Hampton, H.	24721 Harris, H. A.	25418 Hazelby, T.
27922 Hampton, H.	29215 Harris, H. W.	25419 Hazelby, W.
15162 Hampton, J. H.	13834 Harris, J.	16315 Head, L. W.
23769 Hanch, A. E.	14812 Harris, J.	25860 Healey, P.
30985 Hancock, L. S.	21099 Harris, J.	20081 Healey, R. R.
28245 Hand, B.	16331 Harris, J. H.	23797 Healey, W.
25317 Handford, J. G.	28284 Harris, S.	11258 Heard, W. H.
16910 Handley, W.	10891 Harris, S. E.	18628 Hearn, F.
18227 Hands, A. E.	24259 Harris, S. H.	16215 Heasman, F. B.
17811 Hands, J.	28291 Harris, T. E.	
16091 Handy, J.	23660 Harris, W.	23699 Heastie, W. K.
29630 Handy, W. F.	8814 Harris, W.	20375 Heath, C.
25170 Hankin, S.	27916 Harris, W. H.	27168 Heath, E. J.
14760 Hankinson, F. W.	24411 Harrison, A. W.	11090 Heath, F.
	30232 Harrison, C. H.	23431 Heath, J. T.
20257 Hanley, J.	14575 Harrison, C. L.	26893 Heath, P. L.
17576 Hann, F. A.	30570 Harrison, F.	16178 Heathcote, J.
20949 Hannaway, J.	10528 Harrison, G.	28080 Hebblewhite, W.
26526 Hansell, A.	25049 Harrison, G. H.	
25974 Hansford, C. E.	29680 Harrison, H.	17331 Hedge, W.
24693 Hansford, B.	29380 Harrison, H. P.	21222 Henshall, W.
25108 Hanson, S.	19189 Harrison, J.	11265 Henson, R.
24572 Happs, F.	26424 Harrison, J.	18318 Henwood, S. H.
25097 Harber, J. H.	16903 Harrison, J. J.	26433 Herbert, C. H.
17232 Harcombe, F. H.	22128 Harrison, R.	29311 Herbert, F. C.
	27646 Harrison, R. C.	24782 Herbert, P. C.
16159 Harding, A. H.	22824 Harrison, T.	16264 Herbert, S.
13966 Harding, H.	23770 Hart, R. D.	16912 Heritage, E. A.
17010 Harding, J. G. C.	29140 Hart, S.	23103 Hern, G. H.
	28034 Hartland, A.	28489 Herrin, J. H.
23437 Harding, P. T.	22415 Hartley, W.	20809 Herrington, C.
20702 Hardman, J.	17785 Hartopp, H. E.	22099 Hersel, J. F.
28391 Hardwick, W.	9840 Hartwell, C.	26513 Hesketh, M.
22780 Hardy, A. T.	13876 Hartwell, H. G.	28591 Hesketh, T. J.
23659 Hardy, F. H.	18959 Harvey, A.	29926 Hesketh, W.
12026 Hardy, H. O.	29073 Harvey, E.	14574 Heslin, J. E.

NOMINAL ROLL

17852 Hetherington, A. S.	20769 Hodgson, J.	20100 Houghton, J.
28023 Hewes, A. W.	18209 Hodgson, R.	25523 Houghton, R.
30087 Hewetson, F.	26671 Hodgson, T.	24454 Howard, E.
21592 Hewitt, C. E.	20871 Hodgson, W. H.	22666 Howard, F. J.
27437 Hewgill, J.	20276 Hodson, W. T.	26050 Howarth, C. W.
16415 Hewitt, C. J.	30600 Hogg, A. M.	20435 Howarth, F. H.
17674 Hewitt, F. T. W.	17422 Hogg, T. H.	21741 Howarth, J.
	30322 Hoggard, W. E.	24677 Howarth, J.
26213 Hewitt, J.	17534 Hoggins, A. E.	18666 Howell, G.
21265 Heywood, F.	24537 Hogsden, W. G.	28843 Howell, W.
17606 Hibbard, T. J.	23837 Holden, G. J. W.	21381 Howells, F.
14731 Hickey, T.	15270 Holden, P. F. W.	14672 Howes, H. H.
21279 Hickin, A. E.		15235 Hubbard, E.
13133 Hicks, W.	25527 Holden, G.	10022 Hubbard, H.
22499 Higgins, A.	26972 Holden, J.	15907 Hubbard, S. H.
28656 Higgins, E. G.	17922 Holden, J.	24424 Hubble, G. H.
20794 Higgins, J.	21900 Holden, S.	21352 Huckin, W. H.
14554 Higgins, S. R.	23558 Holland, A.	18111 Huckins, E.
24004 Hignett, J.	18277 Holland, L.	22165 Hucklesby, G. F.
17209 Hill, A. F.	17711 Holland, M.	11162 Hudson, T. H.
27969 Hill, A. J.	24505 Hollins, A. J.	26691 Hudson, S.
16902 Hill, C. D.	18045 Hollinshead, J. T.	12492 Huffen, J. H.
18548 Hill, F.		17355 Huffer, C., M.M.
10640 Hill, F.	22396 Hollis, A.	
15388 Hill, F. J.	23713 Holmes, C. A.	21256 Huggett, H.
21166 Hill, H. W. A.	21938 Holmes, G.	27505 Huggins, H.
11974 Hill, J.	11604 Holmes, J.	26734 Hughes, A. C.
14543 Hill, J.	22375 Holmes, J.	29137 Hughes, C.
28675 Hill, J. S.	19166 Holmes, J. H.	14424 Hughes, D. O.
22252 Hill, O.	26923 Holmes, M.	31546 Hughes, H. D.
16708 Hill, W.	13290 Holmes, S. K.	24608 Hull, W. A.
22695 Hillier, H. J.	28632 Holmes, W.	8698 Hulley, G.
14315 Hillier, J.	16796 Holmes, W. E.	25021 Hulme, E.
10684 Hills, F.	26637 Holt, F.	21793 Hulse, H.
23424 Hilton, F.	20704 Holt, J.	19147 Human, A.
14250 Hind, A. E.	22578 Holwill, F.	19447 Humphrey, J. H.
16152 Hind, J.	10461 Holyoak, E. C.	
23632 Hind, W.	25171 Hood, A.	26456 Humphrey, J.
27238 Hindle, H. H.	19052 Hood, J.	29425 Humphrey, J.
27640 Hindle, S.	27240 Hooper, H. J.	21209 Humphreys, A. E.
14884 Hindmoor, R.	11473 Hooton, A.	
17949 Hine, F. J.	20500 Hopkin, T.	24149 Humphreys, F. J.
9027 Hinton, A. E.	13521 Hopkins, A.	
25837 Hinton, E. H.	13406 Hopkins, J.	19962 Humphries, E.
24974 Hiron, T.	16279 Hopkins, R.	16580 Humphries, G.
14364 Hiscock, A.	12398 Hopkins, S.	17329 Hunt, A.
21058 Hislop, H.	15683 Hopkinson, W.	19410 Hunt, C.
21323 Hitchings, W. H.	19856 Horler, H.	26445 Hunt, E.
	25509 Horn, W. G.	25121 Hunt, H.
28498 Hobbs, E.	16814 Horne, F. G.	13791 Hunt, J.
23562 Hobbs, O. C.	19673 Horne, J. L.	18883 Hunt, S.
29035 Hobcroft, H. L.	18550 Horrocks, E.	15240 Hunt, W.
12641 Hobson, W.	18552 Horrocks, F.	27530 Hunt, W.
26652 Hockaday, J.	21266 Horrocks, F.	28882 Hunt, W. C.
19591 Hocking, J.	23569 Horrocks, H. E.	27111 Hunter, A.
24476 Hodgkin, T.	17381 Horton, A.	28153 Hunton, J.
22704 Hodgkiss, E.	18086 Hotson, W. E.	26643 Hurd, J.
18657 Hodgson, J.	19321 Hough, F.	25231 Huntley, E.

APPENDIX IV.

260 THE GRENADIER GUARDS

APPENDIX IV.

19532 Hurdus, A.	28037 Jeffries, R. J.	14497 Jones, P. M.
19398 Hurst, R. G.	31482 Jenkins, A.	8931 Jones, R.
29057 Hutchings, H.	18046 Jenkins, A. F.	16712 Jones, R.
31281 Hutchins, T. A. V.	24100 Jenkins, A. R.	28589 Jones, R.
17599 Hutchinson, S.	29190 Jenkins, H.	30124 Jones, R. F.
20567 Hutchinson, G. W.	10839 Jenkins, J.	15061 Jones, S. A.
27139 Hutchinson, P. D.	19148 Jenkinson, W.	13278 Jones, S. G. A.
29719 Hutchinson, W.	17531 Jennings, J.	28520 Jones, T.
22911 Hutton, F. B.	22996 Jennison, J.	15211 Jones, T. S.
22330 Hyams, H. B.	14513 Jessup, H.	14506 Jones, W.
28676 Hypson, W. A. T.	16340 Jessup, H. S.	17661 Jones, W.
16974 Ibbetson, J.	23324 Jesty, A. V.	21114 Jones, W. J.
27293 Illman, T. G.	11925 Jillians, A.	23354 Jones, W. J.
12577 Ince, H.	23209 Jinks, B. G.	24801 Jones, W. W.
25253 Ingham, H.	12982 Johncey, F.	13149 Jordan, E.
27231 Ingham, J.	22594 Johnson, A.	17330 Jordan, A. E.
26633 Ingham, T. H.	24456 Johnson, A.	22205 Jordan, L. G.
28339 Ingham, T. W.	19727 Johnson, B.	27591 Jowsey, T.
14256 Ingram, A.	14269 Johnson, C.	13690 Joy, A.
28876 Ingram, C. J.	28596 Johnson, E.	28628 Joy, H. G.
30053 Ingram, H. W.	14725 Johnson, F.	18573 Judson, W. T.
15020 Ingram, W.	20660 Johnson, F.	17522 Kane, G.
15223 Insull, R.	17616 Johnson, F. A.	17533 Kay, A. S.
19654 Ions, W.	15140 Johnson, F. C.	28978 Kay, H. E.
14454 Jackman, G.	15594 Johnson, F. S.	19051 Kay, N.
26249 Jackson, A.	20602 Johnson, G. E.	17644 Kay, W. N.
26395 Jackson, A.	22717 Johnson, H.	25365 Kavanagh, A.
27041 Jackson, A.	28077 Johnson, H.	17017 Kear, W.
16411 Jackson, C.	31466 Johnson, H.	27439 Kearney, J. W.
17967 Jackson, E.	28100 Johnson, H. C.	12718 Kearns, A. P.
27748 Jackson, F. W.	23000 Johnson, H. W.	16482 Keay, D. O.
15292 Jackson, G.	28686 Johnson, J.	15843 Keeley, F.
28292 Jackson, H.	29557 Johnson, J. G.	22904 Keeling, W. T.
21999 Jackson, J. B.	25219 Johnston, D. M.	16337 Keen, F. J.
21331 Jackson, J. W.	23272 Johnston, H.	24061 Keen, W.
17258 Jacques, W.	17849 Johnston, W. A.	11267 Keenan, J. A.
10975 Jaggard, J.	20034 Johnstone, J.	13331 Kehoe, N.
27535 James, A.	14610 Jones, A.	10938 Keightley, W.
21059 James, E.	17545 Jones, A., M.M.	18029 Kelcher, H.
15932 James, E.	13470 Jones, A. S.	27045 Kelly, J.
25761 James, F. W.	15443 Jones, C.	30187 Kelly, J. E.
18285 James, L.	19312 Jones, C. E.	18994 Kelly, J. T.
15410 James, S.	22441 Jones, D.	12192 Kembry, W. J.
14671 Jamieson, C. F.	12755 Jones, D. H.	24072 Kemp, A.
30107 Jarratt, J. H.	17720 Jones, D. R.	18827 Kemp, C. J.
22749 Jarvis, A.	16785 Jones, E.	17861 Kennedy, F.
26194 Jarvis, C.	27310 Jones, E.	24390 Kennedy, D. F.
30505 Jarvis, C. H.	20626 Jones, F. J.	24717 Kennerley, W.
18965 Jarvis, E.	14814 Jones, F. P.	27754 Kenny, B.
22131 Jarvis, E. S.	12404 Jones, G.	21514 Kenshole, J.
28378 Jarvis, J. W.	16985 Jones, G., M.M.	23634 Kent, F.
24665 Jarvis, S. W.	28017 Jones, G. B.	13032 Kent, M.
23445 Jay, W.	22916 Jones, G. T.	15414 Kent, P. R.
28786 Jeanes, W. H.	10104 Jones, H.	15398 Kenward, C. H.
22842 Jeffrey, H. S. S.	22000 Jones, H. W.	24091 Kenyon, J. F.
	15633 Jones, J.	13706 Kerr, W.
	22925 Jones, M.	17908 Kershaw, G. C.
	23830 Jones, M.	9704 Kerton, G.
	16666 Jones, P.	28110 Keyte, S. G.

NOMINAL ROLL 261

22880 Keyte, W.	23764 Langley, C.	10858 Lightfoot, I.	APPENDIX IV.
17594 Kibbey, V. R.	21917 Langton, E.	12677 Lightfoot, T.	
18554 Kidd, G.	15826 Lant, F.	20576 Lightwood, C.	
13920 Kidd, H. G.	29925 Larkin, E. S.	16841 Lilley, E. G.	
17962 Kilbee, C.	15701 Launder, R. W.	27125 Lillington, S. F.	
13076 Kilby, W. T.	28280 Law, J.	18715 Lincoln, A.	
12828 King, A.	19021 Law, R.	28141 Lindley, H.	
11398 King, E. M.	20386 Lawley, W.	27156 Lindley, S.	
27851 King, F. W.	19972 Lawlor, J.	16863 Lindop, H.	
11396 King, G. H.	22363 Lawrence, A.	21479 Linford, G. H.	
24392 King, J. W.	26008 Lawrence, F.	29356 Link, O. L. E.	
21340 King, S. C.	23097 Lawrence, G. H.	16322 Linton, P.	
16837 King, T. J.	15464 Lawrence, J.	19020 Lintott, G. T.	
20781 King, W.	12197 Lawrie, W.	24611 Lister, A.	
14462 Kingcott, H. J.	26185 Laws, A. F.	12761 Litchfield, E.	
18276 Kingham, A.	21335 Laws, J. J.	30221 Litchfield, W. H. G.	
12943 Kingston, A. B.	17936 Lawson, H.		
23607 Kirby, H. C.	17938 Lawson, J.	13992 Little, E. J.	
27218 Kirby, E. W.	23173 Lawson, L. A.	19750 Little, R.	
13516 Kirkland, S.	23155 Lawton, J.	9651 Littlehales, J.	
20204 Kirkpatrick, J.	28268 Layton, S. M.	13433 Llewelyn, E.	
15948 Kite, T. J.	13905 Leach, A.	27994 Lloyd, E.	
27594 Kneale, E. J.	19902 Leach, J.	27323 Loader, R.	
17860 Knight, A. C.	20085 Leach, J.	22667 Lock, F.	
8949 Knight, E. F.	27042 Leaman, F.	27006 Locker, T.	
22917 Knight, E. H.	20675 Lears, J.	22055 Lockett, H.	
31202 Knight, G. H.	20714 Leathers, C. V.	21302 Lockwood, J. H.	
30456 Knight, J.	8912 Leckey, A.		
27642 Knight, J. W.	19637 Lee, A.	18966 Lockyer, H.	
14086 Knight, R.	23650 Lee, A.	29180 Loder, R. O.	
20749 Knight, T.	24510 Lee, F. C. W.	14113 Logan, P.	
30138 Knott, J. H.	23682 Lee, G. C.	27528 Lomax, J.	
13550 Knott, L.	18195 Lee, H.	14308 Long, E. W.	
29929 Knowles, E.	26552 Lee, R. S.	17770 Longden, T.	
21758 Knowles, J. R.	21097 Leech, J. Y.	19324 Longhurst, I. R.	
22750 Knowles, W.	13695 Leek, H. G.	20569 Longley, H. H.	
26015 Kreiner, R. H.	15700 Leek, L.	15396 Longley, J.	
29692 Labram, S.	29072 Leeming, R.	11858 Longmore, E.	
13704 Lacey, S.	24308 Lees, M.	7838 Longmore, W.	
16838 Lack, W. C.	12435 Leeson, A.	26871 Longshaw, A.	
12871 Laidlow, T.	14528 Leonard, A. F.	26547 Longworth, T.	
17833 Laird, J.	12388 Leonard, B.	31825 Loomes, J.	
26295 Lake, C.	23135 Letchford, G. A.	12843 Loosley, W. R.	
29703 Lakin, G. A.		21213 Lord, R. W.	
15289 Laking, J. H.	29437 Letherbarrow, A. A.	29040 Lott, E. V.	
21541 Lambert, A. E.		27127 Loughton, F. G.	
25441 Lambert, H.	31944 Letting, T. L.	22741 Loughton, J.	
28224 Lambert, W. C.	30459 Letts, W. H.	21685 Loveday, E. G.	
27892 Lambourne, L. E.	17188 Lewenden, E. J.	24848 Loveday, J.	
	23674 Lewin, W. J.	28183 Lovell, S. J.	
12204 Lambourne, W. J.	21742 Lewington, W. C.	15943 Lovell, T.	
		23758 Lovelock, J. A.	
18420 Lane, A. J.	16197 Lewis, A.	21341 Lovesey, T. M. O.	
12401 Lane, F.	22953 Lewis, A.		
24553 Lane, F.	24594 Lewis, G. W.	26152 Lovett, F. W.	
11344 Lane, J. H.	10495 Lewis, J.	20303 Lowder, W. L.	
11814 Lane, W.	15428 Lewis, N. W.	29935 Lowe, G. R.	
31731 Lang, H. A.	17386 Leyland, W. B.	20620 Lowe, J. W.	
21768 Langford, A.	16038 Lightfoot, A.	21597 Lowe, P.	

262 THE GRENADIER GUARDS

22402 Lowes, A.	17862 Manuel, H. L.	14508 Meadows, W. H.
20406 Lowman, L. A.	18808 Maple, J. E.	9303 Mears, E.
28823 Ludgate, A. W.	18762 Mapstone, B.	18630 Meech, W. E.
24202 Ludlow, H. L. E.	23955 Marcer, C.	29624 Meeking, J. A. A.
	22215 Marchant, H. D.	
28352 Lugard, H. A.	11669 Marks, P.	14226 Melia, J.
28011 Lunt, J.	18212 Markwick, A. V.	20426 Mellanby, J.
15854 Luxmore, W.	26027 Marriott, W. H.	18686 Mellon, J.
28244 Lyddon, F. W.	23186 Marrison, F.	18977 Mellor, J.
15953 Lymer, T.	29062 Marsden, F.	18437 Mellors, G.
20381 Lynn, W. M.	26516 Marsh, E. C.	19699 Melton, E.
17729 Lythgoe, R.	25597 Marsh, F.	19897 Melville, A.
12284 Mabbutt, E.	24650 Marsh, G. A.	14481 Melville, W.
29803 McAllister, A.	26847 Marsh, H. E.	14940 Mendorf, A. W.
15788 McArdle, W.	23090 Marsh, S. C.	20879 Mepham, J. H.
21903 McCabe, T.	13381 Marshall, G.	24746 Meredith, G.
16207 McCarthy, J.	13849 Marshall, G.	13849 Merritt, A.
19222 McDonald, J.	15952 Marshall, G. W.	11441 Merritt, S.
25051 McDonald, P.	17662 Marshall, L.	27797 Merry, W. E.
24304 McGann, F.	32134 Marshall, T.	10000 Message, E. V.
10853 McGillivray, A.	20595 Marshall, W.	20211 Metcalf, T. H.
15013 McGinn, T., M.M.	21562 Martin, H.	12234 Michael, E.
	14923 Martin, J.	20920 Micklewright, C. H.
17951 McIlwain, W.	21946 Martin, R. D.	
26817 McKevitt, H. E.	25142 Martin, R. O.	24142 Middlemiss, J. L.
24702 Macklin, W.	25854 Martin, S. C.	
27022 McKnight, H.	25130 Martin, W.	14164 Middleton, W.
19690 McNeil, W. T.	20035 Martin, W.	24384 Milburn, R.
16254 McPhie, A.	23989 Martin, W. H.	22473 Milburn, W.
19990 McManus, M.	30509 Marvell, W.	25967 Miles, A. J.
26061 McQuaigue, A. C.	21578 Maslin, C.	23181 Miles, C. J.
	26797 Mason, H.	13040 Miles, G.
21394 McShane, E.	15283 Mason, S. J.	34561 Miles, J. H.
27307 Madden, F. H.	28524 Masters, A. P.	28230 Miles, W. C.
13847 Madden, J.	10930 Masters, E. G.	10164 Miller, J. W.
22457 Madden, J. A.	12941 Matcham, E.	15380 Miller, F.
12557 Maddison, F.	21695 Mather, J.	26929 Miller, H. E. B.
26611 Madge, F. W. S.	21902 Mather, W.	27102 Miller, M.
18220 Maguire, E.	27744 Matson, G. W.	19123 Millichamp, B.
19513 Maiden, C. R.	21877 Matson, W. D.	18379 Millins, F. J., M.M.
26907 Maiden, J. E.	15729 Matthews, C.	
29092 Maides, F. J.	28756 Matthews, H. E. T.	14336 Mills, G. T.
25542 Maidlow, A. J. A.		26568 Mills, J.
	21158 Matthews, J.	16313 Mills, T.
26994 Major, R. F.	23450 Matthews, J. E.	16049 Mills, W.
19947 Maker, F. W.	12816 Matthews, W.	10581 Millward, S.
31363 Makins, A.	21157 Matthews, W. J.	23845 Milner, F.
16659 Mallender, P.	23898 Mattich, R. J.	15010 Milton, J. T.
19598 Mallin, F. L.	13997 Maule, W. S.	23417 Minchin, B. R.
27770 Mallows, W. E.	31494 Mawer, R.	15996 Ming, H. W.
10665 Mandeville, J.	17787 May, E.	14466 Mitchell, S.
20292 Mann, A. W.	16607 May, F.	10608 Mitchell, T.
23939 Mann, C. E.	14794 May, H.	29482 Mitchinson, G. D.
26717 Mann, L.	16582 May, S. V.	
21480 Manning, A.	14646 Mayell, W. F.	24372 Mitton, W.
22862 Manning, C.	24890 Mayo, E. W.	13817 Mizon, G.
16789 Mannion, W.	25681 Mayo, R. F.	16005 Mobley, N. W.
28492 Mansell, J. E.	15869 Mead, A.	15528 Moffitt, P.
12851 Mansell, S.	27629 Mead, A.	23297 Moger, T. G.

APPENDIX IV.

NOMINAL ROLL 263

14448 Moisey, C. A. V.	19739 Mumford, P.	18048 Noakes, A.	APPENDIX
26690 Mole, A. E.	28807 Munday,	16301 Nobes, C.	IV.
15497 Mole, S. J.	A. C. T.	31595 Noble, E. S.	
25163 Monk, A. M.	27789 Munton, A. W.	23657 Nolan, W.	
16946 Moody, H.	13520 Murden, D.	25576 Norman, C.	
17398 Mooney, J.	27516 Murphy, A. E.	17405 Norman, N. E.	
23865 Moore, A.	17235 Murphy, C.	28751 Norminton, H.	
14339 Moore, E.	19309 Murphy, J.	22857 North, A.	
18764 Moore, F.	14738 Murphy, M.	23668 North, A.	
17015 Moore, G. J.	28306 Murray, T.	22814 North, J.	
29885 Moore, H. B.	8720 Murray, W.	14191 Nunn, A. E.	
28195 Moore, J. H. S.	13060 Murtagh, P.	19209 Nutkins, F.	
23799 Moore, S.	29797 Murton, A. E.	15039 Nutley, C.	
31336 Moore, S.	15489 Musgrove, F.	25586 Nuttall, J. O.	
22002 Moore, T.	14398 Nash, F. T.	30073 Nuttall, W.	
28526 Moores, R. C.	14551 Nason, H. E.	24766 O'Brien, W. B.	
21835 Morcell, B.	22475 Nathan, W. H.	11239 O'Connor, P.	
20988 Morgan, C. E.	26813 Nattrass, C.	11702 O'Neill, M.,	
28044 Morgan, D. H.	27297 Naylor, J.	M.M.	
24683 Morgan, F.	21812 Naylor, T.,	29946 O'Neill, T.	
16292 Morgan, G.	M.M.	18767 O'Reilly, H.	
16479 Morgan, H. J.,	16893 Neal, F. A.	30290 Oakey, G.	
D.C.M.	27498 Neal, J.	24734 Oakley, C. D.	
12422 Morgan, P.	21084 Needham, L.	22210 Oddy, V.	
12980 Morgan, R.	25042 Needham, T. A.	24362 Odell, H.	
15403 Morgan, S.	24366 Needle, R.	16938 Offord, S. V.	
27923 Morgan, W.	20599 Neighbour, F.	25928 Oglesby, J.	
22945 Morley, E. C.	21862 Nelson, J. W.	16788 Okey, D. J.	
19155 Morley, H.	13438 Nelson, T.	13655 Oldershaw, H.	
29013 Morphew, E.	27630 Nendick, J. E.	20214 Oldham, A.	
21835 Morrell, B.	15519 Nessling, W. J.	19626 Oldham, J.	
21395 Morrey, H.	26622 Nethercott,	15167 Oldham, J. W.	
12666 Morris, A.	R. A.	20933 Oldring, H. J.	
29018 Morris, A.	21813 Nettleton, W.	16300 Oliver, A. V.	
12235 Morris, E.	17997 Nevard, H. W.	31478 Oliver, F.	
24082 Morris, H.	17465 Neville, J.	31739 Oliver, G.	
15520 Morris, S.	25520 Newby, W. P.	30076 Oliver, J. A.	
13969 Morris, S. B.	16960 Newell, B. J.	21474 Oliver, J. W.	
26883 Morris, T.	27369 Newell, S. F.	14272 Oliver, P.	
12080 Morris, T. S.	21065 Newman, C.	16104 Onions, T. H.	
23516 Morris, W.	12868 Newman, F. G.	17537 Orams, F. S.	
15419 Morris, W. J.	17378 Newman, S.	25777 Orange, H.	
28451 Mort, J. W.	27753 Newman, W.	29352 Orpin, C.	
25932 Mortimer, A. G.	29744 Newnham, B.	13235 Orr, C.	
12589 Mortimer, A. W.	29986 Newton, R. C.	25515 Osborn, E.	
24364 Mortimer, R.	28487 Newton, T.	27810 Osborne, G. W.	
28664 Moss, D.	15884 Newton, W.	28580 Otterwell, S.	
9418 Moss, J.	26254 Nichol, J.	24345 Oulton, D. A.	
18072 Mott, W. A.	20234 Nichols,	31096 Over, E. A.	
28445 Mottram, T.	C. N. C.	24901 Owen, F.	
30460 Mould, E. J.	29276 Nicholls, J. C.	10329 Owen, J.	
20810 Mould, J. A.	27043 Nicholls, P. S.	28210 Oxenham, T.	
15916 Moule, J. W.	15928 Nicholls, T.	28477 Oxley, H. S. P.	
12390 Moulson, W. H.	27250 Nicholson, F.	14131 Oxley, P.	
17406 Mountain, A. E.	15733 Nicklinson, J.	24883 Packer, C. H.	
29118 Mowbray, F. C.	25521 Nickolls, P. J.	15437 Packer, R. T.	
31050 Mowbray, W. T.	23693 Nightingale, H.	21422 Page, H.	
15157 Mullins, H. S.	27743 Nightingale,	24555 Page, J. N.	
18213 Mullis, S. E. J.	H. A.	16457 Page, N.	

264 THE GRENADIER GUARDS

APPENDIX IV.

15342 Painter, J.	29042 Pearce, C. M.	24740 Pitcher, C. J.
22663 Painter, J.	15534 Pearce, D. H.	25360 Pitcher, J.
26232 Palmar, H. J.	11216 Pearson, G.	18196 Pittaway, J. W.
27452 Palmer, A.	25880 Pearson, J.	24794 Plackett, F. S.
6260 Palmer, C. W.	28076 Pearson, J. D.	18955 Plant, B.
15501 Palmer, G.	27232 Pearson, J. N.	13715 Player, A. H.
24868 Palmer, H.	24267 Peate, W.	14372 Playsted, W. J.
15024 Palmer, J. B.	22477 Peck, A. W.	22652 Plumb, H.
25797 Palmer, W. P.	29442 Peckitt, E.	28476 Plumb, H.
24262 Paradine, A.	25921 Peel, A. J.	12443 Plummer, L.
25642 Parfitt, A. L.	22170 Pegg, G. W.	22216 Plummer, E.
16290 Pargeter, G.	24955 Pegg, J.	26013 Plummer, E. J., M.M.
26714 Park, H.	16135 Pellett, C. J.	
26586 Parke, H. F.	15463 Pendle, F. J.	17338 Podmore, E.
29589 Parker, F. L.	30513 Penn, W. C.	21032 Pointon, W.
20544 Parker, G.	8363 Percival, W. M.	22819 Pole, D.
20068 Parker, H.	24547 Perkins, P. W. A.	26844 Pollard, G.
29696 Parker, H. J.		17341 Pollard, J. F.
29069 Parker, H. G.	23972 Perkins, R. T.	14838 Pollard, O. P.
17106 Parker, J. F.	20570 Perkins, W.	20454 Pollington, H., M.M.
31646 Parker, R.	21717 Perkins, W. J.	
17804 Parker, W.	28226 Perks, A.	20185 Poole, A.
26803 Parker, W.	20351 Perks, F. H.	14715 Poole, G.
27419 Parker, W.	17468 Perrett, E.	17423 Poole, J. C.
22585 Parker, W. J.	27087 Perry, H. J.	22217 Poole, W. W.
24681 Parkin, J. A.	13054 Perry, W. A.	17283 Porter, H. W.
30531 Parkins, W. R.	13418 Perryman, A. O.	28605 Porter, J.
15189 Parkinson, A., D.C.M.		24359 Porter, J. P.
	22202 Perryman, J.	22555 Potter, A. F.
27560 Parkinson, S. S.	25915 Peters, R. A.	14628 Potter, F.
30613 Parkinson, E.	28988 Pettitt, H.	27526 Potter, J. L.
21194 Parks, G. S.	11360 Petts, G.	25487 Potter, W.
12025 Parks, H.	13572 Phillimore, S.	9193 Potts, G.
13194 Parris, A. L.	28825 Phillips, A.	24660 Potts, T.
16272 Parsons, F.	21328 Phillips, T. M.	11256 Pouncett, A.
24695 Parsons, H. G.	23392 Phillips, W. A.	29959 Powell, C. W.
24671 Parsons, R.	26686 Phillips, W. C.	24536 Powell, E. G.
18050 Parsons, S.	24778 Phillipson, M.	8674 Powell, F. W.
18336 Parsons, W. A.	17745 Phipps, E. W.	19642 Powell, G.
12522 Partridge, J.	14125 Pickard, C.	23740 Powell, J.
28290 Partt, S.	21510 Pickard, G. A.	29893 Power, C. H.
28748 Parvin, A. W.	18118 Pickering, W.	21563 Powlesland, J. W., M.M.
28507 Pascoe, A. H.	27997 Pickford, E.	
11234 Pashley, J. F.	27228 Pickles, H.	23045 Pratley, H.
19864 Patient, A.	29588 Pickles, W. A.	21906 Pratt, P.
20971 Patman, F. J.	28634 Pidgeon, F.	15708 Predith, O.
22926 Patrick, G.	24846 Piggott, J.	8549 Preece, C.
15709 Patten, F. G.	26729 Pike, A. P.	27919 Prentice, J. W.
14735 Paull, F. G.	20477 Pike, M. J.	24240 Prescott, P.
16918 Paul, A.	24462 Pike, R. H.	28680 Prescott, P.
15268 Paxton, A.	29014 Pike, T.	18634 Prescott, W.
15890 Pay, J.	19812 Pike, T.	13894 Press, T.
41410 Payne, C.	28260 Pilch, T.	28603 Prestidge, J. W.
23683 Payne, W.	26296 Pinkney, T. W.	13035 Preston, W. C.
24017 Payne, W.	27011 Pinnington, W.	30512 Pretty, R. J.
13294 Peace, G.	27397 Piper, G.	20593 Price, G.
20226 Peacher, H.	12346 Piper, H.	15453 Price, H. G.
23610 Peacock, F.	26715 Pipkin, H. J.	29115 Price, J. J.
26966 Pearce, A. J.	26539 Pirie, J.	23926 Price, P.

NOMINAL ROLL

			Appendix IV.
18705 Price, R.	24178 Reader, H.	7649 Roadnight, F.	
25706 Price, R.	26848 Reading, S. R.	22568 Roan, C.	
18365 Price, T.	17119 Reaney, M.	22343 Robbins, R. I.	
28389 Price, W. B.	20636 Redfern, W.	10305 Robbins, S.	
18960 Priddy, R.	13404 Redgate, S.	23564 Robbins, W.	
23008 Priest, A.	20180 Redshaw, G. A.	13792 Roberson, W. J.	
20358 Priest, W. C.	16929 Reece, A. E.	26211 Roberts, A.	
22171 Priestley, A.	20248 Reed, A. E.	22596 Roberts, A. B.	
28427 Priestley, H. P.	11221 Reed, J. O.	28358 Roberts, E. W.	
26349 Priestley, N.	15695 Reeves, E. M.	17271 Roberts, E. J.	
15405 Priestley, W. E.	20499 Reeves, W. H.	19835 Roberts, G.	
25517 Prior, A. C.	20274 Regan, F.	12495 Roberts, H.	
17404 Prior, G. D.	11199 Reid, A. E.	9919 Roberts, J.	
30463 Prior, J. O.	14446 Revill, A.	13372 Roberts, J. B.	
23785 Prior, J. T.	20102 Revill, F.	25796 Roberts, O. W.	
23534 Prince, A.	12555 Reynolds, A. J.	16680 Roberts, R.	
28431 Prince, P. W.	22778 Reynolds, F.	18739 Roberts, R. E.	
26253 Pritchard, G. F.	28157 Reynolds, R.	16427 Roberts, R. J.	
25621 Pritchard, S. C.	14848 Reynolds, W.	17715 Roberts, T.	
29161 Pritchett, H.	28111 Rhodes, A. J.	18296 Roberts, W. A.	
22653 Proctor, J.	16989 Rhodes, G. T.	20352 Roberts, T.	
23807 Proudlock, C. W.	22491 Rhodes, J.	25018 Roberts, W.	
	29391 Rhodes, L.	14582 Robins, W.	
18766 Prudames, H. R.	17429 Ribbans, G.	15465 Robinson, A. S.	
	21137 Ribbons, H. T.	22435 Robinson, C.	
27431 Pugh, E.	22016 Rice, E.	20482 Robinson, C. H.	
22595 Pugh, E. J.	29448 Rice, F. H.	22313 Robinson, E.	
10527 Pugh, J.	18556 Richards, A.	18297 Robinson, F.	
25299 Punt, G. E.	16480 Richards, D. J.	22479 Robinson, J. R.	
22133 Purchase, W. J.	20822 Richards, H.	19506 Robinson, J. W.	
27506 Purton, A. W.	24480 Richards, W. E.	23883 Robinson, R.	
21126 Pusey, A.	18609 Richardson, C.	27724 Robinson, R. G.	
16604 Pusey, R. G.	12426 Richardson, F.	20428 Robinson, S.	
18738 Quick, C.	21247 Richardson, R.	13913 Robotham, G. A.	
33311 Quigley, G. R.	26629 Richardson, S.		
16835 Rackham, R.	23217 Richens, A.	17319 Robson, A. W.	
20224 Radford, A.	24429 Richens, F.	27200 Robson, W. C.	
26680 Railton, W.	22285 Riches, E. C.	11648 Roddis, C. A.	
22654 Rainbow, H.	15172 Richings, W. C.	25488 Roden, G. W.	
20056 Ramsdale, A.	24884 Rickard, H.	27554 Roe, A.	
17035 Ramsey, J.	26752 Richmond, E. E.	21062 Rodgers, E.	
19815 Ransome, F.		23810 Rogers, J. J.	
29188 Rapley, A. W.	26427 Riddle, F. N.	15060 Rogers, P. J.	
28364 Ratcliffe, B. S.	17694 Riddoch, A.	20554 Rogers, S.	
27242 Ratcliffe, J.	17282 Rider, W. G.	24461 Rogers, T.	
21359 Rathbone, J.	24340 Ridgway, H.	20678 Rogers, W.	
13066 Ravening, M. A.	11054 Ridout, G.	27884 Rollinson, W.	
17496 Rawle, W.	31620 Riley, D.	25335 Rolfe, G.	
30948 Rawley, A.	24642 Riley, H.	19850 Rolfe, J. J.	
18672 Rawlins, C. W.	20006 Riley, J.	26922 Rooke, A. F.	
29422 Rawlins, G.	21605 Rimmington, J.	15290 Rooke, F. J.	
18541 Rawlinson, R.	12519 Ringer, H. R.	8765 Roome, E. W.	
28068 Ray, F. W.	24147 Risden, W.	21908 Rooney, W.	
25758 Rayment, R. G.	17484 Ritson, N.	19070 Roscoe, W. H.	
13564 Rayner, P.	16212 Rivers, A. L.	24656 Rose, C. W.	
18899 Rayner, W.	12947 Rivers, W.	25833 Rosie, W. C.	
20281 Rayner, W. D.	16072 Roach, B. A. F.	20539 Rossiter, O., M.M.	
19567 Read, G.	11929 Roadley, H.		
27175 Read, G. S.	18503 Roache, G.	26915 Rothwell, W.	

THE GRENADIER GUARDS

Appendix IV.

16253 Roughton, L.	29059 Sawer, A. W.	17964 Shelley, A.
28371 Rouse, A.	28150 Sawyer, A. W.	26238 Shelley, T.
24177 Rouse, W. H.	29009 Sayers, D. E.	25864 Shenton, C. G.
16936 Rousseau, J. G. P.	19863 Scambler, W. M.	11626 Shepley, J.
13369 Rout, R. J.	26744 Schofield, C. V.	11311 Sheppard, C. E.
24826 Rowarth, H.	16914 Scollard, E. J.	17879 Sheppard, G. E.
13760 Rowbottom, E.	30335 Scott, A.	11458 Sheppard, G. T.
20705 Rowe, P. L.	24706 Scott, A. W.	28871 Sheppard, P.
16978 Rowley, J. J.	13599 Scott, E.	19891 Sheppard, S. C.
20507 Rowley, J.	22235 Scott, H.	21458 Sherburn, A.
26154 Rowley, T.	20082 Scott, J.	13998 Sheridan, W.
26693 Rowley, T.	24217 Scott, J. T.	18509 Sherlock, G.
26186 Rowse, W. G.	25466 Scott, J.	20695 Sherratt, J.
29331 Rowson, T. H.	25352 Scott, J. H.	21839 Sherwood, T. W.
25658 Roytherne, A.	21118 Scott, S. W.	27656 Shiner, W. A.
22007 Rudd, C. H.	27478 Scott, Wm.	14345 Shipp, A.
17088 Ruff, B.	12576 Scripps, A.	8402 Shipp, H.
29064 Runge, E.	26623 Scudder, W.	29287 Shipp, L. C.
17487 Russell, A.	27636 Scull, S.	10950 Shipp, W.
17739 Russell, C. E.	28652 Seabrook, A.	21961 Shirley, J. H.
23700 Russell, D.	19452 Seabrook, A. M.	17678 Short, F. V.
26865 Russell, H.	14004 Seagraves, C.	21304 Short, H.
26359 Russell, J.	26675 Seajeant, J.	15313 Shrimpton, L. D.
11481 Russell, M.	22305 Sedgley, A. J.	29647 Sibley, F. G.
22027 Russell, R.	14134 Selby, H. C.	27313 Siddle, A. E.
27142 Rutherford, G.	24712 Seely, J. M.	19787 Sidwell, G. E.
29957 Rutherford, W.	17581 Seewald, F.	16387 Siewertsen, W. T.
31259 Rutter, T.	25356 Self, F.	27948 Sillence, M. A.
20604 Rutter, W. H.	16042 Senior, A. E.	23916 Silva, P. H.
28436 Ryall, F.	12226 Sentence, H.	28227 Silvester, E.
22234 Ryan, C.	26818 Sergeant, H. C.	19267 Simm, J.
17590 Ryde, C. F.	15160 Sergeant, J. C.	27058 Simmonds, A.
9876 Ryles, W.	15680 Sergent, T.	16675 Simmons, F. A.
21621 Sadler, R.	13593 Setterfield, H.	16865 Simons, W. C.
14180 Sage, J.	24123 Settle, W.	26099 Simpson, A. T.
26614 Saint, W. H.	21503 Severn, J.	23009 Simpson, H. W.
31463 Sales, H.	24319 Sewell, J.	14941 Simpson, J.
20236 Salmon, F. E.	28021 Seymour, G. B.	14183 Simpson, R. G.
27475 Salmon, J. W.	16126 Seymour, H. C., M.M.	9302 Sims, E.
11581 Salsbury, J.		10503 Singer, H. R.
29248 Salter, S. G.	16851 Seymour, L.	24859 Sisley, E.
11731 Sampson, A. E.	19335 Shadbolt, W.	25458 Sivills, C.
16177 Sampson, W. G.	10483 Shanley, F.	22106 Siviour, G. T.
30044 Sharman, F.	18532 Sharman, F.	22517 Skarratt, G. F.
34307 Sampson, S.	21163 Sharp, A. H.	25229 Skevington, M. H.
16691 Sanders, W.	8582 Sharp, H. E.	
22669 Sanderson, A.	17993 Sharp, P. C.	20765 Skidmore, L. G.
18408 Sansom, F. J.	11582 Sharples, E.	24028 Skidmore, W.
17538 Sargent, C. D.	15753 Sharrett, G.	20578 Skiller, C. E.
15840 Sargent, G. A.	18482 Shattock, D. L.	22758 Skinley, S. F. J.
16452 Sargent, P. J.	15970 Shaw, E.	23694 Skinner, H.
17916 Sarsfield, W.	21838 Shaw, J.	25187 Slack, F. C.
27619 Saunders, H. R.	18740 Shaw, W.	22436 Slack, H. F.
14165 Saunders, J., M.M.	25197 Shaw, W.	17266 Slade, G. H. T.
	20877 Shaw, W. A.	17418 Slade, L.
29892 Saunders, W.	26740 Sheavyn, W. F.	7790 Slade, W.
18367 Savage, W.	18291 Sheldon, B.	
17361 Savile, J.	26726 Shellard, E. W.	28809 Slater, H.

NOMINAL ROLL

23092 Slater, H.	17740 Smith, W. A.	24558 Stevens, J.
13466 Slater, O. E.	29307 Smith, W. E.	12323 Stevenson, C.
25025 Slater, W. T.	16639 Smith, W. G.	29111 Stevenson, J.
22388 Slee, L.	30000 Smith, W. H.	22572 Stevenson, R.
26387 Smallwood, J.	21024 Smith, W. J.	20008 Stevenson, W.
27984 Smart, F. G.	19402 Smyth, A. P.	20866 Stewart, A.
25394 Smart, W.	13779 Snell, H. W.	26081 Stewart, S. A.
13634 Smiddy, W.	21920 Snelson, J. T. H.	28416 Stiles, V. G.
14163 Smith, A.		20455 Stockell, E. R.
14549 Smith, A.	16187 Soton, W.	14059 Stokes, B.
18010 Smith, A.	28689 Soulsby, J.	16367 Stone, W. C.
19063 Smith, A.	13767 Southan, P.	16267 Stone, W. H.
24954 Smith, A.	29544 Southern, F.	27138 Storey, F. J.
25045 Smith, A.	28259 Southwell, A.	18537 Storey, W.
18306 Smith, A. A.	26635 Spackman, J.	18272 Stott, J.
20788 Smith, A. W. J.	30479 Spalding, A. H., M.M.	24606 Stott, M. M.
15725 Smith, C.		28600 Stowell, S. S.
20743 Smith, C.	27572 Spargo, C. M.	14117 Strange, H.
18515 Smith, C. H.	19752 Sparkes, S. B.	24096 Strange, L. G.
19304 Smith, C. W.	16175 Sparrow, B.	20605 Stratford, F. G.
23957 Smith, C. W.	20306 Speakman, T.	26909 Stratford, P. R.
14587 Smith, E.	15538 Speller, H.	20629 Stratton, E. A.
27890 Smith, E. W.	28392 Spence, A.	25826 Stratton, H.
15739 Smith, F.	17791 Spencer, J. A.	13472 Street, P.
23695 Smith, F.	22927 Spencer, J. H.	17730 Streeter, J. J.
12165 Smith, F. C.	29414 Sporton, E. E.	22990 Streeter, C. W.
22706 Smith, F. L.	27331 Spraggon, G.	25202 Stretton, T. H.
15117 Smith, F. V.	13505 Springhall, W.	29473 Strong, A.
12377 Smith, G.	11338 Springthorpe, A.	29534 Strugnell, C. F.
16189 Smith, G.	17153 Squance, E.	18161 Stuart, J.
29284 Smith, G. F.	19157 Squier, C. E.	16816 Stubbs, H. P.
17417 Smith, G. H.	22664 Squires, B.	18613 Stubbs, L.
27454 Smith, G. W.	19212 Stack, P. F.	9463 Stubbs, W. A.
14950 Smith, H.	25403 Stafford, C. F.	22238 Studholme, G.
20793 Smith, H.	28770 Stafford, E. W.	27691 Sturdy, H.
22541 Smith, H.	30203 Stafford, W. J.	27938 Sturgeon, A.
27449 Smith, H.	29428 Stairs, A.	25852 Sturgess, J. W.
28419 Smith, H.	18920 Stairs, S.	17793 Styles, C.
14951 Smith, H. M.	18741 Staniford, J.	18229 Styles, S.
15915 Smith, J.	24799 Stanley, H. H.	19685 Styles, W. L.
20319 Smith, J. H.	30191 Stannard, H.	27160 Sugden, A.
22859 Smith, J. T.	28789 Stanton, G.	12933 Sullivan, F.
23769 Smith, J. W.	23421 Stapel, E. J.	17273 Sullivan, H. C.
23596 Smith, L. J.	20779 Staples, E.	12174 Summerlin, W. J. B.
13473 Smith, P.	29348 Staples, W.	
16560 Smith, P. W.	26041 Starkie, G. W.	29823 Summer, J.
11650 Smith, R.	19213 Staunton, W.	23031 Summers, A.
16762 Smith, R. H.	19827 Stedman, F.	29007 Summers, A. R.
14156 Smith, S.	12024 Steers, A. E.	21500 Summers, L. J.
22997 Smith, S.	17239 Stenner, J. F.	31173 Sumnall, B.
23560 Smith, S.	17252 Stenning, A., M.M.	16166 Sumner, H. H.
25489 Smith, S.		25168 Surch, P.
12331 Smith, S. J.	23467 Stephenson, R. E.	23373 Surgay, R.
26906 Smith, S. J.		20119 Surtees, R. R.
18423 Smith, T.	13437 Stevens, A.	26386 Sutcliffe, J.
23654 Smith, T.	25234 Stevens, B.	26648 Suter, E. G.
30636 Smith, T.	19004 Stevens, D.	20862 Sutton, F.
17399 Smith, W.	14922 Stevens, G.	18510 Swain, C.
17185 Smith, W. A.	17340 Stevens, G.	18970 Swain, T. J.

APPENDIX IV.

268   THE GRENADIER GUARDS

APPENDIX IV.

21985 Swain, W.	27943 Thomas, G.	31450 Tocknell, C.
21127 Sweet, P.	28943 Thomas, H.	24573 Todd, A.
15279 Swinard, W. E.	30022 Thomas, H. G.	22484 Todd, B. H.
24170 Swinbourne, I.	20844 Thomas, J.	31333 Todd, S. G.
24513 Swinbourne, S. J.	19298 Thomas, T.	15827 Tolley, J. W.
	23775 Thomas, W.	15467 Tomkins, H. J.
30379 Swinfen, H.	10932 Thomas, W. E.	29987 Tomlinson, A.
15572 Swinscoe, A.	12601 Thompson, A.	22051 Tomlinson, H.
11617 Symonds, G. H.	29410 Thompson, F.	19905 Tomlinson, J.
23273 Symonds, F. C.	24085 Thompson, F. C.	19521 Tomlinson, J. W.
20169 Talbot, F.		
10944 Talbot, J.	21778 Thompson, G.	28218 Tomlinson, W.
25104 Tall, W. H.	25064 Thompson, J.	16490 Tomlinson, W.
26005 Tallon, T.	22675 Thompson, J. A.	27215 Toney, H.
19702 Talner, A.		22521 Tonks, H.
21738 Tandy, F.	19413 Thompson, R.	18558 Toon, J. N.
20409 Tanner, F.	26373 Thompson, R.	25080 Toon, J. T.
20452 Tansley, F.	17837 Thompson, T.	26409 Toplis, L. J.
25473 Tarbard, V.	28276 Thompson, T.	26048 Tovey, J. W.
18903 Targitt, W. G.	15847 Thompson, W.	25625 Towler, H. J.
23100 Tasker, J. T.	32008 Thompson, W.	21102 Townsend, T.
25128 Tattersall, W.	24953 Thompson, W. J.	28971 Townsend, W. H.
10935 Taylor, A.		
13392 Taylor, A.	24038 Thompson, W. R.	14289 Tracy, H.
16155 Taylor, A.		23899 Trafford, G.
24489 Taylor, A.	21864 Thorne, E.	23886 Tranter, C.
26464 Taylor, A.	28313 Thorne, J.	17027 Tranter, H. F.
19170 Taylor, E.	24781 Thorneycroft, A.	24257 Treadwell, W.
15416 Taylor, E. A.		10980 Tredall, W.
26266 Taylor, E. A.	18615 Thornton, G. F., M.M.	24237 Trickett, R. A.
25786 Taylor, E. W.		15620 Trigg, G. A.
26991 Taylor, F.	27573 Thorogood, L. J.	27017 Trim, E. J.
22655 Taylor, G.		16310 Trivitt, A. G.
14964 Taylor, H.	24395 Thorp, W. A. G.	19888 Trood, E. J.
23111 Taylor, J.	15712 Thorpe, E.	13604 Trotman, F.
26115 Taylor, J.	27402 Thorpe, H. G.	14664 Trott, B.
26875 Taylor, J.	30110 Thorpe, W.	23508 Trotter, J.
28321 Taylor, J. D.	14270 Thorpe, W. H.	21687 Trow, C.
25300 Taylor, P. D.	22978 Thorley, J.	16124 Trull, C. H.
14660 Taylor, S.	28089 Threadgale, S. H.	18901 Trundle, B.
16419 Taylor, S. J.		24531 Truss, W. G.
15578 Taylor, T.	22742 Tibbitts, F.	19158 Trydell, C.
21732 Taylor, T. E.	20580 Tibble, F.	22634 Tucker, G.
28482 Taylor, V. A.	16629 Tickell, R. E.	24438 Tucker, T.
15287 Taylor, W.	18311 Tickner, J.	21762 Tudbury, J.
26712 Taylor, W.	22275 Tideswell, P.	26401 Tudor, G. H.
26832 Taylor, W.	28250 Tigwell, E.	26455 Tullett, A. E.
27488 Tebbutt, J. C.	27899 Tildesley, E.	17982 Tullett, W. G.
27866 Tector, P. O.	18077 Till, H. P.	25092 Tunnicliffe, A.
19536 Temple, E. C.	21973 Tilley, W. E.	21076 Tunstall, F.
11337 Tetlow, W. H.	14244 Timmins, A. E.	20191 Turley, T.
18557 Tew, C. W.	20766 Timms, B. S.	30409 Turner, C. D.
24058 Thacker, A. E.	17741 Timms, H.	15960 Turner, G.
17926 Thain, M. E.	29066 Timms, J. W.	16738 Turner, G.
29138 Thayre, P. F.	22598 Timperley, H.	27088 Turner, G.
19993 Theaker, J. W.	17502 Tincombe, E.	31590 Turner, G. H.
23178 Thelwell, E. J.	22787 Tinsley, R.	29469 Turner, H.
24645 Theyer, C.	24496 Tipper, W. T.	29374 Turner, J. G.
19171 Thomas, A. C.	23084 Titley, E.	10914 Turner, J. H.

NOMINAL ROLL 269

					APPENDIX IV.
19055	Turner, S.	13557	Walden, G.	11520	Warrener, G.
19933	Turner, T.	12889	Walduck, J.	16749	Warrinton, R.
22108	Turner, T. W.	14450	Walker, A. L.	28057	Warton, J. B.
16220	Turner, W.	19860	Walker, A. V.	23710	Warwick, A.
23547	Turner, W. F.	20384	Walker, C. J.	14552	Washington, H. J.
17742	Turney, A. P.	12493	Walker, E.		
13253	Turton, A.	14734	Walker, F. G.	22784	Wastell, T. W.
11728	Turton, J. S.	21094	Walker, H.	18177	Waterman, W. J.
30339	Turver, E.	18892	Walker, J. W.		
18964	Turvey, A. W.	24568	Walker, N. T.	18585	Wathen, W.
17120	Tutton, H.	16713	Walker, R.	26641	Watkin, F.
30620	Tweddle, R.	14515	Walker, T.	16219	Watkins, J.
30471	Tyas, S.	15715	Walker, T.	23085	Watkinson, G. E.
17065	Tyler, A. G.	16573	Walker, T.		
18837	Tyler, A. H.	28957	Walker, T. W.	23761	Watson, F. J.
26624	Tyson, W. P.	12689	Walker, W.	28209	Watson, H.
23169	Underwood, D.	14568	Walker, W.	16391	Watson, M.
10535	Underwood, G.	30624	Walkley, S. O.	9652	Watson, R.
20977	Upstone, G.	18931	Wall, G. H.	24302	Watson, T.
28092	Upton, F.	25768	Wall, H.	10929	Watson, W.
22397	Upton, J. H.	15559	Wall, T.	24612	Watts, G.
14589	Usherwood, B.	23642	Wallbank, T.	21483	Watts, W. W.
21234	Uttley, R.	12566	Wallington, A.	21090	Weaving, A. G.
19865	Vagg, C.	10757	Wallis, T. C.	14888	Webb, A. J.
16319	Varney, J.	24704	Wallis, W. A.	18618	Webb, H.
26889	Varty, G. H.	26588	Walpole, W.	16813	Webb, H. T.
28916	Vaughan, W. L.	12445	Walsh, M.	8827	Webb, T. C.
27942	Veale, R. W.	16475	Waltham, W.	13771	Webster, A.
21226	Venables, H.	27344	Walton, G.	29141	Webster, A. S.
21227	Venables, W. J.	26644	Walton, H. S.	22522	Webster, F.
23477	Vernon, H.	17764	Walton, J.	13689	Webster, G. J.
18891	Vickers, F. P.	27644	Walton, J. S.	18326	Webster, H.
29727	Vickers, J.	18560	Walton, W. F.	15524	Webster, W.
11525	Vickery, W. N.	11493	Walton, W.	27474	Wedd, P.
17848	Viggers, E. G.	14723	Ward, A. P.	14903	Weedon, H.
17887	Vincent, A. J.	12486	Ward, C. H.	19541	Weekes, W. R.
27767	Vincent, E.	23651	Ward, G.	21219	Welch, A. O.
18401	Vine, M. W.	22549	Ward, H.	17724	Welch, J. G.
27942	Vines, E.	27792	Ward, H.	26155	Welford, J. J.
24042	Viney, P. G.	29405	Ward, J. B.	17023	Weller, J. H.
8064	Vintner, C.	21850	Ward, J. W.	24159	Wells, A.
27904	Vintner, G.	11972	Ward, R.	25970	Wells, A. W.
26702	Volckman, K. P.	15889	Ward, W.	22384	Wells, J. S.
		28780	Wardale, G. S.	24631	Wells, J. W.
28256	Vollans, H.	14994	Wardlaw, W. R. S.	17352	Wells, T. G.
22999	Voss, H.			27545	Wells, W. F.
16968	Wackett, E. E.	26788	Wardle, E. M.	23246	Welsted, E. G.
20752	Wade, A. J.	17421	Wardle, J.	28590	Wensley, W.
23887	Wager, A.	12220	Warhurst, J.	10700	Wesley, J.
17904	Wagstaff, E.	12955	Warland, A.	16592	West, A. E.
23359	Wagstaff, G. A.	14198	Warlock, G.	29867	West, G. W.
13745	Wainwright, T.	11839	Warner, J. W., D.C.M.	21295	West, S.
27317	Waite, C.			20974	West, S. R.
31255	Waite, F.	16827	Warner, L.	21922	Westhead, E.
23032	Waite, H.	10841	Warnes, J.	21306	Westhead, J.
15934	Waite, W.	15023	Warren, E.	28272	Westhead, J.
24861	Waite, W.	11606	Warren, J.	16085	Westlake, B. C.
21201	Wakefield, J.	20117	Warren, M. A.	19580	Weston, T. J.
20139	Wakelin, C. H.	25635	Warren, W.	15552	Westwood, D.

THE GRENADIER GUARDS

APPENDIX IV.

11387	Wetherall, W.	31736 Wickens, T.	23275 Wilson, J.
22219	Whadcoat, C.	24019 Wickstead, H. W.	26862 Wilson, J.
23968	Whall, A.		19828 Wilson, R.
15056	Whalley, W.	28868 Widdowson, H.	28246 Wilson, S. N.
22863	Wheal, E.	26530 Widdup, J. R.	16558 Wimbush, G.
11276	Wheatcroft, W. H.	25078 Wiggett, L. V.	23663 Windeatt, W. H.
		22883 Wiggins, H.	25897 Wing, H. E.
12766	Wheeler, F. G.	18990 Wigglesworth, E.	25310 Winmill, E.
22462	Wheeler, G. C.		20936 Winn, C.
20712	Wheeler, H. J.	25309 Wilcox, W.	27417 Winn, W. C.
17167	Wheeler, J.	20513 Wild, G.	19918 Winterford, A.
19607	Wheeler, J. C.	27109 Wild, J.	26094 Wise, H.
24185	Wheeler, R.	20797 Wildgoose, W.	21198 Wise, T.
21467	Wheeler, W. G.	30621 Wilkins, A. E.	16891 Witham, H.
17671	Wheelock, G. W.	17131 Wilkins, R.	14435 Witson, E.
		29104 Wilkinson, G.	29253 Witt, T. F.
21912	Whild, T.	22135 Wilkinson, J. T.	18369 Wood, C.
28643	Whiley, G.	27513 Wilkinson, P.	20213 Wood, F.
26595	Whipp, T.	22713 Wilkinson, R.	21710 Wood, J.
27327	Whitaker, B. M	28964 Wilkinson, T. E.	27681 Wood, J. W.
17264	Whitaker, J.	14387 Wilkinson, V.	11866 Wood, R.
17214	Whitaker, S.	16226 Williams, A.	21203 Wood, W. W.
26880	Whitaker, T.	16176 Williams, A. T.	29788 Woodall, J. H.
29077	Whitaker, T. E.	26965 Williams, D.	24914 Woodcock, G.
29666	Whitbread, W.	24958 Williams, F.	25210 Woodcock, H. A.
29319	Whitcombe, A.	25181 Williams, F.	
27597	Whitcombe, W. J.	23153 Williams, H.	30946 Woodhams, O. C.
		16623 Williams, H.	
16409	Whitcroft, C. O.	17425 Williams, I.	24550 Woodhead, G.
24972	White, A. J.	27110 Williams, J.	21354 Woodley, J. R.
28136	White, A. J.	12716 Williams, J.	17595 Woodman, H. C.
16352	White, B. C.	29520 Williams, J.	
26240	White, D. G.	26917 Williams, J. W.	17924 Woodrow, R.
19908	White, G. E.	28972 Williams, S.	28113 Woods, H. S.
14480	White, E.	21814 Williams, T.	24381 Woodward, G.
13231	White, H. G.	15282 Williams, T. H.	17158 Woodward, G. H.
16406	White, J.	27037 Williams, T. H.	
26700	White, J. H.	24809 Williamson, A.	29283 Woodward, J.
20440	White, P.	17165 Williamson, H.	28455 Woodward, J. H.
26861	White, W. H. E.	20935 Williamson, T.	
15186	White, W.	27822 Willis, E. J.	19371 Woodward, W.
16259	Whitehall, A.	13942 Willis, H.	24332 Woodward, W.
15298	Whitehead, A. H.	25053 Willis, J. M.	24255 Wooff, J.
		21182 Willis, W.	24726 Wooldridge, D. T.
26023	Whitehead, J. A.	22743 Willis, W.	
		17765 Willman, R.	27457 Wooldridge, B.
12178	Whitmore, J.	12041 Willock, W.	29614 Wooldridge, G. A.
27553	Whitelock, J. E.	26920 Wills, A. H.	
		15182 Wills, C.	23834 Woollett, W.
28053	Whitlock, S. F. H.	18853 Willson, E. R.	27032 Woolley, A.
		28340 Wilshire, F. W.	21450 Woolley, J.
26282	Whitnell, J. W.	13069 Wilson, A. G.	17216 Wootten, J. W.
10078	Whitney, R.	24284 Wilson, C.	28566 Wordley, R. C.
25401	Whittaker, F.	22046 Wilson, C. P.	17262 Workman, R.
24140	Whittall, R. J.	22386 Wilson, E. A.	22954 Wragg, F.
16278	Whitton, A.	14435 Wilson, E.	12828 Wright, A.
12971	Whitty, J.	24324 Wilson, F.	24391 Wright, A. L.
27324	Whybray, N. E.	24840 Wilson, F.	30010 Wright, C. A.
24083	Whyley, B.	27751 Wilson, F.	28267 Wright, F. S.

29734 Wright, G. C.	21275 Wright, W. H.	17374 Yeomans, T.	APPENDIX IV.
16413 Wright, H.	21363 Wyer, H.	28337 Yeowart, J.	
22531 Wright, J.	25499 Wyon, H. V. T.	20665 Young, A. G.	
23783 Wright, J.	21623 Yapp, J.	28811 Young, C.	
26768 Wright, J.	16240 Yarnell, R.	28329 Young, C. W.	
17438 Wright, J. S.	21871 Yates, C.	26030 Young, F.	
11261 Wright, R. S.	9385 Yates, F.	25017 Young, F. J.	
20321 Wright, R. S.	21286 Yates, G. W.	23815 Young, W.	
30473 Wright, T.	9625 Yates, J.	12340 Young, W. H.	
19645 Wright, T.	21070 Yates, J. H.	22777 Youngs, C.	
27821 Wright, W.	24538 Yeomans, L	25893 Zimmer, E. A.	

APPENDIX V

OFFICERS WOUNDED

Major-General

Batt.		Date.
	Ruggles-Brise, H. G., C.B., M.V.O.	2/11/14

Brigadier-Generals

Batt.		Date.
	Ardee, R. le N. Lord, C.B.	1/11/14 4/4/18 (gas)
	Cooper, R. J., C.B., C.V.O.	10/8/15
	Pereira, G. E., C.B., C.M.G., D.S.O.	8/10/15
	Trotter, G. F., C.B., C.M.G., C.B.E., M.V.O., D.S.O.	12/3/15

Colonels

Batt.		Date.
	Scott-Kerr, R., C.B., M.V.O., D.S.O.	1/9/14
1	Corkran, C. E., C.M.G. (Bt.-Col.) (Temp. Brig.-General)	16/6/15
1	Earle, M., C.M.G., D.S.O. (re-patriated prisoner of war)	29/10/14

Lieutenant-Colonel

Batt.		Date.
	Jeffreys, G. D., C.B., C.M.G. (Temp. Major-General)	14/4/16

OFFICERS WOUNDED

APPENDIX V.

MAJORS

Batt.		Date.
4	Hamilton, G. C., C.M.G., D.S.O. (Temp. Col.)	27/9/15
1	Leatham, R. E. K., D.S.O. (Bt.-Lieut.-Col.)	24/10/14
2	Maitland, M. E. M. C., D.S.O. (Temp. Lieut.-Col.)	23/10/14
2	Pike, E. J. L., M.C. (Bt.-Lieut.-Col.)	11/11/14
2	Powell, E. G. H.	11-13/11/14
	Scott, Lord F. G. M. D., D.S.O., Bt.-Lieut.-Col. (with Irish Guards)	31/10/14
3	Sergison-Brooke, B. N., C.M.G., D.S.O. (Bt.-Lieut.-Col.)	14-17/9/16
	Seymour, Lord H. C., D.S.O. (Bt.-Lieut.-Col.) (in West Africa)	{ 25/8/14 30/8/18
s.	Vivian, V., C.M.G., D.S.O., M.V.O. (Bt.-Lieut.-Col.)	18/3/15

CAPTAINS

1	Ames, L. G.	29/10/14
1	Aubrey-Fletcher, H. L., D.S.O., M.V.O. (Temp. Lieut.-Col.)	{ 23/10/14 27/9/15
1	Bailey, Hon. W. R., D.S.O.	24/8/18
4	Britten, C. R., M.C.	{ 25/9/16 28/11/17
2	Craigie, J. C., M.C.	{ 18/5/15 22/9/15 3/10/15 11/10/15

Batt.		Date.
2/3	Dowling, C. M. C.	11-13/11/14 27/9/15 17/10/15
1	Duckworth-King, Sir G. H. J., Bart.	3/11/14
3	Dufferin and Ava, Marquis of, D.S.O.	17/10/15
1	Fisher-Rowe, C. V., M.C. (Bt.-Major)	13/3/15 4/10/18
4/1	Gort, J. S. S. P. V., Viscount, V.C., D.S.O., M.V.O., M.C. (Bt.-Major) (Temp. Lieut.-Col.)	1/12/17 31/7/17 27/9/18
2	Graham, H. A. R.	7/2/15 6/5/15
4	Greville, C. H., D.S.O. (Actg. Major)	31/7/17
2	Harcourt-Vernon, G. C. FitzH., D.S.O., M.C. (Actg. Major)	15/9/16 29/5/16
3	Hughes, J. S., M.C. (Temp. Major)	14-16/9/14 27/11/17
1	Kenyon-Slaney, R. O. R.	29/10/14
1	Kingsmill, A. de P., D.S.O., M.C.	10/3/15
1	Lambert, R. S., M.C.	29/10/14
2	Lascelles, H. G. C., Viscount, D.S.O.	16/6/15 15/9/16
4	Morrison, J. A., D.S.O.	3/5/15 30/4/18
1	Napier, Sir A. L. M., Bart.	29/9/15 9/10/17
2	Needham, Hon. F. E.	1/9/14
2	Newton, C. N., M.C.	19/11/16
1	Percy, Lord W. R., D.S.O. (Temp. Lieut.-Col.)	11/3/15
1	Powell, J. H.	29/10/14

OFFICERS WOUNDED

Batt.		Date.
1	Rhodes, A. T. G.	13/10/17
2	Ridley, E. D., M.C. (Temp. Major)	27/9/14
2	Rose, I. St. C., O.B.E.	31/10/14
	Rowley, C. S.	27/9/15
4	Simpson, J. H. C., M.C.	{ 2/9/18 11/10/18
2	Smith, O. M.	27/8/18
2/4	Spencer-Churchill, E. G., M.C.	{ 25/12/14 22/9/16
1	Stanley, E. M. C., Lord	10/5/16
1	Trench, R. P. le P., M.C.	17/10/15
3	Vivian, G. N., O.B.E.	27/9/15
1	Wakeman, O.	17/10/15
2/3	Walker, C. F. A., M.C.	{ 14-16/9/14 26/10/15
1	Ward, E. S.	15/11/14
2	Wilson, G. B., M.C.	27/3/18
3	Wolrige-Gordon, R.	3/3/16

LIEUTENANTS

4	Abel-Smith, L. R.	{ 15/9/16 1/12/17
2	Acland, A. W., M.C.	{ 1/12/17 22/5/18
3	Adair, A. H. S., M.C.	4/11/18
	Adams, A. C.	27/7/17
3	Agar-Robartes, Hon. A. G., M.C. (Actg. Capt.)	8/10/15
2	Agar-Robartes, Hon. A. V., M.C. (Actg. Capt.)	{ 8/10/15 14/9/16 23/3/18
	Alexander, N. G. A.	25/11/17

APPENDIX V.

THE GRENADIER GUARDS

Batt.		Date.
3	Anson, F., M.C. (Temp. Capt.)	28/9/15 31/7/15
3	Bennett, N. C.	27/3/18
4	Benson, C. E., D.S.O. (Actg. Capt.)	25/3/18
1	Bevan, T. P. M., M.C.	3/12/17
1	Bliss, A. E. D.	21/10/18
4	Bonham-Carter, F. G. (Actg. Capt.)	16/6/16
3	Borthwick, Hon. A. M.	12/9/17
3	Boughey, C. L. F.	27/4/18
1	Bradley, H. G. W. (Actg. Capt.)	9/5/16
	Burman, B.	5/3/17
	Burt, G. C.	13/4/18
1	Brown, A. M., M.C.	27/9/18
3	Campbell, K. A.	4/11/18
3	Carrington, C. W., D.S.O. (Actg. Capt.)	27/3/18
3	Carstairs, C. C., M.C.	4/11/18
2	Carter, H. G.	29/3/16
2	Cary, Hon. P. P. (Actg. Capt.)	18/5/15 23/8/18
3	Cassy, D. W.	14-17/9/16
1	Chambers, A. S., M.C. (Actg. Capt.)	24/8/18
3	Champneys, W. (Actg. Capt.)	14-17/9/16
2	Combe, T. A.	27/9/18
1	Corbett, Hon. T. G. P., M.C.	30/3/18
2	Cornforth, J. C., M.C. (Actg. Capt.)	1/12/17
3	Cornish, G. M., M.C.	14-17/9/16
	Craig, D., D.S.O.	10/10/17
2	Crookshank, H. F. C. (Temp. Capt.)	23/10/15 15/9/16

OFFICERS WOUNDED

Batt.		Date.
2	Crosland, C.	27/9/15
1	Cruttenden, C.	1/12/17
2	Cubitt, C. C. (Temp. Capt.)	15/9/16
3	Dalmeny, A. E. H. M. A., Lord, D.S.O., M.C. (Temp. Lieut.-Col.)	24/7/15
3	De Geijer, E. N., M.C.	11/8/18
3	De Lisle, A. P. J. M. P.	{28/3/18, 27/8/18}
3	Delacombe, R., M.C.	23/8/18
	Denny, J. A.	25/1/15
2	Dent, W. H. S.	1/12/17
1	Dickinson, T. M. (attached from 16th Cavalry I.A.)	16/5/15
2	Drummond, F. H. J., M.C. (Actg. Capt.)	{31/7/17, 1/12/17}
1	Dunville, R. L.	6/5/16
3	Dury, G. A. I., M.C. (Actg. Capt.)	7/9/18
3	Eaton, Hon. H. E.	21/6/16
3	Eliot Cornell, R. W.	19/9/17
3	Elliott, A. G. (Actg. Capt.)	31/7/17
3	Ellison, C. E. M., M.C.	8/12/15
3	Ellison, P. J. M.	28/3/18
2	Eyre, J. B. (Temp. Capt.)	24/12/14
3	Fitzgerald, E. G. A., D.S.O. (Actg. Capt.)	{9/10/17, 7/4/18}
1	Flower, N. A. C.	25/9/16
1	Frere, J. H.	11/5/18
3	Fryer, E. R. M., M.C. (Actg. Capt.)	29/9/16
1	Gardner, S. Y. P., M.C.	5/9/17
2	Giles, C. C. T.	27/8/18
3	Godman, G. W.	4/11/18

APPENDIX V.

THE GRENADIER GUARDS

APPENDIX V.

Batt.		Date.
2	Gordon, C. A., M.C. (Actg. Capt.)	4/11/18
1	Gordon-Lennox, V. C. H.	20/11/16
2	Goschen, G. G.	24/12/14
1	Graham, J. W.	6/5/16
4	Green, G. R., M.C.	12/4/18
4	Greenwood, J. E.	12/4/18
1	Guthrie, C. T. R. S. (Temp. Capt.)	11/3/15
3	Hall, C. A., M.C.	8/17
3	Hanham, Sir J. L., Bart.	27/11/17
2	Hanning, G. H.	12/3/18
4	Hardinge, Hon. A. H. L., M.C. (Actg. Capt.)	1/12/17
1	Hawkesworth, E. G., M.C.	25/8/18
1	Healey, C. H. C.	{25/9/16, 19/5/18}
3	Henderson, K.	31/7/17
3	Hermon-Hodge, L. St. L.	{10/3/16, 6/7/17}
	Hewitt, C. J.	31/7/17
3	Hirst, G. F. R., M.C. (Actg. Capt.)	17/10/15
4	Hoare, E. R. D.	27/9/15
3	Hoare, G. H. R.	27/11/17
3	Holbech, L. (Actg. Capt.), D.S.O., M.C.	1/4/18
3	Hollins, C. B.	27/11/17
3	Hopley, F. J. V. B., D.S.O.	14-17/9/16
4	Irby, C. E., M.C.	11/10/17
2	Irvine, A. F.	25/9/16
2	Jacob, J. H.	{31/7/17, 28/3/18}
2	Jesper, N. McK., M.C.	{15/9/16, 27/8/18}
1	Jones, B. H.	27/9/18

OFFICERS WOUNDED

Batt.		Date.
4	Kendall, R. Y. T.	12/9/16 APPENDIX V.
		1/12/17
3	Knollys, A. C., M.C.	27/3/18
2	Lawford, R. D., M.C.	31/7/17
1	Lawrence, B. L.	30/7/17
2	Layland-Barratt, F. H. G., M.C.	1/12/17
4	Layton, B. C. (Actg. Capt.)	27/7/16
		6/1/18
1	Llewelyn, H.	10-12/9/16
3	Long, E. C.	27/11/17
1	Lovell, W. H., M.C. (Actg. Capt.)	27/9/18
3	Lycett-Greene, F. D.	28/9/15
4	Macmillan, M. H.	27/9/15
		18/7/16
		15/9/16
	Magnay, F. A.	1/12/17
4	Maine, H. C. S.	24/9/16
2	Manners, Hon. F. H., M.C.	30/3/18
2	Mildmay, A. S. L. St. J., M.C. (Temp. Capt.)	11/3/15
2	Minchin, T. W., D.S.O. (Temp. Capt.)	15/9/16
		13/4/18
1	Morley, Hon. C. H.	15-18/5/15
4	Nash, C. S., M.C.	26/11/17
		12/4/18
2	Neill, E. M., M.C.	21/10/18
3	Neville, W. W. S. C., M.C. (Temp. Major)	31/7/17
3	Ogle, H. R.	20/7/17
4	Oliver, F. R.	28/11/17
1	Osborne, R. B.	11/10/18
1	Paget-Cooke, O. D. P.	24/4/18
2	Parker-Jervis, T.	15/9/16
2	Paton, J. A.	27/8/18

THE GRENADIER GUARDS

Appendix V.

Batt.		Date.
2	Pelly, P. V.	27/9/18
2	Penn, A. H., M.C. (Temp. Capt.)	17/5/15
2	Ponsonby, Hon. B. B.	6/5/15
2	Ponsonby, G. A.	12/12/16
2	Ponsonby, M. H.	29/1/18
4	Ridley, M. A. T.	27/9/15
3	Ritchie, A. T. A., M.C. (Actg. Capt.)	27/9/15 15/9/16 31/7/17
	Rodney, Hon. C. C. S.	13/4/18
2	Rumbold, H. C. L.	2/1/15
1	St. Aubyn, F. C.	16/5/15 25/10/15
1	Samuelson, B. G. (Actg. Capt.)	14-16/9/16
4	Selby-Lowndes, J. W. F., M.C.	22/12/16
3	Seymour, E. W.	23/3/18
1	Sharp, C. C. T.	10-12/9/16
2	Sharpe, R. T.	27/9/18
1	Shelley, E. B. (Actg. Capt.)	10-12/9/16
4	Shelley, G. E. (Actg. Capt.)	27/9/15
2	Smith, D. A., M.C. (Actg. Capt.)	5/8/15 29/3/16
	Smith, D. E.	11/10/17
1	Stein, O. F., D.S.O. (Actg. Capt.)	10-12/9/16 19/5/18
	Stephenson, P. K. (Actg. Capt.)	24/11/17
2	Stirling, E. G.	6/7/16
1	Stourton, R. H. P. J.	10-12/9/16
	Sutton, K. H. M.	31/7/17
	Swaine, Y. W.	23/7/17
1	Swift, C. T. (Actg. Capt.)	25/9/16
2	Tabor, J.	9/10/17
3	Tate, E. D.	14/9/17 27/3/18

OFFICERS WOUNDED

APPENDIX V.

Batt.		Date.
2	Terrell, R. (Actg. Capt.)	21/2/17
	Thomas, M. D.	13/4/18
3	Thornhill, N., M.C.	9/10/17
1	Timmis, W. U.	28/3/18
1	Tindal-Atkinson, J. F.	24/4/18
2/3	Towneley-Bertie, Hon. M. H. E. C.	13/9/16 10/5/18
4	Veitch, J. J. M.	1/12/17
1	Vernon, H. B., M.C.	6/3/17 24/8/18
1	Villiers, G. J. T. H.	29/9/15
3	Walker, P. M., M.C. (Actg. Capt.)	25/10/15
1	Webber, R. L.	24/8/18
4	West, R. G., M.C.	5/9/17
1	Westmacott, G. R., D.S.O.	13/3/15
3	Whitehead, A. O.	14-17/9/16
2	Wiggins, H. G., M.C. (Actg. Capt.)	25/9/16
1	Wilkinson, C.	7/4/16
3	Williams, H. St. J.	14-17/9/16
2	Wilton, J. D. C.	17/11/16
2	Wright, R. B. B.	25/9/16
4	Wrixon, M. P. B., M.C.	27/2/18

Second Lieutenants

2	Battye, P. L. M.	8/2/15
2	Bevan, R. C. M.	27/9/18
1	Blunt, J. C.	27/9/18
1	Brutton, C. P.	19/5/18
3	Calvocoressi, S.	7/9/18
1	Campbell, J. L.	30/7/18
2	Chapman, H. M.	12/3/18

Batt.		Date.
1	Clarke, D. H., M.C.	11/10/18
3	Clough-Taylor, E. L. F.	22/8/18
1	Conant, R. J. E.	23/8/18
3	Cooper, H. St. C.	27/11/17
	Cox, P. H.	13/4/18
2	Fitch, C. A.	29/4/18
4	Gilbey, A. J.	23/3/18
3	Gordon, H. P.	3/9/18
1	Hall, C. B., M.C.	21/10/18
3	Henderson, R. K.	7/9/18
1	Holmes, R. E. I.	19/5/18
4	Horne, D. E. A.	1/12/17
	Imeretinsky, Prince G.	29/7/17
3	Inglis-Jones, J. A.	26/5/18
1	Jesper, L. C.	27/9/18
3	Manley, W. B. L.	7/9/18
2	Morgan, H. B. G.	6/9/17
1	Nicholson, J. R.	28/3/18
1	Payne, A. F.	12/9/18
	Philipps, G. P.	13/4/18
4	Sich, H. W.	13/4/18
1	Smith, O. W. D.	23/5/18
	Stewart, H. W.	{ 11/10/17 27/3/18

QUARTERMASTER

1	Teece, J., M.C. (Major and Q.M.)	19/12/14

MISSING

3	Bowes-Lyon, G. P.	27/11/17
2	Gunnis, I. FitzG. S.	3/7/17

CASUALTIES SINCE COMMENCEMENT OF WAR

APPENDIX V.

Detail.	Killed or D. of W.	Wounded.	Missing.	Total.
Officers	203	242	2	447
Other ranks	4508	6939	21	11,468
Totals	4711	7181	23	11,915

Total number of Prisoners of War repatriated, 484.

APPENDIX VI

REWARDS

OFFICERS

[The ranks shown are those held at the time of award]

" V.C. "

Gort, Viscount, Bt.-Major (Actg. Lieut.-Col.), D.S.O., M.V.O., M.C.
Paton, G. H. T., Lieut. (Actg. Capt.), M.C. (Killed in action.)
Pryce, T. T., Lieut. (Actg. Capt.), M.C. (Missing.)

" G.C.B. "

Mackinnon, Sir W. H., General, K.C.B., K.C.V.O.

" K.C.B. "

Cavan, Temp. Gen. The Earl of, K.P., C.B., M.V.O.
Davies, Sir F. J., Lieut.-Gen., K.C.M.G.
Fergusson, Sir C., Bart., Lieut.-Gen., K.C.M.G., M.V.O. D.S.O.

" C.B. "

Ardee, Lord R. le N., Colonel (Temp. Brig.-Gen.)
Cavan, The Earl of, Temp.-Gen., M.V.O.
Clive, G. S., Bt.-Col., D.S.O.
Cooper, R. J., Brig.-Gen., C.V.O.
Corkran, C. E., Bt.-Col. (Temp. Brig.-Gen.).
Crespigny, C. R. C. de, Lieut.-Col., D.S.O.
Earle, M., Colonel, C.M.G., D.S.O.
Gathorne-Hardy, Hon. J. F., Bt.-Col., D.S.O.
Jeffreys, G. D., Bt.-Col. (Temp. Major-Gen.), C.M.G.
Lloyd, A. H. O., Temp. Brig.-Gen., C.M.G., M.V.O.

Loch, Lord E. D., Bt.-Col. (Temp. Brig.-Gen.), C.M.G., D.S.O., M.V.O.
Pereira, G. E., Bt.-Col. (Temp. Brig.-Gen.), C.M.G., D.S.O.
Ruggles-Brise, H. G., Major-Gen., M.V.O.
Trotter, G. F., Bt.-Lieut.-Col. (Temp. Brig.-Gen.), C.M.G., D.S.O., M.V.O.

" G.C.M.G."

Wales, Captain H.R.H. The Prince of (Temp. Major), K.G., G.B.E., M.C.
Cavan, Earl of, Lieut.-Gen., K.P., K.C.B.

" K.C.M.G."

Cheylesmore, Lord, Maj.-Gen., K.C.V.O.
Davies, Sir F. J., Lieut.-Gen., K.C.B.
Fergusson, Sir C., Lieut.-Gen., K.C.B., D.S.O., M.V.O.
Ruggles-Brise, H. G., Maj.-Gen., C.B., M.V.O.

" C.M.G."

Cameron of Lochiel, D. W., Lieut.-Col.
Clive, G. S., Temp. Maj.-Gen., C.B., D.S.O.
Colston, Hon. E. M., Temp. Brig.-Gen., D.S.O., M.V.O.
Corkran, C. E., Bt.-Col. (Temp. Brig.-Gen.).
Crespigny, C. R. C. de, Lieut.-Col., D.S.O.
Earle, M., Lieut.-Col., D.S.O.
V.C. Freyberg, B. C., Capt. (Bt.-Lieut.-Col.), D.S.O.
Gascoigne, E. F. O., Hon. Brig.-Gen., D.S.O.
Gathorne-Hardy, Hon. J. F., Bt.-Col. (Temp. Brig.-Gen.), C.B., D.S.O.
Grigg, E. W. M., Temp. Lieut.-Col., D.S.O., M.C.
Hamilton, G. C., Major (Temp. Col.), D.S.O.
Harrison, C. E., Colonel, C.V.O., M.B., F.R.C.S.
Jeffreys, G. D., Bt.-Col. (Temp. Major-Gen.).
Lloyd, A. H. O., Lieut.-Col. (Temp. Brig.-Gen.), M.V.O. (Shropshire Yeomanry.)
Loch, Lord E. D., Bt.-Col. (Temp. Brig.-Gen.), C.B., D.S.O., M.V.O.
Pakenhem, H. A., Lieut.-Col. (R. Irish Rifles.)
Russell, Hon. A. V. F., Major (Temp. Lieut.-Col.), M.V.O.
Saltoun, A. W. F., Lord, Lieut.-Col.
Scott-Kerr, R., Colonel, C.B., D.S.O., M.V.O.

APPENDIX VI.

Sergison-Brooke, B. N., Bt.-Lt.-Col. (Temp. Brig.-Gen.), D.S.O.
Smith, W. R. A., Lieut.-Col.
Stanley, Hon. F. C., Bt.-Lt.-Col. (Temp. Brig.-Gen.), D.S.O.
Streatfeild, Sir H., Colonel, K.C.V.O., C.B.
Thorne, A. F. A. N., Major, D.S.O.
Trotter, G. F., Bt.-Lieut.-Col. (Temp. Brig.-Gen.), C.B., D.S.O., M.V.O.
Vivian, V., Major (Bt.-Lieut.-Col.), D.S.O, M.V.O..

"D.S.O."

Aubrey-Fletcher, H. L., Capt., M.V.O.
Bailey, Hon. W. R., Capt. (Actg. Major).
Benson, C. E., Lieut. (Actg. Capt.).
Browning, F. A. M. (Actg. Capt.).
Buchanan, J. N., Lieut. (Temp. Capt.), M.C.
Campbell, K. A., Lieut.
Carrington, C. W., Lieut. (Actg. Capt.).
Clive, G. S., Bt.-Col., C.B.
Cooper, A. D., Second Lieutenant.
Colston, Hon. E. M., Temp. Brig.-Gen., C.M.G., M.V.O.
Craig, D., Lieut.
Crespigny, C. R. C. de, Temp. Brig.-Gen., C.M.G.
Dalmeny, Lord, Temp. Lieut.-Col., M.C.
Diggle, W. H., Capt. (Temp. Lieut.-Col.), M.C.
Drury-Lowe, W. D., Capt. (Killed in action.)
Eaton, Hon. F. O. H., Lieut. (Actg. Capt.).
Ellice, E. C., Actg. Major.
Fitzgerald, E. G. A., Lieut.
Gathorne-Hardy, Hon. J. F., Bt.-Col., C.B.
Gerard, C. R., Capt.
V.C. Gort, Viscount, Bt.-Major (Actg. Lieut.-Col.), M.V.O., M.C.
Gosselin, A. B. R. R., Capt. (Died of wounds.)
Greville, C. H. (Actg. Major).
Grey, R., Capt.
Grigg, E. W. M., Temp. Lieut.-Col., M.C.
Hamilton, Lord C. N., Capt., M.V.O.
Hamilton, G. C., Temp. Col.
Harcourt-Vernon, G. C. FitzH., Capt.
Heneage, G. C. W., Major.
Hermon-Hodge, R. H., Major.

REWARDS

APPENDIX VI.

Hervey-Bathurst, Sir F. E. W., Bart., Major.
Heywood-Lonsdale, H. H., Lieut.-Colonel. (Shropshire Yeomanry.)
Holbech, L., Lieut., M.C.
Hopley, F. J. V. B., Lieut. (Actg. Capt.).
Kingsmill, A. de P., Capt. (Actg. Lieut.-Col.), M.C.
Lamont, G. S., Second Lieutenant.
Lascelles, Viscount, Capt. (Actg. Major).
Leatham, R. E. K., Major (Actg. Lieut.-Col.).
Lyttelton, O., Lieut. (Temp. Capt.), M.C.
Maitland, M. E. M. C., Major.
Minchin, T. W., Lieut. (Actg. Capt.).
Mitchell, C., Capt. (Temp. Major).
Morrison, J. A., Capt.
Murray-Threipland, W., Lieut.-Col. (Temp. Col.).
Nicol, W. E., Major.
Percy, Lord W. R., Capt. (Temp. Major).
Pilcher, W. S., Bt.-Major (Actg. Lieut.-Col.).
Rasch, G. E. C., Capt. (Actg. Lieut.-Col.).
Scott, Lord F. G. M. D., Bt.-Lieut.-Col.
Sergison-Brooke, B. N., Bt.-Lieut.-Col. (Temp. Brig.-Gen.).
Seymour, Lord H. C., Major (Bt.-Lieut.-Col.).
Seymour, E., Capt., M.V.O.
Sheppard, E., Capt., M.C.
Stanhope, J. R., Earl, Major (Temp. Lieut.-Col.), M.C.
Stein, O. F., Lieut. (Actg. Capt.).
Streatfeild, H. S. J., Lieut.-Col. (London Regiment.)
Thorne, A. F. A. N., Major (Actg. Lieut.-Col.).
Vaughan, E. N. E. M., Major.
Vivian, V., Major (Bt.-Lieut.-Col.), C.M.G., M.V.O.
Warrender, H. V., Lieut.-Col.
Westmacott, G. R., Temp. Capt.

BAR TO "D.S.O."

Bailey, Hon. W. R., Capt. (Actg. Lieut.-Col.), D.S.O.
V.C. Gort, Viscount, Capt., Bt.-Major (Actg. Lieut.-Col.), D.S.O., M.V.O., M.C.
Lascelles, Viscount, Capt. (Actg. Lieut.-Col.), D.S.O.
Seymour, Lord H. C., Major, Bt.-Lieut.-Col., D.S.O.
Thorne, A. F. A. N., Major (Actg. Lieut.-Col.), D.S.O.

Appendix VI.

SECOND BAR TO "D.S.O."

V.C. Freyberg, B. C., Capt., Bt.-Lieut.-Col., D.S.O.
V.C. Gort, Viscount, Capt., Bt.-Major (Actg. Lieut.-Col.), D.S.O., M.V.O., M.C.
Thorne, A. F. A. N., Major (Actg. Lieut.-Col.), D.S.O.

"M.C."

Acland, A. W., Lieut.
Acraman, W. E., Hon. Capt. and Quartermaster.
Adair, A. H. S., Lieut.
Agar-Robartes, Hon. A. V. (Actg. Major).
Agar-Robartes, Hon. A. G., Lieut. (Actg. Capt.).
Aird, J. R., Lieut.
Alexander, N. G. A., Lieut.
Anson, F., Lieut. (Actg. Capt.).
Arnold-Forster, M. N., Lieut. (Actg. Capt.). (Guards M.G. Regiment.)
Battye, P. L. M., Lieut. (Welsh Guards.)
Beaumont-Nesbitt, F. G., Capt.
Beaumont-Nesbitt, W. H., Lieut. (Actg. Capt.) (Killed in action.)
Bevan, T. P. M., Lieut.
Bicknell, R. A. W., Lieut. (Actg. Capt.).
Briscoe, R. G., Lieut.
Britten, C. R., Capt.
Brown, A. M., Lieut.
Bruce, R. C., Lieut. (3rd Gds. Bde., T.M.B.)
Buchanan, J. N., Lieut. (Temp. Capt.).
Bunbury, E. J., Lieut.
Burke, J. B. M., Lieut. (Actg. Capt.).
Byng, L. G., Lieut.
Carstairs, C. C., Lieut.
Cecil, Hon. W. A., Capt.
Chambers, A. S., Lieut. (Actg. Capt.).
Chapman, M., Lieut. (Actg. Capt.) (Killed in action.)
Clarke, D. H., Lieut.
Clarke, S. T. S., Lieut.
Clive, H. A., Lieut.
Corbett, Hon. T. G. P., Lieut.
Cornforth, J. C., Lieut. (Actg. Capt.).

REWARDS

APPENDIX VI.

Cornish, G. M., Lieut.
Corry, A. V. L., Lieut.
Craigie, J. C., Lieut. (Actg. Capt.).
Cubitt, C. C., Lieut.
Dalmeny, Lord, Temp. Lieut.-Col., D.S.O.
De Geijer, E. N., Lieut.
Delacombe, R., Lieut.
Dent, W. H. S., Lieut.
Diggle, W. H., Capt. (Temp. Lieut.-Col.).
Drummond, F. H. J., Lieut.
Duberly, E. H. J., Lieut. (Temp. Capt.).
Dury, G. A. I., Lieut.
Elliott, A. G., Lieut.
Ellison, C. E. M., Lieut. (Temp. Capt.).
Fairbairn, S. G., Lieut.
Farquhar, R., Lieut. (Died of wounds.)
Farquharson, M. G., 2nd Lieut.
Filmer, Sir R. M., Bart., Capt. (Died of wounds.)
Fisher-Rowe, C. V., Capt.
Fisher-Rowe, L. G., Lieut. (Actg. Capt.). (Died of wounds.)
Fraser, J. C., Lieut.
Fryer, E. R. M., Lieut.
Gardner, S. Y. P., Lieut.
Gibbon, H. J., 2nd Lieut.
Gordon, C. A., Lieut. (Actg. Capt.).
Gort, Viscount, Bt.-Major (Actg. Lieut.-Col.), D.S.O., M.V.O.
Green, G. R., Lieut.
Grigg, E. W. M., Temp. Lieut.-Col., D.S.O.
Gunnis, G. G., Actg. Capt. (Died of wounds.)
Gunther, G. R., 2nd Lieut.
Hague, C. N., Lieut.
Hall, C. A., Lieut. (Actg. Capt.).
Harbord, P. A. A., Lieut. (Died of wounds.)
Harcourt-Vernon, G. C. FitzH., Capt. (Actg. Major), D.S.O.
Harcourt-Vernon, E. G., 2nd Lieut.
Hardinge, Hon. A. H. N., Lieut. (Actg. Capt.).
Hawkesworth, E. G., Lieut.
Heasman, F. J., Lieut. (Actg. Capt.).
Herbert, C. G. Y., Lieut.
Hermon-Hodge, L. St. L., Lieut. (Actg. Capt.).
Hirst, G. F. R., Lieut. (Actg. Capt.).

Holbech, L., Lieut. (Actg. Capt.).
Hope, G. E., Capt. (Actg. Lieut.-Col.) (Presumed killed.)
Hubbard, B. J., Lieut. (Killed in action.)
Hughes, J. S., Capt.
Irby, C. E., Lieut.
Jesper, N. McK., Lieut.
Keith, C. G., Lieut. (Actg. Capt.).
Knollys, A. C., Lieut.
Kingsmill, A. de P., Capt. (Actg. Lieut.-Col.), D.S.O.
Knatchbull-Hugessen, M., Lieut. (Killed in action.)
Lambert, R. S., Capt.
Lawford, R. D., Lieut. (Actg. Capt.).
Lawson-Johnston, A. McW., Lieut. (Died of wounds.)
Layland-Barratt, F. H. G., Lieut.
Leigh-Pemberton, R. D., Lieut. (R.F.C.).
Lovell, W. H., Lieut. (Actg. Capt.).
Lygon, Hon. R., Lieut.-Col., M.V.O.
Lyttelton, O., Lieut. (Actg. Capt.), D.S.O.
Maclear, B. G. H., Lieut. (Killed in action.)
Manners, Hon. F. H., Lieut.
Mildmay, A. S. L. St. J., Lieut.
Moller, A. A., Lieut. (Actg. Capt.).
Morgan, H. B. G., Lieut.
Nash, C. S., Lieut.
Neill, E. M., 2nd Lieut.
Neville, W. W. S. C., Lieut. (Temp. Capt.).
Newton, C. N., Capt.
Osborne, B. R., 2nd Lieut.
Osborne, R. B., Lieut.
Palmer, R. H. R., Lieut.
Parnell, Hon. W. A. D., Lieut. (Killed in action.)
V.C. Paton, G. H. T., Lieut. (Actg. Capt.) (Killed in action.)
Pauling, G. F., Lieut. (Killed in action.)
Pearson-Gregory, P. J. S., Capt.
Penn, A. H., Lieut. (Actg. Capt.).
Pike, E. J. L., Major (Temp. Lieut.-Col.).
V.C. Pryce, T. T., Lieut. (Actg. Capt.). (Missing.)
Riddiford, D. H. S., Lieut.
Ridley, E. D., Capt.
Ritchie, A. T. A., Lieut. (Actg. Capt.).
Selby-Lowndes, J. W. F., Lieut.

REWARDS

Sheppard, E., Capt., D.S.O.
Simmons, P. G., Lieut.
Simpson, J. H. C., Capt.
Skinner, L. P., 2nd Lieut. (Guards M.G.R.).
Sloane-Stanley, H. H., Lieut. (Actg. Capt.). (Killed in action.)
Smith, D. A., Lieut. (Actg. Capt.).
Spence, P. M., Lieut. (Actg. Capt.).
Spencer-Churchill, E. G., Capt.
Stanhope, Earl, Major (Temp. Lieut.-Col.), D.S.O.
Stanley, E. M. C., Lord, Capt.
Stewart, W. A. L., Capt. (Killed in action.)
Teece, J., Hon. Capt. and Quartermaster.
Thornhill, N., Lieut.
Trench, R. P. le P., Lieut.
Tuckwell, E. H., Lieut. (Actg. Capt.).
Vereker, G. G. M., Lieut.
Vernon, H. B., Lieut.
Wall, G. H., Capt. and Quartermaster.
Wales, H.R.H. The Prince of, Capt. (Temp. Major), K.G., G.C.M.G., G.B.E.
Walker, C. F. A., Capt. (Actg. Major).
Walker, P. M., Lieut. (Actg. Capt.).
Wellesley, Lord G., Capt. (Temp. Lieut.-Col.), R.F.C.
West, R. G., Lieut.
Wiggins, H. G., Lieut.
Wilson, G. B., Capt.
Wolrige-Gordon, R., Capt.
Wrixon, M. P. B., Lieut.

BAR TO "M.C."

Adair, A. H. S., Lieut. (Actg. Capt.), M.C.
Cornforth, J. C., Lieut. (Actg. Capt.), M.C.
Fryer, E. R. M., Lieut. (Actg. Capt.), M.C.
Neville, W. W. S. C., Lieut. (Temp. Major), M.C.
Pryce, T. T., Lieut. (Actg. Capt.), V.C., M.C. (Missing.)
Simpson, J. H. C., Capt., M.C.
Spence, P. M., Lieut. (Actg. Capt.).

SECOND BAR TO "M.C."

Cornforth, J. C., Lieut. (Actg. Capt.), M.C.

Appendix VI.

"G.B.E."

Field-Marshal H.R.H. The Duke of Connaught and Strathearn (25-8-17).
Captain (Temp. Major) H.R.H. The Prince of Wales, K.G., M.C., and to be Grand Master of the Order (22-6-17).

"K.B.E."

Bedford, H. A., Duke of, Col., K.G., A.D.C.
Guthrie, C. T. R. S., Lieut.

"C.B.E."

Ardee, R. le N., Lord, Col. (Temp. Brig.-Gen.), C.B.
Bigham, Hon. C. C., Capt., Bt.-Major (Temp. Lieut.-Col.), C.M.G.
Glanusk, J. H. R., Lord, Major and Hon. Col., C.B., D.S.O.
Hobart, C. V. C., Lieut.-Col., D.S.O.
Northumberland, A. I., Duke of, Major (Bt.-Lieut.-Col.).
Trotter, G. F., Major, Bt.-Lieut.-Col. (Temp. Brig.-Gen.), C.B., C.M.G., D.S.O., M.V.O.

"O.B.E."

Blundell-Hollinshead-Blundell, C. L., Lieut. (Temp. Major).
Gregson, L. M., Major.
Hood, G. A. A., Viscount, Major (Temp. Lieut.-Col.).
Hubbard, J. F., Lieut. (Temp. Lieut.-Col.).
Legh, Hon. P. W., Capt.
Lessing, A. E., Lieut. (Actg. Capt.).
Mitchell, C., Capt. (Temp. Major), D.S.O.
Rose, I. St. C., Capt.
Seymour, E., Capt. (Temp. Major), D.S.O., M.V.O.
Taylor, G. P. du Plat, Major.
Vivian, G. N., Capt. (Actg. Major).
Webster, Sir A. F., Bart., Capt. (Temp. Major).

"M.B.E."

Eyre, J. B., Lieut. (Temp. Capt.).

REWARDS

SPECIAL AND BREVET PROMOTIONS

To be Lieutenant-General:

Cavan, Major-Gen. (Temp. Lieut.-Gen.) The Earl of, K.P., K.C.B., M.V.O.
Davies, Major-Gen. (Temp. Lieut.-Gen.) Sir F. J., K.C.B., K.C.M.G.
Lloyd, Major-Gen. Sir F., K.C.B., C.V.O., D.S.O.

To be Major-General:

Cavan, Col. (Temp. Brig.-Gen.) The Earl of, K.P., K.C.B., M.V.O.
Gathorne-Hardy, Lieut.-Col., Bt.-Col. (Temp. Major-Gen.) Hon. J. F., C.B., D.S.O.
Gleichen, Col. (Temp. Brig.-Gen.) A. E. W., Count, K.C.V.O., C.B., C.M.G., D.S.O.
Loch, Lieut.-Col., Bt.-Col. (Temp. Brig.-Gen.) E. D., Lord, C.B., C.M.G., D.S.O., M.V.O.
Ruggles-Brise, Col. (Temp. Major-Gen.) H. G., C.B., M.V.O.

To be Brevet-Colonel:

Clive, Lieut.-Col. G. S., C.B., D.S.O.
Corkran, Lieut.-Col. (Temp. Brig.-Gen.) C. E., C.M.G.
Gathorne-Hardy, Lieut.-Col. (Temp. Brig.-Gen.) Hon. J. F., C.B., D.S.O.
Jeffreys, Bt.-Lieut.-Col. (Temp. Major-Gen.) G. D., C.B., C.M.G.
Loch, Lieut.-Col. (Temp. Brig.-Gen.) E. D., Lord, C.B., C.M.G., D.S.O., M.V.O.
Murray-Threipland, W. (Temp. Col.), D.S.O.
Sheldrake, Surg.-Lieut.-Col. E. N.

To be Brevet-Colonel in Reserve of Officers:

Pereira, Lieut.-Col. (Temp. Brig.-Gen.) G. E., C.B., C.M.G., D.S.O.

To be Brevet-Lieutenant-Colonel:

Colston, Major (Temp. Brig.-Gen.) Hon. E. M., C.M.G., D.S.O., M.V.O.
Crespigny, Major (Temp. Brig.-Gen.) C. R. C. de, C.M.G., D.S.O.

Leatham, Major (Actg. Lieut.-Col.) R. E. K., D.S.O.
Jeffreys, Major (Temp. Major-Gen.) G. D., C.B., C.M.G.
Pike, Major (Temp. Lieut.-Col.) E. J. L., M.C.
Scott, Major Lord F. G. M. D., D.S.O.
Sergison-Brooke, Major (Temp. Brig.-Gen.) B. N., D.S.O.
Seymour, Major Lord H. C., D.S.O.
Vivian, Major V., C.M.G., D.S.O., M.V.O.
Hermon-Hodge, Major R. H., D.S.O., M.V.O.

To be Brevet-Lieutenant-Colonel in Reserve of Officers:

Gascoigne, Brevet-Major (Hon. Brig.-Gen.) E. F. O., C.M.G., D.S.O.
Northumberland, A. I., Duke of (Brevet-Major).
Stanley, Brevet-Major (Temp. Brig.-Gen.) Hon. F. C., D.S.O.
Trotter, Major (Temp. Lieut.-Col.) G. F., C.B., C.M.G., D.S.O., M.V.O.
White, Major G. D.

To be Brevet-Major:

Bailey, Hon. W. R., D.S.O.
Barrington-Kennett, Capt. B. H. (With Royal Flying Corps.)
Rasch, Capt. (Actg. Lieut.-Col.) G. E. C., D.S.O.
Gort, Capt. J. S. S. P. V., Viscount, D.S.O., M.V.O., M.C.
Grey, R., D.S.O.
Pilcher, Capt. W. S. (Temp. Major), D.S.O.
Aubrey-Fletcher, Capt. H. L., D.S.O., M.V.O.
Symons, Capt. T. E. R.

To be Brevet-Major in Reserve of Officers:

Bigham, Capt. (Temp. Lieut.-Col.) Hon. C. C., C.M.G.
Cary, Capt. Hon. L. P. (Master of Falkland).
Fisher-Rowe, Capt. C. V., M.C.
Glyn, Capt. (Temp. Major) A. St. L.
Percy, Lord W. R., Capt. (Temp. Lieut.-Col.), D.S.O.
Percy, Capt. A. I., Earl.
Stanley, Capt. (Temp. Brig.-Gen.) Hon. F. C., D.S.O.
Tryon, Capt. G. C., M.P.
Williams, Capt. M. (Actg. Lieut.-Col.).

REWARDS

Granted next Higher Rate of Pay:

Acraman, Hon. Lieut. and Quartermaster W. E., D.C.M.
Teece, Hon. Lieut. and Quartermaster J.

To be Hon. Colonel under Act 77 R.W.:

Pakenhem (Temp. Lieut.-Col.), H. A., C.M.G.

To be Hon. Lieut.-Colonel:

Garton, Quartermaster and Hon. Major W. G. A. (Ret. Pay) Household Cavalry. (Supplement to London Gazette of 8th August 1917).

APPENDIX VII

REWARDS

WARRANT AND NON-COMMISSIONED OFFICERS AND MEN

"V.C."

Batt.	Name.	Rank.	Regtl. No.	Remarks.
1	Barber, E.	Guardsman	15518	Killed in action.
1	Fuller, W. D.	L.-Cpl.	15624	Discharged.
2	Holmes, W. E.	Guardsman	16796	Killed in action.
3	Rhodes, J. H.	A. Sergt.	15122	Killed in action.

"M.B.E."

	Name	Rank	Regtl. No.	Remarks
R.S.	Fawcett, W.	Suptg.-Clk.	9058	

"M.C."

Batt.	Name	Rank	Regtl. No.	Remarks
3	Aiers, G. A.	C.S.M.	13348	
	Clay, S. R.	C.S.M.	30644	
4	Fremlin, E. J.	A.D.S.	12675	
3	Hill, A. M.	S.M.	5163	
1	Hughes, W.	S.M.	11487	
4	Littler, J.	S.M.	8380	
2	Ludlow, E.	S.M.	4947	Killed during Air Raid in London. To Com. in Rgt.
	Payne, F. J. P.	T.R.S.M.	12096	Attached 7th Bn. London Regt.
	Wall, J.	T.R.S.M.	9671	Attached H.A.C.

"D.C.M."

Batt.	Name	Rank	Regtl. No.	Remarks
4	Abell, W. R.	Guardsman	21887	Discharged.
2	Acton, A.	Guardsman	23299	
2	Albone, W.	Sergeant	10807	Discharged.

REWARDS

APPENDIX VII.

Batt.	Name.	Rank.	Regtl. No.	Remarks.
2	Atkinson, C.	A. Sergt.	13679	
2	Austin, E. J.	A.R.S.M.	14231	
4	Baker, A. A.	Sergeant	15477	
2	Ball, W.	Guardsman	16884	Discharged.
2	Barber, F. L.	L.-Sergt.	23919	
2	Barton, T.	A. Cpl.	15529	
2	Beard, R., M.M.	C.S.M. (D/S)	12909	
2	Beer, W.	A. Sergt.	15074	
	Belcher, W. W.	Sergeant	16634	
2	Bennett, A.	C.S.M.	11755	
3	Bennett, J.	L.-Cpl.	29198	
4	Billing, F. H.	L.-Cpl.	13029	
2	Birtles, F.	Corporal	24989	
2	Blackburn, R., M.M.	Sergeant	22949	
1	Booth, T.	Guardsman	26323	
1	Boreham, G. W.	C.S.M.	14277	
3	Bray, W. J.	Sergeant	19264	
1	Brown, T. W.	Q.M.S.	8277	
3	Browning, C. E., M.M.	L.-Sergt.	20600	
2	Bull, H.	Guardsman	17063	Killed in action.
4	Burtt-Massey, R.	Corporal	28181	
4	Canham, J.	Sergeant	15247	
2	Carter, E.	Sergeant	18523	
	Caulfield, J.	Guardsman	20124	
1	Charlton, H. J.	Sergeant	16363	
2	Clarke, W. H.	Guardsman	14472	
1	Coles, H. E., M.M.	Sergeant	16651	
	Cooke, F. A.	Col.-Sergt.	3825	With Lon. Rgt. to Commission.
2	Cooney, W.	Guardsman	8282	Discharged.
4	Cooper, W. S.	Sergeant	19583	Died from disease.
3	Copping, E.	Q.M.S.	13742	
2	Corrigan, T.	Guardsman	14358	
3	Coulton, E., M.M.	L.-Cpl.	22054	Died of wounds.
4	Cunliffe, J.	Guardsman	21493	
2	Davies, H.	L.-Sergt.	18191	
4	Day, E. W.	A.D.S.	11086	
4	Dickens, T. J.	A. Cpl.	23763	Acc. killed.
2	Diley, A.	L.-Cpl.	25256	
1	Dufty, W. J.	Guardsman	16952	Killed in action.
4	Dyer, R.	Guardsman	21737	
2	Fincham, J.	A. L.-Sergt.	16318	
4	Flaycock, S.	Guardsman	12791	
1	Fleming, J.	L.-Cpl.	22939	

THE GRENADIER GUARDS

Batt.	Name.	Rank.	Regtl. No.	Remarks.
3	Fleming, W.	L.-Cpl.	28198	
4	Fletcher, G.	Guardsman	14238	
1	Frost, E.	C.S.M.	8421	Died of wounds
2	Gardiner, H.	L.-Cpl.	15770	
2	Gladders, H.	Guardsman	17244	
2	Godfrey, W. E., M.M.	Guardsman	12347	
3	Grant, W.	Sergeant	13334	
1	Green, R. B.	Corporal	12479	
2	Greenwood, J.	L.-Cpl.	24877	Discharged med. unfit.
4	Grundy, J.	Guardsman	11477	
3	Habberjam, W.	L.-Sergt.	20614	
2	Harrison, J. C.	Corporal	13841	Killed in action.
1	Hayter, J.	L.-Cpl.	13558	Discharged.
4	Hemsley, C.	A. Cpl.	27312	
3	Hennefer, L.	L.-Sergt.	23050	
1	Heslington, P. J. A.	Guardsman	13171	
3	Hewitt, D.	Guardsman	12657	Discharged.
4	Higgins, J.	Sergeant	11588	Discharged.
3	Hill, A. M.	R.S.M.	5163	
2	Hind, L.	Guardsman	17406	
3	Hobden, F.	L.-Cpl.	24524	
3	Hockings, R.	C.S.M.	11315	
4	Hogbin, G. E.	Guardsman	11434	
2	Holness, H. H. J.	Sergeant	10974	To Commission.
4	Horan, M.	L.-Cpl.	20177	
1	Hull, S.	Sergeant	15310	To M.G. Guards.
1	Hulmes, J.	L.-Cpl.	14707	Discharged.
2	Hunter, G. M.	Guardsman	31698	
1	Jarman, J. H.	Sergeant	15087	
1	Jefferies, G.	Guardsman	24532	
1	Jenkins, J.	Guardsman	16551	
1	Johnston, A. W.	Guardsman	30354	
2	Jones, D. J.	Guardsman	10475	Discharged.
	Jones, E.	T.S.M.	5491	Discharged.
1	Jones, S.	Sergeant	15650	To Commission.
1	Jones, H.	Sergeant	11916	Died of wounds.
2	Lack, W. B.	Sergeant	10840	Died of wounds.
2	Lamplugh, C.	L.-Sergt.	14492	
	Lane, H. W.	Guardsman	15585	To M.G. Guards.
1	Langley, W. J.	Sergeant	14620	Died.
3	Latta, W.	L.-Cpl.	11372	
1	Lavers, W. H.	Sergeant	17070	
2	Leach, A. E., M.M.	C.S.M.	11783	
2	Littler, J.	S.M.	8380	

REWARDS

Batt.	Name.	Rank.	Regtl. No.	Remarks.
1	Llewellyn, D.	Guardsman	20674	
2	Lyes, J. W.	L.-Cpl.	13922	
2	Lyon, J.	A. Sergt.	10371	Killed in action.
3	Marks, F., M.M.	C.S.M.	15261	
1	Martin, W.	Sergeant	18457	
1	Masterman, G. H.	C.S.M.	15175	
2	McCaffrey, A. E.	L.-Sergt.	15802	
2	McCune, A.	Sergeant	12819	
2	McDonnell, P.	L.-Cpl.	16202	To Welsh Gds.
2	Midwinter, A.	Sergeant	16522	
2	Miller, G. H.	Sergeant	11182	
1	Millichap, C. P.	Guardsman	22540	
1	Mills, A. J.	A. Sergt.	14772	Killed in action.
4	Milton, W.	L.-Cpl.	24195	
4	Morgan, H. J.	Guardsman	16479	Killed in action.
2	Murrell, E.	Sergeant	14503	Discharged.
3	Norman, H. J.	L.-Sergt.	15111	
4	Norton, J.	C.S.M.	10330	
3	Oakley, T.	L.-Cpl.	23321	
1	Oldfield, S.	Guardsman	22169	
4	Palethorpe, T. R.	Sergeant	7395	
2	Parker, J.	A. Cpl.	18576	
2	Parkinson, A.	Guardsman	15189	Killed in action.
	Parry, J.	L.-Cpl.	15294	
1	Parnwell, F.	Sergeant	15512	
4	Peacock, G. J.	Sergeant	16372	
2	Penn, H. V.	Drummer	15486	
1	Perceval, W., M.M.	C.S.M.	11591	
1	Phippen, T. C. M.	Sergeant	11467	
4	Pitt, A.	C.Q.M.S.	16390	
3	Pole, F.	C.S.M.	14858	
2	Purnell, C. H.	Guardsman	13778	
2	Randell, G.	L.-Cpl.	27833	
2	Rhodes, J. H.	A. Sergt.	15122	Died of wounds.
4	Richmond, R.	A. Sergt.	26550	
1	Riley, J.	L.-Cpl.	12221	Discharged.
2	Roberts, J. R.	Guardsman	15418	
3	Roe, B.	A. L.-Cpl.	24124	
2	Roots, W. J.	Guardsman	15478	
	Rudlin, W. E.	Sergeant	14597	To M.G. Guards.
2	Sharp, G.	Sergeant	14369	
3	Simm, J. T.	Guardsman	21709	
1	Smith, A. E.	C.Q.M.S.	12597	
1	Smith, J. W.	L.-Cpl.	14427	
	Snook, F.	C.S.M.	9797	To Commission.

APPENDIX VII.

300 THE GRENADIER GUARDS

APPENDIX VII.

Batt.	Name.	Rank.	Regtl. No.	Remarks.
3	Spouge, W., M.M.	Guardsman	16650	
2	Spowage, A.	Sergeant	13211	Killed in action.
2	Stannard, C. H.	Guardsman	27684	
3	Stevenson, W.	Sergeant	9575	
4	Sweetman, W. N.	L.-Cpl.	19678	
4	Taylor, W.	Guardsman	28895	
2	Thomas, G. H.	Sergeant	13486	To Welsh Gds.
2	Thomas, J.	Sergeant	14801	
2	Thomas, W.	L.-Cpl.	14471	Killed in action.
4	Todd, W. J.	Guardsman	24814	
2	Topps, F.	Guardsman	14034	
2	Tullett, H.	Guardsman	17892	
2	Turner, G. F. G.	Corporal	24658	
3	Twiss, C.	Sergeant	17018	
2	Tyrell, A.	Guardsman	15394	
3	Unsworth, H.	L.-Cpl.	20479	
1	Warner, J. W.	Guardsman	11839	Killed in action.
4	Waterfall, T.	A. Sergt.	13713	
3	Watson, J. W.	L.-Cpl.	27844	
3	Watts, A. S., M.M.	Sergeant	13353	
1	Whitaker, W. G. R.	L.-Sergt.	19059	Killed in action.
2	Williams, W.	Guardsman	14356	To M.F.P.
3	Winter, W.	Sergeant	18101	
2	Wonnacott, T. J.	A.C.S.M.	15400	
2	Wood, H.	S.M.	5225	To Com. in Rgt.
1	Worton, H., M.M.	Sergeant	12498	
4	Wright, P.	Sergeant	16557	To Commission.
2	Young, C.	L.-Cpl.	24174	

BAR TO " D.C.M."

Batt.	Name.	Rank.	Regtl. No.	Remarks.
2	Rhodes, J. H.	A. Sergt.	15122	Died of wounds.

" M.M."

Batt.	Name.	Rank.	Regtl. No.	Remarks.
2	Acland, G.	L.-Cpl.	25610	
2	Adams, L. B.	Sergeant	19390	
2	Aderly, P. S.	A. Sergt.	15353	Discharged.
3	Alderson, R.	Guardsman	24371	Killed in action.
	Alexander, R.	Sergeant	13394	To M.G. Guards.
1	Anderson, H. J.	A. Sergt.	26602	
1	Angulatta, C.	L.-Sergt.	18239	
2	Arrowsmith, J.	Guardsman	24679	Killed in action.
1	Ashcroft, J.	Sergeant	6382	
3	Ashe, W.	L.-Sergt.	23284	
2	Ashworth, J. J.	L.-Sergt.	17825	

REWARDS

Batt.	Name.	Rank.	Regtl. No.	Remarks.
3	Ashworth, R. H.	L.-Cpl.	20432	
2	Askew, J.	L.-Cpl.	18418	Attached 1st Gds. Bde. T.M.B.
4	Askey, I.	Guardsman	21851	
2	Aust, C.	Guardsman	22719	
3	Austin, A.	Guardsman	15190	
2	Austin, W. T.	L.-Sergt.	11020	To Commission.
1	Bailey, H. O.	Corporal	12393	
2	Bailey, G.	Guardsman	21214	
1	Baker, J.	Guardsman	28475	
2	Baker, W. H.	C.Q.M.S.	14809	
1	Baker, W.	L.-Cpl.	16832	
1	Baggott, J.	Guardsman	26689	
2	Bagley, G.	Guardsman	25536	
2	Bamping, J.	Guardsman	30364	
4	Bancroft, J.	Guardsman	26573	
3	Bannister, F. C.	L.-Cpl.	22639	
2	Baptist, M.	Guardsman	16274	
1	Barber, D. S.	Guardsman	22800	To M.G. Guards.
4	Barker, S. L.	L.-Cpl.	18708	To R.E.
2	Batchelor, E. T.	Guardsman	25614	
2	Beard, R.	A.S.M.	12909	
1	Beaton, K.	Guardsman	18591	
2	Beever, W.	Guardsman	28086	
4	Belcher, T.	A. Sergt.	20912	
3	Belither, R.	Guardsman	18806	
3	Belleini, A. F. W.	Guardsman	27210	
2	Benjamin, W.	Guardsman	17212	
2	Bennett, C. G. F.	L.-Cpl.	16194	Discharged.
2	Bennett, D.	Sergeant	19112	Died of wounds.
2	Bennett, O. J.	L.-Cpl.	29850	
3	Bennett, H.	L.-Sergt.	21974	
1	Benstead, R.	Guardsman	14114	Discharged.
4	Bent, J.	Guardsman	21023	Missing.
2	Bentley, J.	Guardsman	19370	
2	Benton, J. W.	Guardsman	22788	
1	Bickerstaff, J.	Guardsman	25596	
1	Biggin, T.	Guardsman	11671	
3	Bignell, F.	Guardsman	10966	To Labour Corps.
1	Billing, F. H.	L.-Cpl.	13029	
3	Bird, J.	Guardsman	26808	
2	Blackwell, J. H.	C.S.M.	11300	
3	Bland, E.	Guardsman	31513	
2	Blackburn, L.	Sergeant	22949	
2	Blanks, E. G.	Guardsman	30484	

APPENDIX VII.

302 THE GRENADIER GUARDS

APPENDIX VII.

Batt.	Name.	Rank.	Regtl. No.	Remarks.
3	Blasdale, P. J.	Guardsman	11896	
3	Blundy, R. E.	L.-Cpl.	14603	
3	Bond, B.	Guardsman	16774	
3	Booth, F.	L.-Cpl.	21338	
4	Booth, C. W.	Corporal	22559	
2	Bosworth, J.	Sergeant	10627	Killed in action.
2	Boyle, J.	Guardsman	20231	
1	Boyles, E.	C.Q.M.S.	14220	Discharged.
1	Bradshaw, E. C.	Guardsman	23879	
2	Bray, W. J., D.C.M.	Sergeant	19264	
2	Brierly, P.	Guardsman	23981	
1	Bright, W.	L.-Sergt.	17014	
4	Broadfoot, J.	L.-Cpl.	20817	Missing.
4	Brown, C.	L.-Sergt.	23152	Killed in action.
1	Brown, C. F.	Sergeant	18249	
4	Brown, J. A.	Sergeant	16620	
3	Browning, C. E.	L.-Sergt.	20600	
4	Brownsell, W. I.	Guardsman	22264	Discharged.
3	Bryan, W. K.	A. Sergt.	13494	
2	Bryant, W. T. H.	L.-Cpl.	16400	
3	Buchan, C. M.	L.-Sergt.	24143	
4	Buckle, E.	Sergeant	15494	Killed in action.
1	Burchett, J. G.	Sergeant	17810	
2	Burrows, E.	Guardsman	18594	
3	Burrows, S. N.	L.-Sergt.	24768	
1	Burke, V.	Corporal	11203	Killed in action.
3	Burke, W.	Sergeant	16530	
2	Burton, C. H.	Guardsman	23010	
2	Burton, A. C.	Guardsman	18288	To Labour Corps.
1	Burton, S.	Sergeant	10593	
1	Calder, H.	L.-Sergt.	17228	
4	Canham, J.	Sergeant	15247	
1	Carpenter, S.	L.-Cpl.	12822	
1	Carter, J.	Guardsman	28098	
2	Carter, E.	L.-Sergt.	21720	
1	Carter, W. M.	Guardsman	30387	
3	Carter, A.	Guardsman	21193	
1	Carter, F. J.	Sergeant	11043	To Commission.
1	Casey, P.	Sergeant	13945	
3	Challis, J. A.	L.-Sergt.	22783	Died of wounds.
1	Chambers, E. G.	Guardsman	21206	
2	Chapman, D. W.	A.C.Q.M.S.	8711	
1	Chapman, H.	Guardsman	12795	
2	Chivers, A. E.	Guardsman	24053	
	Churchman, J. A.	Guardsman	25060	

REWARDS

Appendix VII.

Batt.	Name.	Rank.	Regtl. No.	Remarks.
2	Churchyard, H.	Guardsman	28408	
1	Clark, C. W.	Sergeant	18062	To Commission.
1	Clark, E.	Guardsman	17241	
2	Clarke, W. H.	L.-Cpl.	14472	Discharged.
4	Clarkson, J.	Guardsman	17542	Died of wounds.
4	Clay, J.	Guardsman	20805	Discharged.
3	Clayton, C.	Guardsman	21282	
4	Clayton, W.	Guardsman	16383	
3	Clegg, H.	Guardsman	20573	
1	Cliff, N. D.	Guardsman	22360	
3	Clowes, A.	L.-Sergt.	25266	
2	Cole, H. W.	Guardsman	24652	
2	Cole, H. A.	Guardsman	28233	
	Cole, A. J.	Guardsman	25687	
1	Coles, H. E.	Sergeant	16651	
4	Coles, W. H.	Guardsman	8663	
2	Colgate, R. E.	Sergeant	14914	To Commission.
4	Collett, J. W. H.	L.-Cpl.	21876	
	Collier, J.	L.-Cpl.	23934	
	Collier, T.	L.-Cpl.	18568	
1	Collings, E. C.	Guardsman	10061	
1	Collins, E.	Guardsman	18143	
3	Cook, A. H.	L.-Sergt.	19467	Killed in action.
1	Cooke, S.	Sergeant	15664	
3	Coombs, B.	Guardsman	26170	
3	Coonan, T.	Guardsman	18123	To M.G. Guards.
	Cooper, F.	Guardsman	21950	To R.E.
4	Cooper, W. S.	Guardsman	19583	Died.
4	Corcoran, J.	Guardsman	21753	
2	Coton, A.	Guardsman	21392	
3	Coulton, E.	L.-Cpl.	22054	
2	Coutts, H. F.	Guardsman	24718	
2	Coward, W. H.	Guardsman	24790	
3	Cowling, W.	A. L.-Cpl.	28575	
1	Cox, A. L.	Sergeant	13959	
2	Cox, J.	L.-Cpl.	13475	
1	Crick, F.	Guardsman	14818	
4	Crompton, P.	A. Cpl.	20392	
3	Cronin, D.	Guardsman	11492	Discharged.
	Cross, S.	Guardsman	24497	
1	Croucher, R.	A.C.S.M.	11034	
1	Dalling, F.	Guardsman	26667	
4	Darlington, G.	Guardsman	12901	Killed in action.
1	Davidson, S.	Guardsman	18181	
2	Davies, W.	O.R. Sergt.	17780	

THE GRENADIER GUARDS

APPENDIX VII.

Batt.	Name.	Rank.	Regtl. No.	Remarks.
	Davis, T. W.	Guardsman	28294	
4	Dawson, J.	Guardsman	23402	
2	Day, A.	Sergeant	18711	
2	Dean, R.	L.-Cpl.	19317	
4	Deane, F. J.	L.-Cpl.	17187	Killed in action.
3	Dench, E.	Guardsman	29476	
4	Dennison, T.	Guardsman	21611	
4	Devy, G.	Corporal	18167	
2	Dew, A. W.	Guardsman	30493	
2	Dewick, H. B.	Sergeant	15821	
3	Dickenson, J.	Guardsman	28755	
3	Dickson, R.	Sergeant	11900	
2	Dighton, W.	Guardsman	23260	
3	Dix, H.	L.-Sergt.	22974	
	Dobson, W. H.	Sergeant	13610	To M.G. Guards.
4	Docking, R. J.	L-.Cpl.	20151	
2	Donson, H.	Guardsman	16485	
3	Dore, J. G.	Sergeant	14547	
2	Downes, W.	Guardsman	20848	
1	Downs, W. T.	Guardsman	18155	
1	Drew, F.	Guardsman	30326	
2	Drinkwater, P. S.	Guardsman	11183	
1	Driver, G.	Sergeant	15696	
3	Duddell, H. L.	Guardsman	30054	
2	Duddy, J. L.	L.-Cpl.	17551	
4	Duffield, R.	Guardsman	24315	
3	Dunn, G. W.	Sergeant	12138	Died of wounds.
3	Eason, J. E.	C.S.M.	11041	
2	Eccleshall, C.	Sergeant	15574	
1	Eggleton, H. J.	Guardsman	26636	
1	Eglington, H.	L.-Cpl.	18785	
	Elliott, W.	L.-Cpl.	27067	
4	England, J.	Guardsman	10945	
3	England, R. A.	Guardsman	27259	
2	English, G.	Guardsman	26368	
1	Ewell, R. C.	O.R.C.	17673	
	Eyre, G. R.	L.-Cpl.	23638	
	Famfield, C. W.	Guardsman	24646	
3	Fasham, A.	Guardsman	17504	
1	Fenton, E.	Guardsman	18873	Killed in action.
3	Figgis, J.	Guardsman	20345	
3	Files, C. H.	Guardsman	16674	
4	Finch, W. H.	A. Sergt.	19017	
2	Fincham, J.	A. L.-Sergt.	16318	
2	Fitch, S. G.	Guardsman	12744	

REWARDS

Batt.	Name.	Rank.	Regtl. No.	Remarks.
	Fleming, J.	L.-Cpl.	22939	
2	Fletcher, J.	Guardsman	16193	
1	Folke, L. W.	Guardsman	24301	
4	Foster, G.	Guardsman	26408	
	Foster, F.	Guardsman	30061	
	Fox, A. E.	L.-Sergt.	15761	To M.G. Guards.
	Frost, E.	L.-Sergt.	12882	
1	Fryer, G. E.	Guardsman	13130	
4	Fuller, G.	Guardsman	26188	
4	Furness, E.	Sergeant	21568	
4	Gale, B. A.	Guardsman	28387	Died of wounds
2	Galley, P. H.	Guardsman	27141	To A.P.C.
2	Gambrill, W. F.	C.Q.M.S.	13317	
2	Gardiner, H.	L.-Cpl.	15770	
4	Garlick, G.	Sergeant	11670	
1	Gaskin, C.	L.-Cpl.	16233	Killed in action
4	Gibbs, G. A.	L.-Cpl.	21170	
2	Gibson, G. W.	L.-Cpl.	16653	
2	Gipson, J.	Guardsman	14116	
2	Glendenning, J.	Guardsman	28999	
2	Godfrey, W. E.	Guardsman	12347	
1	Golding, W. C.	A.C.Q.M.S.	14771	
3	Goodchild, J. H.	Guardsman	31967	
	Gould, C.	Sergeant	11197	To M.G. Guards.
3	Graham, F. H.	Guardsman	24534	
3	Grant, W.	Sergeant	13334	To K.O.Y.L.I.
	Grayson, T. H.	L.-Cpl.	20055	
2	Greenhalf, W. G.	Guardsman	12191	
3	Greenwood, C.	Sergeant	11579	To Commission.
1	Griffin, G. J.	Sergeant	23304	
1	Griffiths, J.	Guardsman	9849	Discharged.
1	Griffiths, E. J.	Guardsman	12259	
3	Grindley, H.	Guardsman	24467	
3	Haizelden, S.	Guardsman	14569	
4	Hales, C.	Guardsman	19110	
4	Hall, H.	Sergeant	21589	
3	Hall, A. G.	L.-Sergt.	16723	
1	Halls, J.	Guardsman	18001	
	Hallworth, W.	L.-Cpl.	25106	
4	Hames, H. F.	A. Cpl.	22373	
3	Hams, C.	L.-Cpl.	15508	
	Hanis, D. J.	Guardsman	18839	
2	Hankinson, W.	Guardsman	17431	
1	Harcourt, J.	L.-Sergt.	14002	
3	Harris, B.	Guardsman	18759	

APPENDIX VII.

APPENDIX VII.

Batt.	Name.	Rank.	Regtl. No.	Remarks.
1	Harrison, W.	Guardsman	20495	
3	Harrison, W. H.	Guardsman	28045	
3	Harrison, S. F.	L.-Cpl.	24982	
1	Hartga, T. G.	Guardsman	29122	
4	Hartley, M.	A. Sergt.	20768	
2	Hartshorn, C.	L.-Sergt.	13893	
1	Haslem, J.	Guardsman	13524	
4	Hatton, C. G.	Sergeant	13727	Killed in action.
2	Hawcroft, A.	Guardsman	30499	
4	Haycock, S., D.C.M.	Guardsman	12791	
2	Hayes, A. R.	A. Sergt.	17225	
	Haynes, E. W.	L.-Cpl.	22184	
4	Heap, J.	Guardsman	20183	To Labour Corps.
3	Hearn, C.	C.S.M.	10372	Killed in action.
1	Hearn, A. E.	L.-Cpl.	22772	
3	Hemming, A. F.	L.-Cpl.	23862	
4	Hickey, G. F.	Guardsman	16895	
3	Hickman, J. E.	L.-Sergt.	21162	
3	Hicks, W. T.	Sergeant	15556	
4	Higgins, H.	L.-Cpl.	21525	Killed in action.
4	Higgins, J.	Sergeant	11588	Discharged.
	Higham, W.	L.-Cpl.	20476	
3	Hill, C.	L.-Cpl.	20403	
2	Hill, R. M.	Sergeant	15203	
1	Hindley, W.	Sergeant	21676	
	Hiscock, C. H.	Guardsman	29542	
3	Hoare, F. J.	L.-Cpl.	20985	
2	Hodgson, A.	L.-Cpl.	22374	
4	Hodkinson, H.	Sergeant	15085	
4	Holland, A.	L.-Sergt.	21945	Discharged.
2	Holliday, R.	Sergeant	11629	
4	Hollobone, F. R.	Guardsman	25820	
	Holme, A.	Guardsman	11039	
	Holmes, F. W.	L.-Cpl.	10668	
4	Hope, W. S.	Sergeant	12023	Discharged.
	Horler, R. J.	Guardsman	16613	
2	Horton, S.	Guardsman	17382	
4	Houston, R.	L.-Cpl.	20187	
	Hubbard, J. W.	Sergeant	14217	
2	Huffer, C.	Guardsman	17355	Died of wounds.
1	Hughes, F.	Guardsman	16489	
1	Hughes, L. A.	Guardsman	21141	
1	Hughes, T. W.	L.-Sergt.	16917	
1	Hulmes, J., D.C.M.	Sergeant	14707	
1	Humphrey, F. T.	Guardsman	16099	

REWARDS

Batt.	Name.	Rank.	Regtl. No.	Remarks.
1	Hunt, F.	Guardsman	26346	
3	Huntley, E. E.	L.-Cpl.	11031	
1	Illsley, L.	Guardsman	19932	
1	Illsley, W. J.	L.-Cpl.	21998	
3	Ingham, T.	Sergeant	12271	
1	Ironmonger, G.	Guardsman	18350	
2	Ivill, W.	L.-Sergt.	14655	
2	Jacobs, A. C.	L.-Cpl.	29681	
1	Jackson, A.	A. L.-Sergt.	18516	
3	James, E.	Guardsman	14811	
4	James, W. S. G.	L.-Cpl.	23188	
2	Jeanes, J. V.	Sergeant	12813	
2	Jeffreys, C. J.	Guardsman	12111	
1	Jenkins, J.	Guardsman	16551	
1	John, B.	L.-Sergt.	17719	Discharged.
2	Jones, T. L. C.	L.-Cpl.	16167	To Commission.
2	Jones, A.	Guardsman	17545	Died of wounds.
1	Jones, J.	C.Q.M.S.	13526	Discharged.
4	Jones, R. E.	A. Cpl.	10981	
1	Jones, A. F.	Sergeant	15128	Killed in action.
1	Jones, H.	Guardsman	16132	To R.E.
2	Jones, G. H.	Guardsman	20501	To M.G. Guards.
1	Jones, G.	Guardsman	16985	Died of wounds.
1	Jones, W.	Guardsman	14726	
3	Jones, A.	L.-Cpl.	15804	
4	Joyce, A.	Guardsman	12925	
1	Judson, W.	L.-Cpl.	13517	
3	Keate, A. E.	Guardsman	28598	
4	Keep, P.	Corporal	20346	Killed in action.
3	Keggin, W.	L.-Cpl.	28533	
2	Kemp, A.	Guardsman	29083	
4	Kemp, C. W.	Corporal	21175	Missing.
1	Kenlock, A. E.	Guardsman	12599	
3	Kent, W. J.	L.-Sergt.	19019	
1	Kenyon, T.	Guardsman	18012	
3	Keyte, J. G.	L.-Sergt.	14639	
3	Killington, H.	Sergeant	15888	
	King, E. W.	Sergeant	15488	To M.G. Guards.
3	Knight, E.	L.-Sergt.	15592	
1	Knowles, W.	Sergeant	14505	
	Lacey, F. H.	L.-Cpl.	16447	
4	Laming, G. W.	Sergeant	14248	
1	Lancaster, G.	L.-Sergt.	15094	
4	Langford, A.	Guardsman	21768	Missing.
3	Latta, W.	L.-Cpl.	11372	

APPENDIX VII.

THE GRENADIER GUARDS

Appendix VII.	Batt.	Name.	Rank.	Regtl. No.	Remarks.
	1	Lavender, H.	L.-Cpl.	18531	
	1	Lawrance, W. G.	Guardsman	10989	
		Lawrence, J. A.	Guardsman	26997	
	3	Lawrence, W.	Sergeant	14228	
		Lawton, C.	Sergeant	16852	
	2	Leach, A. E.	C.S.M.	11783	
	2	Leech, E. C.	L.-Cpl.	12043	
	1	Lewis, S. T.	Sergeant	13886	Killed in action.
		Lilley, W.	L.-Cpl.	15726	To M.G. Guards.
	3	Little, T.	Guardsman	20603	
	4	Locke, F. C.	L.-Sergt.	19634	Killed in action.
	1	Lockley, J. T.	Guardsman	26141	
	4	Lomas, J.	Guardsman	21684	
	4	Long, W. F.	L.-Cpl.	24996	
	3	Longrigg, J.	L.-Sergt.	23098	
	4	Louth, A.	Corporal	17356	
	4	Lowe, J.	Guardsman	24699	
	1	Lowe, S.	A. L.-Cpl.	12674	
	1	Luker, J.	L.-Sergt.	12910	
	4	Lulham, F. G.	Guardsman	29568	
	4	Lusty, E.	Corporal	11510	
	4	Lynch, M.	Guardsman	23109	
	2	Lyon, J.	Sergeant	10371	Killed in action.
	1	McCarrick, J.	Guardsman	18884	
	4	McEvoy, D.	Guardsman	26621	
	1	McGuin, T.	Guardsman	15013	Died of wounds.
	1	Machin, T. W.	Guardsman	14329	To R.E.
	1	McIntosh, W. A.	Guardsman	17863	
	4	Madeley, F. G.	L.-Cpl.	19176	Discharged.
		Mannion, C.	Guardsman	20424	Att. 2nd Guards Bde., M.G. Co.
	1	Mansell, H.	L.-Sergt.	15493	
	3	Marks, F.	C.S.M.	15261	
	4	Marriott, C. K.	C.S.M.	13729	
	2	Marsden, J.	Guardsman	18332	
	4	Marsh, H.	L.-Sergt.	20306	Missing.
	4	Marshall, A.	Guardsman	20437	Discharged.
		Marshall, W. J.	Guardsman	14449	
	3	Martin, W. J. E.	Guardsman	20348	
	4	Mason, B.	L.-Cpl.	14091	
	1	Masterman, G. H.	C.Q.M.S.	15175	
		Masterman, R.	Guardsman	28010	
	2	Mawby, E.	L.-Sergt.	13725	
	4	Mead, H. R.	Guardsman	27952	
	4	Meikle, H. J.	Guardsman	20190	

REWARDS

Appendix VII.

Batt.	Name.	Rank.	Regtl. No.	Remarks.
1	Merchant, T.	Guardsman	13037	
1	Meredith, A.	L.-Sergt.	12634	
1	Meredith, E. H.	L.-Cpl.	22159	Killed in action.
3	Merry, J. C.	Guardsman	24741	
2	Middleditch, J.	Guardsman	23992	
3	Miles, W.	L.-Sergt.	13109	
4	Miller, W.	A. Sergt.	13872	
2	Millins, F. J.	Guardsman	18379	Killed in action.
2	Mills, A.	Guardsman	19520	
4	Millward, J.	Guardsman	20382	
1	Morris, M.	A.C.Q.M.S.	12640	
1	Morris, W.	Guardsman	10295	
	Morton, W.	Guardsman	21656	
2	Moulding, J.	L.-Cpl.	25819	Died of wounds.
1	Moulton, A.	A.C.S.M.	9712	
2	Moulton, T.	L.-Cpl.	27858	
3	Muff, L.	Guardsman	28190	
4	Mumford, R. J.	Guardsman	26304	
3	Munn, A.	L.-Cpl.	21384	Killed in action.
4	Naylor, T.	Guardsman	21812	Killed in action.
2	Neale, W.	Sergeant	13594	
2	Nelmes, E.	Guardsman	14296	
1	New, C. E.	Sergeant	8606	
4	Newell, B.	Corporal	20907	
2	Newman, H.	L.-Cpl.	14294	
3	Noble, T. E.	Sergeant	14477	To Commission.
1	Norris, T.	Guardsman	24108	
4	Nottage, T. S.	A. Sergt.	22065	
	Nuttall, A.	L.-Sergt.	20762	
3	Nuttall, H.	L.-Sergt.	11091	Killed in action.
1	Oakes, G.	Guardsman	30462	
4	Oakes, H. W.	Sergeant	14716	
3	Ogden, E.	Guardsman	20127	
2	O'Neill, M.	Guardsman	11702	
	O'Neill, T.	Guardsman	29946	
2	Orme, H.	L.-Cpl.	18514	
3	Packman, H. G.	Guardsman	21042	
1	Paddock, F.	Sergeant	16555	Discharged.
1	Page, A. E.	Guardsman	23828	To M.G. Guards.
2	Page, F.	Guardsman	24657	
3	Page, W. W.	Guardsman	20536	Discharged.
	Painter, W. J.	L.-Cpl.	27670	
1	Paintin, H.	Guardsman	12385	
1	Palfrey, E. G.	Corporal	12827	Killed in action.
2	Paradine, H.	Sergeant	15209	Discharged.

Batt.	Name.	Rank.	Regtl. No.	Remarks.
2	Parker, F. C.	Guardsman	12836	
3	Parker, A. A.	L.-Cpl.	15482	
4	Parry, E.	Guardsman	22014	
2	Parry, S. M.	Guardsman	26642	
3	Parry, W.	C.S.M.	10543	Discharged.
3	Parsons, E. W.	A. Sergt.	19971	
3	Partington, J.	L.-Sergt.	23198	
3	Partington, W.	L.-Cpl.	22419	
4	Patefield, E.	L.-Cpl.	19523	
3	Pay, F.	L.-Cpl.	23442	
1	Payne, B. J.	L.-Cpl.	17493	
4	Payne, T.	Corporal	21109	
1	Payne, W.	Guardsman	26459	
2	Peach, J. R.	Guardsman	26727	
1	Pearce, F.	Sergeant	15222	
4	Pearson, A.	L.-Sergt.	28442	
2	Pearson, A. B.	L.-Sergt.	21868	
2	Pearson, T. H.	L.-Sergt.	13414	To Labour Corps.
1	Pearson, W.	Sergeant	23936	
1	Percival, W.	C.S.M.	11591	
	Perkins, H. B.	L.-Sergt.	16872	
	Perrett, G.	Guardsman	31263	
1	Perry, H. N.	L.-Sergt.	18321	
1	Phippin, T. C. M.	Sergeant	11467	
3	Pike, H.	Guardsman	29197	
2	Pinnell, T.	Guardsman	15864	
2	Pitt, W.	L.-Sergt.	9334	Discharged.
	Plimmer, A. G.	Guardsman	35057	
4	Plummer, E. J.	Guardsman	26013	
3	Pollington, H.	Guardsman	20454	
1	Porter, B. R. M.	Sergeant	22909	
2	Portier, J.	Guardsman	22119	
3	Potter, E. P.	Sergeant	19942	Discharged.
2	Potts, W.	Guardsman	20852	
1	Poulter, E. J.	L.-Cpl.	25329	
1	Powell, J. C.	C.Q.M.S.	15543	
4	Powlesland, J.	Guardsman	21563	
	Pratt, G. H. M.	Guardsman	25664	
	Preece, E. A.	L.-Cpl.	26646	
4	Price, H.	Sergeant	14689	
3	Price, J.	Guardsman	19948	
4	Price, W. J.	Guardsman	15637	
1	Price, W. T.	L.-Cpl.	29986	
3	Pugh, W. L.	L.-Cpl.	19273	
3	Pumfrey, H.	Guardsman	27018	

REWARDS

APPENDIX VII.

Batt.	Name.	Rank.	Regtl. No.	Remarks.
3	Purdy, T.	Sergeant	12987	
4	Ralph, W.	L.-Cpl.	21948	
1	Randall, E.	Guardsman	19149	
4	Ratcliffe, A. T.	Guardsman	18874	
4	Ratley, T.	L.-Cpl.	17353	
4	Reynolds, J.	L.-Cpl.	19643	Missing.
3	Reynolds, G. A.	L.-Cpl.	24784	
3	Richards, F. H.	Guardsman	24713	
3	Richardson, R. N.	L.-Cpl.	18855	
2	Richardson, W.	A.C.Q.M.S.	17508	
4	Rider, C.	Guardsman	19156	
4	Roberts, T.	L.-Sergt.	16898	Discharged.
3	Robertson, A.	L.-Sergt.	24770	To Labour Corps.
2	Robinson, C. A.	A. Sergt.	13980	
4	Robinson, J. W.	L.-Cpl.	20219	
2	Robinson, J.	Guardsman	29474	
1	Robinson, S. J.	Guardsman	26311	
4	Robinson, T. W.	Guardsman	26887	
3	Rock, E. D.	Guardsman	25516	
2	Rockley, A.	Guardsman	15507	
4	Roden, H. H.	Guardsman	25551	
3	Rogers, H.	L.-Cpl.	26963	Died of wounds.
2	Roper, W.	L.-Sergt.	16243	
4	Rose, T.	Guardsman	20684	To M.G. Guards.
2	Rosendale, F. J.	Guardsman	15241	To M.G. Guards.
3	Rossiter, O.	Guardsman	20539	Att. 2nd Guards Bde., T.M.B. Killed in action.
4	Round, H.	Guardsman	21465	
1	Round, W. J.	Sergeant	14252	
		89		
4	Rowbotham, S. J.	L.-Cpl.	24266	Missing.
4	Rowbotham, S. R.	Guardsman	27482	
1	Rowe, E. J.	C.Q.M.S.	14068	
4	Rowlett, J.	Sergeant	19211	
4	Rowley, W.	Guardsman	20900	To Labour Corps.
3	Rudge, L. M.	Sergeant	15274	To Commission.
	Ryall, H. E.	A. Cpl.	16116	3rd Guards Bde., M.G. Coy. Killed in action.
2	Ryder, F.	Guardsman	14742	
	Ryder, J.	L.-Cpl.	19473	Att. 1st Guards Bde., T.M.B. Died of wounds.
	Sargent, F. G.	Guardsman	15525	

THE GRENADIER GUARDS

Appendix VII.

Batt.	Name.	Rank.	Regtl. No.	Remarks.
3	Saunders, E. G.	L.-Cpl.	19013	
1	Saunders, H. F.	Guardsman	29124	
2	Saunders, J.	Guardsman	14165	Died of wounds.
4	Saunders, R. W.	Guardsman	23665	
2	Schofield, F.	Guardsman	17527	
	Scott, T.	L.-Cpl.	27433	
2	Scott, J.	L.-Cpl.	15411	
1	Scroggs, A. H.	Guardsman	15675	
2	Sears, F.	Sergeant	16533	
1	Seymour, H. C.	L.-Cpl.	16126	Killed in action.
2	Sharp, G.	Sergeant	14369	
2	Sharples, W.	L.-Cpl.	27122	
4	Shaw, E.	Sergeant	13810	
1	Shaw, J.	Guardsman	22637	
	Shaw, R.	Guardsman	15109	
3	Sheldon, E. S.	Guardsman	28862	
1	Shenton, F.	Sergeant	9936	
1	Shepherd, E.	Guardsman	24152	
1	Sherfield, F.	L.-Cpl.	22297	Att. 3rd Guards Bde., M.G. Coy.
1	Simpson, F. G.	Guardsman	15199	
3	Simpson, F. S.	Guardsman	16567	
	Sims, E.	Guardsman	29203	
3	Skennerton, S.	Guardsman	24898	
	Slater, T. R.	Guardsman	22134	
2	Smart, W.	Guardsman	27764	
	Smith, A.	L.-Cpl.	14239	1st Guards Bde., M.G. Coy., to M.G. Guards.
4	Smith, E. V.	Guardsman	26281	
4	Smith, F.	L.-Cpl.	17076	Died of wounds.
1	Smith, F. J.	Guardsman	14525	
	Smith, G. T.	Guardsman	30380	
2	Smith, J. H.	A.C.Q.M.S.	11899	
2	Smith, J. H. W.	Guardsman	22934	
4	Smith, T.	L.-Cpl.	19408	
4	Smith, T.	Guardsman	24343	
3	Smith, T. H.	L.-Cpl.	24635	
3	Smith, R. J.	Guardsman	11832	
3	Spencer, J.	L.-Sergt.	9887	
1	Spicer, W. W.	Guardsman	22730	
3	Spouge, W.	L.-Cpl.	16650	
4	Spurr, J. W.	Guardsman	26394	
2	Squirrell, S. A.	L.-Cpl.	22633	Died of wounds.
2	Stamp, H.	Guardsman	13865	

REWARDS 313

Batt.	Name.	Rank.	Regtl. No.	Remarks.
4	Stanley, T. W.	Guardsman	24446	
	Stanton, A.	Corporal	17139	3rd Guards Bde., T.M.B.
	Stanton, W. T.	L.-Cpl.	30527	
4	Steele, J. A.	Guardsman	20464	To G.M.G.R.
2	Stenning, A.	Guardsman	17252	Killed in action.
3	Stephenson, G.	A. Sergt.	23846	
2	Stevens, A.	Sergeant	13751	
3	Stevenson, H.	L.-Cpl.	18817	Killed in action.
4	Stevenson, J. H.	Guardsman	14538	
2	Stockdale, F. J.	L.-Sergt.	12353	Killed in action.
1	Street, H.	L.-Cpl.	24791	Died of wounds.
4	Street, T. F.	Guardsman	20395	
	Struggles, W.	Guardsman	25261	
	Sudworth, J.	Sergeant	20359	
3	Summerscales, J.	Guardsman	21863	
1	Swan, L. S.	A.C.Q.M.S.	12794	
1	Swan, T.	Guardsman	17032	
1	Swift, T.	L.-Cpl.	25909	
4	Tapp, T.	L.-Sergt.	13279	
4	Taylor, E. C.	Sergeant	16271	
1	Taylor, G.	Sergeant	10784	Re-enl. New No. 29878.
3	Taylor, G. T.	Sergeant	15328	
	Taylor, J. C.	Guardsman	29577	
2	Teagle, T.	L.-Cpl.	15058	Killed in action.
4	Temple, F. B.	Guardsman	29983	
1	Thackwell, W.	Guardsman	23742	
2	Thomas, H. J.	Sergeant	6268	
	Thomas, J., D.C.M.	Sergeant	14801	
	Thomas, J.	A. L.-Cpl.	26751	
1	Thomas, W. J.	C.Q.M.S.	13716	Killed in action.
2	Thompson, A. G.	A. Sergt.	16321	
1	Thompson, G. W.	Corporal	16326	
3	Thompson, J. T.	Sergeant	18795	
3	Thompson, W.	Guardsman	20194	
4	Thornton, A.	Guardsman	24294	
4	Thornton, J. F.	Guardsman	18615	Died of wounds.
4	Thorpe, I. B.	Guardsman	24393	
	Thraves, R.	Guardsman	13835	
2	Tickner, E. J.	Guardsman	25622	
3	Tilford, G.	A. L.-Cpl.	11450	
1	Titt, W.	Guardsman	18405	To Army Res.
2	Tomkinson, J.	Guardsman	17129	
2	Tomlinson, J.	L.-Sergt.	13769	

APPENDIX VII.

THE GRENADIER GUARDS

APPENDIX VII.

Batt.	Name.	Rank.	Regtl. No.	Remarks.
1	Towns, H.	L.-Cpl.	26374	
4	Trotter, T.	Sergeant	20016	
1	Trueman, R. P.	Guardsman	26101	
4	Tunnell, W.	Sergeant	8596	
2	Turley, W.	Guardsman	18724	
3	Turner, A. G.	A. L.-Sergt.	23863	
3	Underhill, H. G.	Guardsman	20458	
4	Venn, S. E.	Guardsman	15813	
3	Voce, G.	Guardsman	16539	
3	Voyce, W.	L.-Cpl.	25135	
3	Wainwright, W.	L.-Cpl.	23199	
1	Walker, G. R.	A. L.-Sergt.	18282	
2	Wall, A.	L.-Cpl.	12704	Killed in action.
3	Wall, W. J. H.	L.-Cpl.	25072	
	Waller, J.	Guardsman	16514	
2	Wallis, W. D.	L.-Cpl.	12423	
3	Walsh, P.	L.-Sergt.	19488	
1	Walters, H. S.	Guardsman	25277	
2	Walton, B.	Sergeant	14892	Killed in action.
2	Ward, H.	L.-Sergt.	13789	Killed in action.
2	Ward, R. G.	L.-Cpl.	13559	Killed in action.
2	Ward, W.	Sergeant	14371	
2	Warner, F.	Guardsman	14007	
2	Warrender, W.	L.-Sergt.	17882	
4	Waterworth, T.	Guardsman	21764	
1	Watkins, R. J.	L.-Sergt.	11158	Missing.
3	Watts, A. S.	Sergeant	13353	
4	Watts, H.	Corporal	23206	
2	Webb, F. J.	Sergeant	12635	
3	Wentworth, W. H.	Sergeant	15491	Died of wounds.
3	Westmoreland, M.	A. L.-Cpl.	20178	Killed in action.
1	Wharmby, H.	Sergeant	14353	
1	Wheadon, F. J.	Guardsman	18932	Discharged.
1	Whetton, G.	Guardsman	16858	
2	Whiteside, G. S.	L.-Sergt.	23788	
2	Wilding, H. T.	Guardsman	15564	
3	Wilkinson, W. E.	Guardsman	15356	To Army Res.
4	Williams, A. H.	Sergeant	18904	
3	Williams, H.	Sergeant	9426	Killed in action.
4	Williams, H. S.	Sergeant	14355	
2	Williams, W.	Guardsman	14356	To M.F.P.
1	Willmott, A. E.	A. L.-Sergt.	30004	
1	Wilson, A.	Guardsman	24261	
1	Wilson, A.	Corporal	18100	
1	Wilson, C. A.	Guardsman	15333	

REWARDS

Batt.	Name.	Rank.	Regtl. No.	Remarks.
2	Wilson, G. H.	Guardsman	14195	
3	Wilson, S. T.	L.-Cpl.	24491	
3	Wood, A.	Guardsman	19963	
1	Wood, J. A.	L.-Sergt.	19041	Died of wounds.
1	Wood, L.	Guardsman	13097	
	Woodhead, T.	Guardsman	27861	
1	Wooldridge, D.	Guardsman	11998	
1	Worton, H.	Sergeant	12498	
2	Wright, B.	L.-Sergt.	15113	
3	Wright, J.	Guardsman	14675	

APPENDIX VII.

BAR TO "M.M."

Batt.	Name.	Rank.	Regtl. No.	Remarks.
4	Askey, J.	Guardsman	21851	
2	Bailey, G.	Guardsman	21214	
1	Bagot, J., M.M.	Guardsman	26689	
2	Baker, W. H.	C.Q.M.S.	14809	
2	Bryant, W. T. H.	L.-Cpl.	16400	
3	Burke, W.	Sergeant	16530	
2	Coton, A.	Guardsman	21392	
1	Crick, F.	Guardsman	14818	
1	Driver, G.	Sergeant	15696	
3	Greenwood, C.	Sergeant	11579	To Commission.
1	Halls, J.	Guardsman	18001	
1	Jackson, A.	A. L.-Sergt.	18516	
2	Jeanes, F.	Sergeant	12813	
3	Jeffreys, C. J.	A. L.-Cpl.	12111	
3	Keggin, W.	A. L.-Cpl.	28533	
4	Lowe, J.	Guardsman	24699	
2	Lucas, T. H.	A. L.-Cpl.	8942	
2	Nottage, T. S.	Sergeant	22065	
3	Robertson, A. H.	L.-Sergt.	24770	To Labour Corps.
2	Smith, J. H. W.	Guardsman	22934	
3	Spouge, W.	L.-Cpl.	16650	
1	Spur, J. W.	Guardsman	26394	
3	Voce, J.	Guardsman	16539	
3	Webb, F. J.	Sergeant	12635	
2	Warner, F.	Guardsman	14007	
1	Wharmby, H.	Sergeant	14353	
2	Wilding, H. T.	Guardsman	15564	

"MERITORIOUS SERVICE MEDAL"
(For Valuable and Meritorious Service in the Field)

Batt.	Name.	Rank.	Regtl. No.
2	Abbott, H.	Sergeant	6622
	Aldridge, H. N.	O.R.C.S.	7055

Appendix VII.	Batt.	Name.	Rank.	Regtl. No.	Remarks.
	1	Allitt, H.	C.Q.M.S.	14870	
	1	Barker, C.	Sergeant	9718	
	2	Beard, R.	C.S.M.	12909	
	1	Birch, A.	C.S.M.	6498	
	3	Boyles, F.	A.S.M.	9259	Att. 4th Army Inf. School.
	1	Brett, A. E.	Guardsman	12392	
	3	Brown, F. A.	Sergeant	18729	
	4	Burch, A. E.	C.S.M.	11033	
	3	Burgess, T. C.	Corporal	17294	
	1	Burrows, R.	Sergeant	10153	
	4	Burrows, F.	Sergeant	11594	
	2	Capper, J. L.	S.M.	7094	
	3	Card, R.	C.Q.M.S.	7736	
	2	Cartwright, G.	A.Q.M.S.	11889	
		Cooke, H.	Q.M.S.	10738	
	1	Croucher, R.	R.S.M.	11034	
	2	Davis, A.	A. Sergt.	12525	
	3	Fawcett, W.	Q.M.S.	9058	
	3	Fox, W.	Guardsman	12162	
	2	Francombe, O. C.	A.S.M.	6338	
	3	Freeman, A.	C.Q.M.S.	16761	
		French, F.	C.Q.M.S.	11989	
		Gardiner, A. R.	C.Q.M.S.	13368	
	2	Grahame, J. H.	L.-Sergt.	12451	To Commission.
	3	Hawkins, W. E.	A.D.S.	14207	
		Hill, R. H.	C.Q.M.S.	21435	
		Howell, H. G.	Q.M.S.	4866	
	4	Hutchings, W.	C.S.M.	7589	
	2	Kerry, D.	Sergeant	15258	
		Latter, H. E.	C.Q.M.S.	8094	
	3	Loftus, T. D.	Sergeant	13548	
	1	McDonald, V. H.	L.-Sergt.	10787	
	4	Machin, H.	O.R.C.	20691	
	3	Maynard, W. H.	C.S.M.	11253	
	2	Moran, W.	Sergeant	19253	
		Nash, R. E.	Corporal	15985	To R.E.
	3	Noon, W.	O.R.C.	13387	
	2	Oakley, T.	D.S.	7685	
	2	Palmer, E.	Sergeant	11868	
	3	Peters, G.	C.Q.M.S.	14701	
	1	Phillips, C.	S.M.	12425	
	2	Powell, J. C., M.M.	C.S.M.	15543	
	2	Pownall, L.	Sergeant	15143	
	2	Raynor, E. N.	Guardsman	16130	

REWARDS

Batt.	Name.	Rank.	Regtl. No.	Remarks.
4	Richmond, F.	Q.M.S.	11806	
1	Round, W. J.	Sergeant	14252	
	Ruff, R. J.	Sergeant	8837	
2	Sayer, H. W.	Guardsman	22839	
1	Seckington, C.	Sergeant	14245	
	Shelton, J.	C.S.M.	12132	A.R.S.M. Br. Salonika Force.
1	Sims, H.	Guardsman	13232	
	Smart, F. T.	A.Q.M.S.	10432	
2	Smith, A.	Sergeant	18611	
2	Thomas, H. J.	Sergeant	6268	
1	Trotter, G.	C.S.M.	9172	
3	Trotter, H.	C.Q.M.S.	10421	
3	Waspe, A.	Sergeant	16648	
3	West, A.	C.S.M.	8980	
3	Westbrook, A.	C.S.M.	6087	
3	Wombwell, R.	Sergt. Dmr.	5027	

APPENDIX VII.

"ROYAL ALBERT MEDAL" (Second Class)

	Meredith, W. H.	L.-Cpl.	15441
	Warwick, P.	A. L.-Sergt.	18905

"ROYAL VICTORIAN MEDAL" (Second Class)

1	Clayton, C. H.	A.C.Q.M.S.	9809

APPENDIX VIII

"MENTIONED IN DESPATCHES"

Officers

Acraman, W. E., Major and Quartermaster, M.C., D.C.M. (Twice.)
Anderton, W. A. A. G. S., Lieut.-Col.
Ardee, Lord R. le N., Colonel (Temp. Brig.-Gen.), C.B.
Asquith, R., Lieut. (Killed in action.)
Aubrey-Fletcher, H. L., Capt. (Bt.-Major), M.V.O., D.S.O. (Four times.)
Bagot, Hon. W. L., Major.
Bailey, Hon. W. R., Capt. (Actg. Major), Temp. Lieut.-Col., D.S.O. (Four times.)
Barrington-Kennett, B. H., Capt. (Bt.-Major). (Killed in action.)
Beaumont-Nesbitt, F. G., Capt. (Three times.)
Bedford, Duke of, Colonel, K.G.
Benson, C. E., Lieut. (Actg. Capt.), D.S.O.
Bigham, Hon. C. C., Lieut.-Col., C.M.G.
Bonham-Carter, F. G., Lieut. (Temp. Capt.).
Briscoe, R. G., Lieut., M.C.
Browning, F. A. M., Lieut. (Actg. Capt.), D.S.O.
Cameron of Lochiel, D. W., Lieut.-Col., C.M.G., Cameron Highlanders.
Campbell, K. A., Lieut., D.S.O.
Carisbrooke, Marquis of, Capt., G.C.V.O. (Twice.)
Carrington, C. W., Lieut. (Actg. Capt.), D.S.O.
Cavan, Earl of, Lieut.-Gen., K.P., G.C.M.G., K.C.B., M.V.O. (Ten times.)
Cavendish, Hon. W. E., Temp. Brig.-Gen., M.V.O.
Cavendish, R. H. V., Capt., M.V.O.

"MENTIONED IN DESPATCHES" 319

Cecil, Lord E. H., Major, Bt.-Col., K.C.M.G., D.S.O. (Egypt). (Twice.) (Died.)
Cecil, Hon. W. A., Capt., M.C. (Killed in action.)
Cheylesmore, Lord, Major - Gen., K.C.M.G., K.C.V.O. (Twice.)
Clive, G. S., Lieut.-Col. (Bt.-Col.), C.B., D.S.O. (Six times.)
Clive, H. A., Lieut., M.C. (Twice.)
Clive, P. A., Capt. (Temp. Lieut.-Col.). (Killed in action.)
Colby, L. R. V., Major. (Killed in action.)
Colston, Hon. E. M., Major, Bt.-Lieut.-Col. (Temp. Brig.-Gen.), C.M.G., D.S.O., M.V.O. (Six times.)
Combe, T. A., Lieut.
Congleton, H. B. F., Lord. (Killed in action.)
Cooper, A. D., 2nd Lieut., D.S.O.
Cooper, R. J., Brig.-Gen., C.B., C.V.O.
Corkran, C. E., Bt.-Col. (Temp. Brig.-Gen.), C.M.G. (Six times.)
Cornforth, J. C., Lieut., M.C.
Corry, A. V. L., Lieut., M.C. (Killed in action.)
Craig, D., Lieut., D.S.O.
Craigie, J. C., Lieut., M.C. (Actg. Capt.).
Crawley, A. P., Colonel.
Crespigny, C. R. C. de, Lieut.-Col., C.M.G., D.S.O. (Five times.)
Cunninghame, A. K. S., Lieut. (Temp. Capt.) (Killed in action.)
Dalmeny, A. E. H. M. A., Lord, Lieut. (Temp. Lieut.-Col.), D.S.O., M.C. (Four times.)
Darby, M. A. A., Lieut. (Killed in action.)
Davies, Sir F. J., Lieut.-Gen., K.C.B., K.C.M.G. (Seven times.)
Diggle, W. H., Capt. (Temp. Lieut.-Col.), D.S.O., M.C. (Five times.)
Douglas-Pennant, Hon. G. H., Capt. (Killed in action.)
Drury-Lowe, W. D., Capt., D.S.O. (Killed in action.) (Twice.)
Duberly, E. H. J., Lieut., M.C.
Duberly, G. W., Major. (Killed in action.)
Duquenoy, M., Lieut. (Actg. Capt.).
Earle, M., Colonel, C.M.G., D.S.O. (Twice.)

APPENDIX VIII.

APPENDIX VIII.

Eaton, Hon. F. O. H., Lieut., D.S.O.
Ellice, E. C., Capt., D.S.O. (Three times.)
Fergusson, Sir C., Lieut.-Gen., K.C.B., K.C.M.G., M.V.O., D.S.O. (Six times.)
Fisher-Rowe, C. V., Capt. (Bt.-Major), M.C. (Three times.)
Fisher-Rowe, L. R., Lieut.-Col. (Died of wounds.)
Fitzgerald, E. G. A., Lieut. (Temp. Capt.), D.S.O. (Twice.)
Fox-Pitt, W. A. L., Major (Temp. Lieut.-Col.).
Garton, W. G. A., Quartermaster, Hon. Lieut.-Col.
Gascoigne, E. F. O., Hon. Brig.-Gen., C.M.G., D.S.O. (Four times.)
Gathorne-Hardy, Hon. J. F., Lieut.-Col. (Bt.-Col.), C.B., C.M.G., D.S.O. (Nine times.)
Gerard, C. R., Capt., D.S.O. (Twice.)
Glanusk, J. H. R., Lord, Colonel, C.B., C.B.E., D.S.O. (Three times.)
Gleichen, Lord E., Major-Gen., K.C.V.O., C.B., C.M.G., D.S.O., p.s.c. (Twice.)
Glyn, A. St. L., Major. (Twice.)
Gordon-Gilmour, R. G., Colonel (Hon. Brig.-Gen.), C.B., C.V.O., D.S.O. (Twice.)
Gordon-Lennox, Lord B. C., Major. (Killed in action.)
V.C. Gort, Viscount, Bt.-Major, D.S.O., M.V.O., M.C. (Eight times.)
Gosselin, A. B. R. R., Capt., D.S.O. (Died of wounds.)
Greenwood, J. E., Lieut.
Gregson, L. M., Major, O.B.E.
Greville, C. H., Capt. (Actg. Major), D.S.O. (Three times.)
Grey, R., Capt., D.S.O.
Grigg, E. W. M., Lieut. (Temp. Lieut.-Col.), C.M.G., D.S.O., M.C. (Twice.)
Gunnis, G. G., Lieut. (Temp. Capt.), M.C. (Died of wounds.)
Hague, C. N., Lieut., M.C.
Hall, C. A., Lieut., M.C.
Hamilton, Lord C. N., Capt., D.S.O., M.V.O.
Hamilton, G. C., Lieut-Col., C.M.G., D.S.O. (Three times.)
Harcourt-Vernon, G. C. FitzH., Major, D.S.O., M.C.
Harrison, C. E., Col., C.V.O., C.M.G., M.B., F.R.C.S. (Twice.)
Heneage, E., Lieut.
Heneage, G. C. W., Major, D.S.O. (Four times.)
Hermon-Hodge, Hon. R. H., Major, D.S.O. (Twice.)

"MENTIONED IN DESPATCHES" 321

Hervey-Bathurst, Sir F. E. W., Bart., Major, D.S.O. (Three times.)
Hobart, C. V. C., Lieut.-Col., C.B.E., D.S.O. (Twice.)
Holbech, L., Lieut., D.S.O., M.C.
Hood, Viscount, Lieut.-Col., O.B.E. (Twice.)
Hope, G. E., Capt. (Actg. Lieut.-Col.), M.C. (Presumed killed.) (Three times.)
Hopley, F. J. V. B., Lieut., D.S.O.
Hughes, J. S., Capt., M.C.
Ingleby, I. H., Actg. Capt. (Twice.)
Jeffreys, G. D., Lieut.-Col., Bt.-Col. (Temp. Major-Gen.), C.B., C.M.G. (Seven times.)
Joicey-Cecil, Lord J. P., Capt. (Temp. Lieut.-Col., R. Defence Corps).
Kerry, Earl of, Lieut.-Col., M.V.O., D.S.O., Irish Guards.
King, D. L., Lieut.
Kingsmill, A. de P., Lieut.-Col., D.S.O., M.C.
Kinloch, Sir D. A., Bart., Brig.-Gen., C.B., M.V.O. (Twice.)
Knatchbull-Hugessen, M., Lieut., M.C. (Killed in action.) (Twice.)
Lambert, R., Capt., M.C.
Lamont, G. S., 2nd Lieut., D.S.O.
Lascelles, Viscount, Temp. Lieut.-Col., D.S.O. (Twice.)
Leatham, R. E. K., Major, Bt.-Lieut.-Col., D.S.O. (Twice.)
Legh, Hon. P. W., Capt., O.B.E.
Leslie, Sir J., Bart., Col., R. Innis. Fusiliers.
Lessing, E. A., Lieut., O.B.E.
Lloyd, Sir F., Lieut.-Gen., G.C.V.O., K.C.B., D.S.O.
Lloyd, A. H. O., Lieut.-Col. (Temp. Brig.-Gen.), C.M.G., M.V.O., Shropshire Yeomanry. (Three times.)
Lloyd, J. A., Lieut.
Loch, E. D., Lord, Major-Gen., C.B., C.M.G., M.V.O., D.S.O. (Five times.)
Lygon, Hon. R., Lieut.-Col., M.V.O., M.C.
Lyttelton, O., Lieut. (Temp. Capt.), D.S.O., M.C. (Twice.)
Maitland, M. E. M. C., Major (Temp. Lieut.-Col.), D.S.O. (Five times.)
Martin, F., Lieut. (Actg. Capt.).
Minchin, T. W., Lieut. (Actg. Capt.), D.S.O.
Mitchell, C., Capt. (Temp. Major), D.S.O., O.B.E. (Four times.)

APPENDIX VIII.

Morley, Hon. C. Hope, Lieut.
Morrison, J. A., Major, D.S.O. (Twice.)
Murray-Threipland, W., Lieut.-Col. (Temp. Col.), D.S.O. (Three times.)
Nicol, W. E., Major, D.S.O. (Killed in action.)
Northumberland, A. I., Duke of, Major (Temp. Lieut.-Col.)., C.B.E.
Pakenham, H. A., Lieut.-Col., C.B., C.M.G., R. Irish Rifles. (Three times.)
Parker, Hon. M. B., Capt. (Five times.)
Pelly, P. V., Lieut.
Penn, A. H., Lieut. (Actg. Capt.), M.C.
Penn, E. F., Lieut. (Capt.).
Percy, Lord W. R., Capt. (Temp. Col.), D.S.O. (Twice.)
Pereira, G. E., Bt.-Col. (Temp. Brig.-Gen.), C.B., C.M.G., D.S.O. (Six times.)
Pike, E. J. L., Major (Bt.-Lieut.-Col.), M.C. (Three times.)
Pilcher, W. S., Capt., Bt.-Major, D.S.O. (Three times.)
Poltimore, G. W. W., Lord, Capt., R. North Devon Yeomanry. (Twice.)
Ponsonby, Rt. Hon. Sir F. E. G., Bt.-Lieut.-Col., K.C.B., K.C.V.O.
Powell, E. G. H., Major (Actg. Lieut.-Col.), London Regiment. (Twice.)
Powney, C. du P. P., Lieut.-Col.
V.C. Pryce, T. T., Lieut. (Actg. Capt.), M.C. (Missing.)
Quilter, J. A. C., Major (Temp. Lieut.-Col.) (Killed in action.)
Rasch, G. E. C., Capt., Bt.-Major, D.S.O. (Three times.)
Rhodes, A. T. G., Capt. (Twice.)
Ridley, E. D., Capt., M.C.
Ritchie, A. T. A., Lieut., M.C.
Rolinson, J. C., Major and Quartermaster, D.C.M.
Ruggles-Brise, Sir H. G., Major-Gen., K.C.M.G., C.B., M.V.O. (Five times.)
Russell, Hon. A. V. F., Major (Temp. Brig.-Gen.), C.M.G., M.V.O. (Six times.)
Russell, G. B. A., Capt. (Temp. Major).
St. Levan, J. T., Lord, Hon. Brig.-Gen., C.V.O., C.B.
Saltoun, Lord, Lieut.-Col., C.M.G.
Sandeman, H. G. W., Lieut.

"MENTIONED IN DESPATCHES" 323

Scott, Lord F. G. M. D., Major, Bt.-Lieut.-Col., D.S.O.
Scott-Kerr, R., Col., C.B., M.V.O., D.S.O. (Twice.)
Sergison-Brooke, B. N., Lieut.-Col., C.M.G., D.S.O. (Seven times.)
Seymour, E., Major, D.S.O., M.V.O., O.B.E. (Four times.)
Seymour, Lord H. C., Major (Bt.-Lieut.-Col.), D.S.O. (Five times.)
Sheppard, E., Capt., D.S.O., M.C. (Three times.)
Smith, D. A., Lieut. (Actg. Capt.), M.C.
Smith, W. R. A., Lieut.-Col., C.M.G. (Twice.) (Killed in action.)
Spencer-Churchill, E. G., Capt., M.C.
Stanhope, Earl, Major (Temp. Lieut.-Col.), D.S.O., M.C. (Twice.)
Stanley, Hon. F. C., Bt.-Lieut.-Col. (Temp. Brig.-Gen.), C.M.G., D.S.O. (Five times.)
Stein, O. F., Lieut. (Actg. Capt.), D.S.O.
Streatfeild, Sir H., Colonel, K.C.V.O., C.B., C.M.G. (Twice.)
Streatfeild, H. S. J., Lieut.-Col., D.S.O., London Regiment. (Twice.)
Stucley, H. St. L., Major. (Killed in action.)
Swaine, F. L. V., Capt. (Temp. Major).
Swift, C. T., Lieut. (Actg. Capt.). (Twice.)
Symons, T. E. R., Capt. (Bt.-Major).
Teece, J., Major and Quartermaster, M.C. (Three times.)
Thorne, A. F. A. N., Major (Actg. Lieut.-Col.), C.M.G., D.S.O. (Seven times.)
Trench, R. P. le P., Capt., M.C.
Trotter, E. H., Lieut.-Col., D.S.O.
Trotter, G. F., Bt.-Lieut.-Col. (Temp. Brig.-Gen.), C.B., C.M.G., C.B.E., M.V.O., D.S.O. (Four times.)
Tryon, G. C., Bt.-Major, M.P. (Twice.)
Turner, C. R., Lieut.
Vaughan, E. N. E. M., Major, D.S.O.
Vereker, G. G. M., Lieut., M.C.
Vivian, V., Major (Bt.-Lieut.-Col.), C.M.G., M.V.O., D.S.O. (Seven times.)
Vivian, G. N., Major, O.B.E.
Wakeman, E. O. R., Lieut. (Killed in action.)
Wales, H.R.H. The Prince of, Captain, K.G., G.C.M.G., G.B.E., M.C. (Twice.)

APPENDIX VIII.

APPENDIX VIII.

Walker, C. F. A., Capt. (Actg. Major) (Temp. Lieut.-Col.), M.C. (Twice.)
Wall, G. H., Capt. and Quartermaster.
Warrender, H. V., Lieut.-Col., D.S.O. (Twice.)
Webster, Sir A. F. W. E., Bart., Capt. (Temp. Major), O.B.E.
Welby, R. W. G., Lieut. (Killed in action.)
Weld-Forester, Hon. A. O. W. C., Major, M.V.O. (Died of wounds.)
Wellesley, Lord G., Capt. (Temp. Lieut.-Col.), M.C., R.A.F.
Wellesley, Lord R., Capt. (Killed in action.)
Westmacott, G. R., Capt., D.S.O.
White, G. D., Major (Bt.-Lieut.-Col.), M.P. (Three times.)
White, H., Lieut. (Died of wounds.)
Wiggins, A. F. R., Capt. (Twice.)
Williams, M., Bt.-Major (Actg. Lieut.-Col.).
Williams-Bulkely, R. G. W., Major, M.C. (Deceased.)
Windram, R., Lieut. (Twice.)

WARRANT OFFICERS, N.C.O.'s, AND MEN

Batt.	Name.	Rank.	Regtl. No.	Remarks.
2	Abbott, H.	Sergeant	6622	
3	Aston, A.	A.D.S.	11641	To M.G. Guards.
	Ashworth, R. H.	Sergeant	20432	
2	Austin, W. T.	Sergeant	11020	To Commission.
2	Baker, J.	Sergeant	17174	
1	Barker, C.	Sergeant	9718	
2	Beard, R.	D.S.	12909	
3	Beddows, W.	A. Sergeant	20612	
2	Bennett, A.	C.S.M.	11755	
2	Birch, A.	C.S.M.	6498	
2	Blackwell, J. H.	C.S.M.	11300	
4	Blyth, T. J.	C.Q.M.S.	13511	
	Boots, H. S.	Q.M.S.	8230	
3	Boyles, F.	A. Sergt.-Maj.	9259	A.S.M., 4th Army School.
2	Bradley, J. H.	Sergeant	13152	
	Bright, A. E.	A.R.S.M.	4543	
3	Brown, A. A.	Sergeant	20758	
	Brown, F. A.	Sergeant	18729	
	Brown, C. E.	C.S.M.	8652	
1	Bryant, J.	D.S.	10772	
3	Bryan, W. K.	A. Sergeant	13494	
2	Capper, J. L.	R.S.M.	7094	

"MENTIONED IN DESPATCHES" 325

Batt.	Name.	Rank.	Regtl. No.	Remarks.	Appendix
1	Carpenter, S. J.	L.-Cpl.	12822		VIII.
1	Champion, T. K.	Guardsman	12324		
2	Chapman, W. A.	Guardsman	16431	Killed in action.	
1	Chesterman, G. H.	L.-Cpl.	15360		
3	Cook, A. H.	L.-Sergt.	19467	Killed in action.	
2	Cooke, H.	Q.M.S.	10738		
4	Copping, H.	A.D.S.	9043	To Essex Regt.	
3	Cronin, D.	Guardsman	11492	Discharged.	
2	Curtis, E. E.	Sergeant	16707	Missing.	
4	Day, E. W.	C.S.M.	11086		
	Day, E.	Sergeant	18953		
3	Dickson, R.	Sergeant	11900		
	Dobson, W. H.	C.S.M.	13610	To M.G. Guards.	
3	Fawcett, W.	S.C.	9058		
	Fellows, W. J.	Guardsman	19083		
2	Fincham, J.	A. L.-Sergt.	16318		
4	Francis, R. W.	Sergeant	12241		
2	Francis, T. W.	L.-Cpl.	11327	Killed in action.	
3	Freeman, A.	Sergeant	16761		
5	Freeman, J. P.	C.S.M.	5984		
4	Fremlin, E. J.	A.D.S.	12675		
5	French, F.	A.R.S.M.	11989		
4	Frogley, W. D.	Guardsman	17735		
1	Gibson, H. W.	Guardsman	17784		
	Godfrey, F.	A.S.M.	5623	To Commission.	
2	Godfrey, W. E.	Guardsman	12347		
1	Golding, A. J.	Sergeant	12118	To M.F.P.	
1	Golding, W. C.	A.C.Q.M.S.	14711	4th Army Sig. School.	
	Grahame, J. H.	L.-Sergt.	12451	To Commission.	
2	Gudgin, R.	C.S.M.	9855		
	Hales, P. J.	A. Sergt.	16379		
4	Hartley, M.	A. Sergt.	20768		
2	Hawkins, W. E.	A.D.S.	14207		
3	Hill, A. M.	S.M.	5163		
	Howell, H. G.	Q.M.S.	4866		
1	Hughes, W.	S.M.	11487	(Three times.)	
2	Jacques, W. E.	Sergeant	14727	To Army Cyclist Corps.	
1	John, B.	L.-Sergt.	17719	Discharged.	
1	Jones, C.	C.S.M.	10107	To A.G. Staff.	
2	Jones, D. J.	Guardsman	10475	Discharged.	
	Jones, E.	A.R.S.M.	5491		
2	Jones, F. L. C.	L.-Cpl.	16167	To Commission.	
2	Knight, R. J.	Guardsman	14991		

326 THE GRENADIER GUARDS

APPENDIX VIII.

Batt.	Name.	Rank.	Regtl. No.	Remarks.
1	Lambourne, W. J.	Guardsman	12204	Killed in action.
1	Laming, G. W.	Sergeant	14248	
1	Langley, W. J.	C.Q.M.S.	14620	Killed.
3	Latta, W.	L.-Cpl.	11372	Died of wounds.
4	Livick, H. J.	Sergeant	8178	
2	Ludlow, E.	S.M.	4947	To Commission. Killed during Air Raid on London.
4	Littler, J.	S.M.	8380	
	Littlewood, R.	Sergeant	10963	
3	Loftus, J.	Sergeant	13548	
1	Lund, H.	L.-Cpl.	14894	Discharged.
2	McDonald, P.	L.-Cpl.	16202	To Welsh Gds.
4	Marriott, C., M.M.	C.S.M.	13729	
R.S.	Martin, F.	S.C.	5749	To Commission.
3	Matthews, W.	L.-Sergt.	12430	Died of wounds.
1	Miller, W.	A. Sergt.	13872	
3	Munn, A.	L.-Cpl.	21384	
2	Munns, F. J.	Sergeant	10394	Killed in action.
2	Murphy, P.	Guardsman	12434	To R.E.
1	Nash, R. E.	Corporal	15985	To R.E.
2	Nelmes, E.	Guardsman	14296	Hdqrs. 1st Gds. Bde.
	Newcomb, G.	C.S.M.	6966	
3	Noon, W.	Sergeant	13387	
3	North, G. E.	L.-Cpl.	9440	
2	Norton, J.	A.D.S.	10330	
3	Nuttall, H.	L.-Sergt.	11091	Killed in action.
2	Oakley, F.	D. Sergt.	7685	
4	Painter, H.	L.-Cpl.	14498	Died of wounds.
2	Paradine, H.	Sergeant	15209	Discharged.
1	Parkin, J. E.	S.M.	5572	To Commission.
3	Parris, F. T.	L.-Sergt.	13567	
2	Parry, W.	C.S.M.	10453	Discharged.
2	Parsons, F.	Corporal	16272	Died of wounds.
	Payne, F. J.	A.S.M.	12096	To London Regt.
1	Percival, W.	C.S.M.	11591	
4	Pettitt, T.	C.S.M.	10699	
1	Phillips, C.	Q.M.S. (O.R.S.)	12425	
1	Powell, J. C.	C.Q.M.S.	15543	
2	Rhodes, G.	Guardsman	16989	Killed in action.
5	Richmond, F.	Q.M.S.	11806	
1	Roache, G.	Guardsman	18503	Killed in action.
2	Robinson, C. A.	A. Sergt.	13980	

"MENTIONED IN DESPATCHES"

Batt.	Name.	Rank.	Regtl. No.	Remarks.
4	Robinson, J. W.	L.-Cpl.	20219	
1	Rowe, E. J.	C.Q.M.S.	14068	
2	Rule, C.	Guardsman	14224	To M.G. Guards.
2	Sapsford, W. A.	L.-Cpl.	14033	Killed in action.
	Scriven, A.	A.L.C.	8775	
3	Smith, A. E.	C.Q.M.S.	12597	
1	Smith, J.	Sergeant	14785	Died of wounds.
2	Smith, P.	Guardsman	13473	Died.
2	Smith, P. H.	L.-Cpl.	13039	Hdqrs. 14th C.
1	Spencer, J.	Corporal	15132	
3	Stanton, E.	L.-Cpl.	19505	Discharged.
4	Stapleton, O.	Sergeant	13527	
1	Strickland, W.	Guardsman	9877	
2	Thomas, J.	Sergeant	14801	
4	Turner, A.	L.-Cpl.	21622	
3	Underwood, W. C.	O.R.C.S.	15639	
4	Vaughan, A.	L.-Cpl.	17144	
2	Walker, A. E.	Guardsman	14418	
5	Walmsley, J.	A.Q.M.S.	8685	Empl. War O.
3	Walsh, W.	L.-Sergt.	19214	
4	Warwick, P.	A. L.-Sergt.	18905	
1	Waterman, W. J.	Guardsman	18177	Died of wounds.
	Way, W.	L.-Cpl.	14133	
1	West, W.	C.S.M.	8980	
	Whiteman, H.	A. L.-Sergt.	18466	
2	Whitney, G. F.	L.-Cpl.	14347	
4	Wilkinson, A. B.	Guardsman	19844	
4	Williams, H. S.	Sergeant	14355	
	Woodiss, F. G.	Guardsman	22686	
3	Wyeth, W. H.	A. Sergt.	21683	

APPENDIX VIII.

APPENDIX IX

GUARDS DIVISION—"CERTIFICATES FOR GALLANTRY"

Batt.	Name.	Rank.	Regtl. No.	Remarks.
1	Abbott, H.	Sergeant	6622	
3	Ashworth, R. H.	L.-Cpl.	20432	
3	Aston, A.	A.D.S.	11641	To M.G. Guards.
	Austin, O. K.	Guardsman	15190	
1	Barker, C.	Sergeant	9718	
4	Barker, S. L.	L.-Cpl.	18708	To R.E.
2	Bennett, A.	C.S.M.	11755	
2	Birch, A.	C.S.M.	6498	
	Blyth, T. J.	C.Q.M.S.	13511	
1	Boyles, E.	C.Q.M.S.	14220	Discharged.
	Bradley, J. H.	Sergeant	13152	
1	Brown, F. A.	Sergeant	18729	Hdqrs. 2nd Gds. Bde.
1	Brown, T. W.	Q.M.S.	8277	
1	Bryant, J.	D.S.	10772	
1	Carpenter, S.	L.-Cpl.	12822	
2	Chapman, D. W.	A.C.Q.M.S.	8711	
2	Clarke, W. H.	L.-Cpl.	14472	Discharged.
2	Colgate, R. E.	Sergeant	14914	To Commission.
3	Cooke, G.	Guardsman	16644	Killed in action.
3	Coonan, T.	Guardsman	18123	To M.G. Guards.
2	Cox, J.	L.-Cpl.	13475	
3	Cronin, D.	Guardsman	11492	Discharged.
1	Day, E. W.	A.D.S.	11086	(Twice.)
4	Dean, F. J.	L.-Cpl.	17187	Killed in action.
4	Dickens, T. G.	Corporal	23763	Acc. killed.
3	Dickson, R.	Sergeant	11900	
	Dobson, H.	C.S.M.	13610	To M.G. Guards.
4	Fellows, W. J.	Guardsman	19083	
4	Finch, W. H.	A. Sergt.	19017	

"CERTIFICATES FOR GALLANTRY" 329

Batt.	Name.	Rank.	Regtl. No.	Remarks.	Appendix
2	Godfrey, W. E.	Guardsman	12347	1st Gds. Bde., to	IX.
3	Gould, C.	Sergeant	11197	M.G. Guards.	
4	Hall, H.	Sergeant	21589		
4	Hartley, M.	A. Sergt.	20768		
3	Hawkins, W. E.	A.D.S.	14207		
4	Heap, J.	Guardsman	20183	To Labour Corps.	
4	Higgins, H.	Corporal	21525	Killed in action.	
4	Holland, A.	L.-Sergt.	21945	Discharged.	
1	Hughes, W.	S.M.	11487		
3	Kent, W. J.	L.-Sergt.	19019		
3	Keyte, J. G.	L.-Sergt.	14639		
2	Kirkham, C.	L.-Cpl.	14744		
3	Latta, W.	L.-Cpl.	11372		
4	Littler, J.	S.M.	8380		
4	Livock, H.	Sergeant	8178		
3	Loftus, T. D.	Sergeant	13548		
4	Marriott, C. K.	C.S.M.	13729		
4	Matthews, W. C.	Corporal	12430	Died of wounds.	
2	McCune, A.	Sergeant	12819		
1	McGinn, T.	Guardsman	15013	Died of wounds.	
4	Miller, W.	A. Sergt.	13872		
2	Nelmes, E.	Guardsman	14296		
3	Nuttall, H.	Corporal	11091	Killed in action.	
4	Painter, H.	Corporal	14498	Died of wounds.	
2	Percival, G.	C.S.M.	9950	Died.	
4	Pettitt, T.	C.S.M.	10699		
4	Powlesland, J.	Guardsman	21563		
3	Purdy, T.	Sergeant	12987		
2	Robinson, C. A.	A. Sergt.	13980		
4	Robinson, J. W.	L.-Cpl.	20219		
1	Rossiter, E. J.	L.-Cpl.	18661	To R.E.	
1	Rowe, E. J.	C.Q.M.S.	14068		
4	Rowlett, J.	Sergeant	19211	Att. No. 4 O.C. Batt.	
	Ryall, H. E.	L.-Cpl.	16116	3rd Bde. Gds. M.G. Coy. Killed in action.	
2	Scott, J.	Guardsman	15411		
3	Smith, A. E.	C.Q.M.S.	12597		
2	Smith, P.	Guardsman	13473	Died of wounds.	
2	Snooke, F.	C.S.M.	9797	To Commission.	
	Speller, F.	D.S.	9686	2nd Gds. Bde. M.G. Coy., to M.G. Gds.	
4	Steele, J. A.	Guardsman	20464	To G.M.G.R.	

Appendix	Batt.	Name.	Rank.	Regtl. No.	Remarks.
IX.	2	Stevens, A.	Sergeant	13751	
—	2	Thomas, H. J.	Sergeant	6268	
	1	Thomas, W. J.	C.Q.M.S.	13716	Killed in action.
		Vaughan, A.	L.-Cpl.	17144	
	1	Wheadon, G.	Guardsman	18932	Discharged.
	2	Williams, H.	Guardsman	16223	
		Williams, W.	Guardsman	14356	
	2	Wood, H. W.	S.M.	5225	To Commission.

WARRANT OFFICERS, NON-COMMISSIONED OFFICERS, AND MEN WHO HAVE BEEN PROMOTED TO COMMISSIONED RANK SINCE THE COMMENCEMENT OF HOSTILITIES

APPENDIX X.

Battalion.	Regtl. No.	Rank	Rank and Name.	Regiment.	Awards, Promotions, etc.
R.S.	11295	Q.M.S.	Arnold, W. W.	Northumberland Fusiliers	Lieut., Actg. Capt.
3	5360	Sergt.	Ball, J.	Duke of Cornwall's L.I.	Capt., M.C. (Died.)
3	6432	D. Sergt.	Pennington, S.	Royal Warwicks	Temp. Capt. (Killed in action.)
3	10815	C.Q.M.S.	Ricketts, A.	Machine Gun Corps	Lieut., Temp. Capt. (Relinq. Commission, ill-health.)
3	7660	C.Q.M.S.	Hassall, A.	Norfolk Regiment	Actg. Major.
D.	4703	C.S.I.M.	Gache, R.	Royal Irish Regiment	Capt.
3	11123	C.Q.M.S.	Booth, T.	Connaught Rangers	Capt., M.C.
4	9636	C.Q.M.S.	Luckett, J. S.	Royal Irish Regiment	Died.
4	18183	Sergt.	Hayes, J. P.	Royal Irish Fusiliers	Lieut., Temp. Capt.
4	14705	Sergt.	Schroder, F. T.	Suffolk Regiment	Killed in action.
2	9089	C.S.M.	O'Connor, E. R.	R. Munster Fusiliers	Capt., Temp. Lieut.-Col. (Croix de Guerre).
W.A.R.	8925	C.Q.M.S.	Andrew, F. A.	East Yorks Regiment	(Killed in action.)
2	10974	Sergt.	Holness, H. H. J.	Manchester Regiment	Lieut., Actg. Capt., D.C.M.
3	2705	S.M.	Wall, G. H.	Grenadier Guards	Capt. and Qrmr., M.C.
R.S.	3486	S. Clerk	Dabell, W. B.	Welsh Guards	Capt. and Qrmr., M.C.
R.S.	6534	Q.M.S.	Holland, A. N.	East Lancs Regiment	Lieut.
1	6546	Q.M.S.	White, H. P.	Cheshire Regiment	Lieut., M.C.
4	11060	C.S.M.	Maywood, J. H.	Duke of Cornwall's L.I.	Lieut. (Died.)
P.S.	6873	Sergt.	Watkins, T.	Royal Berks Regiment	(Killed in action.)
S.	12988	Sergt.	Hassell, J.	K.O.Y.L.I.	Lieut., D.S.O., M.C.
2	13664	Sergt.	Rochfort, R. A.	Royal Warwicks	Capt., D.S.O., M.C.
R.S.	7732	Q.M.S.	Heath, S. J.	Welsh Regiment	Capt., Temp. Lieut.-Col., M.C.
5	8415	S.M.	White, G.	Northumberland Fusiliers	Actg. Major, M.C.
5	12997	Sergt.	Bailey, J.	Northumberland Fusiliers	Temp. Capt.
5	14502	L.-Sergt.	Hine, E. E.	East Lancs Regiment	Actg. Capt., M.C.

332 THE GRENADIER GUARDS

APPENDIX X.—PROMOTED TO COMMISSIONS (contd.).

Battalion.	Regtl. No.		Rank and Name.	Regiment.	Awards, Promotions, etc.
1	16576	Sergt.	Matson, C.	Machine Gun Corps	Actg. Major, M.C.
R.S.	6156	Q.M.S.	Baker, C. W.	Leicester Regiment	Temp. Major, M.C.
2	4947	S.M.	Ludlow, E.	Grenadier Guards	M.C. (Killed in London.)
1	17512	Pte.	Drew, J. B.	R. W. Surrey Regiment	Lieut.
A.G.S.	10107	C.S.M.	Jones, C.	Northumberland Fusiliers	Actg. Capt. (Relinq. Commission, ill-health.)
P.S.	3825	A.S.M.	Cooke, F. A.	London Regiment	Capt. and Qrmr.
1	5572	S.M.	Parkin, J. E.	R.A.F.	Lieut.-Col., M.B.E.
1	22485	L.-Cpl.	Wilson, C. V.	Royal Berks Regiment	Lieut. (Died from wounds.)
1	18454	Guardsman	Jones, A. C.	Lincoln Regiment	Capt., M.C. (Killed in action.)
1	17940	Guardsman	Perry, C.	Middlesex Regiment	(Killed in action.)
1	13127	C.S.M.	Pritchard, G.	Wiltshire Regiment	Actg. Capt.
3	19893	L.-Cpl.	Bennison, M.	Yorks Regiment	(Died.)
1	6702	S.M.	Young, H.	K.O. Royal Lancs.	Actg. Capt., Adjt., M.C.
M.G.C.	18394	Sergt.	Alexander, R.	Gds. Machine Gun Regt.	Lieut., M.M.
5	24160	L.-Sergt.	Smith, F. A.	Royal Warwicks Regiment	M.C.
3	11720	L.-Sergt.	Clayson, S. C.	Royal Warwicks Regiment	
P.S.	5623	D. Sergt.	Godfrey, F.	Royal Fusiliers	Temp. Capt. (Killed in action.)
P.S.	4543	S.M.	Bright, A. C.	Royal Fusiliers	
2	14914	Sergt.	Colgate, R. E.	Gloucester Regiment	(Killed in action.)
3	14144	C.S.M.	Bloomfield, A. H.	Gloucester Regiment	(Killed in action.)
4	14755	Sergt.	Virgo, E. W.	Worcester Regiment	Lieut., M.C.
3	14274	C.Q.M.S.	Rudge, L. M.	Essex Regiment	Temp. Capt. and Adjt., M.M.
S.L.	11469	Sergt.	Parks, J. B.	Essex Regiment	Temp. Major, M.C.
4	14172	C.Q.M.S.	Storer, S.	N. Staffs Regiment	
2	9797	C.S.M.	Snook, F.	General List	Actg. Major, M.C., D.C.M.
A.G.S.	5888	S.M.	Bailey, C.	Border Regiment	Temp. Major.
4	12688	C.S.M.	Grellis, J.	East Kent Regiment	Lieut., Actg. Capt., M.C.
2	21398	Guardsman	Reid, G. R.		(Killed in action.)

PROMOTED TO COMMISSIONS

APPENDIX X.

Battalion.	Regtl. No.	Rank and Name.		Regiment.	Awards, Promotions, etc.
R.S.	5749	S. Clerk	Martin, F.	Grenadier Guards	Actg. Capt.
5	15484	Corpl.	Ford, F. W.	Welsh Regiment	Capt.
1	18125	Corpl.	Penn, P.	R. Irish Fusiliers	(Died.)
5	22033	Guardsman	Grice, H. T.	Scottish Rifles	(Relq. Commission, ill-health.)
3	17946	L.-Cpl.	Cruickshank, J. A. B.	R. Innis. Fusiliers	Actg. Capt.
5	21018	Guardsman	Beech, A. H.	North Staffs Regiment	Major and Qrmr.
S.	215	C. Sergt.	Crook, A.	General List	M.C.
3	11961	Sergt.	Morris, C. T.	Gloucester Regiment	
5	10424	Sergt.	Burry, E. T.	Wiltshire Regiment	Lieut.
5	10862	Sergt.	Bayley, E. A.	Liverpool Regiment	M.M.
5	11043	Sergt.	Carter, F. J.	Yorkshire L.I.	M.M. (Killed in action.)
5	16167	L.-Cpl.	Jones, F. L. C.	R. Welsh Fusiliers	(Killed in action.)
5	13408	Sergt.	Willett, N. H.	Royal Fusiliers	M.C., M.M.
3	14477	Sergt.	Noble, T. E. W.	Welsh Regiment	Actg. Capt. and Adjt., M.C.
3	13399	L.-Cpl.	Richings, A. W.	South Lancs Regiment	
3	14235	Sergt.	Fox, E. C.	East Lancs Regiment	
3	15352	Sergt.	Shaw, L.	Royal Warwick Regiment	
3	11579	Sergt.	Greenwood, C.	Royal Lancs Regiment	M.M. (Killed in action.)
2	12451	L.-Sergt.	Grahame, J. H.	K.O. Scottish Borderers	
5	16557	Sergt.	Wright, L. G.	Essex Regiment	D.C.M.
4	15651	Sergt.	Price, W. A. W.	Somerset L.I.	Actg. Capt.
5	14590	A.C.Q.M.S.	Cole, G. F.	Wilts Regiment	
2	14016	Sergt.	Hibbard, R.	K.O.S.L.I.	
5	5225	S.M.	Wood, H.	Grenadier Guards	Actg. Qrmr., D.C.M.
1	16734	Sergt.	Halls, F.	Somerset L.I.	2nd Lieut.
1	15650	Sergt.	Jones, S.	Royal West Surrey Regt.	D.C.M.
3	16754	Sergt.	Morris, A. J.	Manchester Regiment	

R.S.—Regimental Staff. D.—Depots. W.A.R.—West African Regiment. P.S.—Permanent Staff. M.G.C.—Machine Gun Company. A.G.S.—Army Gymnastic Staff. S.L.—Supernumerary List.

APPENDIX X.

Ex-Warrant and Non-Commissioned Officers and Men appointed to Commissions since Commencement of Hostilities. Rank now held according to March 1919 Army List

Lieut.-Cols.	Majors.	Captains.	Lieutenants.	2nd Lieutenants.	Hon. Lieuts. and Qrmrs.	Total.
4	10	24	14	18	9	79

Non-Commissioned Officers and Men discharged to take up Temporary Commissions with New Army. Rank now held according to March 1919 Army List

Captains.	Lieutenants.	2nd Lieutenants.	Total.
30	64	199	293

INDEX TO NAMES OF OFFICERS

Abbey, N. R., ii. 245, 262, 381, iii. 8, 34, 36, 39, 48, 237
Abel-Smith, L. R., ii. 23-4, 132, 134, 284, 286, 309, 312, iii. 275
Acland, A. W., M.C., ii. 179, 181, 240, 250, 331, 333, 334, 371, iii. 24, 26, 275, 288
Acraman, W. E., M.C., D.C.M., i. 220, 255, 297, 329, 366, 373, ii. 165, 179, 181, 240, 360, iii. 24, 79, 288, 295, 318
Adair, A. H. S., M.C., ii. 187, 373, iii. 28, 91, 95, 96, 97, 133, 159, 160, 161, 182, 184, 185, 186, 188, 275, 288, 291
Adams, A. C., ii. 158, iii. 275
Adams, C. J. N., iii. 152, 155, 179, 239
Agar-Robartes, Hon. A. G., M.C., i. 299, 339, 341, ii. 169, 187, 188, 242, 254, 372, 375, iii. 28, 90, 275, 288
Agar-Robartes, Hon. A. V., M.C., i. 297, 329, 366, iii. 275, 288
Aird, J. R., M.C., iii. 288
Aldridge, E. A., Capt. (R.A.M.C.), i. 298, 329
Alexander, Capt. (Irish Guards), ii. 103, 104
Alexander, H., i. 324-5, iii. 209, 239
Alexander, N. G. A., M.C., ii. 329, iii. 275, 288
Alington, A. F., iii. 56, 155
Allenby, Sir E., Gen., i. 15, ii. 267, 349, iii. 105, 136
Ames, A., ii. 352, 353, iii. 17
Ames, L. G., i. 88, 130, iii. 273
Anderson, A. D., iii. 172, 176, 239
Anderson, R., Capt. (R.A.M.C.), iii. 91
Anderton, W. A. A. G. S., iii. 318
Andrews, J. A., Capt., M.C. (R.A.M.C.), i. 366, 373, ii. 57, 66, 78, 166, 179, 182, 227, 241, 250, 331, 361
Andrews, N. P., iii. 122, 141, 147, 172
Anson, A., i. 299, 339, 340, iii. 237
Anson, F., M.C., i. 300, 305, 306, ii. 169, iii. 159, 160, 162, 183, 187, 276, 288
Antoine, Gen., ii. 180-81
Antrobus, E., i. 88, 116, 130, iii. 237
Arbuthnot, G. A., i. 372, 373, 377, ii. 78, 80, 85, iii. 239
Arbuthnott, J., i. 367, 373, ii. 57, 60, 65, iii. 239
Ardee, Lord, Brig.-Gen., C.B., C.B.E., i. 76, ii. 362, 383, iii. 7, 9, 10, 11, 13, 272, 284, 292, 318
Arnold - Forster, M. N., Lieut., M.C. (Guards Machine Gun Regiment), iii. 288
Ashton, Capt. (Welsh Guards), ii. 112
Asquith, R., i. 343, ii. 1, 87, 97, 107, iii. 209, 237, 318
Aubrey-Fletcher, H. L., D.S.O., M.V.O., i. 87, 115, 130, 308, 309, 310, 314, 315, 318, iii. 273, 286, 294, 318
Ayles, F. P., iii. 239

Bagot, Hon. W. L., iii. 318
Bailey, Hon. G. S., i. 218, 221, 255, 279, iii. 239
Bailey, Hon. W. R., D.S.O., i. 144, 166, 175, 201, 206, 220, 255, 297, 329, 366, 373, ii. 51, 52, 56, 63, 78, 83, 151, 165, 179, 181, 184, 360, 362, 363, 371, iii. 23, 66, 69, 70, 73, 74, 78, 140, 141, 143, 146, 147, 148, 151, 171, 173, 174, 176, 177-8, 273, 286, 287, 294, 318

Baker, C. D., i. 355, ii. 162, 176, 177, 216, 217, iii. 235
Ball, W. B., ii. 341, 346, 373, iii. 5, 28
Barber, G. E., iii. 71, 74, 239
Baring, G., Lieut.-Col. (Coldstream Guards), ii. 102
Barrington-Kennett, B. H., i. 218, 221, 255, 258, 260, iii. 234, 294, 318
Battenberg, H.H. Prince Alexander of, Lieut., i. 12, 72
Battye, P.L.M., Lieut., M.C. (Welsh Guards), i. 214, iii. 281, 288
Beaumont-Nesbitt, F. G., M.C., i. 144, 201, 206, 297, iii. 288, 318
Beaumont-Nesbitt, W. H., M.C., i. 329, 333, 366, 373, ii. 56, 63, 78, 85, 242, 254, 255, 340, 342, iii. 235, 288
Bedford, Duke of, K.G., K.B.E., A.D.C., iii. 292, 318
Bedford, C. H., ii. 169, 348, 373, 374, iii. 28, 91
Bennett, N. C., ii. 373, 376, 378, iii. 276
Benson, C. E., D.S.O., ii. 171, 191, 194, 243, 244, 381, iii. 3, 8, 11, 276, 286, 318
Bentinck, Capt. (Coldstream Guards), i. 60
Bentley, F. D. (Machine Gun Company), iii. 239
Benyon, J. W. A., iii. 209
Benzie, Col., i. 288
Berkley, W., Capt. (Welsh Guards), i. 315
Best, Rev. E., iii. 56, 57
Bevan, R. C. M., iii. 24, 27, 79, 123, 125, 281
Bevan, T. P. M., M.C., ii. 149, 162, 175, 177, 219, 237, 238, 324, iii. 276, 288
Bibby, J. P., ii. 16, 17, 237, 238, 258, 260, iii. 237
Bibby, K. B., iii. 123, 152, 155, 179
Bicknell, R. A. W., M.C., ii. 151, 166, 179, 241, 250, 361, iii. 24, 288
Bigham, Hon. C. C., C.M.G., C.B.E., iii. 292, 294, 318
Bingham, R., Lieut.-Col. (Guards Machine Gun Regiment), iii. 186
Bird, H., ii. 162, 176
Blackett, W. S. B., iii. 235
Blackwood, Lord F. T. H. T., D.S.O., i. 341, 342, ii. 151, 166

Blackwood, Lord I. B. G. T., ii. 151, 166, 179, 181, 182, 183-4, iii. 239
Bliss, E. A. D., iii. 122, 141, 142, 147, 148, 150, 276
Blundell-Hollinshead-Blundell, C. L., O.B.E., i. 141, 308, 344, ii. 12, 15, 17, 18
Blunt, J. C., iii. 115, 122, 141, 147, 171, 281
Bolton, Lieut.-Col. (Scots Guards), i. 119
Bonham-Carter, F. G., i. 319, 323, ii. 12, iii. 209, 276, 318
Borthwick, Hon. A. M., ii. 187, 189, 210, 214, 242, iii. 276
Botha, General, i. 189, 265
Boughey, C. L. F., ii. 242, 254, iii. 28, 30, 151, 155, 276
Bowes-Lyon, G. P., i. 299, 339, ii. 1, 6, 242, 340, 342, 343, iii. 282
Boyton, H. J., ii. 158, 159, iii. 237
Brabourne, Lord, i. 190, 198, 225, 228, 230, 244, iii. 237
Bradford, Gen., V.C., ii. 302
Bradley, H. G. W., i. 359, 360, iii. 276
Brierley, H., Capt., M.C. (Coldstream Guards), ii. 337
Briscoe, R. G., M.C., ii. 179, 181, 227, 360, iii. 23, 79, 82, 83, 90, 123, 151, 179, 288, 318
Britten, C. R., M.C., i. 206, 214, 308, 344, 346, ii. 12, 132, 381, 143, 284, 286, 302, 305, iii. 273, 288
Brooke, Capt. (20th Brigade Staff), i. 133, 134
Brough, Lieut.-Col. (Royal Engineers), i. 368-9
Brown, A. M., M.C., iii. 67, 115, 116, 122, 147, 276, 288
Brown, C. C., iii. 28, 91, 95, 100
Browning, F. A. M., D.S.O., i. 335, 366, ii. 150, 165, 179, 181, 240, 250, 331, 333, 335, 336, 360, 364, 367, 369, 370, iii. 24, 27, 79, 286, 381
Bruce, R. C., M.C., ii. 238, 324, 350, 353, iii. 18, 288
Brunton, E. R., Lieut. (R.A.M.C.), i. 308, 344, 345
Brutton, C. P., iii. 22, 281
Buchanan, J. N., D.S.O., M.C., i. 206, 220, 255, 297, 329, ii. 153, 165, 179, 181, 227, 229, 230, 231, 240, iii. 286, 288

INDEX TO NAMES OF OFFICERS 337

Buchanan, R. G., iii. 67, 115, 147, 171
Bulfin, Brig.-Gen., i. 11, 131, 134, 152, 159
Bullough, I., Lieut. (Coldstream Guards), iii. 201, 203
Bunbury, E. J., M.C., ii. 348, 373, iii. 28, 91, 132, 133, 159, 160, 162, 164, 183, 189, 288
Burke, J. B. M., M.C., ii. 22, 172, 191, 194, 222, 224, 243, 244, 262, 263, 264, 309, 310, 311, 313, iii. 235, 288
Burman, B., ii. 12, 13, 17, 132, 171, 173, iii. 276
Burnand, C. F., i. 192, 198, 225, 228, 230, 244, iii. 239
Burnett, Capt. (Gordon Highlanders), i. 127
Burt, G. C., ii. 193, iii. 8, 34, 40, 47, 48, 276
Burton, J. S., i. 371, 372, iii. 240
Bury, H. S. E., i. 206, 211, iii. 240
Butler, Hon. L. J. P., Brig.-Gen., iii. 33, 34, 35, 38, 39, 40, 44, 53-4, 56
Butt, J. G., Lieut. (R.A.M.C.), i. 88, 129
Byng, Sir J., Gen., ii. 266, 267-8, 269, iii. 27-8, 59, 60
Byng, L. G., M.C., ii. 238, 258, 260, 318, 350, iii. 17, 67, 71, 74, 237, 288

Cain, R. C., ii. 149
Calvocoressi, S., iii. 92, 130, 281
Cameron of Lochiel, D. W., Lieut-Col., C.M.G. (Cameron Highlanders), iii. 285, 318
Campbell, J. L., iii. 67, 68, 281
Campbell, J. V., Lieut.-Col., V.C., C.M.G., D.S.O. (Coldstream Guards), ii. 57-8, 59, 70, 71, 72, 102, iii. 168
Campbell, K. A., D.S.O., iii. 159, 182, 184, 185, 186, 187, 188, 195, 276, 286, 318
Capper, T. B., Maj.-Gen., C.B., D.S.O., i. 83, 88, 94, 103, 104, 110, 111, 115, 118, 133-4, 136, 138, 140-41, 197, 229, 238, 244, 270-71
Carisbrooke, Marquis of, G.C.V.O., iii. 318. See Battenberg, Prince Alexander of
Carrington, C. W., D.S.O., ii. 187, 189, 210, 215, 242, 341, 342, 343, 344, 346, 347, 373, 376, 378, iii. 276, 286, 318
Carson, R. H., ii. 237, iii. 240
Carstairs, C. C., M.C., ii. 107, 242, 340, 341, 346, iii. 91, 95, 133, 182, 185-6, 276, 288
Carter, H. G., i. 339, 366, 371, iii. 276
Carter, J. S., ii. 361, 367, 371, iii. 24, 79, 115, 116, 117, 122, 235
Cary, Hon. L. P., i. 87, iii. 208, 209, 294
Cary, Hon. P. P., i. 221, 255, 260, 328, 355, 361, ii. 237, 238, 318, 353, iii. 18, 67, 70, 71, 72, 208, 276
Cassy, D. W., i. 378, ii. 87, 103, 107, iii. 276
Castle, H. H., Capt. (R.A.M.C.), ii. 317, 318, 350
Cator, A., Lieut.-Col. (Scots Guards), i. 136, 138, 250, 313, 317, 345, 346
Cavan, Earl of, Gen., K.P., K.C.B., G.C.M.G., M.V.O., i. 75, 145, 152, 153, 154, 155, 156, 157, 158, 159-60, 161, 164, 165, 166, 167, 168, 169, 171, 179, 183-4, 186, 205, 207, 212, 219, 261, 262, 267-8, 274, 281, 284, 289, 294, 295, 298, 306-7, 312, 314, 334-5, 349, 359, 368, 369, 375, ii. 9, 24, 42, 49-50, 58, 64, 83, 143, 146, 167, 195, 200, iii. 197, 230, 231, 232, 284, 285, 293, 318
Cavendish, R. H. V., M.V.O., i. 143, 144, 179, 183, 201, 203, 205, 206, 220, 274, 297, 329, 332, 333, 366, 373, ii. 372, 373-4, iii. 28, 29, 318
Cavendish, Hon. W. E., Brig.-Gen., M.V.O., iii. 318
Cecil, A. W. J., iii. 208
Cecil, Lord E. H., K.C.M.G., D.S.O., iii. 319
Cecil, G. E., i. 13, 35, 36 (*note*), iii. 240
Cecil, Hon. W. A., M.C., i. 12, 27, 61, 71-2, iii. 235, 288, 319
Challands, R. S., iii. 122, 141, 145, 147, 148, 172, 175
Chamberlain, N. G., ii. 176, 178, 237, 318, 323, 324, iii. 237
Chambers, A. S., M.C., ii. 176, 178, 219, 238, 258, iii. 18, 71, 74, 276, 288

VOL. III Z

Champneys, W., ii. 3, 6, 87, 107, 348, 373, iii. 276
Chapman, H. M., ii. 361, 366, iii. 281
Chapman, J., ii. 242, 254, iii. 30, 91, 95, 133
Chapman, M., M.C., i. 345, ii. 12, 17, 23, 243, 244, 261, 285, 288, 289, 290, 304, 306, 309, 310, 380, iii. 8, 11, 33, 36, 38-9, 48, 209, 235, 288
Chapple, J. W., ii. 176, 178, 219, 221, iii. 240
Charteris, Hon. I. A., i. 319, 323, 324-5, 326, iii. 209, 240
Cheylesmore, Lord, Major-Gen., K.C.M.G., K.C.V.O., iii. 285, 319
Chitty, J. M., ii. 192, 193, 222, 244, 309, 313, iii. 237
Cholmeley, H. V., i. 328, 355, 358, iii. 240
Cholmeley, Sir M. R. A., Bart., i. 203, 204, iii. 235
Churchill, Rt. Hon. Winston, i. 336
Clarke, D. H., M.C., iii. 115, 118, 119, 141, 144, 282, 288
Clarke, S. T. S., M.C., ii. 325, 361, 364, 365, 367, 369, 372, iii. 24, 79, 155, 288
Clive, G. S., C.B., D.S.O., iii. 284, 285, 286, 293, 319
Clive, H. A., M.C., i. 273, 297, 329, 331, 332, 333, iii. 288, 319
Clive, P. A., i. 203, 206, 215, 220, 255, 258, 261, 278, iii. 234, 319
Clough-Taylor, E. L. F., iii. 29, 91, 95, 99, 195, 282
Clutterbuck, Major, iii. 201
Coffin, E. L., Lieut. (R.A.M.C.), iii. 152, 155, 179
Colby, L. R. V., i. 88, 95, 104, 115, 130, iii. 234, 319
Colquhoun, Sir I., Capt. (Scots Guards), ii. 103-4, 105
Colston, Hon. E. M., C.M.G., D.S.O., M.V.O., i. 12, 27, 47, 76, 78, iii. 285, 286, 293, 319
Colville, Viscount, iii. 216
Combe, T. A., i. 334, 366, 373, 374, ii. 165, 179, iii. 81, 123, 125, 209, 276, 319
Conant, R. J. E., iii. 70, 72, 282
Congleton, Lord, i. 76, 144, 167, 169, 171, 181, iii. 237, 319
Connaught, H.R.H. the Duke of, Field-Marshal, i. 196-7, 286-7,
289, ii. 149, 154, 158, 317, 339, iii. 27, 55, 292
Constable, D. O., ii. 13, 17, 18, 23, 138, 139, 143, iii. 240
Cookson, Lieut.-Col., i. 84
Cooper, A. D., D.S.O., iii. 95, 97-8, 99, 133, 286, 319
Cooper, H. St. C., ii. 340, 343, iii. 91, 281
Cooper, R. J., Brig.-Gen., C.B., C.V.O., iii. 272, 284, 319
Corbett, Hon. T. G. P., M.C., ii. 353, 359, iii. 276, 288
Corbyn, E. C., Lieut.-Col. (Bengal Lancers), ii. 336
Corkran, C. E., Brig.-Gen., C.B., C.M.G., i. 190, 245, 247, 248, 250, 251, 252, 267, 268-9, ii. 24, 109, 112, 115, 119, 120, 126, 129, 157, iii. 272, 284, 285, 293, 319
Corkran, R. S., i. 255, 274, iii. 240
Cornforth, J. C., M.C., i. 371, ii. 165, 167, 179, 181, 240, 250, 252, 331, 333, 334, iii. 26, 79, 83, 84, 87, 88, 90, 152, 153, 276, 288, 291, 319
Cornish, G. M., M.C., ii. 12, 87, 103, 107, iii. 31, 91, 130, 131, 182, 276, 389
Corry, A. V. L., M.C., i. 221, 222, 246, 255, 260, 279, ii. 108, 114, 130, iii. 237, 289, 319
Corry, N. A. L., D.S.O., i. 12, 17, 20, 21, 35, 41, 48, 51, 299, 301, 306, 339, 340, 344, ii. 1, 2
Cottle, W. E. W., Lieut. (Machine Gun Company), ii. 232, iii. 237
Coventry, St. J. H., iii. 208
Cox, P. H., iii. 36, 48, 282
Crabbe, C. T. E., i. 299, 303, 304, 306, iii. 237
Craig, D., D.S.O., iii. 276, 286, 319
Craigie, J. C., M.C., i. 206, 220, 255, 329, 330, 331, 332, ii. 169, 187, 188, 242, 254, 255, iii. 273, 289, 319
Cranborne, Viscount, i. 216, 221, 255, 260-61
Crawfurd, Lieut.-Col. (Coldstream Guards), ii. 201
Crawley, A. P., iii. 319
Creed, C. O., i. 208, 220, 255, 260, iii. 240
Crespigny, C. R. C. de, Brig.-Gen., C.B., C.M.G., D.S.O., i. 143, 167, 185, 217, 221, 255, 258, 286, 319, 320, 323, 355, 356,

INDEX TO NAMES OF OFFICERS 339

367, 373, 375, 376, ii. 50, 52, 54, 56, 59, 60, 75, 78, 83, 134, 165, 168, 179, 181, 182, 184, 227, 228, 229, 240, 276-7, 279, 280, 327, 328, 330, 332, 362, iii. 65, 69, 81, 90, 110, 111, 120, 167, 169, 284, 285, 286, 293, 319
Crichton, H. F., Major (Irish Guards), i. 36, iii. 234
Crisp, F. E. F., i. 198-9, iii. 240
Crookshank, H. F. C., i. 275, 278, 297, 329, 335, 373, ii. 56, 63, 65, iii. 276
Crosland, C., i. 298, iii. 209, 277
Cruttenden, C., ii. 317, 318, 324, iii. 70, 75, 78, 277
Cubitt, C. C., M.C., i. 378, ii. 56, 66, 123, 152, 155, 179, 180, 277, 289
Cunliffe-Owen, Col., i. 177
Cunninghame, A. K. S., i. 13, 144, 201, 206, 220, 255, 297, 366, 373, ii. 56, 59, 64, 78, 80, 85, iii. 235, 319

Dalhousie, Lord, Lieut. (Scots Guards), i. 122
Dalkeith, Earl of, i. 245, 248, 319, 323, 355, 361
Dalmeny, Lord, D.S.O., M.C., iii. 277, 286, 289, 319
Dalrymple, Viscount, Major (Scots Guards), i. 117, 119
Darby, M. A. A., i. 88, 130, 138, 198, 200, 226, 231, 244, iii. 237, 319
Darrell, Lieut.-Col., i. 281, 368
Dashwood, W. J., ii. 120, 150, 162, 163, 175, 177, 218, 219, 220, iii. 237
Davies, Col. (Oxfordshire Light Infantry), i. 169, 176
Davies, Sir F. J., Lieut.-Gen., K.C.B., K.C.M.G., i. 11, 190, iii. 284, 285, 293, 319
Dawnay, H., Col. (Household Cavalry), i. 168
Dawson-Greene, C. J., ii. 316, 381, iii. 8, 12, 240
Dearden, H., Lieut. (R.A.M.C.), ii. 189, 242, 254, 341
De Cerjat, C. S., ii. 162
De Geijer, E. N., M.C., ii. 376, iii. 28, 91, 94, 95, 96, 133, 134, 183, 186, 277, 289
Delacombe, R., M.C., iii. 29, 91, 95, 99, 277, 289

De Lisle, A. P. J. M. P., ii. 363, 367, 370, iii. 81, 83, 86, 90, 277
De Lisle, Sir H. de B., Lieut.-Gen., iii. 33, 48-9
Denman, R. C., ii. 192, 193, 244, 262, 286, 309, 311, iii. 240
Denny, J. A., i. 211, iii. 277
Dent, W. H. S., M.C., ii. 150, 240, 331, 334, iii. 24, 79, 123, 124, 151, 179, 195, 277, 289
Derby, Earl of, i. 214, 268
D'Erlanger, L. F. A., iii. 67, 115, 147, 172
Derriman, G. L., i. 220, 255, 276-7, iii. 235
D'Esperey, Franchet, Gen., i. 43
Des Vœux, F. W., i. 12, 61, 62, iii. 237
Dickinson, T. M., i. 246, 248, 249, iii. 277
Diggle, W. H., D.S.O., M.C., iii. 286, 289, 319
Donnison, F. S. V., ii. 242, 373, iii. 133, 163, 164
Douglas-Pennant, Hon. A. G. S., i. 88, 130, iii. 237
Douglas-Pennant, Hon. G. H., i. 192, 198, 225, 228, 243-4, iii. 235, 319
Dowling, C. M. C., i. 144, 178, 181, 300, 304, 306, 340, 342, iii. 274
Drummond, F. H. J., M.C., ii. 182, 227, 231, 232, 234, 328, 331, 334, iii. 24, 25, 80, 123, 124, 277, 289
Drury-Lowe, W. D., D.S.O., i. 364, ii. 108, 113, 118, 123, 125, 126, iii. 235, 286, 319
Duberly, E. H. J., M.C., i. 192, 197, 225, 231, 239, 243, 248, 250, 319, 323, 355, 361, ii. 108, 123, 162, iii. 289, 319
Duberly, G. W., i. 141, 225, 228, 233, 238, 239, 240, 243, iii. 206, 234, 319
Du Cane, Sir J. P., Lieut.-Gen., iii. 32
Duckworth-King, Sir G., Bart., i. 88, 116, 130, 136-7, iii. 208, 274
Dudley-Smith, C. J., i. 246, 248, 258, 267, iii. 240
Dufferin and Ava, Marquis of, D.S.O., iii. 274
Dunlop, B. J., ii. 188, 189, 210, 213-14, iii. 237
Dunlop, L. E., ii. 189

Dunville, R. L., iii. 277
Duquenoy, M., ii. 8, 169, 187, 188, 242, iii. 319
D'Urbal, Gen., i. 187
Durbin, P., ii. 373, 374, 376, 377, iii. 240
Dury, G. A. I., M.C., ii. 187, 373, 375, iii. 28, 91, 128, 130, 277, 289

Earle, M., C.B., C.M.G., D.S.O., i. 87, 108, 116, 119, 121, 129, iii. 272, 284, 285, 319
Early, J. L., Capt. (U.S.M.O.R.C.), iii. 24, 80
East, G. W., Capt. (R.A.M.C.), ii. 210, 215
Eastwood, J. F., ii. 162, 176
Eaton, Hon. F. O. H., D.S.O., i. 299, 303, 305, 339, 341, ii. 1, 6, 169, 187, 188, 210, 211, 212, 213, 214, iii. 286, 320
Eaton, Hon. H. E., i. 343, ii. 1, 11, 242, 254, iii. 277
Echlin, R. F. W., i. 355, 361, ii. 123, 165, 176, 178, 351, 354, iii. 17, 67, 115, 147
Edwards, G., Capt. (Coldstream Guards), i. 180
Eliot-Cornell, R. W., ii. 242, iii. 277
Ellice, A. R., ii. 135, 138, 143, iii. 237
Ellice, E. C., D.S.O., iii. 201, 202, 205, 208, 286, 320
Elliott, A. G., M.C., ii. 187, 188, 209, 215, iii. 28, 91, 277, 289
Ellison, C. E. M., M.C., i. 307, 311, 314, 344, iii. 277, 289
Ellison, P. J. M., ii. 373, 375, 380
Ennor, F. H., ii. 237, 238, 258, 324, 350, 352
Ethelston, H. W., i. 198, 225, 228, 230, 232, 233, 239, 244, iii. 237
Evans, W. B., Lieut. (U.S. M.O.R.C.), iii. 18, 67, 71, 113
Eyre, J. B., M.B.E., i. 204, iii. 209, 277, 292

Fairbairn, S. G., M.C., iii. 92, 95, 133, 159, 183, 186, 289
Farquhar, R., M.C., ii. 26, 132, 133, 138, 142, 157, 172, 191, 193, 222, 244, iii. 209, 237, 289
Farquharson, M. G., M.C., iii. 122, 141, 147, 172, 195, 289

Feilding, G., Maj.-Gen., i. 41, 48, 57, 58, 61, 274-5, 277, 278, 280, 284, 295, 298, 336, 350-51, 368, ii. 3, 9, 24, 32, 38, 41, 58, 64, 106, 133, 146, 157, 172, 192, 195, 201, 204, 246, 249, 270, 271, 272, 276, 277, 280, 303, 326, 353, 383, iii. 62, 65, 90, 107, 197, 205
Fergusson, Sir C., Bart., Lieut.-Gen., K.C.B., K.C.M.G., D.S.O., M.V.O., i. 12, 264, ii. 362, iii. 1, 284, 285, 320
Ffoulkes, Capt. (R.A.M.C.), iii. 28
Filmer, Sir R. M., Bart., M.C., i. 288, 340, 347, 348, 349, ii. 13-14, iii. 235, 289
Filmer-Strangways-Rogers, A. E. F., iii. 159, 183, 185, 240
Finch, H. A., iii. 26, 83, 90, 240
Fish, H. C., Lieut. (U.S.R.), ii. 373, 376, 378
Fisher-Rowe, C. V., M.C., i. 141, 197, 225, 235, 238-9, 240, 244, ii. 150, 176, iii. 274, 289, 294, 320
Fisher-Rowe, L. G., M.C., i. 355, 362, ii. 108, 113, 114, 118, 162, 163, 164, 176, 177, 217, 238, 258, 318, iii. 289
Fisher-Rowe, L. R., i. 190, 197, 198-9, 225, 228, 230, 236, 243, 245, iii. 234, 320
Fitch, C. A., iii. 24, 25, 172, 282
FitzClarence, C., Brig.-Gen., V.C., i. 100, 174, 176
Fitzgerald, E. G. A., D.S.O., ii. 188, 242, 254, 257, 373, 375, 379, iii. 28, 90, 133, 159, 277, 286, 320
Fleet, W. A., ii. 236, 237, 353, iii. 18, 19, 22, 240
Fletcher, G. H., i. 211, iii. 240
Flower, A. C., ii. 25, 132, 138, 143, iii. 240
Flower, N. A. C., ii. 123, 125, iii. 277
Foch, General, i. 43, iii. 16, 59, 105, 166
Follett, G. B. S., Brig.-Gen., ii. 328, 362, 375, iii. 63, 69, 78, 110, 114
Forbes, A. H., ii. 317, 325, iii. 98
Forbes, Lord, iii. 210
Fortune, Capt. (Black Watch), i. 176
Forgety, C. A., Lieut. (U.S. M.O.R.C.), ii. 354

INDEX TO NAMES OF OFFICERS

Foster, A. C., i. 226, 228, 230, 244, iii. 240
Foulkes, Major (Royal Engineers), i. 215
Fox, Capt. (Scots Guards), i. 117, 119
Fox-Pitt, W. A. L., iii. 320
Fraser, J. C., M.C. (Machine Gun Company), iii. 237, 289
Freeman-Greene, H., iii. 151, 172, 175, 176
French, Sir John, Field-Marshal, i. 18, 21, 22, 29, 32, 35-6, 44-5, 46, 54-6, 68, 79, 80, 84, 97, 106, 107, 111, 141-2, 143, 149, 151, 163-4, 172, 187, 224, 244-5, 247, 282, 287, 290, 322
Frere, J. H., ii. 318, 351, 353, iii. 277
Freyberg, B. C., V.C., C.M.G., D.S.O., iii. 285, 288
Fryer, E. R. M., M.C., i. 278, 298, 329, 330, 340, ii. 1, 6, 187, 188, 209, 211, 212, 214, 215, 242, iii. 30, 91, 95, 96, 98, 99, 128, 133, 159, 160, 277, 289, 291

Gardner, C. G., ii. 12, 87, 98, 107, iii. 237
Gardner, S. Y. P., M.C., ii. 163, 176, 177, 219, 237, iii. 277, 289
Garton, W., O.B.E., iii. 225, 295, 320
Gascoigne, E. F. O., C.M.G., D.S.O., iii. 294, 320
Gascoigne, I. C., ii. 317, 352, iii. 237, 285
Gathorne-Hardy, Hon. J. F., C.B., C.M.G., D.S.O., iii. 284, 285, 286, 293, 320
Gault, R. A., ii. 17, 132, 134-5, iii. 240
Gelderd-Somervell, R. F. C., i. 199, 226, 231, 232, 244, iii. 240
George, S. C. K., ii. 338, 361, 367, iii. 79, 82
George V., H.M. King, i. 10, 15-16, 172, 191-2, 195, 201-2, 245, 286, 288-9, 326-7, 342, 364-5, ii. 12, 143-4, iii. 195, 196, 197, 198-9, 213, 233
Gerard, C. R., D.S.O., i. 144, 201, 206, ii. 193, 222, 244, 285, 306, 309, 313, 380, iii. 8, 33, 36, 38, 54, 55, 56, 286, 320
Gibbon, H. J., M.C., iii. 29, 91, 133, 134, 135, 159, 183, 289

Gibbs, 2nd Lieut. (Scots Guards), i. 122
Gilbey, A. J., iii. 8, 10, 282
Giles, C. C. T., ii. 338, 360, iii. 83, 87, 90, 277
Gillett, H. V., iii. 55, 56, 57
Gillilan, Major (Coldstream Guards), iii. 54
Gladwin, Lieut. (Scots Guards), i. 117
Glanusk, Lord, C.B., C.B.E., D.S.O., iii. 292, 320
Gleichen, Lord E., K.C.V.O., C.B., C.M.G., D.S.O., iii. 293, 320
Glyn, A. St. L., i. 335, 336, 357, 360, 361, 363, 366, 367, 370, iii. 208, 294, 320
Godman, G. W., ii. 338, 373, iii. 28, 91, 183, 186, 277
Gordon, C. A., M.C., iii. 26, 278, 289
Gordon, H. P., iii. 92, 130, 282
Gordon-Gilmour, R. G., C.B., C.V.O., D.S.O., iii. 216, 320
Gordon-Lennox, Lord B. C., i. 12, 17, 26, 28, 40, 48, 57, 64, 70, 73, 76, 144, 148, 153, 155, 157, 161, 171, 181, 210, iii. 234, 320
Gordon-Lennox, V. C. H., ii. 150, iii. 209, 278
Gort, Viscount, V.C., D.S.O., M.V.O., M.C., i. 262, ii. 191, 193, 194, 222, 225, 226, 244, 261, 262, 274, 285, 288, 304, 306, 307, 308, 309, 314, 352, 354, 356, iii. 17, 21, 61, 66, 69, 74, 75, 76, 77, 78, 107, 111, 112, 113, 114, 115, 116, 117-19, 121-122, 126, 274, 284, 286, 287, 288, 289, 295, 320
Goschen, C. G., i. 192, 198, 225, 228, 231, 239, 243, 248, 269, ii. 16, 17, 18, 130, 138, 139, 143, iii. 235
Goschen, G. G., i. 204, iii. 278
Gosselin, A. B. R. R., D.S.O., i. 12, 40, 61, 62, 72, 206, 214, iii. 235, 286, 320
Gough, Capt., i. 185
Gough, H., Lieut.-Gen., i. 81, 266, 270, 277, 291
Graff, J. H., Capt. (U.S.M.O.R.C.), iii. 95, 133, 159
Graham, A. C., i. 359, 362, ii. 108, 109, 113, 114, 130, iii. 235

Graham, H. A. R., i. 214, iii. 208, 274
Graham, J. W., i. 359, 360, iii. 278
Grant, A., iii. 67, 115, 120, 122, 240
Grant, J. C. B., Capt. (R.A.M.C.), i. 355, 362, ii. 162, 176, 178, 219, 236, 258
Green, G. R., M.C., ii. 191, 193, 222, 244, 381, iii. 8, 34, 35, 36, 48, 278
Greenhill, F. W. R., ii. 187, 189, 210, 242, 254, 257, iii. 240
Greenwood, J. E., iii. 8, 34, 36, 48, 56, 57, 278, 320
Greer, E. B., Lieut.-Col. (Irish Guards), ii. 206
Gregson, L. M., O.B.E., iii. 292, 320
Gregson-Ellis, P. G. S., iii. 53, 55, 56, 57
Grellier, N., Capt., M.C. (R.A.M.C.), ii. 132, 138, 172, 191, 194, 222, 245, 262, 286, 381, iii. 8, 34, 36, 56, 57
Greville, C. H., D.S.O., i. 192, 245, 246, 248, 323, ii. 172, 191, 193, 194, 222, 226, 353, iii. 17, 171, 274, 286, 320
Grey, R., D.S.O., i. 79, iii. 286, 295, 320
Grigg, E. W. M., C.M.G., D.S.O., M.C., i. 275, 297, 329, 366, ii. 93, 94, iii. 285, 286, 289, 320
Guernsey, Lord (Irish Guards), i. 62
Gunnis, G. G., M.C., i. 299, 339, 341, ii. 1, 6, 87, 98, iii. 236, 289, 320
Gunnis, I. FitzG. S., ii. 179, 180, 181, 182, 184-5, iii. 282
Gunther, G. R., M.C., iii. 91, 133, 159, 163, 182, 186, 240, 289
Guthrie, Sir C. T. R. S., K.B.E., i. 192, 198, 225, 228, 244, iii. 278, 292
Gwyer, C., iii. 25, 83, 86, 90, 237

Hague, C. N., M.C., iii. 289, 320
Haig, Sir Douglas, Field-Marshal, i. 10, 15, 48, 98, 99, 102, 113, 151, 155, 158, 184, 225, 247, 281, 290, 293, 322, 349, ii. 27, 28, 144, 145-6, 160, 266, 267, 268, 284, 339, iii. 50-51, 59, 105, 137
Haking, Lieut.-Gen., i. 11, 285, 368
Halford, C. H., iii. 208

Hall, C. A., M.C., ii. 169, 187, 189, iii. 278, 289, 320
Hall, C. B., iii. 141, 147, 150, 282
Hall-Watt, R., ii. 237, 238, 258, 261, iii. 240
Hambro, C. J., Lieut. (Coldstream Guards), ii. 201
Hamilton, Lieut. (Gordon Highlanders), i. 135
Hamilton, Maj.-Gen., i. 12
Hamilton, Lord C. N., D.S.O., M.V.O., i. 87, 109, 117, 138, 269, 273, 356, iii. 286, 320
Hamilton, G. C., C.M.G., D.S.O., i. 12, 26, 57, 59, 144, 153, 161, 166, 177, 288, 289, 307, 308, 310, 313, 318, ii. 159, 171, 190, iii. 209, 210, 273, 285, 286, 320
Hamilton, G. E. A. A. FitzG., ii. 354, iii. 18, 22, 240
Hanbury, Lieut. (Irish Guards), iii. 202
Hanham, Sir J. L., Bart., ii. 341, 344, iii. 278
Hanning, G. H., ii. 240, 241, 361, 366, iii. 278
Harbord, P. A. A., M.C., ii. 181, 227, 240, 331, 334, iii. 240, 289
Harcourt-Vernon, E. G., M.C., iii. 152, 155, 179, 289
Harcourt-Vernon, G. C. FitzH., D.S.O., M.C., i. 12, 63, 373, ii. 51, 57, 63, 78, 85, 167, 179, 181, 241, 250, 330, 331, 337, 361, 362, 367, iii. 24, 27, 79, 122, 123, 124, 125, 208, 274, 286, 289, 320
Hardinge, Hon. A. H. L., M.C., ii. 158, 172, 191, 284, 309, 311, 312, 381, iii. 34, 56, 57, 278, 289
Hargreaves, Capt. (Irish Guards), ii. 126
Hargreaves, S. J., ii. 317, 318, 350, iii. 18, 22, 240
Harrison, C. E., C.M.G., C.V.O., M.B., F.R.G.S., iii. 285, 320
Harter, H. H., iii. 238
Hartley, 2nd Lieut. (Coldstream Guards), iii. 227
Harvard, K. O'G., ii. 123, 125, 166, 167, 179, 181, 227, 231, 233, iii. 238
Harvard, L. de J., i. 356, 362, ii. 108, 179, 238, 258, 318, 320, 350, 353, 354, 358, iii. 241
Harvey, D., i. 367, 373, 378, ii. 57, 66, 368, 370, iii. 241
Hasler, A., i. 378, ii. 57, 60, 65, iii. 241

INDEX TO NAMES OF OFFICERS 343

Hawkesworth, E. G., M.C., ii. 258, 318, 350, 353, iii. 17, 67, 69, 70, 74, 75, 76, 78, 278, 289
Hay, Lord A. (Irish Guards), i. 62
Hay, Lord E. D. J., ii. 193, 194
Head, Major (R.H.A.), i. 109
Healy, C. H. C., ii. 120, 125, iii. 278
Heasman, F. J., M.C., ii. 7, 187, 210, 211, 215, 242, 254, 373, iii. 28, 91, 289
Henderson, K., ii. 187, 188, 209, 212-13, 215, iii. 278
Henderson, R. K., iii. 28, 91, 130, 282
Heneage, E., i. 319, 323, iii. 320
Heneage, G. C. W., D.S.O., i. 287, iii. 286, 320
Herbert, C. G. Y., M.C., iii. 289
Hermon-Hodge, Hon. L. St. L., M.C., i. 297, 329, 330, 340, ii. 1, 4, 186, iii. 27, 79, 123, 124, 155, 156, 179, 278, 289
Hermon-Hodge, Hon. R. H., D.S.O., iii. 286, 294, 320
Hervey-Bathurst, Sir F. E. W., Bart., D.S.O., i. 287, iii. 287, 321
Hewitt, C. J., iii. 278
Heywood, C. P., Brig.-Gen., ii. 35, iii. 139, 146, 168, 175
Heywood-Lonsdale, H. H., D.S.O., iii. 287
Heyworth, F. J., Brig.-Gen., D.S.O., i. 190, 227, 229, 230, 239, 252, 268, 285, 289, 295, 307, 308, 309, 310, 311, 312, 313, 315, 317, 320, 347, 360-61, 368, ii. 15, 21
Higginson, Sir G., Gen., iii. 209-10
Higginson, T. C., i. 300, iii. 238
Hilton-Parry, W., Capt. (R.A.M.C.), ii. 13
Hirst, G. F. R., M.C., i. 300, 305, 340, 342, ii. 11, 87, 169, 187, 189, 242, 254, 255, iii. 80, 91, 95, 96, 97, 128, 278, 289
Hoare, E., i. 359, 360, iii. 241
Hoare, E. R. D., i. 308, 309, 319, ii. 191, 245, 262, 286, 381, iii. 278
Hoare, G. H. R., ii. 338, 340, 341, 342, iii. 278
Hobart, C. V. C., C.B.E., D.S.O., iii. 292, 321
Holbech, L., D.S.O., M.C., ii. 169, 187, 189, 209, 242, 373, 375, 376, 380, iii. 151, 153, 155, 156, 157, 179, 195, 278, 287, 290, 321

Hollins, C. B., ii. 242, 340, 343, iii. 133, 159, 278
Holmes, R. E. I., iii. 18, 19, 22, 282
Home, Hon. W. S. D., Maj.-Gen., iii. 226
Hood, Viscount, O.B.E., iii. 292, 321
Hope, G. E., M.C., i. 88, 119, 130, 137, iii. 234, 290, 321
Hope, P. S., i. 362
Hopley, F. J. V. B., D.S.O., i. 336, ii. 1, 6, 87, 106, 107, iii. 209, 278, 287, 321
Hopley, G. W. V., i. 206, 212, iii. 241
Hore-Ruthven, Hon. W. P., G.S.O.I., i. 160, 368
Hornby, M. C. St. J., iii. 58
Horne, D. E. A., ii. 309, 311, iii. 282
Horne, H. S., Gen., i. 272, 277, 280-81, iii. 48, 49-50
Houstoun-Boswall, Sir G., Bart., i. 307, 310, 312, 314, 318, iii. 236
Howell, F. D. G., Capt. (R.A.M.C.), i. 72, 201, 206, 221, 255
Hubbard, B. J., M.C., ii. 172, 191, 193, 222, 223, 245, 309, 310, 311, iii. 241, 290
Hubbard, J. F., O.B.E., iii. 292
Huggan, Lieut. (R.A.M.C.), i. 70
Hughes, G., iii. 67, 69, 238
Hughes, J. S., M.C., i. 143, 144, 166, 180, 201, 206, 217, 245, 248, 250, 251, ii. 341, 343, 344, iii. 57, 274, 290, 321
Hulme, Lieut., iii. 98

Imeritinsky, Prince G., iii. 282
Ingleby, I. H., i. 297, 329, ii. 12, 17, 171, 191, 193, 222, 244, 303, 308, 380, iii. 8, 33, 55, 56, 321
Inglis, G., i. 326, 355
Inglis-Jones, J. A., iii. 126, 282
Irby, C. E., M.C., ii. 172, 191, 193, 222, 244, 285, 309, 314, 315, 381, iii. 8, 34, 55, 56, 57, 278, 290
Irvine, A. F., i. 336, 366, 373, 374, 376, ii. 78, 80, 85, iii. 209, 278

Jackson, G. D., ii. 3, 6, 87, 103, 107, iii. 241
Jackson, H. K., Brig.-Gen., D.S.O., i. 84

Jacob, J. H., ii. 151, 179, 182, 227, 231, 234, 368, 371, iii. 278
Jeffreys, G. D., C.B., C.M.G., i. 13, 20, 35, 38, 48, 49, 59, 61, 64, 65, 67, 70, 72, 144, 163, 174, 180, 201, 206, 220, 255, 258, 261, 262, 273, 297, 329, 331, 334, 335-6, 337, 366, 367, ii. 2, 153, 208, 240, iii. 155, 272, 284, 285, 293, 294, 321
Jesper, L. C., iii. 115, 117, 122, 282
Jesper, N. McK., M.C., i. 339, 366, 373, ii. 56, 61, 66, iii. 27, 80, 83, 85, 87, 90, 278, 290
Joffre, General, i. 18, 21, 32, 44, 80, 191, 266, 290, ii. 27, 145
Johnson, H. J. G., ii. 176, 178, 219, 236, iii. 238
Johnston, C. F., ii. 107
Joicey-Cecil, J. F. J., ii. 26, 136, 138, 143, iii. 209, 238
Joicey-Cecil, Lord J. P., iii. 321
Jones, B. H., iii. 67, 115, 116, 120, 122, 278
Jones, Capt., iii. 201

Kaye, Capt. (Manchester Regiment), iii. 67
Keating, H. S., iii. 238
Keith, C. G., M.C., ii. 13, 17, 18, 132, 133, 138, 141, 142, 171, 191, 193, 194, iii. 290
Kemble, Capt. (Scots Guards), i. 122
Kendall, R. Y. T., ii. 26, 131, 240, 331, 334, iii. 209, 279
Kennaway, C. G., iii. 115, 122, 141, 142, 147, 148, 172, 173, 175
Kenyon-Slaney, R. O. R., i. 87, 130, iii. 208, 274
Kerr, C., Lieut. (Australian Infantry), iii. 51, 52
Kerry, Earl of, Lieut.-Col., D.S.O., M.V.O., (Irish Guards), iii. 321
Keyes, Sir Roger, iii. 136
King, D. L., iii. 81, 123, 152, 155, 179, 321
King, E. G. L., i. 359, 362, ii. 108, 109, 176, 177, 178, iii. 241
Kingsmill, A. de P., D.S.O., M.C., i. 208, 298, 329, 366, iii. 274, 287, 290, 321
Kinloch, Sir D. A., Bart., Brig.-Gen., C.B., M.V.O., iii. 321
Kitchener, Earl, Field-Marshal, i. 9, 13-14, 172, 286, 287, 297, 354, 362, 367

Knatchbull-Hugessen, M. A., M.C., i. 275, 298, 329, 366, ii. 76, 78, 80-81, 85, iii. 238, 290, 321
Knight, D. J., ii. 193, 245, 262, 381
Knollys, A. C., M.C., ii. 242, 341, 342, 345, 346, 373, 376, 378, iii. 24, 279, 290

Lambert, R. S., M.C., i. 88, 116, 117, 130, 344, ii. 12, 17, 132, 138, 171, 190, iii. 274, 290, 321
Lambton, G., Lieut. (Coldstream Guards), i. 36 (note)
Lamont, G. S., D.S.O., iii. 71, 115, 147, 172, 173, 241, 287, 321
Landon, Brig.-Gen., i. 11
Lang, A. H., i. 208, 211, iii. 241
Langley, F. J., ii. 338, 361, 367, 372, iii. 27, 79, 83, 87, 90, 241
Lascelles, Viscount, D.S.O., i. 266, 267, 319, 323, 324, 325, 355, 356, 362, 363, ii. 56, 64, 65, 177, 237, 350, 351, iii. 29, 30, 90, 127, 128, 129, 130, 131, 132, 133, 134, 159, 160, 161, 163, 164, 182, 184, 186, 187, 189, 201, 274, 287, 321
Lawford, A. B., i. 245, 248
Lawford, R. D., M.C., i. 216, 221, 355, 362, ii. 123, 125, 162, 176, 177, 218, 219, 220, 317, 318, 320, 323, 350, 353, iii. 17, 66, 114, 279, 290
Lawford, S., Brig.-Gen., i. 83, 90
Lawrence, B. L., ii. 149, 162, 177, iii. 279
Lawrence, G. F., iii. 24, 25, 79, 82, 83, 90, 238
Lawes, R. L. M., ii. 245, 381, iii. 8, 34, 40, 54, 55, 57
Lawson, J., Capt. (R.A.M.C.), iii. 183
Lawson-Johnston, A. McW., M.C., ii. 78, 81, 165, 167-8, iii. 238, 290
Layland-Barratt, F. H. G., M.C., ii. 78, 81, 165, 179, 181, 227, 240, 328, 331, 336, iii. 279, 290
Layton, B. C., i. 308, 316, 344, ii. 13, 17, 20, 26, 309, 315, 381, iii. 56, 57, 279
Leatham, R. E. K., D.S.O., i. 88, 116, 130, iii. 273, 287, 294, 321
Lee-Steere, J. H. G., i. 178, 179, 181, iii. 241
Leeke, C., i. 319, 323, 358, iii. 238

INDEX TO NAMES OF OFFICERS

Legh, Hon. P. W., O.B.E., iii. 292, 321
Leigh-Pemberton, R. D., M.C., i. 308, 344, iii. 58, 290
Leslie, Sir J., Bart., Col. (R. Innis. Fusiliers), iii. 321
Lessing, A. E., O.B.E., iii. 292, 321
Lethbridge, Sir W. P. C., Bart., iii. 208
Leveson-Gower, R. H. G., ii. 172, 191, 193
Lewis, Lieut. (R.F.A.), iii. 39
Lindsay, W., Capt. (R.A.M.C.), iii. 119, 141, 147, 172
Lister, W. H., Capt., D.S.O., M.C. (R.A.M.C.), ii. 368
Llewelyn, H., ii. 109, iii. 209, 279
Lloyd, A. H. O., Brig.-Gen., C.B., C.M.G., M.V.O., iii. 285, 321
Lloyd, Sir F., Lieut.-Gen., G.C.V.O., K.C.B., D.S.O., iii. 107, 209, 293, 321
Lloyd, J. A., ii. 237, 258, 318, 350, 353, 354, iii. 17, 67, 70, 141, 171, 195, 321
Lloyd, M. K. A., i. 376, ii. 56, 59, 65, iii. 202, 203, 236
Loch, Lord, C.B., C.M.G., D.S.O., M.V.O., i. 12, 13, 17, iii. 284, 285, 293, 321
Loftus, D. F., iii. 208
Loftus, F. P., ii. 331, 336, 361, iii. 24, 80, 209
Logan, A. T., Lieut. (R.A.M.C.), i. 300, 340, ii. 1, 6, 87
Lomax, Major-Gen., i. 11, 100, 156
Long, E. C., ii. 338, 340, 343, iii. 279
Long, H. M., Lieut. (U.S.A.M.S.), ii. 361
Lovell, W. H., M.C., i. 365, ii. 108, 162, 176, 177, 218, 318, 350, 352, iii. 114, 116, 121, 122, 279, 290
Lowther, H. C., Brig.-Gen., i. 287
Lubbock, Hon. H. F. P., ii. 371, iii. 24-5, 238
Ludlow, E., i. 307, 344, ii. 12, 17, iii. 7
Lyautey, Gen., ii. 173
Lycett-Green, F. D., i. 299, 304, 306, iii. 279
Lygon, Hon. R., M.V.O., M.C., i. 141, 198, 226, 231, 233, 234-5, 239, 240, 241-2, 243, iii. 208, 290, 321
Lyon, F. C., ii. 12, 316, 381, iii. 8, 11, 34, 40, 42, 47, 48, 238

Lyttelton, Rev. Hon. C. F., M.C., ii. 182, 241, iii. 24, 80
Lyttelton, O., D.S.O., M.C., i. 216, 221, 255, 281, 341, ii. 1, 6, 86, 101, 103, 104, 105, 169, iii. 287, 290, 321

Macdonald, G. G., iii. 208
Macdonald, I., iii. 8
MacDougall, I., i. 12, 35, iii. 236
M'Ewen, Col. (Camerons), i. 176
Mackay, Lieut. (Machine Gun Guards), ii. 345, 346
Mackenzie, A. K., i. 12, 49, 63, ii. 7, 87, 97, 107, iii. 236
Mackenzie, H. W. R., i. 88, 135, 138
Mackinnon, Sir W. H., Gen., G.C.B., K.C.B., K.C.V.O., iii. 284
MacLear, B. G. H., M.C., ii. 16, 17, 18, 25-6, iii. 238, 290
MacMahon, Gen., ii. 170
Macmillan, M. H., i. 308, 316, 317, 319, 373, 375-6, ii. 51, 56, 60, 61, 65, iii. 279
Magnay, F. A., ii. 186, 240, 331, 334, iii. 28, 279
Maine, H. C. S., ii. 135, 138, 139, 143, iii. 279
Maitland, Lieut. (Scots Guards), iii. 202
Major, E. L., Lieut. (U.S. Army), iii. 83, 123
Makgill - Crichton - Maitland, M. E., D.S.O., i. 143, 144, 146, 181, 245, 248, 250, 251, 319, 323, 327, 343, 363, ii. 1, 4, 6, 11, 108, 109, 118, 123, 162, 164, 175, 176, 177, 218, 221, 237, 258, 262, 318, 321, 350, 352, iii. 210, 273, 287, 321
Malcolm, P., i. 308, 318, iii. 17, 67, 70, 75, 78, 236
Manley, W. B. L., iii. 29, 91, 130, 282
Manners, Hon. F. H., M.C., ii. 150, 165, 179, 181, 240, 250, 251, 361, 371, 372, iii. 209, 279, 290
Manners, Hon. J. N., i. 12, 34, 35, iii. 238
Marshall, Major (Manchester Regiment), iii. 67
Marshall, F. G., i. 144, 201, 206, 217, iii. 238
Marshall, Sir W. R., Gen., ii. 267, 349

Marsham, Hon. S. E., iii. 55, 56, 123
Martin, F., iii. 321
Matheson, T. G., Major-Gen., C.B., i. 64, 65, iii. 108, 110, 114, 137, 146, 169
Maude, Sir S., Gen., ii. 161, 175, 236, 267
Maunoury, Gen., i. 43, 46
Maurice, F. T., ii. 176, 237, iii. 238
Maxwell, A. E., i. 86, iii. 236
Mays, C. C., ii. 237, 238, 258, 318, 350, 353, 354, 358, iii. 241
Meikle, R. M., ii. 382
Mildmay, A. S. L. St. J., M.C., i. 198, 226, 231, 244, ii. 181, 227, 230, 231, 232, 234, iii. 208, 279, 290
Miller, D., i. 78, 146
Miller, E. E., iii. 209
Miller, F. W. J. M., i. 12, 144, 181, iii. 238
Minchin, T. W., D.S.O., i. 339, 366, 373, ii. 51, 52, 57, 66, 382, iii. 8, 13, 34, 40, 41, 42, 43, 47, 279, 287, 321
Minne, Monsieur, ii. 6
Mitchell, C., D.S.O., O.B.E., i. 137, 138, 193, 198, 245, 246, 248, ii. 26, 127, iii. 287, 292, 321
Moller, A. A., M.C., i. 198, 319, 323, 355, ii. 237, 238, 258, 350, 352, iii. 17, 67, 290
Molyneux - Montgomerie, G. F., i. 299, 301, 302, 305, 339, 342, iii. 234
Monro, Sir C., Lieut.-Gen., i. 11, 37, 38, 173, 209, 272
Montagu, Hon. S. A. S., ii. 361, 367, 370, 371, iii. 24, 79
Montagu-Douglas-Scott, Lord F. G., D.S.O., iii. 210, 225
Morgan, H. B. G., M.C., ii. 239, 250, 361, 367, iii. 79, 83, 84, 88, 89, 90, 155, 156, 282, 290
Morley, Hon. C. H., i. 245, 248, 251, iii. 279, 322
Morris, A. A., iii. 55, 70, 75, 115, 120, 122, 238
Morris, Hon. G., Col. (Irish Guards), i. 20, 36
Morrison, J. A., D.S.O., i. 190, 194, 197, 198, 199, 246, 307, 309, 311, 315-16, 317, 318, 328, 344, 345, ii. 12, 16, iii. 210, 274, 287, 322
Moss, G. C. G., i. 88, 245, 248, 250, 251

Moussy, Gen., i. 146
Murray, Sir A., Gen., ii. 161
Murray, W. R. C., i. 86, 300, 305, 306, iii. 236
Murray-Threipland, W., D.S.O., i. 311, 312, ii. 109, 110, 111, 119, iii. 287, 293, 322
Mylne, Lieut. (Irish Guards), ii. 102, 103

Nairn, E. W., i. 345, ii. 13, 17, 20, iii. 56, 57, 209
Napier, Sir A. L. M., Bart., i. 268, 319, 321, ii. 181, 227, 230, 240, 250, 252, 253, iii. 274
Napier, R. G. C., ii. 179, 181, 227, 230, 234, iii. 238
Nash, C. S., M.C., ii. 22, 172, 191, 193, 222, 245, 261, 262, 264, 286, 302, iii. 35, 36, 37, 48, 279, 290
Neale, G. D., iii. 17, 22, 241
Needham, Hon. F. E., i. 12, 34, 35, ii. 157, 171, 191, 193, 194, 222, 226, 244, iii. 53, 54, 55, 208, 274
Neill, E. M., M.C., iii. 123, 151, 155, 158, 279, 290
Nevill, J. H. G., i. 204, iii. 241
Neville, W. W. S. C., M.C., ii. 11, 169, 187, 189, 210, 211, 212, 213, 214, 215, 216, iii. 279, 290, 291
Newey, A. F., ii. 16, 17, 132
Newton, C. N., M.C., ii. 56, 152, 239, 240, 250, 253, 361, iii. 274, 290
Nicholson, J. R., ii. 351, 357, iii. 282
Nicol, W. E., D.S.O., i. 198, 225, 237, 245, 248, 251, 319, 321, iii. 234, 287, 322
Nivelle, Gen., ii. 164
Noble, E. H., i. 275, 297, 329, 366
North, J. B., iii. 209
Northumberland, Duke of, C.B.E., iii. 292, 294, 322. *See* Percy, Earl
Nugent, G. C., Brig.-Gen., i. 266, iii. 234
Nugent, G. G. B., i. 13, 299, 339

O'Brien, Capt. (Irish Guards), iii. 12
Ogle, H. R., ii. 189, 190, iii. 279
Oliver, F. R., ii. 192, 194, 222, 245, 286, 305, iii. 279
Oliver, R. E. H., i. 373, ii. 179, 182

INDEX TO NAMES OF OFFICERS 347

Oliver, R. M., ii. 227, 231, iii. 26, 79, 83, 87, 90, 238
Orriss, W. G., ii. 169, 170, 376, 380, iii. 238
Osborn, W. S., Brig.-Gen., iii. 114
Osborne, B. R., M.C., ii. 316, 381, iii. 152, 153, 155, 179, 180, 241, 290
Osborne, R. B., M.C., iii. 8, 34, 36-7, 122, 141, 144, 147, 279, 290

Paget, F. E. H., i. 266, 319, 323, 355
Paget-Cooke, O. D. P., iii. 20, 279
Pakenham, H. A., Lieut-Col., C.B., C.M.G. (R. Irish Rifles), iii. 285, 295, 322
Palmer, Capt., i. 234
Palmer, R. H. R., M.C., ii. 239, 361, 364, 372, iii. 24, 27, 79, 123, 124, 152, 153, 179, 181, 290
Papillon, R. P., iii. 30, 91, 92, 95, 133, 159
Parker, L. E., i. 246, 248
Parker, Hon. M. B., iii. 322
Parker, R. W., i. 341, ii. 1, 3, 6, 169, 171, 187, 189, 373, 375, 378, iii. 209, 236
Parker, W., ii. 1
Parker-Jervis, T., i. 192, 198, 371, 373, 375, ii. 56, 65, iii. 208, 279
Parnell, Hon. W. A. D., M.C., i. 282, 298, 329, 337, 338, 339, 366, 373, ii. 78, 80, 85, iii. 238, 290
Parry, Capt. (R.A.M.C.), i. 346
Paton, G. H. T., V.C., M.C., ii. 25, 132, 172, 191, 193, 194, 222, 245, 286, 289, 302, 306, 309, 310, 313, iii. 236, 284, 290
Paton, J. A., iii. 24, 25, 80, 83, 90, 279
Pauling, G. F., M.C., ii. 108, 123, 126, 162, 177, 216, 218, 376, 377, iii. 238, 290
Payne, A. F., iii. 113, 282
Payne-Gallwey, M. H. F., ii. 16, 17, 20, 132, 138, 143, iii. 238
Payne-Gallwey, Sir W. T., Bart., M.V.O., i. 36, iii. 236
Paynter, Capt. (Scots Guards), i. 135
Pearce, N. A., ii. 191, 192, 193, 222, 244, 285, 303, iii. 241
Pearson, S. H., ii. 186, 240, 250, 331, 334, iii. 241
Pearson-Gregory, P. J. S., M.C., ii. 150, 162, 164, 175, 177, 218, 238, 258, 350, 352, iii. 208, 290

Pelly, P. V., ii. 366, 371, iii. 24, 80, 123, 125, 280, 322
Pembroke, W. A., ii. 348, 373, 375, iii. 28, 151, 172
Penfold, A. H., ii. 12
Penn, A. H., M.C., i. 216, 220, 255, 258, ii. 151, 165, 179, 181, 227, 240, 328, 331, 360, 367, iii. 23, 79, 81-2, 280, 290, 322
Penn, E. F., i. 308, 316, 344, 345, 346, iii. 236, 322
Percy, Earl, iii. 294
Percy, Lord W. R., D.S.O., i. 190, 198, 226, 231, 244, iii. 274, 287, 294, 322
Pereira, G. E., Major-Gen., C.B., C.M.G., D.S.O., i. 368, 376, ii. 43, 60, 64, 66, 68, 82, 83, 84, 85-6, 153, iii. 272, 285, 293, 322
Petit, G., Capt. (R.A.M.C.), i. 226, 243, 248, 319, 323, 328-9
Philipps, G. P., iii. 36, 45, 48, 282
Phillimore, Rev. S., M.C., ii. 254, 257, 341, 373, iii. 28, 91, 95, 159, 183, 187-8
Phillipps, R. W., i. 324, 326, iii. 241
Pickersgill-Cunliffe, J. R., i. 13, 60, iii. 241
Pike, E. J. L., M.C., i. 12, 35, 70, 144, 174, 181, iii. 273, 290, 294, 322
Pilcher, W. S., D.S.O., i. 87, 119, 128, 130, 246, 248, 319, 323, 355, 361, ii. 171, 190, 193, 244, 309, 315, 380, 381, 383, iii. 1, 2, 8, 9, 11, 14, 33, 34, 36, 38, 40, 41, 43, 53, 54, 55, 56, 196, 287, 294, 322
Pixley, J. N. F., ii. 171, 191, 193, 194, 222, 223, 225-6, 244, 262, 264, iii. 236
Plumer, Sir H., Gen., i. 371
Poltimore, Lord, Capt. (R. North Devon Yeomanry), iii. 322
Ponsonby, Hon. B. B., i. 298, 329, 333, 366, 372, iii. 280
Ponsonby, Hon. C. M. B., M.V.O., i. 88, 126, 130, 307, 308, 309, 310, 312, 313-14, 315, 318, iii. 235
Ponsonby, Rt. Hon. Sir F. E. G., K.C.B., K.C.V.O., iii. 322
Ponsonby, G. A., i. 307, 344, 348, iii. 280
Ponsonby, J., Major-Gen., i. 284, 287, 295, 301, 303, 304, 305, 306-7, 368, ii. 84, 106, 271, 272, 288, 289, 303

Ponsonby, M. H., ii. 17, 360, 363, iii. 81, 83, 84, 85, 90, 238, 280
Powell, E. G. H., i. 12, 70, 144, 153, 155-6, 161, 169, 171, 181, 300, 302, 303, 340, iii. 273, 322
Powell, J. H., i. 87, 130, iii. 274
Powney, C. du P. P., iii. 322
Pryce, T. T., V.C., M.C., ii. 191, 193, 196, 244, 262, 263, 264, 381, iii. 8, 13, 14, 34, 35, 36, 37, 38, 41, 42, 44, 45, 46, 47, 48, 238, 284, 290, 291, 322
Pulteney, Sir W., Lieut.-Gen., i. 51, 97, 140, ii. 284

Quilter, J. A. C., i. 86, iii. 235, 322

Radcliffe, D. J. J., iii. 238
Ranney, R. van T., ii., 376, 378, iii. 241
Rasch, G. E. C., D.S.O., i. 87, 124, 127, 128, 130, 135, 138, ii. 169, 170, 171, 187, 188, 189, 239, 240, 250, 281, 328, 330, 331, 333, 336, 337, 360, 362, 367, 371, iii. 23, 27, 79, 83, 84, 87, 89, 151, 210, 287, 294, 322
Rawlinson, Sir H., Lieut.-Gen., i. 89, 96, 103, 106, 107, 140, 291, ii. 144, 146-7, iii. 59, 60
Rennie, G., i. 88, 125, 127, 130, iii. 236
Reuter, R. C. G. de, iii. 29, 91, 93, 95, 133, 159, 182
Rhodes, A. T. G., ii. 236, 238, 258, 261, 315, 318, 320, 321, 323, 324, 351, iii. 17, 67, 275, 322
Richardson, R. D., ii. 316, 381, iii. 8, 34, 54, 241
Riddiford, D. H. S., M.C., i. 361, ii. 162, 175, 177, 238, 258, iii. 290
Ridley, Lord (Northumberland Hussars), i. 84
Ridley, E. D., M.C., i. 40, 69, 76, 78-9, 144, 152, 161, 162, 171, 176, 181, 201, 203, 206, 216-17, 308, 309, 310, 312, 344, ii. 188, 189, 242, 338, 340, iii. 275, 290, 322
Ridley, M. A. T., i. 308, 310, 314, 315, 318, iii. 280
Ritchie, A. T. A., M.C., i. 288, 299, 303, 304, 305, 306, 378, ii. 56, 62, 65, 166, 179, 181, 227, 229, 230, 234, iii. 280, 290, 322
Rocke, Major (Irish Guards), ii. 103, 104, 105
Rocke, C. O., iii. 67, 70, 72, 241

Rodney, Hon. C. C. S., ii. 316, 381, iii. 8, 34, 36, 48, 280
Rolfe, R. H., ii. 165, 176, 178, iii. 8, 34, 54, 239
Rolinson, J. C., D.C.M., iii. 206, 209, 322
Romilly, Lieut.-Col. (Scots Guards), ii. 206
Roper, W. H. S., ii. 190, 242, 254, 257, iii. 241
Rose, Capt. (Royal Engineers), i. 191
Rose, I. St. C., O.B.E., i. 143, 144, 150, 155, 181, 221, 255, ii. 151, 154, 169, iii. 275, 292
Rowley, C. S., i. 192, 299, 304, 306, iii. 275
Ruggles-Brise, Sir H. G., Major-Gen., K.C.M.G., C.B., M.V.O., i. 83, 84, 90, 108, 112, 119, 122, 132, 136, iii. 272, 285, 293, 322
Rumbold, H. C. L., i. 206, 208, iii. 209, 280
Russell, Hon. A. V. F., C.M.G., M.V.O., iii. 285, 322
Russell, G. B. A., iii. 322

St. Aubyn, F. C., i. 246, 248, 249, 324, 326, ii. 149, 162, iii. 208, 280
St. Levan, Lord, Brig.-Gen., C.V.O., C.B., iii. 323
Saltoun, Lord, C.M.G., iii. 285, 322
Samuelson, B. G., i. 365, ii. 108, 118, 119, iii. 223, 280
Sandeman, H. G. W., i. 282, 297, 329, 330, 331, 332, 366, 373, iii. 322
Sanderson, H. W., iii. 29
Sarrail, Gen., i. 354
Sartorius, E. F. F., i. 199, 226, 231, 244, iii. 236
Scott, Lord F. G. M. D., D.S.O., i. 76, iii. 273, 287, 294, 322
Scott-Kerr, R., Brig.-Gen., C.M.G., C.B., D.S.O., M.V.O., i. 19, 20, 35, iii. 215, 272, 285, 323
Scott-Russell, O., iii. 58
Selby-Lowndes, G. W., ii. 286, 380, 383, iii. 8, 34, 55
Selby-Lowndes, J. W. F., M.C., ii. 26, 132, 138, 142. 159, iii. 280, 290
Sergison-Brooke, B. N., Brig.-Gen., C.M.G., D.S.O., ii. 2, 4, 6, 86, 91, 98, 106, 272, 274, 275, 304, 306, 339, 375, iii. 62, 63, 70, 94, 167, 273, 286, 287, 294, 323

INDEX TO NAMES OF OFFICERS 349

Seymour, E., C.B.E., D.S.O., M.V.O., iii. 287, 292, 323
Seymour, E. W., ii. 151, 165, 242, 254, 373, 375, 376, iii. 280
Seymour, Lord H. C., Brig.-Gen., D.S.O., i. 212, 217, 220, 245, 255, 258, 261, 297, 329, 332, 334, 346, 349, ii. 12, 16, 18, 109, 130, 132, 134, 138, 158, 164, 170, 216, 218, 247, 280, 302, 307, 308, 320, 322, 354, iii. 1, 273, 287, 294, 323
Sharp, C. C. T., i. 363, ii. 108, 110, 112, iii. 280
Sharpe, R. T., ii. 338, 361, 371, iii. 24, 123, 126, 280
Sheldrake, E. N., iii. 293
Shelley, E. B., i. 363, ii. 108, 109, iii. 79, 113, 236, 280
Shelley, G. E., i. 307, 318, ii. 171, iii. 280
Sheppard, E., D.S.O., M.C., ii. 107, 123, 125, iii. 287, 291, 323
Sich, G. W., iii. 36, 48, 282
Siltzer, F. J., ii. 187, 188, 209
Sim, L. G. E., i. 365, ii. 118, 119, iii. 241
Simmons, P. G., M.C., ii. 165, 176, 177, 219, 238, 258, 350, iii. 17, 291
Simpson, J. H. C., M.C., iii. 55, 79, 113, 115, 116, 119, 120, 141, 142, 144, 147, 275, 291
Singh, Sir Pertab, Major-Gen., i. 191
Sitwell, F. O. S., i. 192, 198, 297, 329, 345, ii. 13, 17, iii. 208
Skidmore, J. H., i. 12, 144, 201, 206
Skinner, L. P., 2nd Lieut., M.C. (Guards Machine Gun Regiment), iii. 291
Sloane-Stanley, G. C., i. 345, ii. 13, 17, 172, 191, 193, 244, 261, 381, iii. 8, 13, 14, 34, 209
Sloane-Stanley, H. H., M.C., i. 346, ii. 12, 17, 20, 22, 23, 245, 262, 263, 285, 302, 306, 309, 310, 314, 315, 380, iii. 8, 13, 34, 35, 36, 42, 47, 48, 209, 236, 291
Smith, Capt. (Tank Corps), iii. 96
Smith, D. A., M.C., i. 208, 220, 255, 279, 297, 329, 366, iii. 280, 291, 322
Smith, D. E., iii. 280
Smith, H. I'B., iii. 133, 159, 163
Smith, M. B., ii. 49, 73, 74-5
Smith, O. M., ii. 325, 361, 364, 367, 368, 369, 371, iii. 24, 79, 83, 84, 86, 90, 275
Smith, O. W. D., iii. 18, 23, 282
Smith, T., ii. 179
Smith, W. R. A., C.M.G., i. 75, 76, 144, 148, 152, 153, 154, 155, 156, 157, 159, 160, 163, 166, 169, 173, 174, 178, 183, 184, 185, 197, 201, 204, 206, 210, 218, 219, 220, 255, 257-8, 261, 272, 336, iii. 234, 286
Smith-Dorrien, Sir Horace, Gen., i. 11, 15, 24, 29, 97, 111
Smuts, J. C., Gen., i. 353, 354
Snelling, A. G., iii. 56, 57
Somerset, N. A. H., i. 88, 113, 114, 130, iii. 241
Sordet, Gen., i. 24
Spence, P. M., M.C., i. 361, ii. 123, 126, 162, 176, 177, 218, 237, 238, 315, 318, 320, 322, 323, iii. 122, 141, 142, 143, 147, 171, 172, 175, 291
Spencer-Churchill, E. G., M.C., i. 205, ii. 26, 130, 131, 132, 134, 136-7, 137-8, 143, 157, 172, 191, iii. 93, 94, 275, 291, 323
Stainton, W. A., ii. 11, 87, 103, 107, iii. 239
Stanhope, Earl, D.S.O., M.C., i. 190, 198, 199, iii. 287, 291, 323
Stanhope, Hon. R. P., i. 341, ii. 1, 5, 6, 87, 103, 107, iii. 208, 236
Stanley, Hon. F. C., Brig.-Gen., C.M.G., D.S.O., iii. 286, 294, 295, 323
Stanley, Lord, M.C., i. 245, 248, 269, 270, 319, 323, 326, 355, 361, iii. 275, 291
Stein, O. F., D.S.O., ii. 108, 110, 111, 112, 163, 176, 177, 219, 258, 350, 353, 354, 359, iii. 18, 22, 280, 287, 323
Stephen, D. C. L., i. 12, 26, 47-8, 50, iii. 236
Stephenson, P. K., i. 218, 248, 319, 323, iii. 280
Stepney, H., Major (Irish Guards), i. 49
Stewart, E. O., i. 192, 341, ii. 150, 157, 165, 193, iii. 208
Stewart, H. W., iii. 241, 282
Stewart, W. A. L., i. 65, 72, ii. 7, 130, 132, 134, 138, 139, 143, iii. 208, 236, 291
Stirling, Lieut.-Col. (Scots Guards), iii. 168, 175
Stirling, E. G., iii. 280

Stocks, M. G., i. 12, 38, 144, 171, 181, iii. 239
Stopford, Gen., i. 287
Stourton, R. H. P. J., i. 359, 362, ii. 108, 113, 280
Stratford, H. D., ii. 240, 250, 253, iii. 36, 48, 239
Streatfeild, Sir H., K.C.V.O., C.B., C.M.G., i. 183, 194, 210, 245, 268, 286, 288, ii. 149, 154, 158, iii. 78, 218, 224, 230, 233, 286, 323
Streatfield, H. S. J., D.S.O., iii. 287, 323
Stucley, H. St. L., i. 87, 116, 124, 126, 129, iii. 235, 323
Sutton, K. H. M., iii. 280
Swaine, F. L. V., i. 246, 248, 250, 251, 319, 323, 355, iii. 323
Swaine, Y. W., iii. 280
Swift, C. T., i. 356, 362, ii. 123, 125, iii. 280, 323
Sykes, C. A. V., i. 141
Symes-Thompson, C., i. 12, 40, 59, 76, 144, 178, 181, iii. 236
Symons, T. E. R., i. 88, 96, iii. 294, 323

Tabor, J., ii. 166, 179, 182, 241, 250, 253, iii. 280
Tate, E. D., ii. 242, 373, 375, 378, iii. 280
Taylor, G. P. du Plat, O.B.E., iii. 208, 292
Taylor, E. R., iii. 208
Teece, J., M.C., i. 87, 138, 193, 225, 248, 323, 355, 361, ii. 162, 175, 177, 238, 350, 354, iii. 17, 67, 171, 282, 291, 295, 323
Tennant, Hon. E. W., i. 308, 344, ii. 13, 17, 137, 143, iii. 239
Terrell, R., ii. 166, 167, iii. 281
Tetley, J. C. D., ii. 187, 189, 242, 254, 255, 257, iii. 239
Thomas, M. D., i. 364, ii. 382, iii. 8, 34, 36, 37, 48, 281
Thomas, O. C. (Machine Gun Company), iii. 239
Thorne, A. F. A. N., C.M.G., D.S.O., i. 359, 360, 361, ii. 120, 169, 171, 187, 189, 209, 214, 229, 242, 254, 306, 340, 341, 344, 345, 346, 372, 373, 375, 376, iii. 28, 29, 30, 90, 95, 98, 99, 126-7, 286, 287, 288, 323
Thorne, T. F. J. N., i. 288, 307, 310, 313, 314, 315, 318, iii. 226, 237

Thornhill, N., M.C., ii. 187, 189, 242, 254, 257, iii. 281, 291
Thoseby, J. N. L., Capt. (R.A.M.C.), ii. 169, 187
Thrupp, M., ii. 7, 8, 87, 103, 107, 163, 177, 218, 219, iii. 241
Thynne, Sir R., Major-Gen., i. 194, iii. 216, 218, 219, 223
Timmis, W. U., ii. 237, 238, 318, 350, 357, iii. 281
Tindal-Atkinson, J. F., ii. 237, 238, 258, 350, iii. 18, 20, 281
Tisdall, Capt. (Irish Guards), i. 36 (*note*)
Tompson, A. H., i. 308, 316, 318, iii. 241
Tompson, R. F. C., ii. 130, iii. 239
Topham, D. B., ii. 317
Towneley-Bertie, Hon. M. H. E. C., i. 373, iii. 30, 281
Townshend, Gen., i. 354
Trench, R. P. le P., M.C., i. 248, 319, 323, 325-6, 364, ii. 108, 123, 162, 175, 178, 238, 258, 350, iii. 55, 275, 291, 323
Trotter, E. H., D.S.O., iii. 234, 323
Trotter, G. F., Brig.-Gen., C.B., C.M.G., C.B.E., D.S.O., M.V.O., i. 191, 197, 225, 234, 235-6, 243, 244, 245, 248, 252, 269, 270, 319, 320, 323, 324, 325, 355, 357, 370, iii. 272, 285, 286, 292, 294, 323
Tryon, G. C., M.P., iii. 294, 323
Tuckwell, E. H., M.C., ii. 158, 171, 191, 193, 222, 244, 262, 285, 302, 381, iii. 8, 34, 55, 291
Tudway, H. R. C., i. 171, 181, iii. 239
Tufnell, C. W., i. 144, 166, 167, 181, iii. 239
Tufnell, N. C., ii. 348, 373, iii. 91, 95, 96, 97
Turner, C. R., i. 355, iii. 323

Van Neck, P., i. 88, 118, 120, 130, iii. 239
Vaughan, E. N. E. M., D.S.O., i. 342, 373. ii. 1, 6, 108, 109, 110, 111, 112, 162, 175, iii. 206, 208, 287, 323
Veitch, J. J. M., ii. 192, 193, 222, 309, 311, iii. 281
Venables, Rev. C., iii. 115, 141, 147, 172
Venables, Rev. J. O., iii. 113
Vereker, G. G. M., M.C., i. 366,

INDEX TO NAMES OF OFFICERS 351

373, ii. 165, 179, 240, 360, iii. 24, 27, 79, 291, 323
Vereker, R. H. M., i. 13, 28, iii. 242
Verelst, Capt. (Coldstream Guards), ii. 82
Vernon, H. B., M.C., ii. 164, 351, 360, iii. 18, 67, 70, 71, 74, 281, 291
Vernon, H. D., i. 300, iii. 239
Viand, Lieut. (Coldstream Guards), iii. 202
Villiers, G. J. T. H., i. 268, 319, 321, iii. 281
Vivian, G. N., O.B.E., i. 299, 303, 304, 306, iii. 275, 292, 323
Vivian, V., C.M.G., D.S.O., M.V.O., iii. 273, 286, 287, 294, 323

Wakeman, E. O. R., i. 246, 248, 251, iii. 242, 323
Wakeman, O., i. 248, 319, 323, 324, 325, iii. 275
Wales, H.R.H. the Prince of, K.G., G.C.M.G., G.B.E., M.C., i. 191, 193, 208, 219-20, 245, 269, 273, 278, 356, iii. 195, 197, 225, 285, 291, 292, 323
Walker, Gen., ii. 308
Walker, C. F. A., M.C., i. 12, 63, 299, 303, 304, 306, 339, 341, ii. 151, 165, 179, 181, 184, 227, 239, 380, 381, iii. 33, 55, 151, 153, 154, 155, 179, 275, 291, 324
Walker, Sir H. B., Major-Gen., K.C.B., D.S.O., iii. 50
Walker, P. M., M.C., i. 341, 373, ii. 56, 169, iii. 209, 281, 291
Wall, G. H., M.C., i. 299, 339, ii. 1, 6, 169, 187, 188, 242, iii. 28, 91, 291, 324
Wall, L. E. G., iii. 147
Wall, R. B. St. Q., ii. 165, 238
Wall, V. A. N., ii. 258, 325, 350
Walter, S., i. 88, 113, 114, 130, iii. 242
Ward, E. S., i. 141, 191, ii. 6, iii. 208, 275
Wardrop, Brig.-Gen., i. 368
Warner, A. A. J., iii. 67, 71, 74, 242
Warner, E. C., i. 360, ii. 117, 122
Warren, Capt. (Border Regiment), i. 135
Watts, H., Brig.-Gen., C.B., i. 83, 90, 111

Warrender, H. V., D.S.O., iii. 287, 324
Wearne, W. R., iii. 56, 57
Webber, R. L., ii. 360, iii. 18, 67, 71, 74, 281
Webster, Sir A. F. W. E., Bart., O.B.E., iii. 208, 292, 324
Webster, G. V. G. A., ii. 189, 190, 241, iii. 242
Welby, R. W. G., i. 12, 62, 70, iii. 239, 324
Weld-Forester, Hon. A. O. W. C., M.V.O., i. 87, 104, 119, 120, 121, 126, 129, iii. 235, 324
Wellesley, Lord G., Capt., M.C. (R.A.F.), iii. 324
Wellesley, Lord R., i. 88, 95, 105, 126, 130, iii. 237, 291
Wells, P. H., Capt. (R.A.M.C.), ii. 236, 238, 317
West, R. G., M.C., ii. 192, 193, 222, 244, iii. 91, 95, 100, 281, 291
Westmacott, Brig.-Gen., i. 176
Westmacott, G. R., D.S.O., i. 192, 198, 226, 231, 233, 234, 236, 237, 238, 239-40, 243, 244, ii. 186, 241, 250, 253, 331, 333, 335, 336, 361, iii. 208, 281, 287, 324
White, G. D., iii. 206, 208, 209, 294, 324
White, H., ii. 239, 240, 250, 361, iii. 24, 79, 83, 87, 90, 242, 324
Whitehead, A. O., ii. 87, 98, 107, iii. 223, 281
Wiggins, A. F. R., i. 221, 297, 329, 366, 373, 374-5, 376, ii. 52, iii. 28, 91, 324
Wiggins, H. G., M.C., ii. 78, 80, 85, 317, 318, 323, iii. 55, 57, 281, 291
Wigram, C., i. 245, 288
Wilkinson, C., i. 328, 355, 358, ii. 149, 162, 163, 176, 237, iii. 281
Williams, A., ii. 170, 179, iii. 212, 213
Williams, E. G., i. 206, 221, 255, 279, iii. 239
Williams, H. St. J., ii. 12, 87, 98, 107, iii. 28, 281
Williams, M. G., i. 204, 206, 307, 311, 314-15, 317, 318, 344, ii. 158, 191, iii. 208, 294, 324
Williams, R., i. 190, 195-6, 299, 340, iii. 242
Williams-Bulkeley, R. G. W., M.C., iii. 324

Willoughby, Hon. C., Lieut.-Col. (Tank Corps), ii. 280
Wilson, G., Col. (Household Cavalry), i. 167-8
Wilson, G. B., M.C., i. 328, 355, 359, ii. 338, 360, 367, 369, 370, iii. 151, 153, 155, 156, 275, 291
Wilson, H. M., ii. 166, 179, 181, 227, 240
Wilton, J. D. C., ii. 151, iii. 281
Windeler, H. W., ii. 192, 193, 222, 244, 262, 286, 305, iii. 226, 242
Windram, R., iii. 324
Wolrige-Gordon, R., M.C., i. 12, 268, 323, 340, ii. 1, 5, 7, 87, 99, 100, iii. 18, 56, 57, 67, 71, 74, 75, 77, 275, 291

Wood, Lieut.-Col. (Border Regiment), i. 238, 249
Worsley, E. G., i. 343, ii. 107, iii. 242
Worsley, J. F., ii. 1, 6, 7, 87, 98, 107, 187, 189, 210, 215, 254, 340, 343, iii. 209, 239
Wright, R. B. B., ii. 78, 85, iii. 281
Wrixon, M. P. B., M.C., ii. 191, 382, iii. 3-4, 55, 56, 57, 281, 291
Wynne, E. H. J., i. 299, 339, ii. 1, 6, 87, 97-8, 107, iii. 239

Yorke, Hon. A. E. F., ii. 1, 6, iii. 209
Yorke, B. E., i. 343

THE END

Printed by R. & R. CLARK, LIMITED, *Edinburgh.*

www.ingramcontent.com/pod-product-compliance
Lightning Source LLC
Chambersburg PA
CBHW061929220426
43662CB00012B/1848